Issues and Environments

GCSE Geography for AQA specification C

David Payne | Sue Jennings

Heinemann

Heinemann Educational Publishers
Halley Court, Jordan Hill, Oxford, OX2 8EJ
Part of Harcourt Limited
Heinemann is the registered trademark of Harcourt Educational Limited

© 2002 David Payne and Sue Jennings

Copyright notice
All rights reserved. No part of this publication may be reproduced in any material form (including photocopying or storing it in any medium by electronic means and whether or not transiently or incidentally to some other use of this publication) without the prior written permission of the copyright owner, except in accordance with the provisions of the Copyright, Designs and Patents Act 1988 or under the terms of a licence issued by the Copyright Licensing Agency Ltd, 90 Tottenham Court Road, London W1P 0LP. Applications for the copyright owner's written permission to reproduce any part of this publication should be addressed to the publisher.

First published date 2002

10-digit ISBN: 0 435353 59 4
13-digit ISBN: 978 0 435353 59 9

06
10 9 8 7

Edited by Katherine James

Designed by Roarr Design
Typeset and illustrated by Hardlines Ltd

Printed and bound in Spain by Edelvives

Photograph acknowledgements
The authors and publishers would like to thank the following for permission to use photographs:
Cover photo by SPL
Environmental images: p. 5 Katherine Miles, pp. 13, 89, 183 Jim Holmes, pp. 48, 53, 55, 59, 68 (both), 70, 72, 75 164 Martin Bond, p. 92 Edwin Maynard, p. 129 Rob Visner, p. 147 Matt Sampson, p. 152 Kam Y Sung, p. 158 Steve Morgan, p. 159 Chris Westwood, p. 165 John Morrison, p. 180 Irene R Lengui, p. 197 Dorothy Burrows, p. 203 Robert Brook, p. 227 David Sims; *Still Pictures*: pp. 7, 30, 35, 37, 51, 175, 180, 215 Mark Edwards, p. 14 Andy Crump, pp. 17, 132 Ron Giling, pp. 21, 135, 199, 232 Hartmut Schwarzbach, pp. 25, 41, 200 John Maier, p. 28 Jorgen Schytte, p. 36 Edward Parker, p. 39 Martin Wright, Bojan Brecelj, p. 84 Dylan Garcia, pp. 93, 232 B & C Alexander, p. 103 Alan Watson, p. 112 Don Hinrichson, p. 131 Jim Wark, p. 154 Klein Hubert, p. 161 JP Delobelle, pp. 204, 241 Gerard & Margi Ross, p. 208 Daniel Dancer, pp. 220, 225 Shehzad Noorani, p. 223 Savran p. 231 Nigel Dickinson, p. 242 Dianne Blell, p. 244 Roland Seitre, p. 245 Magnus Andersson; *Panos Pictures*: p. 12 Chris Johnson, pp. 16, 135, 141, 226 Sean Sprague, pp. 29, 32 Martin Adler, pp. 29, 133 Betty Press, pp. 31, 137, 226 Jeremy Hartley, pp. 34, 240 Roderick Johnson, p. 43 Chris Stowers, pp. 52, 154 David Reed, p. 54 Philip Wolmuth, p. 125 Fred Hoogervorst, p. 139 Ray Wood, pp. 144, 152 John Leo Dugast, p. 151 Liba Taylor, pp. 181, 240 Guy Mansfield, p. 185 Bruce Paton, p. 241 Dermot Tatlow; *Sally and Richard Greenhill*: pp. 19, 56; *Rex*: pp. 19, 42, 128, 232, 234, p. 247 Trevor Humphries, p. 45 Roger Scruton; *Popperfoto*: pp. 46 (both), 123; *Popperfoto/ Reuter*: p. 97 Kimimasa Mayama, p. 98 El Tiempo, p. 105 Royal Navy, p. 117 Andrew Winning, p. 127a Dylan Martinez, b Ian Hodgson, p. 213 Goran Tomasevic; *Popperfoto/ AFP*: p. 107 Yuri Cortez, p. 119 Robert Sullivan, p. 226 *Ace*: p. 47 John Searle; *Robert Harding Picture Library*: p. 57 N Francis, p. 64 G Hellier, p. 237 Michael Busselle; *Collections*: p. 58 Liz Stares, p. 62 Andy Hibbert, p. 63 Sam Walsh, p. 123 John Gollop, p. 164 Simon Warner, p. 166 Ashley Cooper, p. 189 Brian Shuel; p. 202 Gina Davies, p. 211 Roger Scruton; *Format*: p. 64 Maggie Murray; pp. 65, 66, 71, 88, 157 Garrett Nagle; p. 68a Mark Ridout; p. 79 Katherine James; p. 81 *Aerofilms*; pp. 82, 83 *Phototheque Eparmarne*; p. 97 *Pictor International*; pp. 110, 112, 126, 142 University of Dundee; p. 138 Wateraid/ Jim Holmes; p. 138 Josh Hobbins; pp. 154, 159b, 162, 236 John Pallister; p. 161 *Geoscience Features*/ Dr B Booth; pp. 172, 173 Oasis Forest Holiday Villages; p. 184 Mark Ridout; p. 186 Bruce Coleman; p. 187 UNDP; pp. 190, 191 Teesside Development Corporation; p. 193 *Science Photo Library*/ David Nunuk; p. 213 *Science Photo Library*/ Novosti; p. 216 *Science Photo Library*/ NASA; p. 202 *Hulton Archive*; p. 224 *South American Pictures*: Tony Morrison.
The publishers have made every effort to trace the copyright holders, but if they have inadvertently overlooked any, they will be pleased to make the necessary arrangements at the first opportunity.
Picture research by Thelma Gilbert

Text and artwork acknowledgements
The Guardian: p. 13 22/09/1999, p. 15 20/11/1999, p. 16 7/11/2000, pp. 17, 18 22/09/1999, p. 20 11/09/1994, p. 21 August 1994, p. 22 15/08/1994, p. 54 25/10/2000, p.58 18/04/2001, p.61 16/02/1999, p.75 15/02/1997, p.79 16/10/1999, p.96 18/01/1995, p. 225 7/02/2001; SEG: p. 24 SEG1999, p. 64 SEG 1998, pp. 86, 87 SEG 2000, p. 130 SEG, p. 192 26/04/1996, p. 199 16/12/2000; p. 38 Garrett Nagle, *Advanced Geography*/ OUP 2000; pp. 44, 230, 248 AQA; p.61 Norwich City Council; *The Times*: p. 61 27/12/2000, p. 95 22/09/1999, p. 117 4/11/1998, p. 119 28/09/1998, p. 210 4/10/1994, p. 239 22/07/2000; p. 123 *The Sunday Times* 31/08/1997; p.72 Beazer Homes; p.75 Bluewater Shopping Centre; p.76 www.stortford-residents.org.uk/CAUSE; p.85 www.west-quay.co.uk; p. 93 *Time Magazine* 5/11/1989; p. 109 The *Daily Telegraph* 19/08/2000, p. 213 February 2000; p. 127 The *Sunday Mirror* 5/11/2000; *Global Eye*: pp.118, 130, 144, 187 Spring 1999/ Worldaware; p.141 *Global Eye*, Spring 2000/ Worldaware; p. 137 Oxfam; pp. 138, 139, 145 WaterAid; p. 139 The World Resources Institute; p. 140 The World Health Organization; p. 146 E. Newby, *Slowly Down the Ganges* / Picador; p. 147 The *Sunday Telegraph* 29/03/1998; p. 161 The *Daily Express* 13/01/2001; pp. 163, 169, 203, 250 Maps reproduced from Ordnance Survey maps with the permission of the Controller of Her Majesty's Stationary Office © Crown Copyright; License No; 10000230; p. 168 Yorkshire Dales National Park Committee 1989; p. 173 Oasis Forest Holiday Villages; p. 186 Rainforest Action Network; p. 189 *The Observer* 1991, p. 212 28/09/1997; p. 196 US DOE EIA International Energy Outlook 2000; p. 198 Guardian Education Resources 18/03/1997; p. 201 *Why time is running out for Brazil's Indians*, 1993, reproduced with permission of Oxfam Publishing, 274 Banbury Road, Oxford OX2 7DZ; p. 207 The Environment Agency; p. 219 The Electronic Telegraph 27/08/1997; p. 219 The *National Forecaster* August 1998; p. 221 The *Sunday Express* 18/02/2001; p. 227 The World Wildlife Fund www.panda.org; p. 229 Sustainable Development International; p. 229 www.sustravel.com; p.233 World Tourist Organization; p.236 The Spanish National Tourist Office; p.246 Thompson Holidays.

Websites
Links to appropriate websites are given throughout the book. Although these were up to date at the time of writing, it is essential for teachers to preview these sites before using them with students. This will ensure that the web address (URL) is still accurate and the content is suitable for your needs. We suggest that you bookmark useful sites and consider enabling students to access them through the school intranet. We are bringing this to your attention as we are aware of legitimate sites being appropriated illegally by people wanting to distribute unsuitable or offensive material. We strongly advise you to purchase suitable screening software so that students are protected from unsuitable sites and their material. If you do find that the links given no longer work, or the content is unsuitable, please let us know. Details of changes will be posted on our website.

Contents

CS : Case study

1 Population change — 5
Measuring population change — 6
Causes of population change — 8
The demographic transition model — 10
World population growth — 12
The challenge of population change – MEDCs: Japan **CS** — 14
The challenge of population change – LEDCs: Kenya **CS** — 16
Strategies for change – MEDCs — 18
Strategies for change – LEDCs — 20
Global futures — 22
Exam practice questions — 24

2 Rural–urban migration in LEDCs — 25
What is rural–urban migration? — 26
Push factors from rural areas — 28
Attraction to the urban areas — 30
Problems in LEDC cities — 32
Contrasts in countries Case Study: India — 34
Brazil **CS** — 36
Cairo in Egypt **CS** — 38
Are there solutions to city problems? — 40
Rural change — 42
Exam practice questions — 44

3 Changing city and town centres — 45
How have MEDC town and city centres developed? — 46
Changes in land use in city and town centres — 48
Changing transport in city and town centres — 50
Managing traffic — 52
Living in poor inner city areas — 54
Retail changes and city and town centres — 56
Managing parts of city and town centres: Glasgow **CS** — 58
Solutions to problems – if people agree — 60
Manchester, a changing city **CS** — 62
Exam practice questions — 64

4 Pressure at the rural/urban fringe — 65
Why have changes occurred? — 66
What has happened to housing? — 68
What activities have moved to the rural/urban fringe? — 70
What are the consequences of pressure at the rural/urban fringe? — 72
What do people think about developments in the rural/urban fringe? — 74
Pressure groups – urban change — 76
How can change at the rural/urban fringe be managed? — 78
Green belts and new towns — 80
Marne-la-Vallée – a new town in France — 82
Environmental protection and redevelopment — 84
Decision-making exercise: a new town for Hampshire – Micheldever Station — 86
Exam practice questions — 88

5 Living with tectonic hazards — 89
Earthquakes and volcanoes — 90
Why do people live in hazardous areas? — 92
Earthquake activity — 94
The Kobe earthquake, January 1995 **CS** — 96
The Colombian earthquake, January 1999 **CS** — 98
Volcanic activity — 100
Eruption of Mount St Helens – 18 May 1980 **CS** — 102
The Soufrière Hills eruption – Montserrat 1997 **CS** — 104
Exam practice questions — 106

6 Weather hazards — 107
The climate of the British Isles — 108
Weather systems — 110
Anticyclones: high pressure systems — 112
Tropical storms — 114
Hurricane Mitch, 1998 **CS** — 116

Rebuilding Nicaragua after Hurricane Mitch CS	118
Hurricane Georges, 1998 CS	119
The hydrological cycle	120
The Lynmouth flood, 1952 CS	122
Flooding in Bangladesh CS	124
The autumn 2000 floods in the British Isles CS	126
River management – the Mississippi, USA CS	128
Exam practice questions	130

7 Water and food supply — 131

The causes of poor food supplies	132
Global distribution of food supplies	134
Drought and desertification	136
Water, water everywhere?	138
The effects of contaminated water	140
Alternative strategies to improve food and water supplies	142
Sustainable food and water projects in LEDCs	144
Managing the River Ganga, India CS	146
Water management in the western USA CS	148
Exam practice questions	150

8 Pressures on the physical environment — 151

What makes natural landscapes attractive?	152
Weathering and erosion	154
Coastal environments – the Wessex coast CS	156
Glaciation	158
Glaciation – erosion	160
Glaciation – deposition	162
The Lake District National Park CS	164
Managing visitors in the Lake District CS	166
National parks: choices for the future	168
National parks in the USA CS	170
Decision-making exercise: Oasis Holiday Village, Cumbria	172
Exam practice questions	174

9 Contrasting levels of development — 175

Contrasts in development	176
The quality of life	178
Contrasting living standards	180
Reducing the development gap	182
Large-scale development projects in LEDCs	184
Sustainable development	186
Industrial change, Teesside, north-east England CS	188
Recent developments in Teesside	190
Exam practice questions	192

10 Resource depletion — 193

The depletion of resources	194
Fossil fuels and minerals	196
Renewable resources	198
Brazil, the Amazon Basin and the effects of deforestation CS	200
The effects of coal mining in South Wales CS	202
Renewable energy	204
Recycling – a way to conserve resources	206
A changing resource: the US temperate forests CS	208
Exam practice questions	210

11 Managing economic development — 211

Economic development and the global environment	212
Acid rain	214
The ozone layer	216
Global warming	218
Rising sea-level	220
Development, pollution, health and accidents CS	222
Sustainable strategies for development CS	224
Appropriate technology and sustainability	226
International agreements and responses to climate change	228
Exam practice questions	230

12 Tourism and development — 231

The growth of global tourism	232
Tourism in Europe	234
Changing patterns of tourism in Spain CS	236
Tourism and development	238
Tourism in Africa	240
Tourism and the environment: East Africa CS	242
Tourism in fragile environments: The Amazon rainforest CS	244
Decision-making exercise: a potential tourist development in Barbados	246
Exam practice questions	248
Revise your map-reading skills	249
Glossary	251

MANAGING CHANGE IN THE HUMAN ENVIRONMENT

1 Population change

How do people in LEDCs and MEDCs meet the challenges of population change?

Managing Change in the Human Environment

1.1 Measuring population change

On 12 October 1999 the United Nations estimated that the total world population had reached 6 billion people. The population had doubled since 1985. The rate of growth is beginning to slow down but it is predicted that world population will rise to 10 billion by 2050 (B).

The population is changing in every country. Changes in the number of births, deaths and life expectancy alter the structure of the population. Migration affects the total number of people who live in a place. Governments need to know about these changes so that they can plan for the future.

How data is collected

The estimated figure of 6 billion was based on data collected from 227 countries in 1998. In More Economically Developed Countries (MEDCs) information about a population is collected through a **census**, which is carried out by a government every 10 years. The head of the household must record data about gender, age, marital status, ethnic background, language, etc. All births and deaths are registered, so the number of people is recorded quite accurately. In Less Economically Developed Countries (LEDCs) it is not so easy to count people. Some countries, like Ethiopia and Afghanistan, have held very few censuses. People who cannot write, who live in remote or very overcrowded areas, or who move frequently, are difficult to count. Births and deaths may not be registered in these areas.

Recording population change

- The **birth rate** gives the number of births per 1000 people.
- The **death rate** gives the number of deaths per 1000 people.
- The **infant mortality rate** gives the number of deaths of babies under the age of 1 year per 1000 babies born. The infant mortality rate in Sierra Leone (West Africa) in 1999 was 174 and in the UK it was 6.
- The **total fertility rate** is the average number of children born to a woman in her lifetime. The total fertility rate in the UK in 1995 was 1.8, but in Sierra Leone it was 6.5. The total fertility rate is a useful figure to use to look at population change.
- **Life expectancy** measures the average number of years a person can expect to live, at birth.

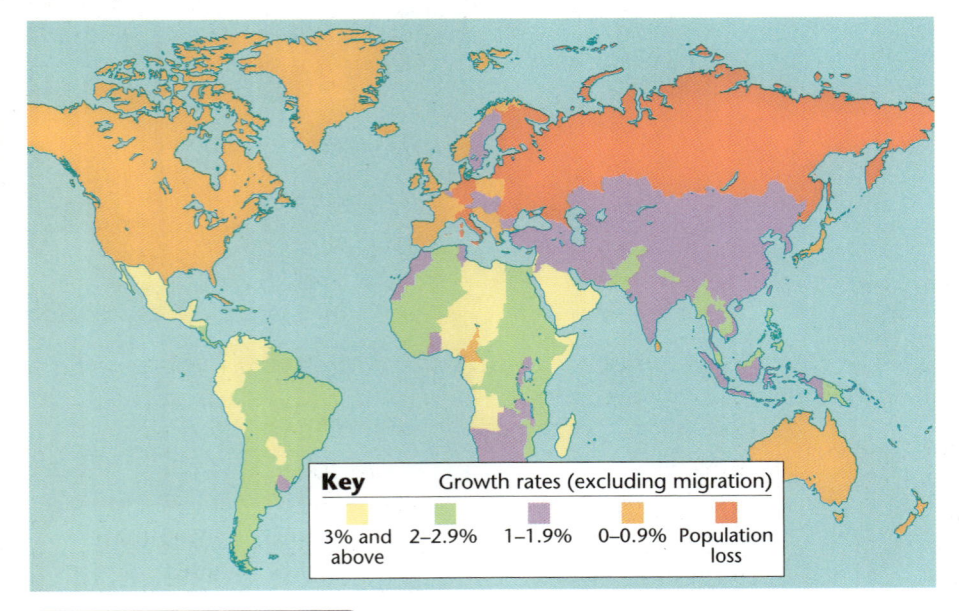

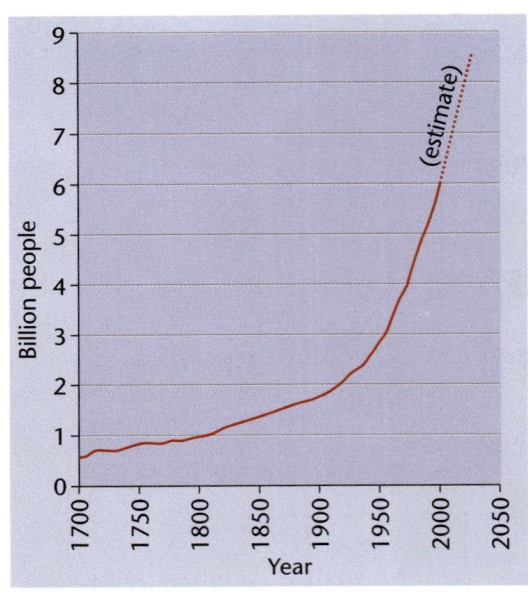

A – World population growth

B – World population, 1700–2050

1 Population change

- **The rate of natural increase** is the difference between the birth rate and the death rate.
- **Migration** is the movement of people from one place to another. **Population change** is found using migration figures, birth rates and death rates.
- A **population pyramid** is a way of illustrating the structure of a population (**C**). It is a type of bar graph. The population is divided into age groups on the vertical axis. The percentages of the total populations are given on the horizontal axis.

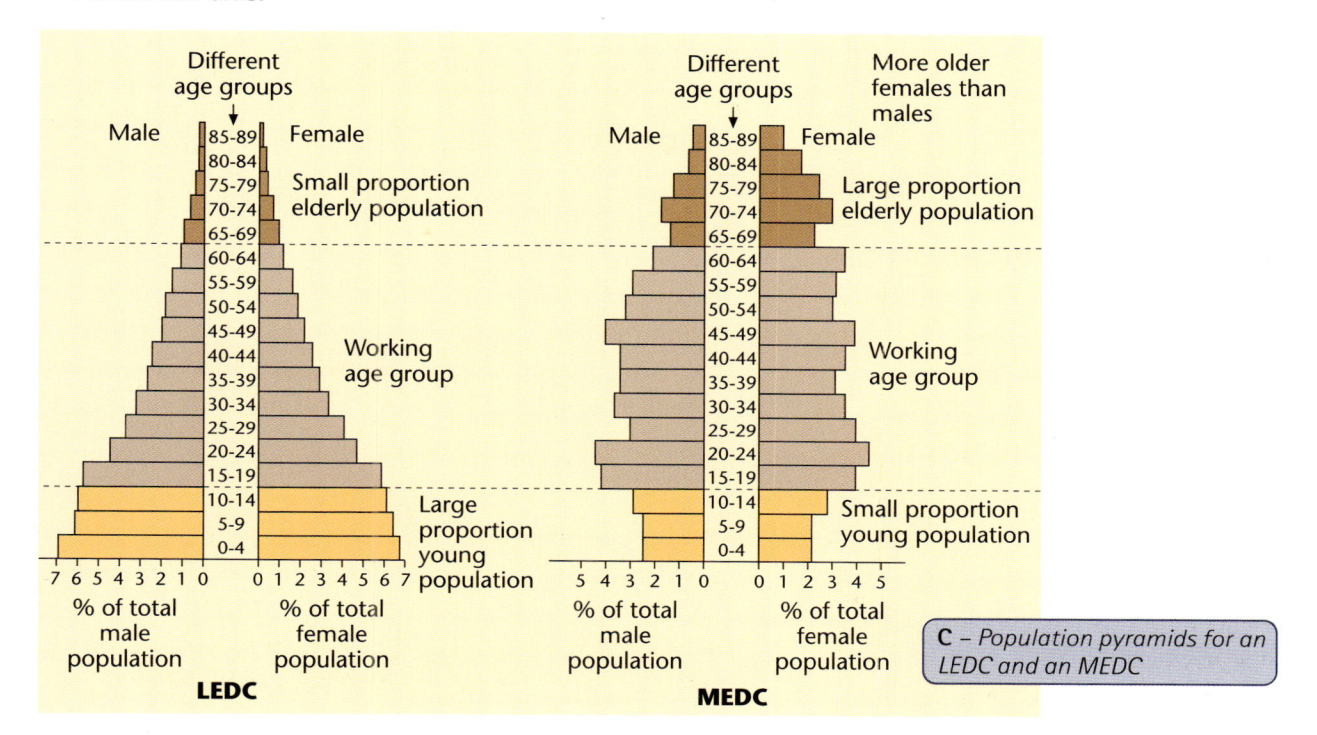

C – Population pyramids for an LEDC and an MEDC

Questions

1. How is population recorded? Suggest five reasons why, in a poor, developing country, it is difficult to count how many people there are.

2. In Nigeria (West Africa) in 1995, the birth rate was 45 per 1000, the death rate 15 per 1000. What was the rate of natural increase?

3. What differences can population pyramids show about a population in an LEDC and an MEDC?

4. Why is it important for planners in a country to know fertility rates as well as birth and death rates?

5. a) Using E, draw bar graphs to show the birth rate and death rate figures for India and the UK.
   b) Describe the differences between the two countries.
   c) Why might the death rate be similar in LEDCs and MEDCs?

D – Young people, a small proportion of the MEDC population

2000	India (LEDC)	UK (MEDC)
Birth rate	27 per 1000	10 per 1000
Death rate	9 per 1000	11 per 1000
Total population	1002 million	59 million
Doubling time (years)	39	546

E – Population change in India and the UK

Managing Change in the Human Environment

1.2 Causes of population change

Populations change in different ways in MEDCs and LEDCs. The population in many LEDCs is still growing rapidly but in most MEDCs it is growing very slowly or declining. Population change takes place at different rates in different parts of countries, so one region may grow rapidly while another declines. The urban areas of Rio de Janeiro and São Paulo in south-east Brazil are expanding quickly, whilst people are still leaving the poor north-east region. South-eastern England is growing, and the highlands of Scotland are losing population.

POPULATION INCREASE

... in LEDCs

The improvement of healthcare in an LEDC is followed by a reduction in the death rate, particularly the infant mortality rate. Traditionally, many families in LEDCs had several children because they were needed to work and care for each other. Many died before they were 5 years old. If more of these children live, the population will increase. When these children have their own children, the population growth will be rapid. It is useful to know the fertility rate, because if each woman has only one child, as in China, the population will grow a lot more slowly than in a country like Sierra Leone, for example, where the average fertility rate is 6.5 children.

... in MEDCs

The life expectancy in an MEDC is longer, so more people stay alive and total population numbers can increase, even if the birth rate is low. People live longer because of better healthcare, improved diet, education, and a good standard of living. The population can also increase with immigration.

A – Population increase

Factors affecting population change

- Some *religions and cultures* welcome as many children as possible — the Roman Catholic Church teaches that abortion and contraception are immoral. In other cultures small families are acceptable. In some places, for example parts of China, boys are valued more than girls.

- *Poverty* increases the death rate and shortens life expectancy. Poverty pushes people to migrate to find food and water, or a better quality of life. As wealth increases, some people have smaller families. Poor people in LEDCs often have more children to help them work the land and to care for them in their old age.

- The higher the levels of *education and healthcare*, the lower the birth rate.

- The greater the *level of development*, the more slowly the population grows.

- *Governments* can influence where people live and how many children they have. China allows one child per family. France pays a high rate of family allowance to encourage people to have children.

- People *migrate* between countries or within countries, often in order to achieve a better quality of life.

- Most *wars and conflicts* now are civil wars (wars between people within one country) and many people can be displaced or become refugees. 'Ethnic cleansing', or the forced expulsion of thousands of people from one place, is a common feature of civil war.

- *Disease* kills millions of people each year, and malaria kills the most. HIV/Aids now affects 33 million, mostly in LEDCs, particularly in Africa. In Botswana (southern Africa), 25 per cent of adults aged 15–49 are **HIV positive**.

POPULATION DECLINE

...in LEDCs

A decline in population growth in an LEDC, can be the result of a variety of factors. Education (particularly for women), healthcare, improved diet and standard of living, and access to contraception, can all bring a reduction in family size. Families may decide to have fewer children if they can see that infant mortality is falling and living standards improving. In Bangladesh, the average family size has fallen from 5 to 2.8, so the growth rate has reduced. War, civil disturbance, or natural disasters like floods or famine, can cause a sudden reduction in population. **Aids** is changing the population structure and growth in many countries, especially in Africa.

...in MEDCs

There are increasing numbers of older people in all MEDCs, and these countries are said to have an ageing population. The death rate in the UK is unlikely to drop below 11 per 1000 because there are now so many people over 65 years old, who will inevitably die in due course. There are fewer babies being born — in some countries, e.g. Italy and Japan, there are so few that there are not enough to replace the people who die.

B – Population decline

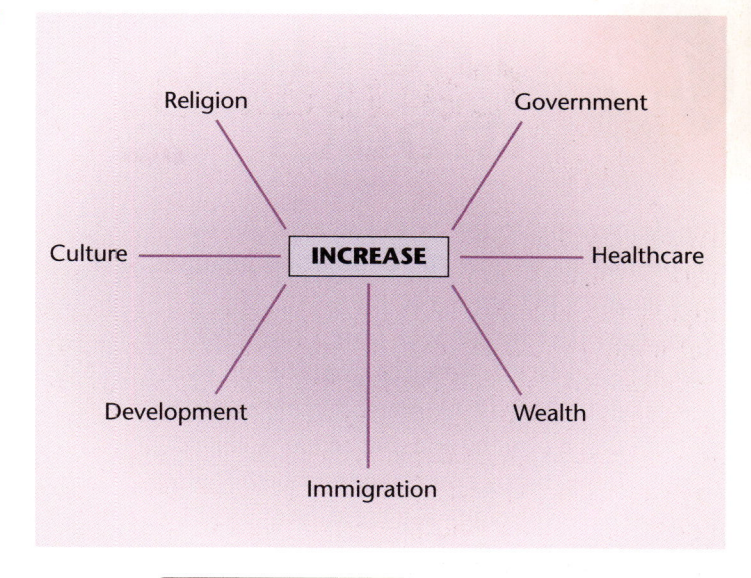

C – What factors affect an increasing population?
(INCREASE: Religion, Government, Culture, Healthcare, Development, Wealth, Immigration)

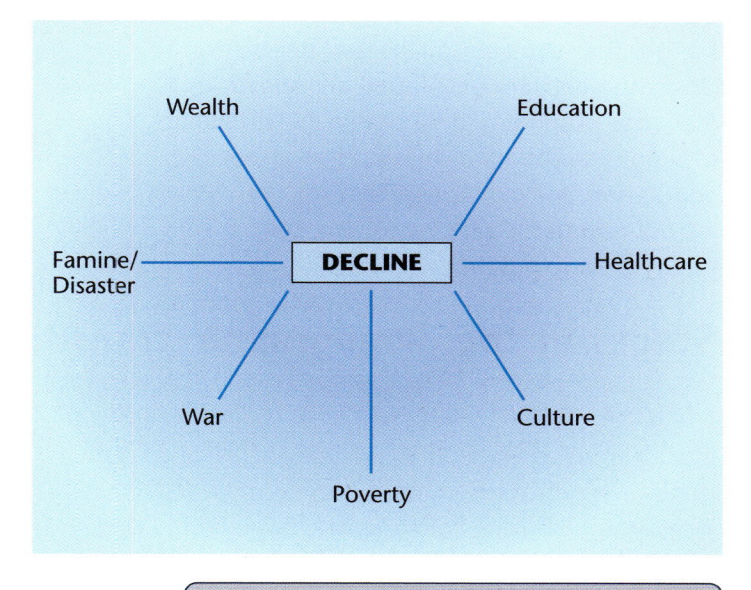

D – What factors affect a declining population?
(DECLINE: Wealth, Education, Famine/Disaster, Healthcare, War, Culture, Poverty)

Questions

1) Draw a table with four columns:

Increase in LEDC population	Decline in LEDC population	Increase in MEDC population	Decline in MEDC population

Using A and B, in each column list at least five factors affecting population change.

2) Using your answer to question 1, and C and D, explain why populations are increasing more rapidly in LEDCs than in MEDCs.

1.3 The demographic transition model

The **demographic transition model (A)** was devised to show how the population changes as a country becomes economically developed. The model was based on what had happened in North America and Europe over the previous 150–200 years. It is now used to help us to understand the reasons for population growth and change in developing countries. Four stages are identified, although there may be a fifth stage in some MEDCs.

Population pyramids can be used to illustrate the population structure at each stage. The factors that affected births and deaths in the UK as the country developed are shown in **B**. A similar graph could be drawn for all places to highlight the main things that affect the population, for example a famine, the introduction of a vaccine, or the start of a family planning policy.

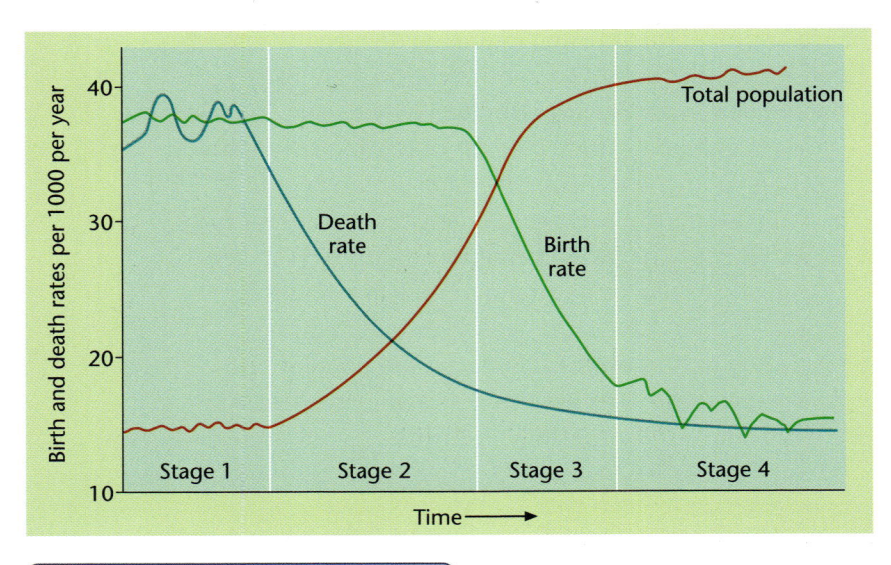

A – The demographic transition model

Stages in the demographic transition model

Stage 1
Birth and death rates are high, about 35 per 1000. There is very little healthcare, so death rates vary with disease and disaster. Most people live off the land. Britain and Europe were like this before 1750 (before industrialization), and some parts of the poorest countries are at this stage now.

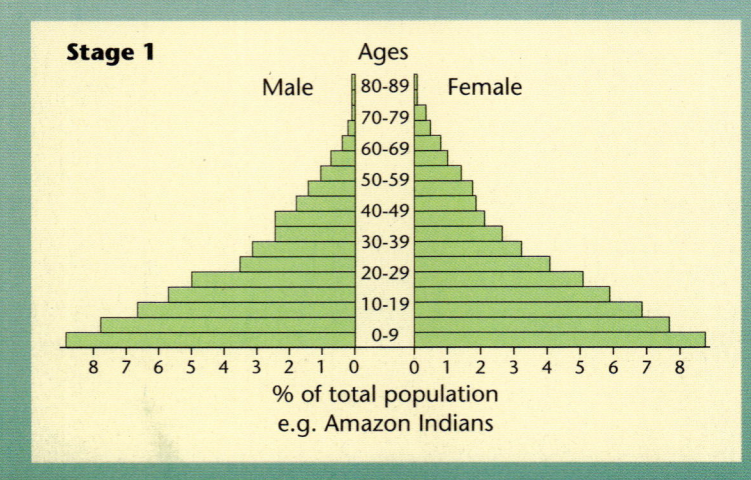

% of total population
e.g. Amazon Indians

Stage 2
Death rates begin to fall to less than 20 per 1000 as better healthcare reduces infant mortality and deaths from disease. The birth rate remains high, so the population grows rapidly. This is sometimes called the *early expanding stage*. Britain was in this stage towards the end of the 19th century, and countries like Sri Lanka have these characteristics today.

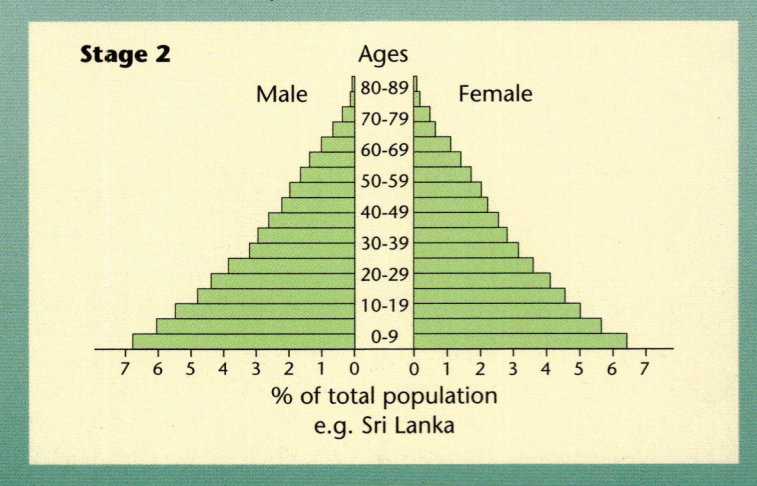

% of total population
e.g. Sri Lanka

1 Population change

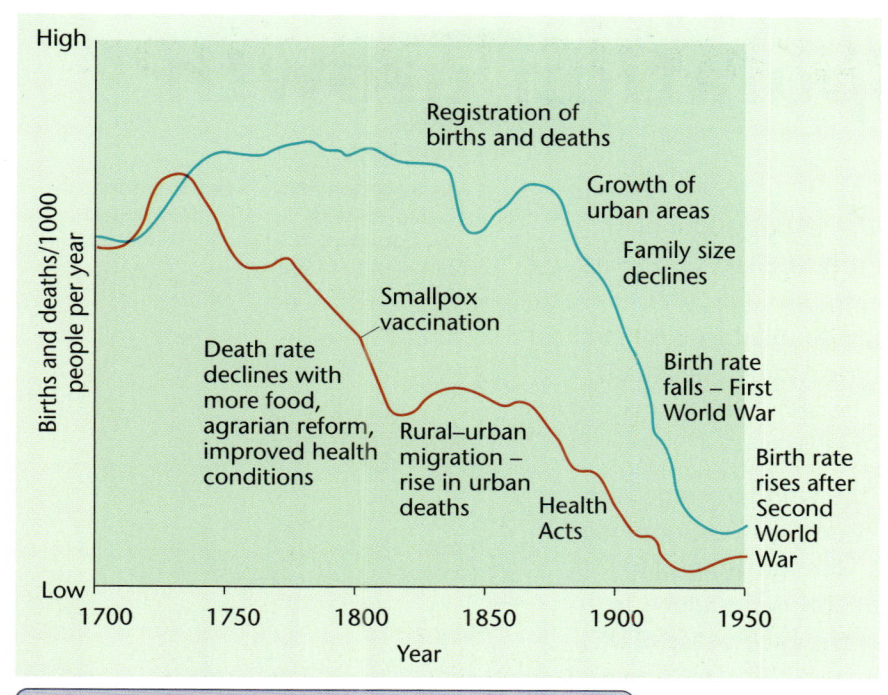

B – *The UK in transition: changes in fertility, 1700–1950*

Questions

1) State five things that cause changes in the birth rate and five things that cause changes in the death rate.

2) a) What is the purpose of a demographic transition model?
   b) Sketch the outline of each of the four population pyramids representing each stage. Describe the changes in the birth rate and the death rate at each stage.
   c) Give an example of a country now at each stage of the demographic transition model.

Stage 3

The death rate continues to fall, and the birth rate falls to about 20 per 1000 as the quality of life improves. More people are employed in industry and family size is reduced. Population growth slows down. Britain was like this in the first half of the 20th century, and developing countries like China and Cuba are in this position today.

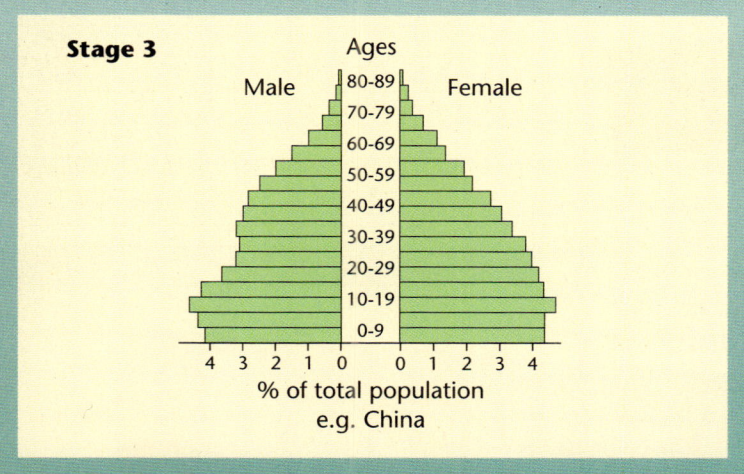

Stage 4

At this stage, birth rates and death rates are similar, about 12 per 1000. Population growth is low. Much of Europe was in this stage after 1940, along with Japan, the USA and, now, other developed countries. Birth and death rates fluctuate with disaster, conflict and fashion.

There was an increase in the birth rate at the end of the Second World War (1945) when soldiers returned from fighting abroad, creating the 'baby boom'.

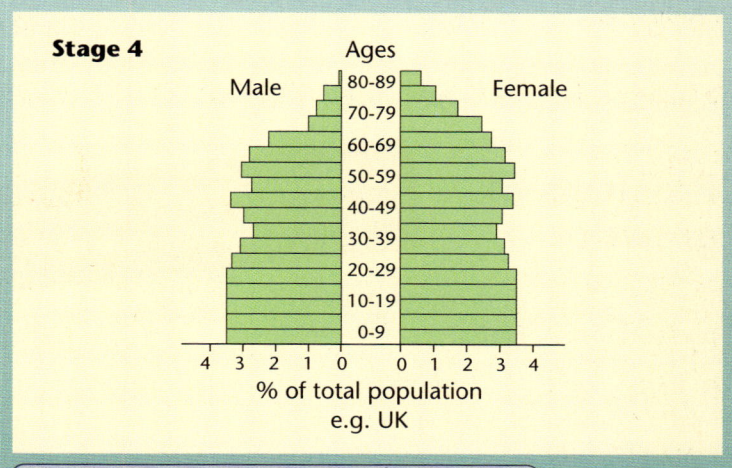

C – *Stages in the demographic transition model*

The future

Some countries are unlikely to become highly industrialized places in the near future, so they may not go through all the stages.

With rapid industrialization and a strict population policy, China has moved through the stages in a much shorter time than the UK. Although 60 per cent of people in China still live in rural areas, it is likely that the population growth rate will continue to fall.

Managing Change in the Human Environment

1.4 World population growth

Two thousand years ago, the world population was about 300 million. The population grew slowly until about 1750, but in the last 250 years growth has been very rapid and is still accelerating. Around 1960, the world population was 3 billion but by 1999 it had doubled to 6 billion. The doubling time of MEDC populations is estimated to be about 800 years. In LEDCs, the doubling time is thought to be about 40 years – and 97 per cent of world population growth is in LEDCs.

The rate of growth has also increased. In 2000, the world average rate of natural increase was 1.4 per cent, but some countries were growing much faster than that. Many countries in Africa were growing at 2–4.5 per cent a year. This means that 20–45 people were added to the population for every 1000 people in the country, each year. MEDCs were growing much more slowly, and some countries had a declining population. The growth rate in Japan was 0.3 per cent, so only 3 people per 1000 were added to the population each year. The rate in Hungary was –0.4, a loss of 4 people per 1000 each year.

A country with a growth rate of 4 per cent will double in size in 17 years, while one with a growth rate of 3 per cent will double in 25 years. LEDCs are growing very much more quickly than MEDCs, and now form a greater proportion of the world's population. There may be 6 billion people in LEDCs alone by 2004.

Problems of growth

2 billion people go hungry in the developing world every day.

The rapid growth in world population puts pressure on all resources and creates complex problems.

- *Clean water, food and firewood* are in short supply in many countries (C). Some people have to walk long distances each day to get water to survive. Water could well become *the* most serious issue in the 21st century. Often the water is not clean, and it is estimated that one child dies every four minutes from drinking contaminated water. In Asia and Africa 14 million children are thought to die each year from diseases caused by malnutrition (not enough of the right kinds of food). In 1999, enough food was produced in the world to give everybody an adequate diet of 2740 calories per day, but people in Sierra Leone averaged only 1694 calories per day. In contrast, people in the USA averaged 3732 calories – more than twice as much. It is estimated

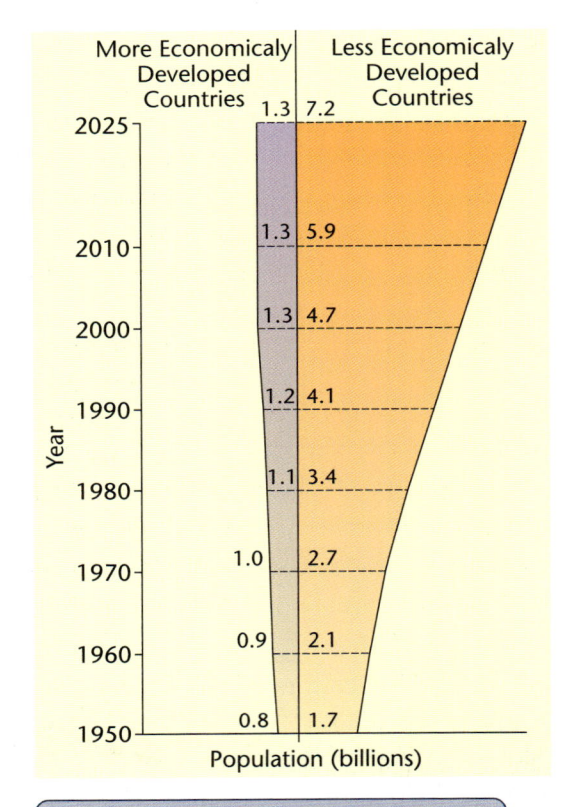

A – World population growth, 1950–2025

Continent	1950	2000
Africa	224	800
Latin America	166	517
North America	172	306
Asia	1402	3685
Europe	547	727
Oceania	12	31

B – Population totals in millions, 1950 and 2000

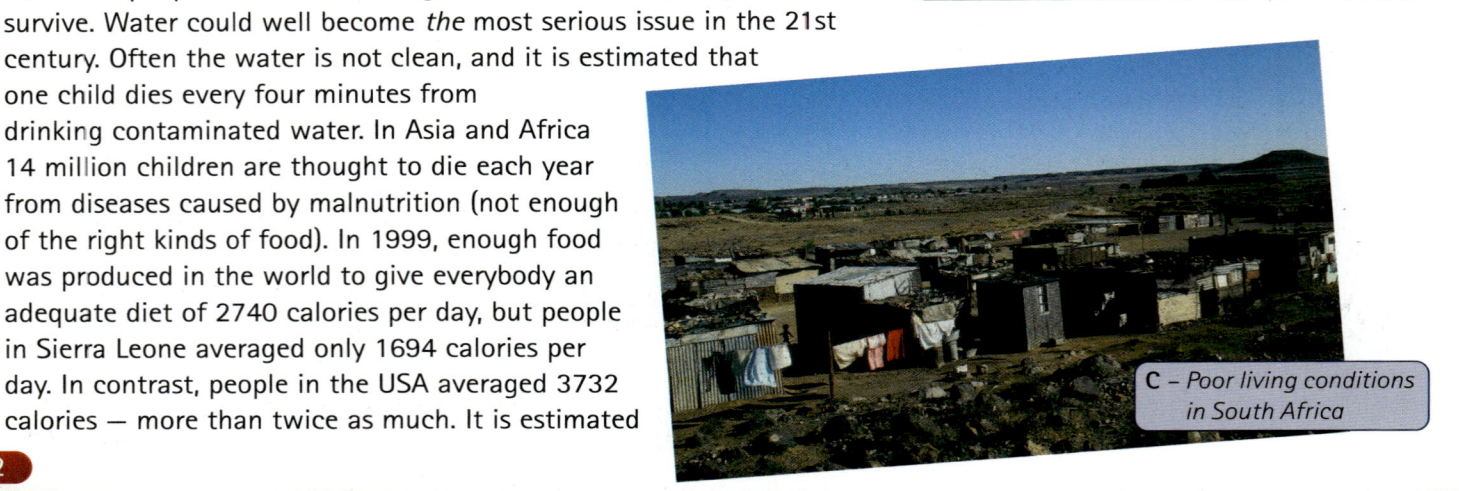

C – Poor living conditions in South Africa

that world food supplies can only keep pace with population growth for the next 10 years. Subsistence agriculture has not been able to supply enough food for the increasing rural populations in many LEDCs, so many people are forced to move to the cities.

- *Rural–urban migration* – many people move from the countryside to the cities, attracted by the prospect of a better quality of life there. Cities have grown at a phenomenal rate in the last 100 years. Nearly half the world's total population now live in cities, but it is thought that by 2015 this figure will be 70 per cent, with most people living in cities in LEDCs. The majority of **mega-cities** (cities with over 10 million people) are in LEDCs, as these cities have grown more rapidly than those in MEDCs.

- *Pollution, congestion, poverty and unemployment* are all problems in areas of rapid population growth, especially in urban areas (D). Healthcare, education and transport services are all put under pressure by changing populations. The needs are different in each country. More healthcare for the elderly is needed in MEDCs like the UK and Sweden, where 17.3 per cent of people were over 65 in 1997. In an LEDC like Mauritania in West Africa, where the majority of people are under 30 years old and 74 per cent of women and 50 per cent of men are illiterate, education is the great need.

D – *Traffic congestion in Karachi*

Poverty is the biggest problem to result from the explosion in world population.

Action needed now to avert disaster

October 12 has been designated as the day when the world's population hits 6 billion. It has doubled since 1960, and could rise to 10 billion in the next 50 years.

John Vidal

Today the world will gain another 230,000 people. Every day a city the size of Sunderland, every week another Birmingham, every month a London, and every year another Germany to feed, water and clothe.

All but three in every 100 of the newcomers will be born in a country whose finances are stretched, whose cities are swelling, where millions go hungry, and where the water and food is often scarce.

But the population explosion is a developing world phenomenon, with 2 billion people going hungry every day due to a combination of inequitable land distribution, soil erosion, lack of infrastructure, grinding poverty in cities, and people unable to buy food from the world market.

Food also depends on water, widely expected to be the most serious issue in the next century.

With population growth inevitable, if present consumption and climatic patterns continue, says the United Nations, two of every three people will have limited access to fresh water by 2025, with up to 2 billion in acute shortage.

There are thought to be more than 50 million environmental refugees -- people forced to flee lands that are uneconomic or impossible to work -- and the total is expected to rise.

Environmental concerns are growing. Global warming exacerbated by human activity is accepted by the consensus of world scientists as having started, and unpredictable and deleterious effects are expected. Deserts are growing, marine resources are at their limit, and air pollution has reached crisis situation in many African and developing country cities.

If trends continue, toxic emissions are likely to triple in rich countries and rise by 500 per cent in poor countries, posing ecological and human health threats. Carbon dioxide emissions, the prime source of global warming, are expected to more than double.

E – *From the* Guardian, *22 September 1999*

Questions

1. Use A to describe how world population growth has changed over time.

2. Use B to draw bar graphs showing the changes in population in the continents between 1950 and 2000. Describe the changes shown and try to give reasons for them.

3. Study the information on problems of population growth, and E. Devise a fund-raising pamphlet for a non-governmental organisation (NGO) like Oxfam, to explain to people in the UK why the population explosion is a problem in LEDCs.

4. Why is poverty the biggest problem resulting from the world population explosion?

Managing Change in the Human Environment

1.5 The challenge of population change

Japan

The Japanese Institute for Population Problems

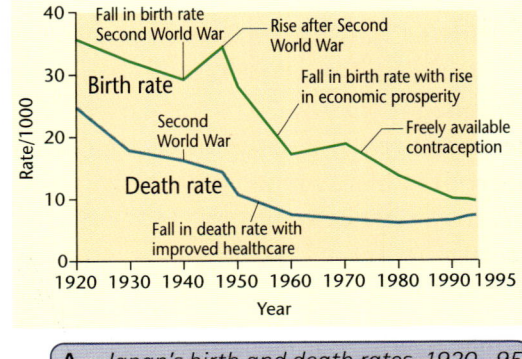

'No other country in the world is ageing as quickly as Japan.'

Some of the most crowded places in the world are in Japan. The average density of population is about 330/km² (240/km² in the UK), but 80 per cent of the land area is mountainous, so millions of people live on the 20 per cent of flat land. The total population of Japan was 127 million in 2000, and about 32 million people live in the Greater Tokyo Metropolitan Area. About 8.5 million live in Tokyo city, where population densities are very high at 5500 people/km².

Development was rapid in Japan after 1945 and industrial growth turned Japan into an extremely rich MEDC. Much money was invested in health and education and the population structure changed quickly. Fewer children were born and people lived longer. Now, with a birth rate of 9 per 1000 and a death rate of 8 per 1000, it will take 462 years for the population to double. One population projection suggests that the population may shrink to 100 million by 2050.

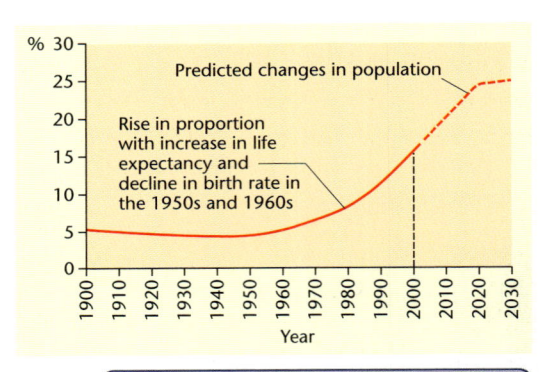

A – Japan's birth and death rates, 1920–95

B – Population in Japan aged over 65, 1900–2030

What are the problems?

Seventeen per cent of the total population are over 65 years of age, so Japan is faced with an ageing population. Can a small proportion of workers support a growing dependant population of the elderly? The number of people needing hospital care, housing and pensions will increase and by 2020, 25.5 per cent of the population will be over 65 years old. The problems will remain, even if people stay in work for longer and take up pensions at a much later age than in the UK.

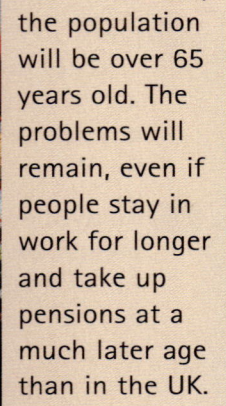

C – Urban concentrations: Japan

About 43 per cent of the Japanese population live in three major **urban concentrations** around Tokyo, Osaka and Nagoya. These are very crowded urban areas with typical urban problems of congestion, pollution and shortage of housing. Some people need to use oxygen and facemasks because of the air pollution from traffic. Thousands commute each day from suburban 'bed towns' in the Tokyo Metropolitan Area to the city for work, putting still more pressure on the already overstretched transport system.

Housing is in very short supply and expensive. Most urban housing was destroyed in the Second World War and replaced by high-rise apartment blocks. Traditional houses were small with limited living space although in the early 1900s each family averaged 165m^2 of floor space. The average floor space per unit is now 92m^2 but in Tokyo the demand is so great, the average floor space is 62m^2 per family unit.

Some inner city residents are elderly, living in apartments which they moved into as they were built 50 years ago. Some of the apartments are now old and substandard but people are reluctant to move out of neighbourhoods that they know. A high proportion of the elderly are women, many with no family to support them. Single elderly people living on their own may need help but cannot always afford it.

Questions

1) Why is the population structure in Japan changing? Refer to the birth rate and the death rate in your answer.

2) What are the problems that result from those changes?

3) Read E.
   a) What is Italy's 'baby crisis'?
   b) Make a list of five changes happening in the village of Vastogirardi as it gets smaller.
   c) Why is Italy's birth rate falling so rapidly? Give three reasons.
   d) Describe and explain three different effects on Italy if the population structure changes in all villages.

Italy's baby crisis

Too busy hunting boar, making wine or playing football to settle down, the ageing bachelors of a dying Italian village have been catapulted into infamy by their mayor's ultimatum: marry or pay a singles' tax.

Vastogirardi, founded almost 2000 years ago on a mountain in southern Italy, will soon cease to exist unless its citizens start having children. In the latest symptom of a demographic timebomb that church and state are powerless to defuse, the mayor has declared war on the self-sufficient old boys who cluster in bars every night and return to empty homes.

Mr Venditti, the mayor, intends to levy a tax on the 50 men and 20 women who show no desire to marry or have children, despite prominently advertised government aid to families.

'We are reaching the point of no return. When the school dies, society dies,' he said. Funerals in the village outnumber weddings by three to one. There is no secondary school, not enough children to fill the primary school, and the kindergarten will close within three years unless more babies are born.

One was born last year, none this year. In three decades the population has shrivelled from more than 3000 to 823. Once famed for its delicate handmade mozzarella cheese, Vastogirardi no longer has a bank, plumber, shoemaker or priest. Its pulse is slowing to a stop.

But for the bachelors life is sweet. Hunting, fishing, a football field, three bars and wine-making to fill their free time. Some of them have been engaged to women for more than 20 years.

'It suits us,' grinned Antonio Bisciotti, 29, sitting in the Bar Central with friends sunk into padded anoraks. 'We're lazy. We like our lives.'

Guiseppe di Benedetto, 40, a forest ranger, drained his Campari and proclaimed a desire to marry his girlfriend next year.

'Hah!' exploded the mayor, standing behind. 'If only.'

Italy's average rate of 1.2 children per woman is the lowest in the world.

Many of the bachelors are part of Italy's army of so-called *mammoni*, grown-up sons who never leave their mothers and the comforts of home. Sociologists cannot agree on an explanation for the phenomenon, which carries no stigma in Italy.

Like their male counterparts, the village's new generation of educated, career-driven single women are in no rush to bag partners.

- Population expected to fall from 57.3m to 51.3m over next 25 years.
- Number of live annual births halved to 521,000 in past 30 years.
- Average fertility rate of 1.2 children per woman is lowest in the world. Rate needed for a couple to 'replace' itself is 2.1.
- 90 per cent of couples use contraception.
- Average age of first-time mother: over 27. In 1981: under 24.

The changing population structure is similar in all MEDCs. In the UK, 18 per cent of the population are of **pensionable age**. In the future the working population will be supporting a larger dependant population, both young and old, and the elderly will need more in the form of pensions, healthcare and different types of housing. Italy is trying to take positive steps to stop its decline.

E – *From the Guardian, 20 November 1999*

Managing Change in the Human Environment

1.6 The challenge of population change

Kenya

In the *mid-1980s*, Kenya (Africa) was known as 'the world's fastest growing nation'.

- The population doubling time was 20 years.
- Women averaged 8 children each.
- The birth rate remained high at over 50 per 1000.
- Life expectancy had increased to 55.
- The infant mortality rate was becoming the lowest in Africa.
- The growth rate was 4.12 per cent.

With a high birth rate and a falling death rate, Kenya was facing a **population explosion**. Only 20 per cent of the land could be farmed and food was imported. Pressure on the land meant that marginal land was being used, leading to soil erosion and land degradation. The rural–urban movement of people to cities increased, particularly to Nairobi. Slum areas grew rapidly around many of the larger towns and cities. The development of healthcare, education, housing and employment could not keep up with rapidly increasing numbers.

Why did the death rate fall so dramatically?

Fewer babies and young children died and more people lived longer. Immunisation of young children against polio, TB and measles was increasingly effective and basic healthcare improved (new health centres were built). The quality of life began to improve and life expectancy increased.

Why did the birth rate remain so high?

Children were needed to work, especially in rural and poor areas. They were also needed to look after parents in old age. Use of contraceptives and education about birth control was not widespread. The cultures of the different groups of people in Kenya all depended on families having many children, who were seen as a status symbol.

A proposal by the world's leading pharmaceutical companies to slash the cost of Aids drugs in Kenya is 'cynical and hypocritical', Dr Mohammed Abdullah, the chairman of the country's Aids Control Council, said yesterday.

Earlier this week the Kenyan Minister of State, Marsden Madoka, estimated that the Aids pandemic was costing Kenya's barely solvent economy more than £1.8m a day in medical care, lost labour and funeral expenses. In less than five years the figure would be almost £17.5m a day, he said.

In the west, anti-retroviral drugs have delayed the development of full-blown Aids by up to 10 years, turning a killer disease into a chronic illness. But in sub-Saharan Africa, where 90% of the infected people live, they are out of reach and unknown to the vast majority.

Government figures show that up to 25% of Kenyans are HIV-positive, but only 2% can afford the recommended cocktail of anti-retroviral medicines.

At about 432 000 Kenyan shillings (£3800) for a year's course, the cost of treating all the infected Kenyans would exceed the national budget.

'Instead, our people are left to succumb to what doctors in Kenya have become adept at doing: simply managing their decline and death,' Dr Chris Ouma of the charity ActionAid said.

'The Ministry of Health cannot provide the most basic medicines,' Dr Abdullah said. 'It cannot treat diarrhoea, and it will never be able to treat Aids at any western price.'

'Extraordinary means call for extraordinary measures. We must re-examine the whole patenting issue. If the disease continues unchecked it will be like exploding a neutron bomb in our country. There will be buildings but there will be no human beings.'

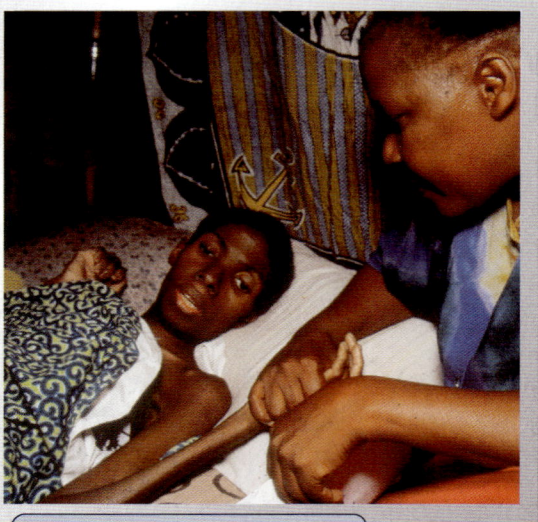

B – *A young Kenyan Aids victim*

A – *From the* Guardian, *7 November 2000*

Why was it necessary to limit population growth?

By *1990* half the population of Kenya was under 15 years old. By *2000* many of these people had had several children and the growth rate escalated.

In *1994*:
- the population was 27 million
- the infant mortality rate was 66
- 49 per cent were under 15 years
- 2 per cent were over 65 years
- the birth rate was 44 per 1000
- the death rate was 10 per 1000
- the rate of increase was 3.3
- the doubling time was 21 years
- life expectancy at birth was 59 years.

And by *2000*:
- the population was about 30 million
- the infant mortality rate was 74
- 46 per cent were under 15 years
- only 3 per cent were over 65 years
- the birth rate was 34 per 1000
- the death rate was 13 per 1000 —

but...
- the rate of increase was down 2.1 per cent
- the doubling time was 33 years
- and life expectancy was 49 years.

What brought about the changes?

The Kenyan government supported population control and wanted to reduce the growth rate to 2.5 per cent by 2000. It encouraged families to have four children and no more. Education of women and the setting up of women's groups contributed to better family planning. An increase in paid employment encouraged some people to look for a better quality of life and fewer children.

Sadly, since the late 1990s HIV/Aids has had a huge impact on the population structure (**A**). Now, 12 per cent of people aged between 15 and 49 have HIV/Aids. By 2020 the workforce will be 15 per cent lower than it would have been without Aids, creating more child labour and slowing the advancement of women.

And in Ghana...

Twin track

Kofi and Efia, humans 5 999 978 623 and 624 (more or less) were born on Friday to Rhoda Mensab in Korle-bu. They are asleep, Rhoda is resting, and civil servant dad Philip looks worried, not quite understanding how his personal population explosion happened. There is no history of twins in either family, he says.

Next year's census is expected to show population at 20 million, a 500% rise in 50 years. Rhoda and Philip's families illustrate Ghana's rising and and now slowing population curve in the last 40 years. Their grandparents had seven and eight children respectively: their parents five and four. They will have one more child. 'That's enough,' says Rhoda. The crude birth rate is falling but so is the mortality rate of children, and Ghanaian mums bear 4.4 children on average. It's far less than nearby Nigeria, but there's nothing anyone can do about the next stage of the explosion.

Almost one in five Ghanaians are now under five, half are under 15 and 62% under 25. The momentum in this country of the young is unstoppable, and will define Ghana in the next century. At best, the government can reduce the long-term numbers but it expects there to be 30m by 2025, perhaps as many as 38m. The national plan is to reduce the birth rate to 4.0 by 2003 and then bring it, as fast as possible, to 3.5. That doesn't sound difficult but it represents a herculean task in educating people and providing contraception. The culture in the countryside, where 70% of people live, is still to see children as assets, conferring status, wealth and recognition.

Cosmos Offei works with the Ghanaian family planning association and is in the personal and professional front line. He is the youngest of eight children, and his brothers and sisters have 26 children between them. He has just two and is unlikely to have more, he says, because prices are high, and life hard, in Accra.

D – A rising population in Ghana, West Africa

C – From the Guardian, 22 September 1999

Questions

1. Divide your page into three columns:

Kenya mid-1980s	Kenya 1994	Kenya 2000

   Use the figures given on these two pages to complete your table and describe what happened to the population at each time.

2. Using the figures for 2000, the text and newspaper articles, pick out five ways in which the HIV/Aids issue affects Kenya and other African countries now, or will do in the future.

3. Why is it difficult to predict future population levels in Africa?

4. What does **C** tell you about Ghana's population structure now and in the future?

Managing Change in the Human Environment

1.7 Strategies for change — MEDCs

How is the population in the UK changing?

The UK population in mid-1999 was estimated to be 59.5 million, with 7.2 million living in London. By 2008 London is expected to grow by 7 per cent to 7.7 million, but the numbers are difficult to predict because of international migration. The figures assume that 91 000 people per year will come from other countries, but this could change. The biggest growth in the UK will be in Cambridge (11 per cent). The biggest decline will be in Merseyside (4 per cent). Built-up areas are estimated to decline by 1 per cent as people move out. Some regions are expected to grow as people move to rural and coastal areas and as the population ages. Population in south-west England may grow by 5.8 per cent.

What are the costs of an ageing population?

The proportion of the UK population over 65 is now 18 per cent, and the proportion will grow in the next decade. After the Second World War (1945), the birth rate rose. Babies born then will be 60 in 2005. In the 1960s and 1970s the birth rate fell, partly because of the introduction of the contraceptive pill and because the trend was to have smaller families. This smaller group of people born in the 1970s and 1980s will be the working population who will have to support the increasing proportion of people over 65.

The National Health Service (NHS) compiles much of the data on population change because it needs to know the proportion of

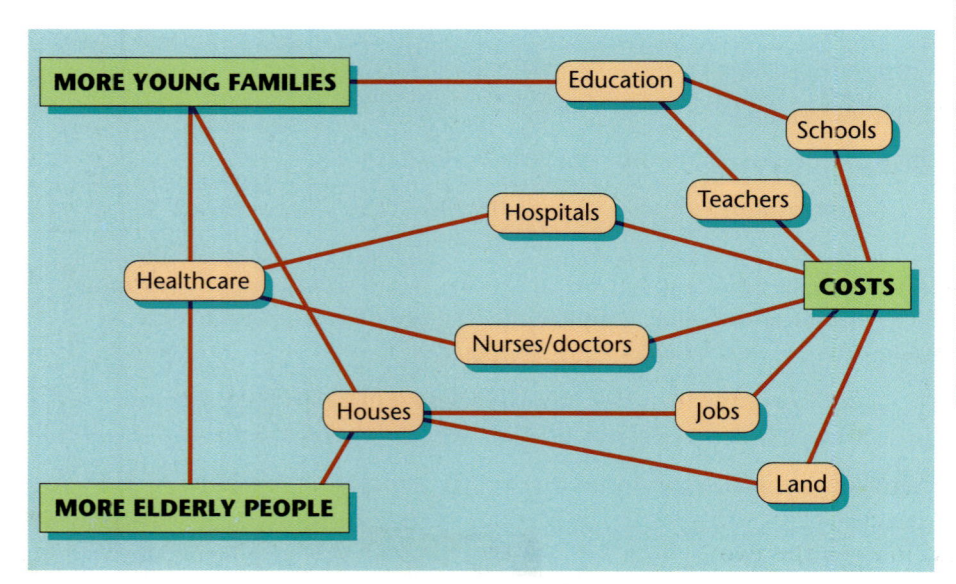

A – Some costs of a changing population

Pressure on crowded island

Britain. Unlike most of Europe, numbers will grow to new peak by 2023

John Vidal

In the next 25 years the United Kingdom is expected to grow by 3.3m people, the equivalent of three cities the size of Birmingham.

Compared with Africa, India and Asia this is nothing, but it will add to the pressures of life in one of the most crowded islands in the world.

There is little doubt that our economy can cope with the extra numbers, but unless we become healthier, and learn to live together more and use less power, it will mean significant extra spending on schools, hospitals, housing, pollution, infrastructure, and water supplies.

Britain led the way in population explosions during the industrial revolution. In 1801 we had fewer than 11m people. By 1891 we had 33m and now, after a series of rapid rises due to baby booms and immigration, we are at about 57.8m.

We do not know exactly what our numbers are, partly because so many students and others did not fill in their census forms in 1991 due to the poll tax, and also because population is subject to unexpected social and economic changes.

Nevertheless, Britain is one of Europe's few countries expecting an increase in numbers. We should peak in 2023 at 61.5m, then fall back slowly to a mid-1980s figure of about 54m, says the Office for National Statistics.

Apart from Ireland, we are Europe's youngest country with almost 20% of people under 14. Where most other EU countries have a declining population, we have more teenage births and one-parent families than any other. Women in Britain on average are giving birth to more children than anywhere else except Ireland and Sweden.

The population shifts between regions are dramatic. Central London is growing again, after decades of falling numbers, but the old northern industrial cities like Liverpool and Glasgow are expected to shrink significantly. The Office for National Statistics expects hundreds of thousands of northerners to move to the south-east over the next 20 years.

B – From the Guardian, 22 September 1999

people in each age group in order to provide appropriate resources. Elderly people need more healthcare, so health authorities have to respond appropriately.

The elderly want different leisure activities to 20-year-olds, different holidays, shops and facilities in cities and rural areas. Many elderly people retire to semi-rural areas and villages, and find it difficult to cope with the decline of shops, public transport and other facilities. More of the elderly are living alone in their own homes, which increases the demand for houses. Local authorities have to manage some of these changes.

In Cambridge, the population is expanding because of the development of high-tech industry, which presents planners with other challenges. Here, there are more families and young people. More schools and colleges are needed, healthcare for a younger generation, and considerably more houses, shops and leisure facilities.

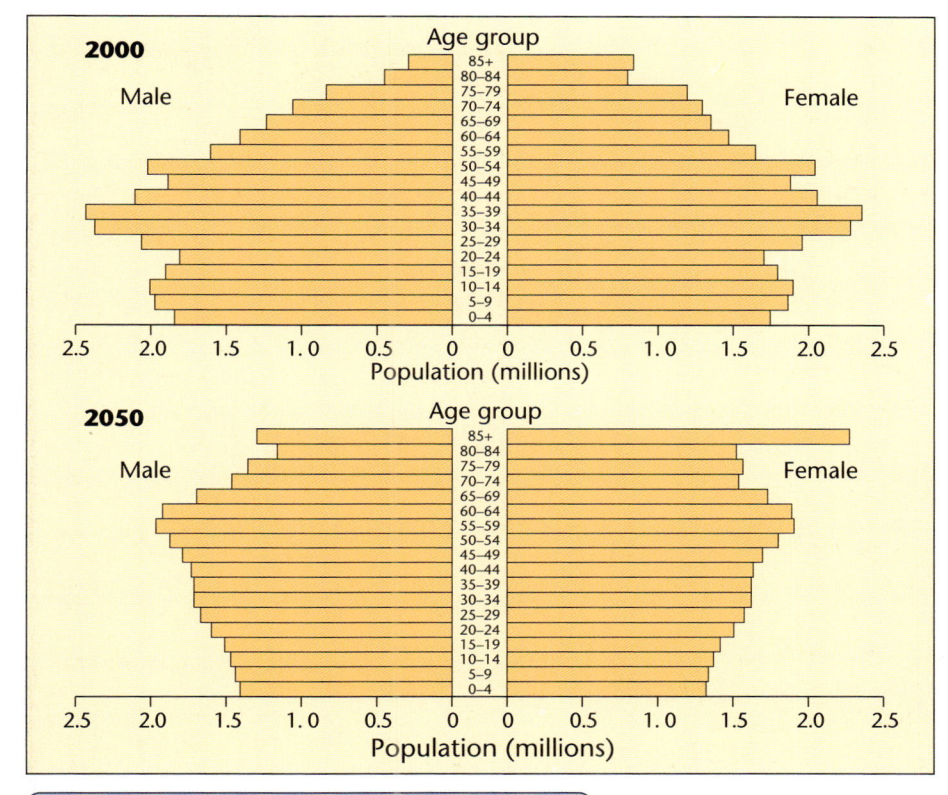

C – Population pyramids for the UK, 2000 and 2050

D – An ageing UK population

Questions

1) What changes are taking place in the UK population?

2) a) Name regions in the UK where population is:
   • declining   • growing   • ageing.
   b) What healthcare, housing and services will be needed in each region?

3) Refer to C.
   a) If people are aged 35 in 2000, when were they born? How old will they be in 2050?
   b) How many males and how many females will be aged over 65 in 2050? How many people will there be in that age group altogether?
   c) How many will be under 20?
   d) What does this mean for housing in 2050 in the UK?
   e) What will happen to the number and size of schools by 2050? Describe and explain the differences between the two pyramids for 2000 and 2050.

4) Use B. How is the UK population different to other parts of Europe?

E – There are more young people in growth areas

19

Managing Change in the Human Environment

1.8 Strategies for change — LEDCs

The global population explosion needs global discussion as well as national strategies. People need to talk, as 18 000 people did in 1994 at a Population Summit in Cairo organized by the United Nations. The aim was to stabilize world population in the 21st century. Many of the delegates were women and it became clear that supporting and educating women and girls would lead to a reduction in the birth rate. This has happened in Bangladesh and parts of India. In China the government enforced its **one-child policy** to reduce family size: now the rate of natural increase there is 0.87.

Bangladesh

Bangladesh is one of the poorest and most densely populated countries in the world: 120 million people live in a space the size of England and Wales, and 49 per cent of the population are under 15. The UN predicts that the population will double by 2030, but over the last 10 years the government has actively encouraged family planning. It is a Muslim country but family planning information groups for women and men have been set up. 'One is enough' leaflets and condoms have been delivered to millions of homes. Women can get access to contraception and almost half the country's married women use it. The fertility rate has reduced to 3.3 but the government aim is for families to have only two children. The government advertising is supported by many NGOs working with local community groups.

China

China has a population of 1264 million (1 in 4 people in the world, mid-2000 estimate), with 69 per cent of the population living in rural areas. In 1950 there were 550 million people and the fertility rate was 6. By the 1970s, it became clear that if all the children born survived to have children, the people would outstrip the food supply and resources and there would be devastating famines.

In 1978 the government introduced the one-child policy, allowing each couple just one child. Healthcare and education came with that one child, but benefits were lost if you had more than one, and money had to be repaid to the government. The average age of marriage increased and couples were told when they could try for a child. Abortion was freely available. The birth rate fell spectacularly and the fertility

Fighting to hold back the flood

In Bangladesh, the world's most densely populated country, where 120 million people compete for space in an area the size of England and Wales, half of which is flooded most years, family planning has become an issue of national survival.

Almost half the country's married women use contraceptives and the move to smaller families is fostering a social revolution.

For 10 years the Bangladeshis have been inundated with advertisements emphasising the economic benefits of contraception and repeating slogans such as 'One is enough'. Health workers have delivered leaflets and condoms to a majority of the 15 million Bangladeshi homes in more conservative rural communities. Abortions, carried out under the euphemism of 'menstrual regulation', are officially approved for 10 weeks after conception.

Moderate imams [Muslim religions leaders] have lent their support. 'I know of one who married a couple and then handed them a family planning leaflet straight afterwards,' said Dr Mohammed Alamgir, health programme manager in Bangladesh for the development agency Concern Worldwide. He has spent 20 years working in family planning. 'When I first started, it was very difficult to discuss these issues,' he says, 'but now men and women are very open about contraception. We are Muslims but not strict followers of Islam.'

Deep in the slums of Dhaka, 12-year-old Parvin shares a 12ft square hut with her parents, her teenage sister and a baby brother and sister. 'I started working in a garment factory one and a half years ago,' she says. 'I wanted to stay on at school, but I needed to earn money to help to feed my family.'

Parvin's mother, like millions of other Bangladeshi women, is now using contraception for the first time. As a result, she has found time to learn sewing skills at a Concern training centre and she is saving to buy a sewing machine. Like millions of poor Bangladeshi women, she is finding birth control a liberating experience.

A generation ago few Bangladesh women worked. But a social revolution is following in the wake of family planning programmes, as tens of thousands of illiterate women receive rudimentary education which gives them a new-found status and power within the family.

On the island of Demra, Abul Hossain's wife is receiving a basic education and learning handicrafts at a Concern-run women's training centre. 'Before, I never took any notice of what my wife said,' Hossain says. 'Now she has been educated about children's health and she has learnt to sew saris so she can make some more money for the family. Now I will talk to her more and we will make decisions together, good decisions.'

A – *From the* Guardian, *11 September 1994*

1 Population change

With millions more males than females, finding a wife is tough. Now their scarcity value could raise women's status

Philip Shenon in Beijing

In the free markets of the new China, young men are coming to realize that there is something even more precious than a new car, an electronic pager or a Swiss-made watch. And that rare commodity – an unmarried woman – is becoming harder and harder to find.

There are not nearly enough of them, a situation that is creating anguish for millions of Chinese men and has at least the potential of revolutionizing the status of women in this traditionally sexist society.

For Chinese men in search of love, the offerings of the Chinese state statistical bureau are downright heartbreaking. The 1990 census showed that of a total population of 1.2 billion, about 205 million Chinese over the age of 15 are single. And of them, there are nearly three men for every two women.

A three-to-two ratio might seem bad enough to most men. But the numbers suggest that the situation becomes far, far bleaker for a Chinese man the longer he stays unmarried. The government's figures show that while the vast majority of Chinese adults marry by the time they turn 30, 8 million people in their 30s were still single in 1990. And in that age group, the men outnumbered the women by nearly 10 to 1.

China's strict rule of one child per family, imposed in the late 1970s and meant to defuse a population time bomb, has only worsened the insistence on having male heirs. Ultrasound machines and ready access to abortion have made it relatively simple for parents to guarantee that their one child is a boy. The numbers suggest that tens of millions of men alive at the turn of the century will be lifelong bachelors because there will simply not be enough women available as wives.

'I do think this shortage of women will play a positive role in improving the status of all women,' said Guo Daofu, a senior economist with the state statistical bureau. 'I think this will lead to changes in society. Men will have to become more open-minded.'

Figures compiled by the United Nations show that the world's second most populous country, India, with nearly 900 million people, has nearly 133 single men for every 100 single women. As in China, Indian custom demands that couples produce male heirs.

In the industrialized world, the ratios are much smaller, and in some countries, such as the United States and Japan, single women outnumber single men.

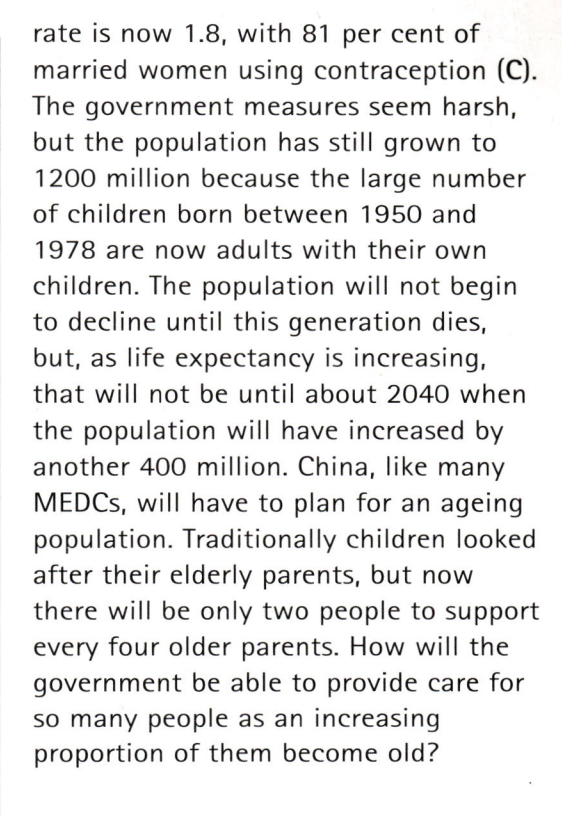

B – A one-child family in China

C – From the Guardian, mid-August 1994

rate is now 1.8, with 81 per cent of married women using contraception (**C**). The government measures seem harsh, but the population has still grown to 1200 million because the large number of children born between 1950 and 1978 are now adults with their own children. The population will not begin to decline until this generation dies, but, as life expectancy is increasing, that will not be until about 2040 when the population will have increased by another 400 million. China, like many MEDCs, will have to plan for an ageing population. Traditionally children looked after their elderly parents, but now there will be only two people to support every four older parents. How will the government be able to provide care for so many people as an increasing proportion of them become old?

India

In India the population growth varies between the regions. The country's 1000 million population will grow rapidly in the next 20 years but not in the states of Goa and Kerala where improvements in healthcare and education of women have reduced the birth rate. In other poorer regions such as Rajasthan and Bihar, the growth rates are still high (**D**).

	Kerala, south-west India	India	USA
Infant mortality	20	94	10
Life expectancy	70	56	75
Female literacy	87%	40%	95%

D – A comparison of populations in Kerala, India and the USA

Questions

1. Divide a page into two parts, heading one part 'Advantages of China's one-child policy' and the other 'Disadvantages of China's one-child policy'. List five points in each section, and try to explain each one.
2. How has Bangladesh managed to reduce its birth rate?
3. a) Use the figures in **D** to draw bar graphs for Kerala, India and the USA.
   b) Describe your graphs and try to suggest reasons for the differences.

1.9 Global futures

The global population is unevenly distributed across the world. One-tenth of the land area, in China, Bangladesh and India, is home to nearly half the world's population. Areas of high population density can become **overpopulated** where the resources are insufficient to adequately support the population. It is possible to have a high population density and a good standard of living, as in South Korea, or a high population density and a low standard of living, as in Bangladesh. Areas that are too hot, too cold or too dry, and most mountainous regions, support low levels of population.

Some places are **underpopulated**: the resources could support a bigger population. Canada and Australia, for example, have a high standard of living and the natural resources to provide for more people.

Population change and the impact on resources

- LEDCs have used very little *energy* in the past compared with MEDCs like the USA, which uses more than one-quarter of the world's oil. Developing economies with large populations will need increasing amounts of energy. China already burns huge quantities of coal and will soon be the biggest producer of carbon dioxide. LEDCs cannot afford to produce 'clean' energy to supply growing industrial and urban areas.

- *Clean water* is a major problem for LEDCs. Millions of women walk long distances each day to collect water. In north-east Somalia (East Africa), an area of frequent drought, the Red Cross delivers water to 70 000 people each day. Population growth makes problems like these worse. On the very densely populated Ganges delta in Bangladesh, 60 million people are at risk of arsenic poisoning from water which is extracted from deep underground.

- *Food* is not evenly distributed, so some people have more than they can use while others do not have enough. The greater use of pesticides and fertilizers has increased food production but caused environmental problems.

- *Hardwoods* and *minerals* are being exhausted at an increasingly rapid rate.

Overcrowding points to global famine

An alarming report on world population growth to be published today forecasts severe global shortages in the next 40 years, leading to famine on an unprecedented scale.

But the Worldwatch Institute report, which precedes next month's United Nations conference on population in Cairo, goes beyond orthodox extrapolations and stagnating grain production. It argues that the threat is worsened by the disproportionate ecological damage inflicted by the world's rich and the very poor.

'Food scarcity, not military aggression, is the principal threat to our future,' the Washington-based institute says.

The biggest increases in population are expected in some of the poorest areas, such as Africa and southern Asia.

The projected yearly grain supplies would be 239kg per person, the report says. That is a quarter of the average American's present consumption, and only 20% above consumption in India.

The UN Population Fund unveiled a proposal last April to try to stabilize world population at 7.8 billion by 2050.

But food supplies would be inadequate to feed the world even if that goal were reached, said one co-author of the Worldwatch study. Global population growth, rising by 70m a year in the past four decades, is beginning to rise by 90m a year, a figure which looks stable for the next four decades.

After decades of steady growth, world farm production will no longer be able to keep up with increasing demands, the study predicts.

The rice yield in Japan peaked at 4.7 tonnes/ha in 1984, and has not risen since.

The report continues: 'People at either end of the income spectrum are far more likely than those in the middle to damage the Earth's ecological health -- the rich because of their high consumption of energy, raw materials and manufactured goods, and the poor because they most often cut trees, grow crops or graze cattle in ways harmful to the Earth simply in order to survive.'

The report recommends a 'massive re-ordering of priorities', from intensified family planning and an attack on underlying causes of high fertility such as illiteracy and poverty, to protecting soil and water resources and raising investment in agriculture.

It says demand in food-importing countries will soon exceed global exportable supplies.

A – *From the Guardian, 15 August 1994*

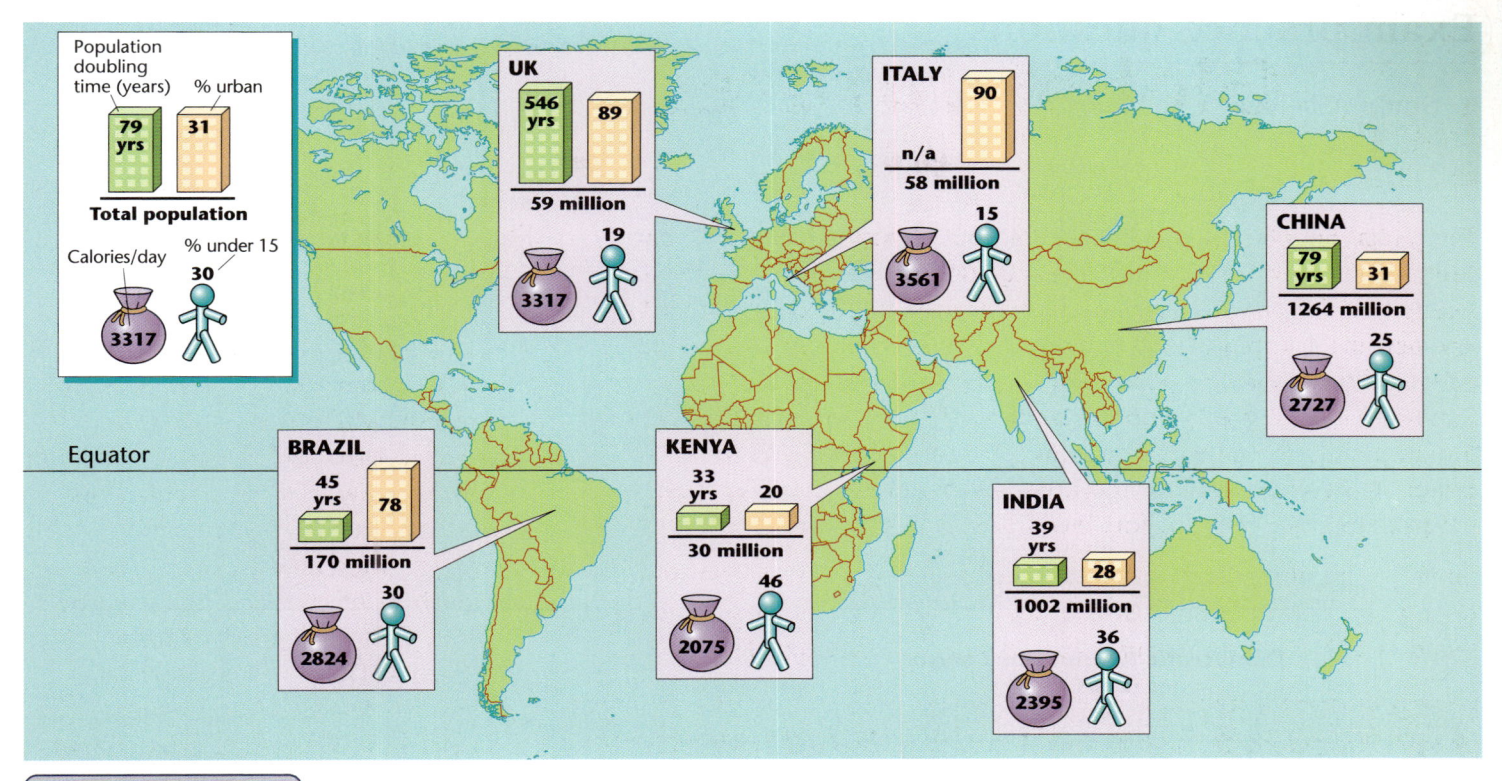

1 Population change

B – Population statistics for six countries

Legend:
- Population doubling time (years): 79 yrs
- % urban: 31
- Total population
- Calories/day: 3317
- % under 15: 30

UK: 546 yrs, 89% urban, 59 million, 19% under 15, 3317 calories/day

ITALY: n/a, 90% urban, 58 million, 15% under 15, 3561 calories/day

CHINA: 79 yrs, 31% urban, 1264 million, 25% under 15, 2727 calories/day

BRAZIL: 45 yrs, 78% urban, 170 million, 30% under 15, 2824 calories/day

KENYA: 33 yrs, 20% urban, 30 million, 46% under 15, 2075 calories/day

INDIA: 39 yrs, 28% urban, 1002 million, 36% under 15, 2395 calories/day

What will affect predictions of growth?

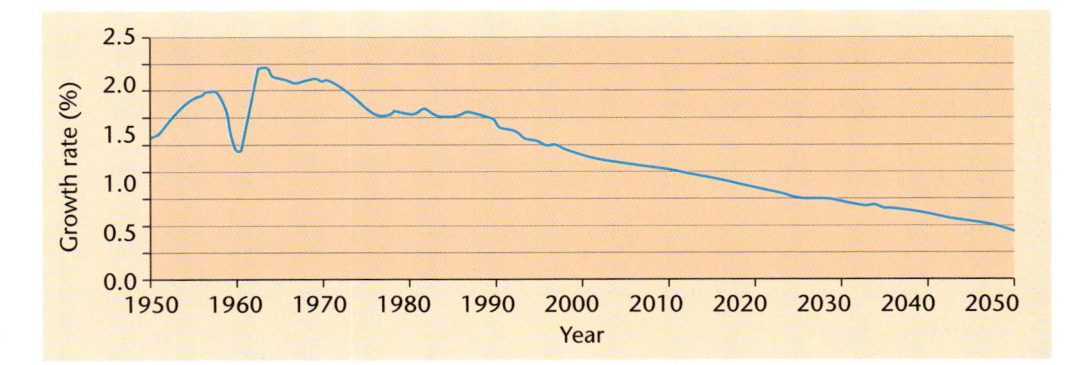

- *HIV/Aids* is having a significant effect on the composition, future growth and welfare of some populations, especially in Africa. The death of 11.5 million people of working age in Botswana, Kenya, Malawi, Mozambique, Namibia, South Africa, Uganda and Zimbabwe before 2020 will reduce the growth rate and life expectancy and slow development. Companies are training two or three people for the same job in order to cope with future deaths.

- *Religion and education* both have an impact on the number of children women have. If women receive an education, the birth rate falls. LEDCs with high female literacy rates, like Sri Lanka and Jamaica, have low rates of natural increase, while countries with low levels of literacy have high rates of increase, e.g. Afghanistan.

- *Wealth and prosperity* also influence the number of children people have. The rate of development of LEDCs will have an impact on family size.

C – World population growth rate predicted to 2050

Question

Use the information on these two pages to write and illustrate a front page for a newspaper for 1 January 2050, describing the global population in 2049. Use the statistics from B and refer to the six countries.

23

Managing Change in the Human Environment

Population change

Exam practice questions

Mark schemes can be found on the book's website, at www.heinemann.co.uk/issuesmarkschemes

1 Study A below.

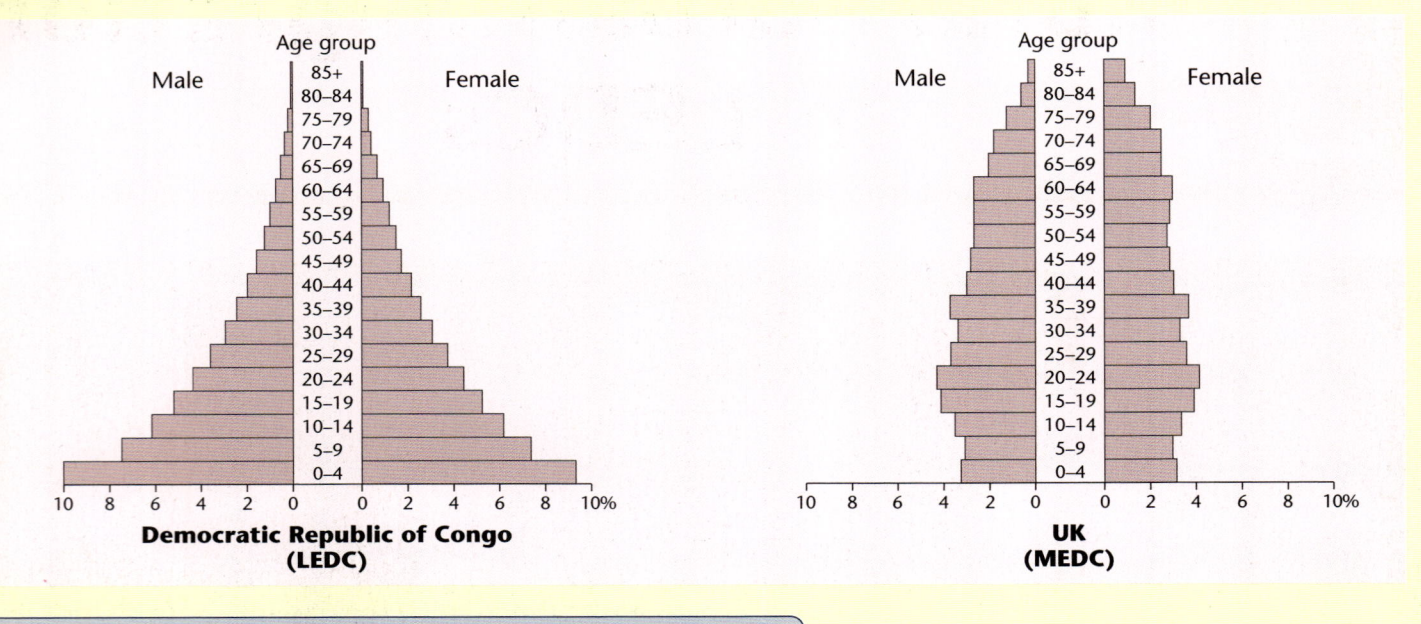

Democratic Republic of Congo (LEDC)

UK (MEDC)

A – Population structures of the Democratic Republic of Congo and the UK

   a) Which age group has the largest percentage in the Democratic Republic of Congo? (1)
   b) Which age group has the largest percentage in the UK? (1)

2 a) Why do some countries have a high birth rate? (3)
   b) Why do some countries have a high rate of natural increase? (3)
   c) The percentage of elderly people is usually smaller in LEDCs than in MEDCs. Suggest reasons for this. (6)

3 Governments study the population structure in their country in order to plan for the future. The UK population is ageing. The population of the Democratic Republic of Congo is youthful. Suggest how this may affect government planning in each country. (8)

4 Some areas of the world have a high population density. With reference to named examples, explain why such high population densities develop. (8)

5 a) Use the figures given in B on page 23 to complete a copy of this table:

Country	Population	Doubling time	% under 15	% urban	Calories/day

   b) Now use your table to answer these questions:
     i) Which country is growing most quickly?
     ii) Where would you live longest?
     iii) Where may people be short of food in the future?
     iv) Which countries may have problems resulting from obesity?
     v) In which countries is a large proportion of the population under 15? What could the population structure in these countries be like in 20 years' time?
     vi) Which countries seem to have most food? Do they have a high rural or a high urban population? (10 marks)

MANAGING CHANGE IN THE HUMAN ENVIRONMENT

2 Rural—urban migration in LEDCs

People from rural areas in LEDCs are moving to urban areas. How are the causes and consequences of rural–urban migration managed in LEDCs?

Managing Change in the Human Environment

2.1 What is rural–urban migration?

Rural–urban migration is the movement of people from the countryside to the city. People may leave the countryside because of drastic changes like famine, or they may be attracted to greater opportunities in the city. One person may go to the city and send money back to the family, or the whole family may migrate. The fastest-growing cities are in LEDCs, particularly in Asia and South America as more people move from rural to urban areas.

Two things are happening:

1 **Urban growth** — towns and cities are expanding, covering a greater area of land.
2 **Urbanization** — an increasing proportion of people are living in towns and cities.

Rural **depopulation** occurs when numbers of working-age people migrate from the countryside to earn money in the city, leaving behind the old and the young.

Since 1800 the percentage of people living in urban areas has risen from 5 per cent to 50 per cent, or 3 billion people, but the most rapid urban growth has been since the 1970s, in LEDCs: 97 per cent of population growth is in LEDCs. The majority of people live in **millionaire cities** — cities with over 1 million people — and the number of these has increased rapidly. **Mega-cities** are those with over 10 million people. In 1950 there were only two really large cities, London and New York. In 2000 there were probably 21 mega-cities; most in LEDCs and a few in MEDCs. Cities are growing at different rates, with some LEDC cities growing very rapidly and others more slowly. MEDC cities are growing very slowly or, like London, are declining.

Mumbai, (India), a mega-city has grown very rapidly and was estimated to have a population of 18 million in 2000. The population had increased by 2 million since 1995, and the suburb Dharavi is said to be the largest slum area in Asia with over 1 million people.

Is rural–urban migration important in the growth of cities?

LEDC cities have grown rapidly. In 1995 it was estimated that 63 per cent of city growth was the result of natural change and 37 per cent was due to inward migration.

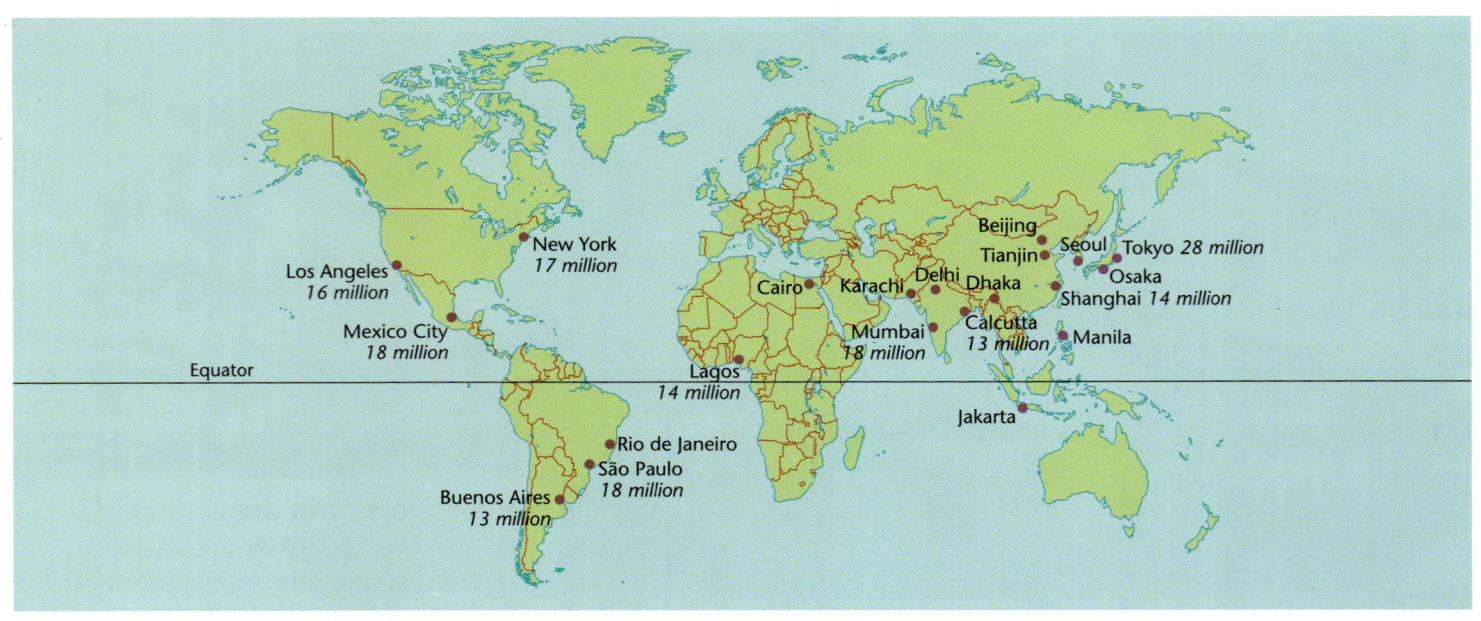

A – Populations of the ten largest cities in 2000

- Los Angeles 16 million
- New York 17 million
- Mexico City 18 million
- Buenos Aires 13 million
- Rio de Janeiro
- São Paulo 18 million
- Lagos 14 million
- Cairo
- Karachi
- Delhi
- Dhaka
- Beijing
- Tianjin
- Seoul
- Tokyo 28 million
- Osaka
- Shanghai 14 million
- Mumbai 18 million
- Calcutta 13 million
- Manila
- Jakarta

2 Rural–urban migration in LEDCs

Natural population change — the difference between births and deaths — is lower in urban areas than in rural areas, as is the birth rate. However, the rate of population growth in urban areas is greater than in rural areas, because of migration into the cities. Many people go directly from the countryside to the cities, but some move to a small town and then to a larger urban area, and this **inter–urban migration** is increasing.

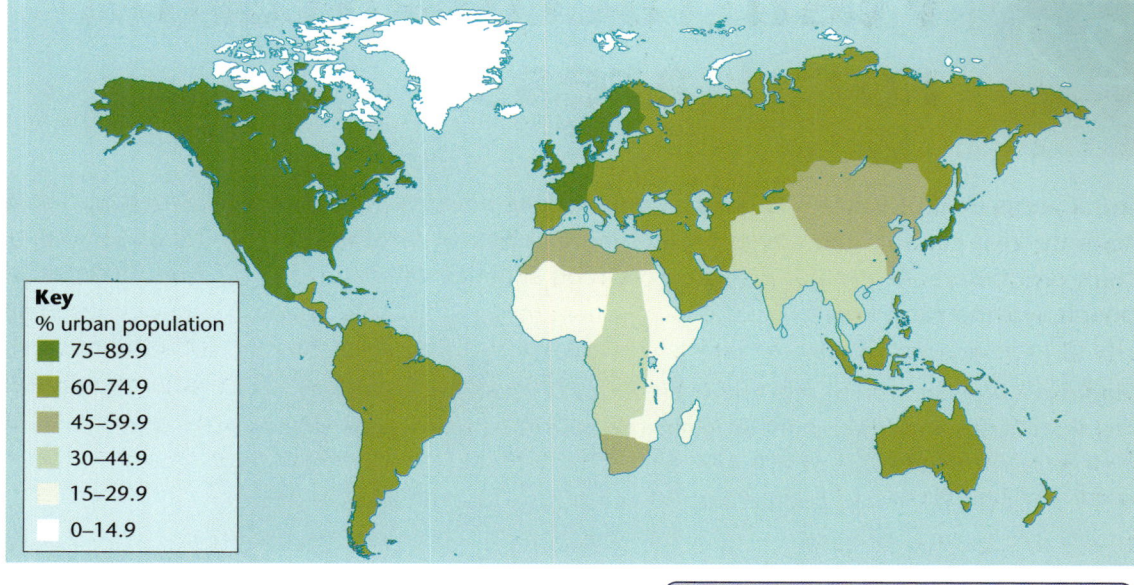

Key
% urban population
- 75–89.9
- 60–74.9
- 45–59.9
- 30–44.9
- 15–29.9
- 0–14.9

B – A simplified map of world urbanization

Why do people move from rural to urban areas?

Living conditions are very basic for the poorest city dweller, but urban healthcare and education provision can still be better than those found in rural areas. The city is seen as a place of opportunity where work can be found and money made. The **pull factors** — the attractions of the city — may seem more important to people than the **push factors** — the problems and deprivation of the rural areas, which push people away from poor rural areas.

Push factors
- Famine, drought and natural disaster
- Poor living conditions, particularly housing, education and healthcare
- Agricultural change
- Unemployment, lack of work
- War and civil conflict

Pull factors
- Work, employment
- Higher incomes
- Better healthcare and education
- Urban facilities and way of life
- Protection from conflict

Questions

1. What is rural–urban migration?
2. Why do people leave the countryside (push factors)? What attracts them to the cities (pull factors)?
3. What is the difference between **urban growth** and **urbanization**?
4. a) Using A, B and an atlas, copy and complete the following table:

Mega-city	Continent	Country	% of people living in urban areas

b) Describe the pattern shown, giving at least five different points.

2.2 Push factors from rural areas

Rural areas in LEDCs have changed as populations have grown. Natural hazards, civil conflict and poverty affect more people in rural areas than ever before. Any major disruption in food supplies will result in people leaving rural areas.

Rapid population growth and the increase in the number of people trying to farm and make a living from the land puts enormous pressure on the countryside:
- 72 per cent of Indian people and 80 per cent of Bangladeshi people still live in rural villages.
- 80 per cent of Kenyan and other East African people live in rural areas.
- 69 per cent of Chinese people live in small villages.

Land ownership is an issue in many LEDCs. In Brazil, three-quarters of the people live in cities, but millions of people still live on the land. A tiny proportion (1 per cent) of the farmers own over 40 per cent of the arable land, and there are about 15 million very poor farmers and agricultural workers who own little or no land. Land reform would mean breaking up the big estates, but estate owners are powerful people. Land conflicts can result in violent clashes between landless people and landowners. The government has begun some redistribution of land, but many people simply move to the nearest big city.

The *modernization of agriculture* in countries such as Brazil, South Africa and Kenya has resulted in mechanization and the need for fewer workers. Many of the workers have migrated to the nearest big city, like São Paulo, Cape Town or Nairobi.

Commercial agriculture has replaced subsistence farming in some countries, so workers and their families are displaced and have to move to the cities to survive.

The *decline of traditional village industries* such as textiles and metal-working in some places means that some people have had to move to an urban area to look for work.

Flooding displaces many people, and changes the landscape. Floods in 1999 and 2000 in Mozambique (East Africa), and in Bangladesh (Asia), destroyed the food crops for millions of people. In these circumstances people may have no option but to move to the city.

PUSH FACTORS FROM RURAL AREAS

A – Mechanization of agriculture in Burkina Faso

2 Rural–urban migration in LEDCs

Drought is a constant problem in parts of the world such as India, East Africa and north-east Brazil. The *sertao*, a part of north-east Brazil, is semi-arid with dry scrub vegetation called *caatinga*. People there have always had a hard life. Living standards are low and there are often food shortages. When droughts occur, people leave for cities like São Paulo, or Salvador on the coast, which is now the third largest city in Brazil. In Kenya, 80 per cent of cattle belonging to the Maasai people have died from drought in Kenya since 1997, forcing people to look for other opportunities.

Drought and *conflict* can result in huge refugee movements from the land. Often these people end up in refugee camps, but some will eventually drift to the cities. In Ethiopia in the mid-1980s, drought was made worse by fighting which destroyed the crops, and famine resulted. At one point, 200 000 people walked for 80 days from Ethiopia to Sudan – an estimated 30 000 of them died on the journey. The survivors were settled in camps but many never returned to the land.

Land degradation causes subsistence farmers to move out.

The provision of *healthcare and education* tends to be less well organized in rural areas than in urban areas. Remote villages in the high Andes in Ecuador, and densely populated villages in India, have similar problems, with too few qualified people and too little medicine. Poor or non-existent facilities in rural areas will make people look for something better, and help to 'push' people off the land.

C – *Provision of education is very poor in many rural areas*

B – *African refugees fleeing from conflict in their country*

Question

Either draw a table like this:

Push factors: reasons for leaving	Location or example	Natural or human reason?
1 Rapid population growth		

Complete your table listing 10 reasons why people leave rural areas. *Or* Using examples, explain why people leave rural areas.

Managing Change in the Human Environment

2.3 Attraction to the urban areas

People are attracted to urban areas because they think that the opportunities there will be greater than in the country. For many life is better but some end up in desperate poverty. There are more services and facilities, and people think that they will be able to provide a better quality of life for their children, but their future depends on making money, either in the **informal sector** or the **formal sector**. Rapidly growing MEDC cities often have more **service activities** than manufacturing industries, and jobs can be short-term and offer low pay. However, living in houses that the people have built themselves, in a squatter settlement or shanty town, may provide a better quality of life than living in the country.

Where do people live?

People moving into the city build houses out of anything they can find: packing cases, pallets, cardboard and other materials are all used. Houses are built on unused land that is not wanted at the time, for example on steep hillsides or derelict land along main roads into cities, or around a single water supply. Settlements of many small, crowded homes grow quickly in an informal way, with narrow alleyways, gutters for drains, and no running water or power. Often these **shanty towns** or squatter settlements grow into very densely populated settlements with many thousands of people.

Over time, the buildings may become more permanent homes, built out of concrete and brick. Some of the shanty towns or *favelas* in Brazil (page 25) have become established suburbs with water and power supplies. In Nairobi (Kenya), some shanty areas are as poor and flimsy as when they were put up in the 1980s, and can very easily be bulldozed by developers, since the inhabitants have no legal right to the land. Some street dwellers in Mumbai in India have lived on

A – *Squatters in Mumbai*

2 Rural–urban migration in LEDCs

B – Living on the pavement in Calcutta

the same pavement for 20 years and even have post delivered to them — but they may still only have a canvas cover for protection. Some of the shanty housing in dry areas like Cairo (Egypt) is on the flat roofs of inner city buildings.

What are the communities like?

As squatter settlements grow, they can become communities organized with **residents' associations**. Electricity may come by tapping into overhead lines or by putting pressure on the authorities to put in a basic infrastructure. Small bars, shops and other facilities develop, and with enough local support schools may be set up in someone's house or in a small local building. In Mumbai the school may be held on a pavement alongside a heavily congested road. Some people travel to work in the city, while others make a living in the informal economy, doing whatever jobs they can.

They may have common features, but all the shanty towns grow and change in different ways. In Brazil they are called *favelas*, *bustees* in India, *barrios* in Colombia, and *bidonvilles* in North Africa.

LEDC urban models

Rapidly growing cities in LEDCs develop different patterns to cities in MEDCs, which have grown more slowly, often over hundreds of years. The **Central Business District**, the **CBD**, is the commercial centre where most of the city's business activities take place. Factories, businesses and expensive apartment blocks may develop along main roads out of the cities. The really poor shanty town areas tend to be on the edge of the city or along the main roads rather than near the centre where poor housing is found in many MEDC cities. Shanty towns near the centre of an LEDC city may be more substantial than the new ones on the outside. Figure **C** is a model to show the structure of a 'typical' South American city — but remember that large cities and mega-cities in different parts of the world show different patterns.

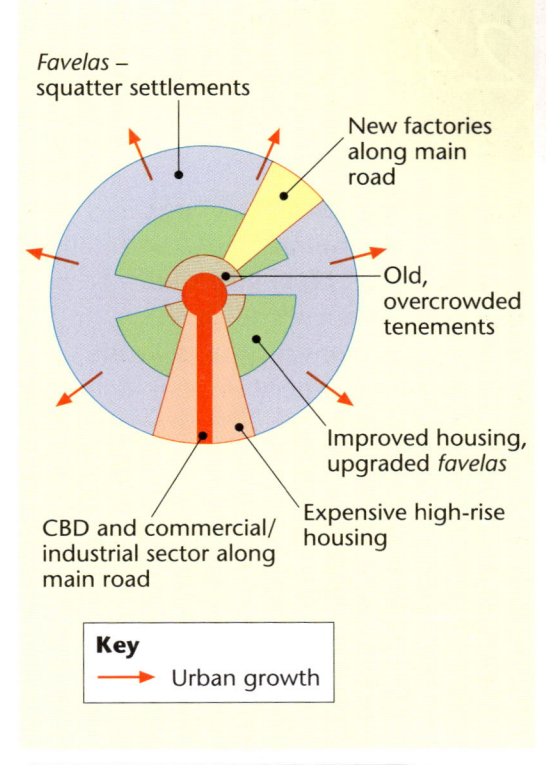

C – Model of a South American city

Questions

1. Describe five features of shanty towns that are common to all squatter settlements.

2. Look carefully at the photographs on these pages and page 25. *Either:*
   a) Draw a simple sketch of a shanty town home. Label your diagram to show the building materials, size and shape of the house.
   Or
   b) Draw an annotated sketch of a photograph.

Managing Change in the Human Environment

2.4 Problems in LEDC cities

There are problems in all large urban areas, both in MEDCs and LEDCs, but the rapid growth of LEDC cities has created some extreme problems for the residents and the city planners.

Electricity and power supplies are also variable. Some people in shanty towns tap into existing supplies of electricity, others cook with wood, oil or coal. This can contribute to air pollution, as for example in Beijing (China) where millions of the poor people cook with coal.

Traffic is a major problem in all large cities. Bangkok (Thailand) has huge congestion problems, 1000 deaths a year from accidents, severe air pollution at times, an *average* speed of less than 10 miles an hour — and it has had a 24-hour traffic jam!

Everyone, everywhere needs *shelter*. Millions of people around the world are living in poor-quality housing or home-made shelters. Ill health is common, and millions of people suffer from damp conditions, disease, unclean water and a lack of sewerage systems.

Pollution comes from vehicles, industrial processes, cooking and heating. Half the people in Calcutta (India) have some sort of respiratory problem. The rapid increase in the number of vehicles in Mexico City is putting children at risk. Pollution is everywhere — in the air, in the water, and on the land (creating an ugly environment).

Access to *clean drinking water* varies across the world. The poorest people have the least reliable supplies, and they may have to buy it at high prices. More wealthy areas tend to have better supplies.

Poverty is the biggest problem of all, and the biggest killer. Money can buy food, clean water and medicine, which enable people to survive even in poor-quality living conditions.

Sewerage systems are needed to deal with human waste, but many of these systems fail to keep up with rapidly expanding cities. Where they do exist, as in Cairo (Egypt) or Bangkok (Thailand), they become overburdened as the population increases. Development schemes struggle to keep up. Many cities have only open sewers or pits.

2 Rural—urban migration in LEDCs

Overcrowding is a problem in most cities, but it especially affects the poorest people. Shanty towns and squatter settlements are the most densely populated parts of any LEDC city.

Rubbish collection is often unregulated and haphazard. Some very poor people can make money from other people's rubbish by recycling items thrown onto the city's rubbish tips.

Education and health provision are two of the most important items for city planners to manage. Even when children do get a primary education, as most children in São Paulo do, those from the *favelas* are more likely to drop out when they are still very young and not move into paid employment.

Employment opportunities cannot keep up with the number of new arrivals in most LEDC cities, so people make a subsistence living by street trading, selling food and other services, or making craft items, often for the tourist industry.

A – Living in an LEDC city

Drugs, gangs and violence are part of everyday life in many shanty settlements. Often, as in some *favelas* in Brazil, the shanties are under the control of drug gangs. The police may or may not have control of squatter settlements, and keeping control in these areas may lead to violence, whether in Lagos in Nigeria, Rio de Janeiro in Brazil, or Beijing in China.

Resulting problems in rural areas

Rural areas become **depopulated** if many people leave to go to the cities. When the people of working age move to the city they leave behind the young and the old who have to look after themselves or depend on money sent back from the city. If complete families leave, then the whole rural area may be in decline.

Questions

1. Think about the problems in a rapidly growing LEDC city. Which ones need solutions most urgently?

   Draw a table with four columns:

Problems	Ranking	Reason for ranking	Example city

   Look very carefully at all the information on these two pages. Then list the problems from 1 to 12, with 1 being the most important one to be tackled first, and 12 the least important. Give reasons for the order in which you put them.

2. Which problems could be solved easily if more money is available? Which are more difficult to solve?

Managing Change in the Human Environment

2.5 Contrasts in countries

Different countries have different problems as their cities grow very rapidly. On pages 34–39 we look at the situation in three countries: India, Brazil and Egypt.

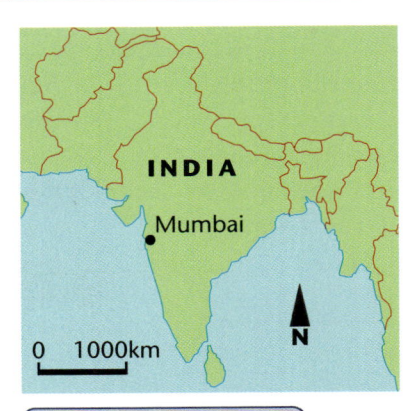

CS India

Cities in India are growing very rapidly, but the proportion of people living in cities is still only 30 per cent, with nearly 70 per cent or 700 million people in rural areas.

In Mumbai, one of the biggest cities in the world, there are now approximately 18 million people, and the city is still growing rapidly. The huge industrial area grew around the port and is very important to India's economy. People who are desperate for work are attracted to the city, and the population probably increased by 2 million people between 1998 and 2000. Many people are very rich and live in expensive housing developments, but even more people are so poor that they live on the roadside, along the railway tracks or on the pavements. Land and housing are expensive, so it is difficult for poor people to move out of the slums even when they do find work. Employed people who cannot afford to live in the city have to commute from the suburbs each day on the very crowded trains or roads.

One of the suburbs, Dharavi, probably the largest slum in Asia, has a population of 1 million and is still growing. It began when poor craftsmen from the surrounding region arrived 50 years ago and put up 'temporary' shelters. These structures are still there, along with thousands of others built out of whatever was available at the time. Families found work and made a better life for themselves — but stayed in Dharavi. Outdoor toilets are filthy, and water and power supplies scarce, but televisions and satellite dishes are not uncommon. As in all shanty town areas in India, the informal economy is most important, and the narrow alleyways are crowded with people who live and work together, making an assortment of things, including food, clothing and cigarettes.

A – Location of Mumbai

B – Mumbai, one of the world's mega-cities

C – Dharavi, probably the largest shanty town in Asia

Is it better to live in a city in India?

- *Roads* are badly congested day and night, and **air pollution** is a huge problem. Many people suffer from breathing problems, especially children, but there are more doctors here than in the rural areas.
- The *infant mortality rate* is lower in urban areas than in rural parts, as are the birth and death rates.
- *Clean water* is in very short supply, but it is still easier for more people to get clean water than in some rural areas.
- *Sewage and rubbish* are problems in urban areas. Possibly 300 million people — five times the population of the UK — need to dispose of waste every day in cities in India. But it is a problem for the 700 million people in the rural areas, too.

- On average, city households have more *money* than those in rural areas.
- *Self-help schemes* are important everywhere, but especially in cities. Women have been effective in organizing themselves into groups to improve the quality of housing, education, etc.

Conclusion: The quality of life probably is better in the city than in the countryside for many people.

Year	Population (millions)
1900	0.8
1950	2.9
1960	4.1
1970	5.8
1980	8.1
1990	12.2
2000	18.1
2010 (est.)	24.3

D – Growth of the population of Mumbai, 1900–2010

Questions

1. Look at **D**.
   a) Use the figures to draw bar graphs of population growth in Mumbai from 1900 to 2010.
   b) Describe the pattern of growth and try to explain why the city has grown so rapidly.
2. Why do so many people want to live in the city rather than in the countryside? Imagine you live in rural India. Make a list of the reasons why you might want to move to live in Mumbai.
3. Use **B**, **C** and the text to describe the problems facing people living in Mumbai.

Managing Change in the Human Environment

2.6 cs Brazil

In the 1960s, half the population lived in rural areas in Brazil. By 2000, more than 35 million people had moved to the cities leaving 30 per cent of people in the countryside. The first stop was usually a *favela* or shanty town on the edge of the urban area. São Paulo, Rio de Janeiro, Recife and Salvador have grown rapidly, with people from rural and poor parts of Brazil moving in.

A – Brazil

São Paulo

São Paulo (see photograph on page 25) is now a cosmopolitan, industrial city of nearly 18 million people, with 11 shopping malls, numerous condominiums (apartment blocks) for the rich, and lots of entertainment. Many parts are extremely prosperous and it is possible to live there without ever seeing the poor in the *favelas*. Like all megacities, congestion is a problem, so one way the rich can travel from block to block is by helicopter. A three-minute helicopter journey would take hours by road — some busy, rich São Paulo people need never set foot on the ground.

In the early 1970s the city was one of the fastest-growing places in South America with 150 migrants arriving every hour, attracted by the prospect of jobs in the newly developing industries. Many of these migrants from the countryside put up shacks on land that was at the edge of the city, and in the next 25 years most of the housing was built with very little control or regulation. Conditions were poor, living spaces cramped, clean water was expensive and sewage a problem. Crime was rife and new rural families were very vulnerable to gangs who occupied land and illegally sold off plots to newcomers.

B – The vast sprawl of São Paulo

C – A favela in Rio de Janeiro

How have people helped themselves?

Heliopolis is a *favela* that grew in the early 1970s on land 8km from the centre of São Paulo, near a major industrial area. The *favela* grew rapidly and so did the problems. People grouped together to campaign for protection against gangs and for water and electricity. The local authorities were persuaded to take control of the area in the late 1980s and put in basic amenities. Then the authorities put in apartment blocks for middle-income people, so the very poor local residents had to campaign again and they were provided with materials to build their own houses. Once land was secure, people began to buy and sell houses, and Heliopolis is now an ordinary residential neighbourhood, 10km away from the rural edge of the city and home to 50 000 people. People are still very poor and some may not know where the next meal will come from but housing has improved.

Rio de Janeiro

Rio de Janeiro is not growing as rapidly as São Paulo but is still a mega-city of 10.2 million people. The mountains that surround the bay have restricted growth and the city is congested, noisy and polluted (a lot of sewage goes into the sea untreated). The south side and Copocobana beach are particularly busy. *Favelas* grew on the very steep hillsides, and some parts of these can be washed away in severe rainstorms. In 1988, 200 people died when mudslides engulfed them. Some of the earliest *favelas*, more than 30 years old, are now well established brick and stone-built 'suburbs' with houses of three or four storeys.

How has Roçinha *favela* changed?

Roçinha, perched on a steep hillside in Rio de Janeiro, is the biggest favela in the city and houses 100 000 people. The pathways between the buildings are too narrow for cars and everything has to be moved by hand. Houses are small but solid and if another room is needed, it is built on the top of the house. There are schools, bars, shops and some health provision here, and a lot of community support. People may move out when they make sufficient money and Rio de Janeiro is losing population from the centre. The middle classes are moving to new towns, particularly to Barra down the coast.

Barra, a new town

This town — now with a population of 100 000 — was built on coastal flat land that was developed after tunnels were built to open up the way through the mountains. It is said to be the 'Miami of the South', and shops line a 5km stretch of road. The standard of living is as high as in any MEDC, and many rich people live safely in 'condos' (condominiums, or blocks of flats), which are protected by security guards. The town has grown so quickly that the infrastructure has not always kept up with developments, and at times the smell of sewage hangs over the whole town.

Questions

1. Describe the *favela* shown in **C** and on page 25. Mention the housing, size, shape and building materials, paths, surface and width of road, rubbish, and services (infrastructure) like water and electricity.

2. How have people in the *favelas* in Rio de Janeiro and São Paulo improved the quality of their lives?

3. a) Try to suggest some differences in the way of life of someone living in Dharavi in Mumbai, and someone living in Roçinha in Rio de Janeiro.
   b) Are there any similarities between the two places?

Managing Change in the Human Environment

2.7 CS Cairo in Egypt

Cairo is the mega-city of Africa and may have a population of 13 million people, or more. It is a **primate city** — one that dominates the country, as probably as many as 35—40 per cent of the population of Egypt live in the Greater Cairo area. Some problems in Cairo are similar to those in other LEDC mega-cities, but added to these is the fact that Cairo is 5000 years old. The city grew on the edge of the Nile delta, about 200km from the sea. Every year the Nile flooded, so the oldest parts of the city are on slightly higher land away from the river. Over time the old parts of the city have changed in character and function, but have often become home to poor people moving from rural areas.

In the 20th century the river flood was controlled by the building upriver of the Aswan Dam. Also, a new CBD grew up on the banks and islands of the Nile. The city expanded onto valuable, and scarce, fertile farmland around the river, but that expansion had to be restricted so the city grew upwards as well as outwards.

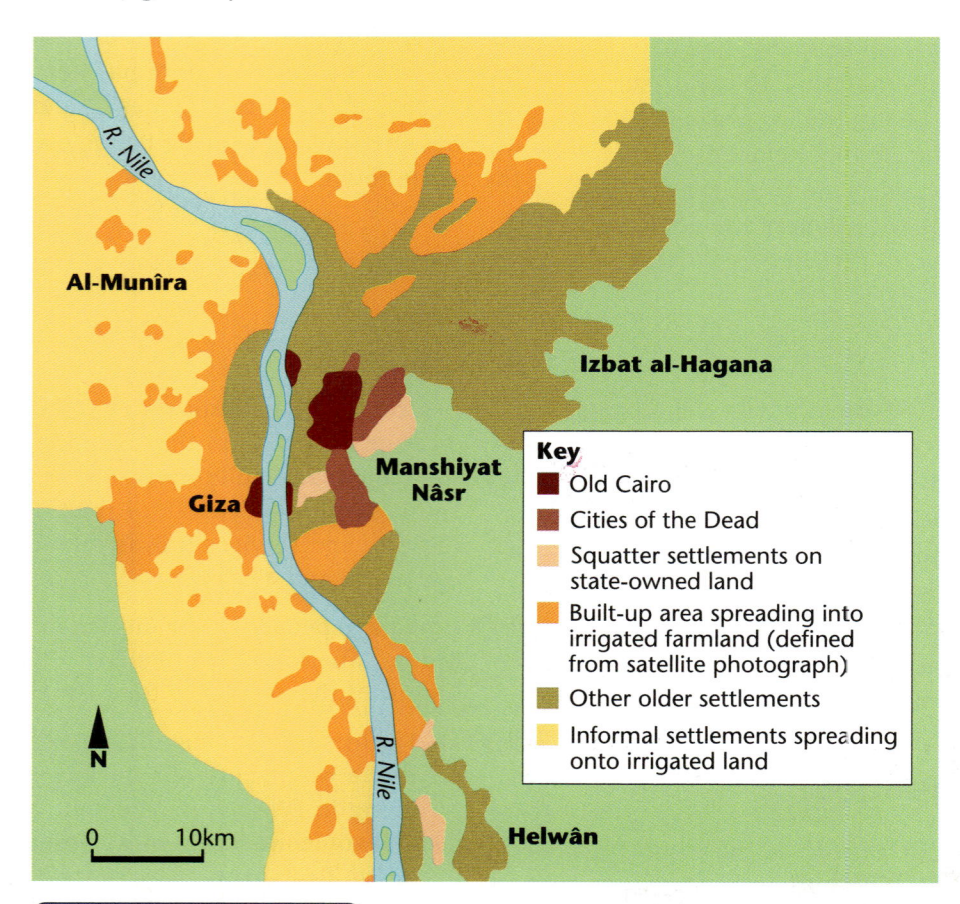

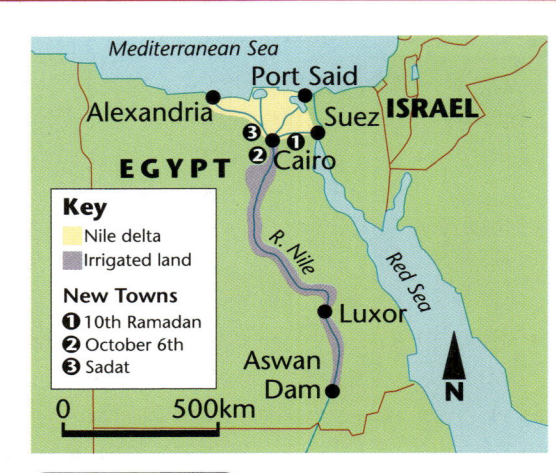

A – Cairo in Egypt

Tenement blocks of flats have extra storeys added when more living space is needed, and the poorest people, possibly 1 million of them, live on the rooftops (**D**). The population density is very high, perhaps 100 000/km² in places. Some very poor families have actually made their homes in the tombs in the old cemeteries, called the Cities of the Dead. Thousands of people live here and in some parts the authorities have put in basic amenities like water and electricity. Self-help schemes are important in establishing schools and some medical help in these informal settlements.

The infrastructure of the entire city is suffering:

- *Electricity* is variable.
- *Water supplies* do not reach all parts of the city, and the pipe network is old and in a poor state of repair.
- *Sewage* is a real problem and sometimes floods the streets. Three-quarters of the city is connected to a sewerage system, but only about a quarter of the sewage is treated. New systems have been put in but by the time they can be used, the population has grown again.

B – The changing city of Cairo

2 Rural–urban migration in LEDCs

- *Rubbish collection* for 13 million people is a challenge. Much of the city's waste is still collected using small carts and sorted at the dumps on the edge of the city by the Zabaleen people who live and work there (**C**). These people are well organized and look after themselves. Rubbish is recycled through this informal economy, including food waste, which is fed to pigs. If all rubbish collection were to be mechanized, these people would be displaced and no longer able to make a living.
- *Traffic congestion* in the city is a major problem because of the number of vehicles (perhaps 1.5 million cars), the old city streets, and the volume of through traffic. Cars can hardly fit through the narrow streets in the old parts, and horse-drawn carts, taxis, lorries, buses and cars all create noise and congestion. Concrete flyovers built in previous decades look out of place in this historic city and have not solved the problem. A motorway ring-road to take through traffic would damage heritage sites, and tourism.
- *Air pollution* created by the traffic is made worse by climatic conditions and dry desert air.
- *New housing* is in constant demand. One solution has been to build a number of **new towns** around Cairo, designed to be self-supporting, with work and housing together for between 250 000 and 1 million people. The most successful of these is probably 10th Ramadan, which was begun in 1977 about 50km from Cairo in the desert. New industries have been established and apartment blocks built. However, poor rural migrants do not to get to live in this new housing, and many people still commute each day from the new town to Cairo, adding to the traffic congestion. In addition, desert towns have particular problems — for example, water supplies are unreliable and may be infrequent. The problem of housing for the rural poor has not been solved by the new towns.

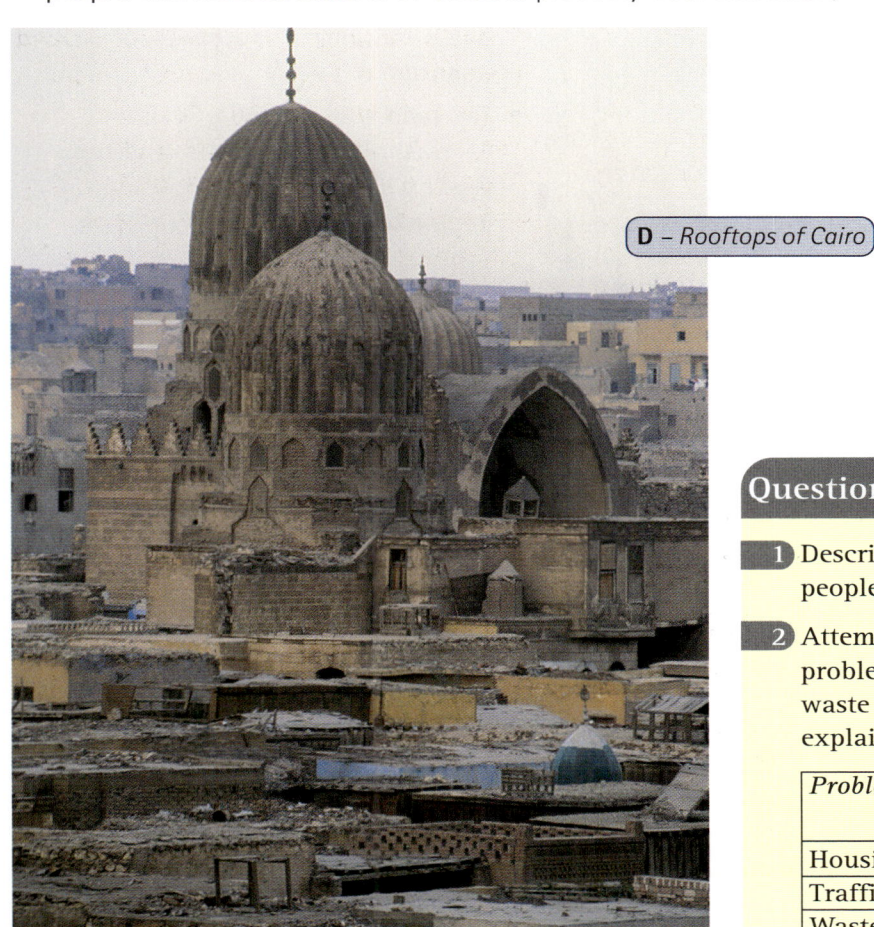

C – *The Zabaleen people make a living by recycling the city's waste*

D – *Rooftops of Cairo*

Questions

1. Describe some of the different places where poor people live in Cairo.

2. Attempts have been made to find solutions to Cairo's problems. For the problems of housing, traffic and waste rubbish, complete a large copy of this table, explaining the problem first:

Problem	Possible solution	Disadvantage of this solution
Housing		
Traffic		
Waste/rubbish		

Managing Change in the Human Environment

2.8 Improving life for the urban poor

Rural–urban migration involves millions of people globally, both rich and poor. The problems of rural–urban migration are greatest in LEDC cities and in the rural areas that these people leave. Migration is very difficult to stop, even when it is between countries, and people who are desperate for work will travel (often illegally) for thousands of miles to other places. Some governments, for example in China, may try to control rural-urban migration.

Migrants usually have little money and no power or rights. They are vulnerable to intimidation by gangsters, police, developers and governments. Shanty towns are easily bulldozed and water, for example, can be sold to newcomers at very high prices.

However, the quality of life in the cities *can* be improved and problems in the country tackled to encourage people to stay in rural areas.

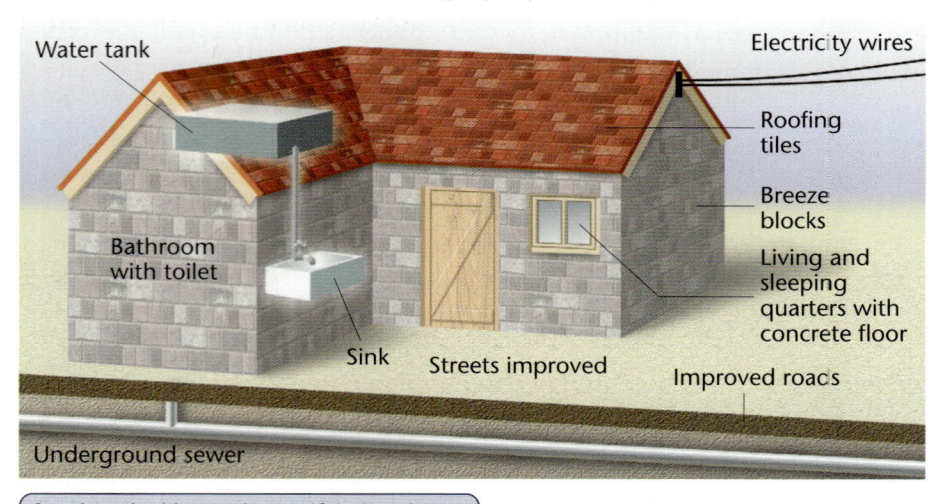

A – A typical house in a self-help scheme

How is city life being improved?

- *Self-help* (when people work together to improve their own living conditions) has been vital in all countries.
- *Government assistance* (local and national) has helped shanty town dwellers by improving the infrastructure (water, electricity, health facilities).
- Governments have also provided self-help groups with *money* and *materials* for building small, low-cost housing units (**A**).
- Some *NGOs*, like Save the Children Fund, help community programmes.

Successful schemes are those that the local people want, not necessarily those that the authorities think they want.

The Cingapora project, São Paulo

The Cingapora project in Brazil was named after Singapore's huge slum clearance programme. It aims to replace hundreds of *favelas* with low-rise blocks of flats which could house 500 000 people – but there are problems:

- 20 per cent of people in São Paulo live in *favelas* and half a million live on the streets – the scheme could help only a small proportion of people.
- Many *favela* people have occasional work or none at all, so they could not buy a flat with a mortgage, or maintain it.
- The land was cleared of existing favelas to build the flats, and there was no guarantee of rehousing people who were made homeless.
- Businesses were broken up.
- Many people in *favelas* voted against the project.

Curitiba, Brazil: a sustainable city

Curitiba, the capital city of the state of Parana, has grown rapidly from 500 000 in 1971 to over 2 million in 2000. The United Nations has called it 'The Ecological Capital' because it is trying to be a sustainable city with policies that will not lead to a decline in the quality of life with urban growth. Curitiba has the highest average standard of living in Brazil and is the most planned green LEDC city. The project began in the 1970s.

2 Rural–urban migration in LEDCs

B – Curitiba: 'The Ecological Capital' of Brazil

What has been done?

- *Transport* is high-quality, cheap and public so that people travel quickly and easily with minimum air and noise pollution. An integrated transport system uses bus and cycle lanes and special buses to carry over 200 people at a time. Platforms at boarding points enable people to walk on quickly without climbing steps. The CBD is **pedestrianized**.
- *Recycling* accounts for two-thirds of the city's waste and people from *favelas* can exchange their waste for food or for bus tickets. The food comes from local farmers, so many people are helped by the recycling scheme and the *favelas* do not have the old metal and junk lying around as is common in many other urban areas.
- 95 per cent of people have access to *clean water*, and nearly as many to sewerage facilities.
- 1.5 million *trees* have been planted, parks made and river flooding prevented by creating *lakes* and *wetland* habitats.
- *Healthcare* is provided 24 hours a day, with special facilities for children.
- *Education* is compulsory between the ages of 7 and 14. There are many libraries, and an Open University of the Environment.
- *Street children* are fed and the urban poor are all involved in decisions about the city.
- *Industry* has been attracted to the city, providing employment.

Questions

1. Why is self-help so important for people in LEDC cities?
2. What is the Cingapora project? How successful has it been?
3. Why is Curitiba called 'The Ecological Capital'? Describe five ways in which poor people have been helped by the city's development.

Managing Change in the Human Environment

2.9 Rural change and urban farming

GREEDY CITIES: Are they taking too much from the Earth?

A – Are the world's cities taking too much?

Rural—urban migration could be slowed if changes were made in the countryside to enable people to live there with a good lifestyle, with adequate supplies of food and water, and if cities were more sustainable.

Natural hazards are hard for people to manage. For example, droughts in north-east Brazil have caused famines, and in 1985 perhaps as many as 1 million people abandoned their small farms and moved to the cities, or north to the Amazon area. In 1993, 6—7 million people were saved from starvation by government work schemes. Farmers in north-east Brazil are poor and cannot afford expensive water storage systems, but they could be helped if the government put in new water systems.

Land reform is another issue in many LEDCs. In Brazil, much of the land is still in large estates (*latifundios*) and more than half the land is owned by fewer than 5 per cent of farmers. The government has declared that it will break up the big estates and give small patches of land to peasant farmers, but change has been slow. Small farms produce more per hectare than large ones, but modern commercial mechanized farming is more efficient on large areas of land. In the 1990s in Brazil, 100 000 jobs a year were lost as a result of mechanization so workers either had to find alternative places to farm, or move to the cities to find work.

In 1995, 40 000 families were resettled, but perhaps as many as 12 million rural people had become landless. Trade unionists, landless farmers and Catholic clergy have led land occupations to try to force change, but this has sometimes ended in violence. In one incident in 1996, 19 people were killed in police gunfire as a demonstration was broken up in Amazonia.

2 Rural–urban migration in LEDCs

B – An urban farm

In the Nilgiri Hills in southern India, the expansion of tea plantations caused conflict over land rights with the local people. Here, a local charity helped the people, who successfully employed a land rights lawyer to help them safeguard their land from further commercial expansion of tea plantations – 30 000 people joined in the peaceful demonstration supporting this.

Global food production has increased since the 1940s, helped by the **'Green Revolution'**. New high-yielding varieties of staple crops were developed, like rice, maize and wheat. The new dwarf strains of wheat and rice could withstand strong wind, heavy rain and drought. In the 1960s, technologists thought that the world food problem had been solved, but in the 1970s it became clear that it had not. The new plants needed huge quantities of fertilizers and pesticides, and irrigation. Small farmers could not afford these. The new plants were not so resistant to disease, and the rice did not seem to taste the same. Genetic engineering or modification (GM) is the latest controversial attempt at increasing food production – but will it help the small farmers as well as large-scale commercial farmers?

Food supplies are critical for big cities. A city of 10 million people may need 5000–6000 tonnes of food to be brought in each day, which has an impact on surrounding rural areas. **Urban farming** is helping to improve nutrition and health, and an estimated 800 million city people grow food or keep livestock to eat or sell. In Mexico City, sheep graze on the central reservations of dual carriageways, tended by street children. In China, 90 per cent of the vegetables eaten by urban residents are grown in the cities. Urban farming can also help the environment by using composted waste. It is a way forward in developing sustainable cities and rural areas, but authorities do not always appreciate this and may clear the land for building development.

Questions

1. a) Describe two problems faced by small farmers in Brazil, one natural, one created by people.
   b) How could the government help with these problems? Why is it difficult for an individual farmer to tackle the problems?
   c) How have some groups of people in Brazil and India worked together to improve and safeguard their rights to farm land?

2. How did the Green Revolution help global food production? Which group of people were not helped by it? Why not?

3. How can urban farming help:
   - cities
   - the individual city dweller
   - rural people?

Managing Change in the Human Environment — Rural–urban migration in LEDCs

Exam practice questions

Mark schemes can be found on the book's website, at www.heinemann.co.uk/issuesmarkschemes

1 Study A. In less economically developed countries (LEDCs), people may migrate to cities.

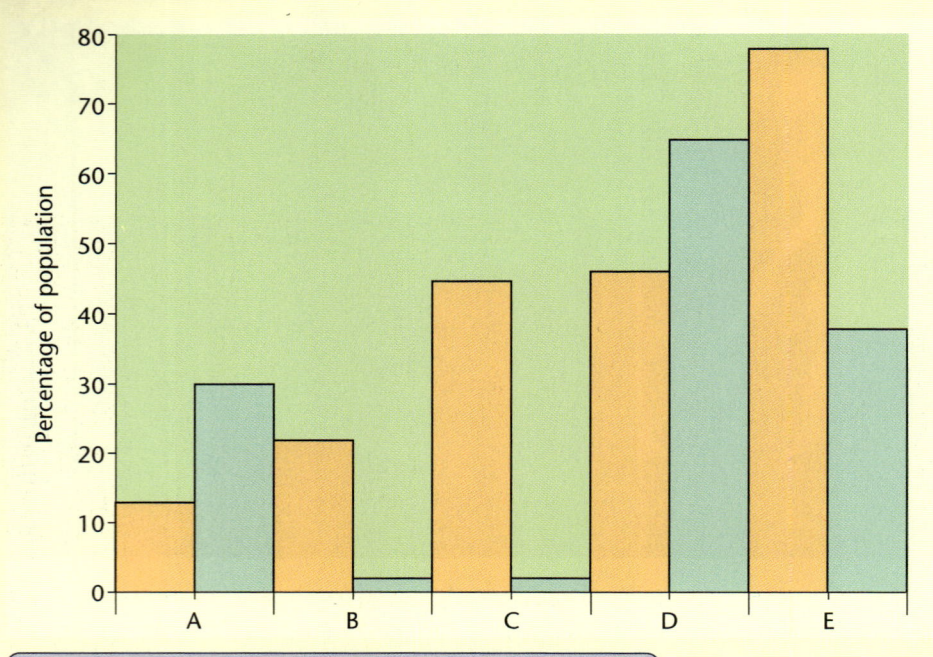

Key
- Urban areas
- Rural areas

Aspects of life
A Female population with no education
B Households with a television
C Households with a flush toilet
D Infant mortality rate
E Women with access to a midwife

A – Some aspects of urban and rural life in Kenya (an LEDC)

a) What is meant by a 'push factor'? (1)
b) What is meant by a 'pull factor'? (1)

2 Using evidence from A and your own knowledge, explain why people may migrate to cities. (6)

3 Rural–urban migration can lead to the setting-up of shanty towns (squatter settlements) in LEDC cities. This problem has to be managed.

Look at B. Describe some other ways of managing the problem of shanty towns. Suggest why these may be better than the method shown in B. (6)

B – One way to manage the squatter problem in an LEDC

MANAGING CHANGE IN THE HUMAN ENVIRONMENT

3 Changing city and town centres

How are changes in and around city and town centres in MEDCs being managed?

Managing Change in the Human Environment

3.1 How have MEDC town and city centres developed?

The centre of a town or city is the **CBD**, the **Central Business District**. The centre is constantly changing, and how the changes are managed has an important impact on our lives. Most town and city centres are experiencing some social, economic or environmental problems.

When did cities grow?

Cities in the UK grew rapidly as industry developed from the late 18th century. The type of industry that developed affects what they are like now. In 1757 Manchester had a population of 17 100, but the cotton industry was growing and the town too grew rapidly. Some of the spinning mills that were built in 1797 are now, in the 21st century, being turned into flats. Figure **B** shows the growth and change in population in the city between 1757 and 2000.

Why did cities grow?

Industries grew up around **raw materials** that were heavy to transport, like coal. Railways began to be built in the early 1800s, and they provided quick and easy transport. The Manchester–Leeds railway was built in 1839.

Factories were built around the central area and alongside the railways and canals. Houses were built around the factories to cope with the rapid increase in population.

The population increased quickly because:
- rural–urban migration brought more people to work in these factories
- healthcare and water quality improved, so…
- the death rate fell
- people lived longer
- fewer children died in infancy, and
- the rate of natural increase accelerated.

What happened to the centres?

Between 1850 and 1950 the city centre became the most important part of the city, with administration, shops, industry and high-density housing, but as they grew some centres turned into congested, overcrowded, polluted, noisy and expensive places. By the 1960s and 1970s many people thought that the way to get rid of the problems of the old CBDs was to knock them down and to redevelop the whole

A – Liverpool in the 1960s: an old industrial city

Year	Population
1757	17 101
1838	181 708
1891	563 638
1921	730 307
1971	541 468
1996	405 803
2000	412 965
Greater Manchester	2.5 million

B – Population growth of Manchester, 1757–2000

C – Glasgow in the 1970s: redevelopment

3 Changing city and town centres

D - A modern CBD

area. Some that were redeveloped, like Birmingham, are changing again. Not all towns were redeveloped, and some look much as they did 50 years ago.

What features are common to city and town centres now?

- Land is expensive because businesses and shops want to be in the middle of the city, and will pay high costs. They need to be accessible to large numbers of people.
- 'High-rise' buildings may have three or four storeys in a small town or 30 storeys in a large city.
- Many buildings are multi-functional, with a different use on each floor.
- Traffic is congested and the speed of travel is slow.
- There are many places where people can find food (restaurants, fast food), drink (pubs, wine bars), and entertainment (cinema, theatre, clubs, gym).

- Here also are the banks, finance companies, offices and public administration.
- The residential population is low, with few homes and few people living there.
- There is now little manufacturing industry.

What is the inner city?

On the edge of the central area is the inner city, which may have some or all of the following features:

- old terraced housing
- old factories
- brownfield sites where old factories and houses have been demolished
- car parks on cleared sites
- high-rise blocks of flats built in the 1960s or 1970s when older slums were cleared.

Inner city areas often suffer from particular problems resulting from poverty, pollution and change.

Questions

1. Use the photographs and text on these pages. Describe how CBDs have changed since the 1960s.
2. a) What are the things you would see in a city centre that make it different from other areas?
   b) How does the CBD differ from the inner city?
3. Make a list of the different reasons why people use the CBD, in the daytime and at night.
4. Make a sketch of D. Label (annotate) your sketch to show all the features of a city centre in 2000.

3.2 Changes in land use in city and town centres

The CBD is the centre of the city. The land use here varies, depending on the cost of the land, how easy it is to get to (the **accessibility**), and the original use. The competition for space in the middle results in very high land prices and high-rise buildings, with cheaper land and lower buildings away from the centre.

The **core** of the CBD contains large department stores, high-rise office blocks and some smaller shops. National chain stores like John Lewis or Marks & Spencer need access to millions of shoppers to make them financially viable, to cover the cost of being in the centre. Prestige office blocks house the headquarters of companies, banks and financial institutions. Any small shops here are likely to be specialist stores, selling high-value products like jewellery. These areas can become very quiet at night when the shops and offices close. Also in this inner core there may be theatres, restaurants, bars and smaller shops serving the huge number of people using the CBD in the daytime.

Around the core is a **framework** of other services like bus and coach stations, multi-storey car parks, wholesale distribution, education, public offices and smaller shops. In this area land use can change quickly, so the site of a demolished old Victorian factory may be a car park today and an office block tomorrow.

The whole CBD may get bigger. It may merge into a more accessible residential area where houses are converted into offices and this then becomes a **zone of advance** or **assimilation**, part of the busy, sought-after city centre. The buildings in this area are well cared for and land prices become higher.

In other less attractive areas the CBD may contract, because buildings are too difficult to upgrade, or because they are no longer accessible. This becomes a **zone of retreat** or **discard** where the buildings are run down and decaying.

When more and more people try to use the city centre, traffic congestion becomes a real problem, as do air

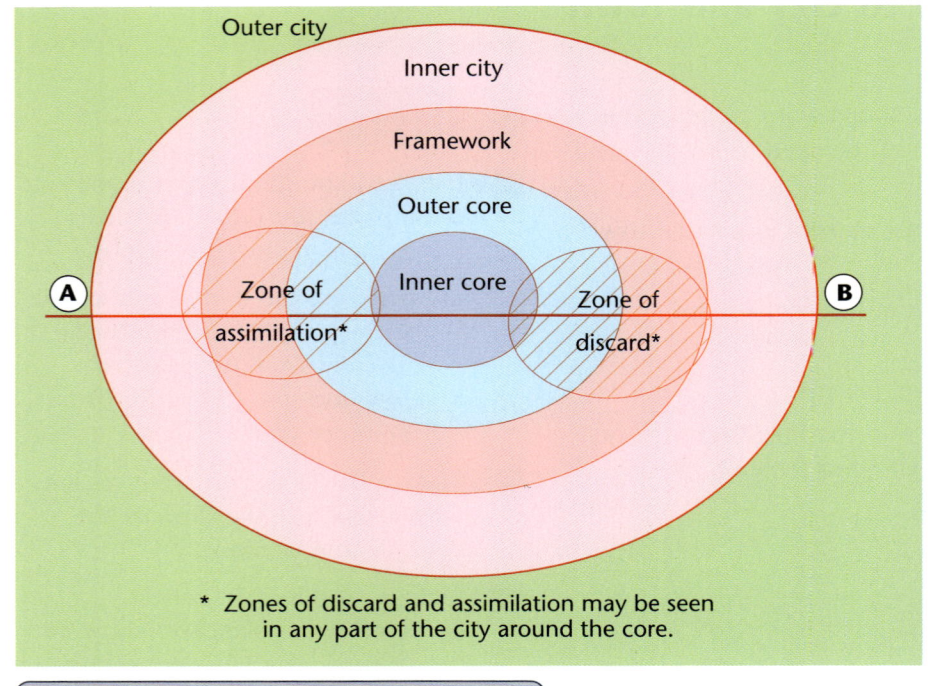

* Zones of discard and assimilation may be seen in any part of the city around the core.

A – Land use changes away from the city centre

B – A zone of discard

3 Changing city and town centres

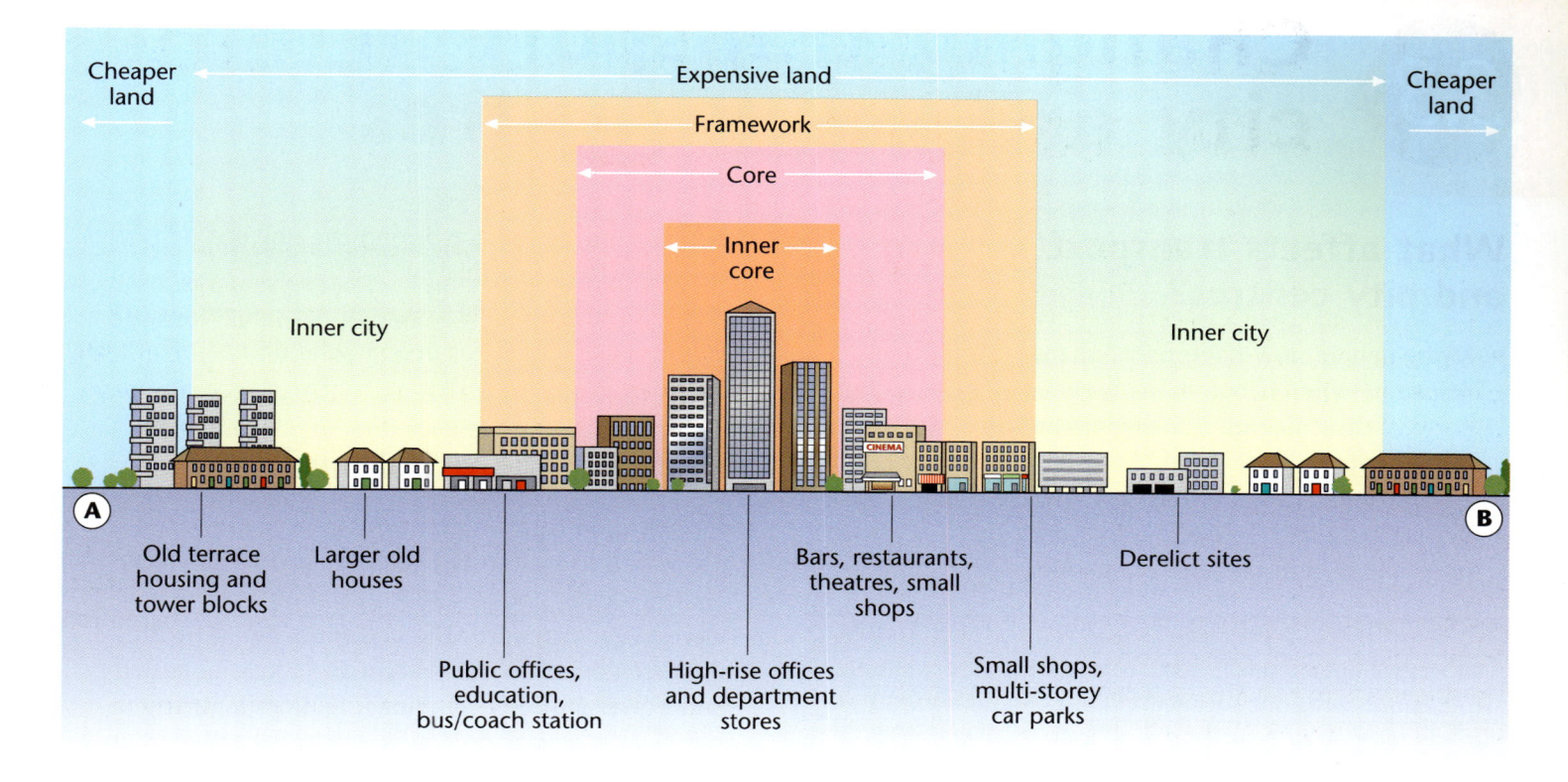

C – Cross-section of a city centre

Labels on diagram:
- Cheaper land (left) | Expensive land | Cheaper land (right)
- Framework
- Core
- Inner core
- Inner city (both sides)
- A (left edge), B (right edge)
- Old terrace housing and tower blocks
- Larger old houses
- Public offices, education, bus/coach station
- High-rise offices and department stores
- Bars, restaurants, theatres, small shops
- Small shops, multi-storey car parks
- Derelict sites

pollution, noise and overcrowding. If the financial or environmental costs of being in the centre become too high, people and businesses move out. This movement away from the centre to the edges is **decentralization**.

Many UK towns and cities originally grew around manufacturing, but industrial activities moved out to the suburbs some time ago, and so too did many of the people who had lived in the centre. Land in the suburbs was cheaper, access easier and quicker, and the quality of life was better.

In the 1980s there was a big change in most of our CBDs, when **retailing** began to leave the centres of many cities. Ninety per cent of shop floor space in the UK was in city centres in 1980, but two decades later this had reduced to 63 per cent. During the 1980s and early 1990s, retailing moved to suburban sites, to regional centres (like Merry Hill outside Dudley), to factory outlets, and to fashion centres on motorways and retail parks. In the late 1990s, out-of-town expansion was discouraged and retail development is now taking place in city centres, as in WestQuay in Southampton, one of the biggest city centre mall developments in 2000. In extreme cases the city centre becomes quite empty, with all the important activities going on around the edges.

Questions

1. a) Make a large copy of C to show the land use in the centre of a city. Label (annotate) each area of your diagram to describe the land use and what you might see there.
   b) Why are highest buildings in the city centre?
   c) In which part do people live?
   d) Which part may be busy at night?
   e) Which part may be empty at night?

2. a) What are zones of discard and zones of assimilation?
   b) How might land use and buildings change in each of these areas?

3. Describe an area of change in your nearest city or town centre and explain why the changes are taking place.

3.3 Changing transport in city and town centres

What affects transport in town and city centres?

- Many people now have *cars* but few had private transport when urban areas grew in the 19th and early 20th centuries. Car ownership (330 cars per 1000 people) in the UK is lower than in Europe, but car usage is higher. In the USA there are 650 cars per 1000 people. In every urban area there is a rush hour and a high demand for parking spaces.

	1985	1995	1998
All road vehicles (millions)	21.2	25.4	27.5
Households without cars (%)	38	30	20
Goods moved by road (billion tonne km)	103	150	160

A – *Vehicles in the UK, 1985–98*

- The *layout* of central city areas is different in each case, but inner city roads in old urban areas in the UK tend to be narrow, increasing congestion. By contrast, Los Angeles, like many American cities, grew up around the car and developed a huge system of urban freeways. There the distances are so great between shops, houses and work that a car is essential. Paris has wide boulevards, built in the 19th century, but they were designed to stop people from barricading the roads and rioting – not to make travel easier. Even here although the roads are wide they are still congested.
- *Urban areas* have got bigger and the number of people living in urban areas has increased in all MEDCs. A huge total of 25 million people live in the Tokyo greater metropolitan area. The major cities are now growing more slowly, but the area of land covered is increasing, with urban sprawl pushing into the countryside. People tend to move out of central areas to live, and commute to work, so the number of people travelling has increased, as has the distance they travel.
- *Goods transport* is mostly by lorry and the volume of materials carried has increased. Some cities ban lorries from the centre during the day but deliveries still have to be made.
- *Public transport* is necessary to get people into the centre, particularly for people who do not own a car, but road space is limited.

What are the problems?

- *Air pollution* from vehicle emissions in the UK is estimated to hasten between 16 000 and 24 000 deaths a year, and in 1998 a total of 3421 people were killed in road traffic accidents. Road traffic produces more pollution than all industrial activity and power stations combined, and emits nearly all the carbon monoxide. Many emissions are carcinogenic (cause cancer). Vehicle pollution can trigger asthma attacks, and Britain has the highest level of childhood asthma in the world. Healthcare to treat these illnesses is expensive. In certain weather conditions, pollution can be so bad that vehicles are banned from central areas, as in Athens in winter. Air pollution damages buildings as well as people – a particular problem for 'heritage' cities like Bath.
- *Traffic congestion* is a problem in and around every urban area, however small or large. **Gridlock** happens when vehicles cannot move at all, either because of an accident or because there are simply too many vehicles trying to use the roads, and delays can last for hours.
- The *speed of travel* is slowing and in 2000 the average speed across London was almost the same as it was in 1900 – about 4 miles per hour (6km/h). The 18-lane highway through Houston, Texas, is reduced to 18 miles per hour in 'rush' hours! The slow speed of travel can also affect the emergency services, which may be unable to get to the scene of an emergency.
- *Accidents* to pedestrians and people in vehicles increase with congestion – around 1200 pedestrians are killed in UK cities each year.
- A *poor environment* results from heavily congested urban areas and people and businesses may move

3 **Changing city and town centres**

B – A busy city centre street

away, leading to a decline in the economy and quality of city centres.
- *Public transport* is also slowed by car congestion, with the result that fewer people choose to use it.
- *Parking* is a problem for people who want to go into a city and stay there for some hours, and for people who live around the central areas and want to park close to where they live. Residents often have to buy an expensive permit in order to park close to their own home. Everywhere there are insufficient parking places for people's needs, and parking spaces are expensive. Illegally parked cars increase congestion.

Questions

1. Use the figures in A to explain how road traffic in the UK has changed since 1985.

2. What particular problems are caused by traffic in cities? Make a list, using source B, and put the problems in rank order, with 1 being the worst. Try to add two more problems not mentioned on these pages, and explain each problem.

3. List five of the worst traffic problems in your nearest inner town or city. Explain what you think has caused them.

3.4 Managing traffic

Early attempts at solving traffic congestion problems in city centres involved building huge multi-storey car parks, flyovers, ring roads and urban motorways. These solutions produced their own problems. Motorways attracted more vehicles, car parks and flyovers have disfigured city centres, and ring roads have led to out-of-town developments and a decline in services in the centre.

Towns and cities in MEDCs are looking for more environmentally sensitive solutions to traffic problems, although the traffic is growing as fast as solutions are put in place. Zurich and Manchester, for example, have trams, and Dutch cities have extensive cycleways.

A – City centre traffic problems

How can traffic be managed in the city centre?

Traffic in the centre can be managed to make it move faster or to be less of a problem for people using the centre.

- Computerized traffic lights, to speed flow.
- Traffic calming to reduce speed.
- Parking restrictions and high charges to deter people from driving in, clamping, and permits for residents.
- One-way systems, restricted routes and narrow roads to force drivers to find other routes.
- Traffic pricing, to make people pay to use a road into a city centre.
- Pedestrians-only areas.
- Constant information on the radio about hold-ups, to inform people and so help traffic flow.
- Buses run on gas, or electric trams, to reduce air pollution.
- Motorways and ring roads built as by-passes or flyovers to speed traffic around city centres (the M25 was built around London, but is now itself often reduced to a crawl).

How can people be encouraged to change the way they travel?

More people now travel further each day, but they can be encouraged to travel in a different way by schemes often put in place by local authorities.

- Park and ride schemes.
- Cycleway networks.
- Car-sharing incentives.
- Preferential road lanes for buses and trams, to make public transport faster than travelling by car.
- Better public transport — trams, buses, light railways, underground railways that are attractive to use.
- Increase in the costs of running a car — the government increases the costs of petrol and car tax, in order to persuade people to use cars less (part of a plan to reduce air pollution).
- School-run alternatives, like 'walking buses', to encourage parents not to drive their children to school.

How can public transport be developed?

Public transport is very important in managing traffic in city centres. In Zurich (Switzerland), trams run every 7 minutes. Quick, efficient, environmentally clean old tram systems are still in use in many other European cities, but most UK cities ripped them up 50 years ago. Places like Manchester, Sheffield and Birmingham are now putting back supertrams, and 24 schemes are under way in the UK.

Public transport can be made more attractive to encourage more people to use it, for example:

- low floors and raised waiting areas for easier access
- multiple doors to get people on and off quickly
- articulated buses with standing room for lots of people
- city traffic lights system giving buses priority over cars, and bus lanes, to make public transport faster and more reliable.

A city transport policy: Greater Nottingham

Some places are now looking at **integrated policies** to cover city centres and the surrounding areas, as the problems are interlinked. Greater Nottingham (population 650 000) has produced an integrated transport and land use plan for 2001–2006, to improve the quality of life:

- park and ride sites for 4000 cars, used by 500 000 people a year
- re-allocation of road space to buses, pedestrians and cyclists
- regulation of traffic signals
- encouraging organizations to make travel plans for employees
- better public transport (600 new buses, 100 raised-kerb loading points, low-floor buses)
- tram system and rail project, with public transport interchanges at key locations
- a clear zone in the city centre with restricted access.

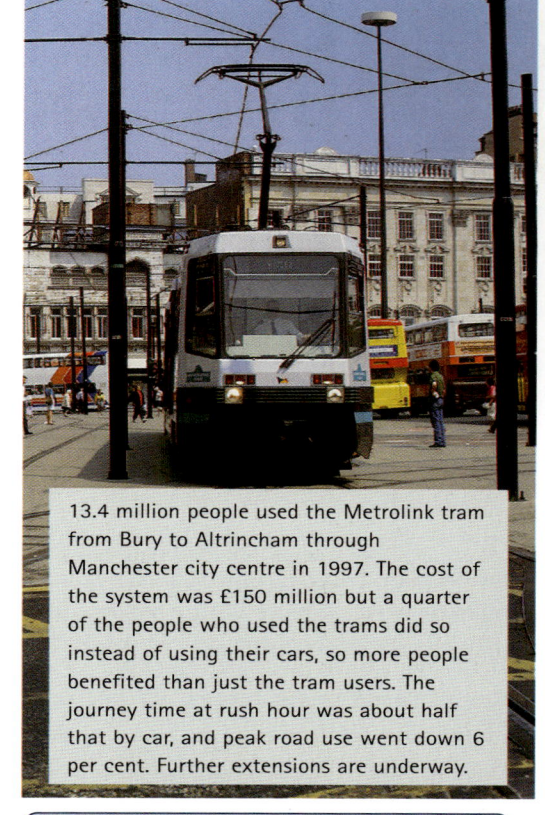

13.4 million people used the Metrolink tram from Bury to Altrincham through Manchester city centre in 1997. The cost of the system was £150 million but a quarter of the people who used the trams did so instead of using their cars, so more people benefited than just the tram users. The journey time at rush hour was about half that by car, and peak road use went down 6 per cent. Further extensions are underway.

B – Manchester's Metrolink tramway system

	1981	1991
Used a car to get to work	48%	61%
Used a bus to get to work	26%	17%
Lived and worked in the city	53%	47%

C – Getting to work in Nottingham

Questions

1. a) Why are some early attempts at traffic control not popular now?
   b) Drivers and residents may have different views on traffic management. Which form of traffic management would be preferred by: • drivers • local residents?

2. a) Draw a table with the following headings:

Ways to encourage people to travel differently	Mother with two children and a buggy	Elderly lady	Middle-aged person	Teenager

   Complete the first column with seven ways to encourage people to change the way they travel, and tick the boxes you think appropriate.

   b) Look again at C. Explain why Nottingham needs a transport policy. How is the city tackling traffic growth?

Managing Change in the Human Environment

3.5 Living in poor inner city areas

Until the 1960s, most inner city housing in the UK was small terraced houses built for workers in the 19th century, or larger houses for richer people, some now subdivided into flats or offices.

The terraced housing was very run down and decaying, and local councils wanted people to have better places to live, with bathrooms and kitchens (A). The solution in the 1970s was to **redevelop** neighbourhoods, demolishing everything and putting up new tower blocks or very high-density housing. In Glasgow, 262 multi-storey blocks with 8–31 floors were built.

Many of these tower blocks did not provide good housing and some have been demolished, only 30 years after they were built. There were problems with damp, condensation, cracks, and expensive heating systems that people could not afford to run. Some communities had been broken up and people often felt isolated and alone high up in blocks where the lifts might be vandalized and children had nothing to do. Many of these inner city areas became bleak, windswept places often broken up by flyovers and multi-storey car parks.

A – Inner city decay

In the 1970s and the 1980s, inner city areas continued to decline as social, economic and environmental problems increased. Riots broke out in Brixton, Liverpool and Manchester and led to a government enquiry. A new phase of inner city **regeneration** rather than redevelopment is now attempting to tackle the problems. Local people were involved in some of the most successful schemes to tackle urban deprivation in the 1990s.

There are still many deprived areas in inner cities. It is thought that one in every four children in the UK today is growing up in poverty or deprivation.

One definition of deprivation is:
'When an individual's well-being falls below a level generally regarded as a reasonable minimum for Britain today'.

Dense idea demolished

Tough lessons from the rise and fall of the Marquess estate

The Marquess estate was built in 1977 in Islington, north London. In a deliberate contrast to 1960s tower blocks, the estate was designed as a series of streets and alleys of mostly family houses with gardens around a series of green spaces.

But the Marquess became a disaster. It quickly gained a fearsome reputation as an area of high crime, with twice as much vandalism as anywhere else in the borough. Its tightly compact and intricate layout was seen as a major cause of crime and fear of crime on the estate. The police said the design 'lends itself to crime'. The Marquess's compact layout meant that very few people walked through the estate. So there was actually less self-policing.

The problems at the Marquess, which also included damp and noisy flats, became so acute that Islington took the drastic step of deciding to tear down 463 of the homes. It is now rebuilding the estate, on a more simple street pattern, in partnership with Southern Housing Group (SHG).

Renamed New River Green, the estate is being opened up to encourage more people to walk through. More homes for sale and shared ownership are also being provided in an attempt to promote a mixture of incomes on the estate.

The remodelled estate now has significantly fewer homes. Regeneration of the estate 'would not work' without reducing the density – but the reduction in density is not in line with current policy. To avoid suburban sprawl, we need to get more homes into the inner city.

B – From Guardian Society, *25 October 2000*

3 Changing city and town centres

Social problems	Economic problems	Environmental problems
A high proportion of poor people who are often: • old and young • students • ethnic minorities • single-parent families People cannot move out because of lack of money or skills High levels of illness and disease and a shorter life expectancy and higher infant mortality rate than more wealthy areas Lack of things for children to do Drugs Crime, theft, vandalism, mugging, damage to property, joy riding Poor police and community relations	A cycle of poverty: people simply get poorer with no money coming into the community High levels of unemployment, particularly for men Low wages and low-skilled work Declining industries, few new jobs Lack of facilities/infrastructure	Air pollution from traffic or industry which is often old Land pollution, rubbish, derelict sites Water pollution (rivers and canals) Lack of open, green space that people feel able to use Old decaying terraces, newer decaying tower blocks Poor-quality housing and declining 1970s housing estates

C – *Social, economic and environmental problems experienced by people in the inner city*

D – *Redevelopment in Gateshand, Tynside*

Questions

1 a) What was wrong with inner city housing by 1970?
   b) How did local authorities try to tackle the problems?
   c) What went wrong with some of the solutions? Refer to **B** and explain at least five different points.

2 *Either*
   Use **C** and the photographs on these pages to describe social, economic and environmental problems for people living in inner city areas. *or*
   Sketch an outline of each photograph. Annotate each one to illustrate at least three problems of inner city living.

3.6 Retail changes and city and town centres

Shopping habits changed in the 1970s and 1980s when most people got access to a car and had more money and leisure time. Shopping for daily necessities like food changed from the small shop in the local area to a supermarket, usually further away from the inner city where land costs were lower. People were able to choose where to shop for other goods and where to go for leisure, and were not dependent on public transport.

Regional shopping centres and retail parks

Shopping moved away from the city centre to **retail parks** on the urban edges, or to regional shopping centres like Meadowhall outside Sheffield and Bluewater in Kent. Nine million people live within one hour's drive of Meadowhall, and nearly half the shoppers do all their shopping there. Before it was opened in 1990, they would have spent their money in neighbouring towns and cities.

As retail parks opened in the rural/urban fringe, city and town centre shops declined. Urban areas of all sizes have been affected, from towns of just 5000 people to cities of 200 000 and more. City centres have seen shops boarded up, fewer customers and falling trade, as congested, polluted centres became less attractive places to shop in than the out-of-town retail parks. In the 1990s, development of out-of-town sites was restricted, and the focus is now returning to the city centre.

Leisure in the city and town centre

The main activities in many city and town centres at night are in the pubs, clubs, restaurants and fast food places. These bring people in to the centre but there are problems too: drunkenness, violence and noise may deter some people from using the centre. CCTV, extra policing and private security guards are being used to tackle some of the problems. Banning drinking in the streets has also made some centres calmer.

A – Shut-up shops in a city centre

Shopping malls

Shopping malls — bright, attractive, pleasant places — originated in the USA and were introduced in the UK in the 1980s and 1990s. Montreal and Toronto in Canada have extensive underground malls to cope with the extremes of climate there: from −30°C in the winter to 30°C in the summer. Shopping malls in the UK may have other facilities such as cinemas and restaurants, and community facilities like a library integrated with the shops. Shopping malls bring different problems to those in inner cities:

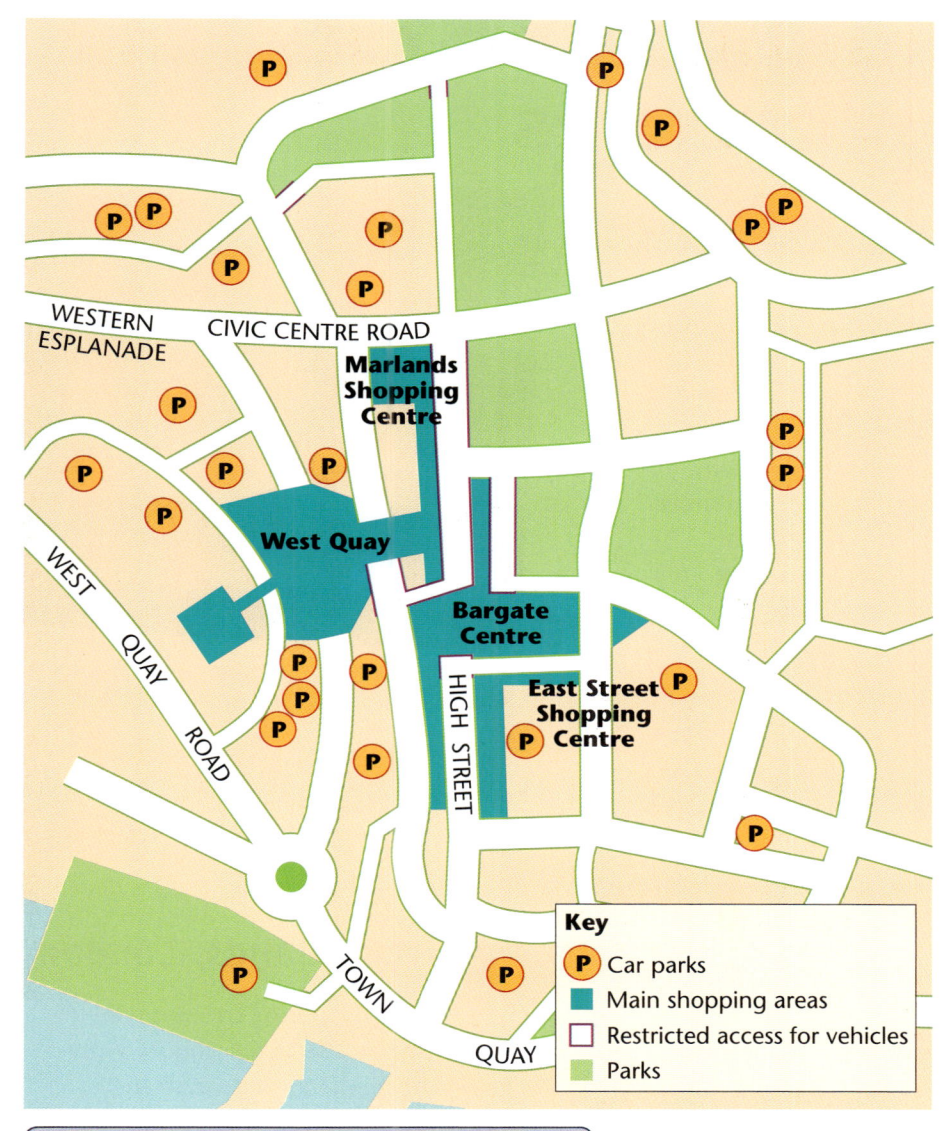

3 Changing city and town centres

B – Location of the shopping malls in Southampton

C – A shopping mall

- While they may be busy, bustling places in the daytime, they can be empty, frightening places at night, making the problem of a 'dead' city centre even worse. In the USA, some of the older malls are being demolished in order to bring people, cars and life back to the city centres. In Southhampton, Marlands, Bargate and WestQuay malls are part of the retail centre, surrounded by extensive parking with all the facilities of an out-of-town retail park.
- They may become unpopular and are then little used by shoppers. Land use in the CBD changes — they may even become part of a zone of discard.
- They are privately owned, controlled by security guards, so people may not be able to sit, eat or sleep there as they would if it was a public place.
- Like retail parks, they may be the cause of the decline of other parts of the city centre.

Questions

1. a) List five reasons why shopping malls are attractive places to shop.
   b) Now list five negative effects of malls. (Use figures B and C).

2. a) Think about where you/your family go to do most of your shopping, including your food shopping. Is it the nearest town or city to where you live? Explain why you go there to shop.
   b) Do you go to the same place to do your non-food shopping? Why/Why not?

3. a) Suggest why leisure activities in the CBD might be the source of problems. Why? Who for?
   b) How should such problems be tackled?

57

Managing Change in the Human Environment

3.7 Managing parts of city and town centres

Local authorities are attempting to manage change in inner city areas and build sustainable urban communities.

CS Glasgow

The local authority in Glasgow has tried a number of different schemes to improve the quality of life for people, starting with housing but now developing policies to tackle social, environmental and economic problems together. Between 1957 and 1974, comprehensive redevelopment of slum tenements meant clearing the whole area and putting people into tower blocks or outer city council estates, often splitting up communities and even families.

When the problems with this type of development became clear in the 1970s, other policies were tried. *GEAR*, the Glasgow Eastern Area Renewal project (1976–87), was a response to the mistakes of slum clearance: 1200 houses were refurbished and 2000 new ones built, with 300 factories to provide employment.

In 1988, inner city derelict dockland was transformed in the *Glasgow Garden Festival*, a government initiative to bring 'green' development to derelict inner cities. Eventually the Glasgow site had 1100 houses and flats, a business park and a large green open space.

The *Govan initiative* aimed to use public and private money to regenerate the economy of the declining dock area. By the mid-1990s there were new jobs, training, new housing and a better environment. Social, economic and environmental problems were tackled together.

A – *Recent development in central Glasgow*

Despite all the work, much council housing is still in poor condition, and £1.2 billion is needed to repair existing homes.

CS Docklands, London

The Docklands area of London was in decline in the 1980s. The docks were redundant, housing was poor and unemployment high. The *Docklands Development Corporation* was set up

---

Transforming a century-old former doss house into more than 100 flats in an area with a desperate housing shortage would seem, on the face of it, good news. But critics say that the conversion of Tower House – a brooding 700-room building in Whitechapel, east London – into £200,000 apartments will only add to the problems of an area with some of the highest levels of homelessness in the country.

Property development is booming in the East End. Workers who want to live just two stops on the Dockland Light Railway from Canary Wharf, and 10 minutes' walk from the City of London, are snapping up factory and warehouse conversions. But this popularity puts more pressure on an area of extreme poverty and high levels of immigration from Africa, Asia and now the former Soviet Union and the Balkans. With fewer empty buildings, the homeless are being forced towards the margins.

Tower Hamlets Council says that more than 8,500 families are living in overcrowded conditions. The council housing sell-offs of the mid-1980s mean that the authority does not have the housing stock to offer transfers, and families cannot afford the £160,000 cost of a three-bedroom, ex-council flat. In the private sector, Victorian terrace houses have reached the £500,000 mark.

B – *From* Guardian Unlimited, *18 April 2001*

3 Changing city and town centres

C – Transformation of the London Docklands

with public and private money to regenerate the area, which has now been transformed.

What is there now?
- Canary Wharf and other high-rise buildings, centres of commerce, printing and publishing and finance businesses
- 25 000 flats, apartments and housing units
- Docklands Light Railway, to speed communications with the centre of London
- City Airport for use by smaller aircraft
- marina and other leisure facilities
- bars, restaurants, shops.

Millions of pounds have transformed the area – but for whom? The houses and flats, and goods in the shops, are too expensive (B) for the people who lived in and used the area before redevelopment. Fewer than 1000 new council houses have been built. Most of the people who work in Docklands come from outside the area (by rapid transit). So who has benefited from the transformation?

Gentrification

Some inner city areas change as people move within the city. Certain parts become sought-after places to live for people who want to be nearer their work in the city. Old housing is 'done up', house prices rise and neighbourhoods become fashionable. This is a process called **gentrification**. Poorer people may move out to somewhere else in the inner city that is cheaper.

Who decides?

Should local planners stop developments that displace people? (see B). Areas may need improving, but the local council may not have enough money to do this. If developers are willing to pay a high price for land in a city, should it be sold so that the money can be spent on improving other areas in the same city?

Questions

1. Describe the changes made to parts of Glasgow to improve the quality of life for people living there.

2. What are the advantages and disadvantages of the Docklands development for:
   - local people
   - the City of London
   - the new residents of Docklands?

   You could write your answers in the form of a table.

3. a) Use B and C. How have derelict industrial sites been redeveloped?
   b) How would you improve the site for the benefit of local people and the environment?

4. Do you think gentrification in some places is a 'good thing' or a 'bad thing'? Who is it good/bad for? Explain your answer.

3.8 Solutions to problems — if people agree

Urban issues involve two main groups of people: the decision makers and planners who try to find solutions, and the people who are affected by the problem. Solving an urban problem means change, and every solution has advantages and disadvantages for different people. Consultation between the two groups of people is important. Some problems affect an urban area that is wider than the city centre, and then agreement can be difficult to find.

As early as 1956 in the USA, it was evident that traffic was clogging the San Francisco Bay area roads and bridges and that problems would get worse. BART, the San Francisco Bay Area Rapid Transit system, was devised to link major city, commercial and suburban subcentres around the Bay with a high-speed rapid rail network, but there was considerable disagreement about the costs and the detail. Construction began in 1964 but it was 1972 before the first passengers travelled on the system and by then the delays meant that traffic problems were very much worse.

Change may be halted altogether if people disagree. Efforts to improve public transport in Los Angeles (USA) have met with opposition from different groups of people. From 1990, new Metro Rail lines were built as part of a $130 billion rapid transport network to tackle traffic congestion, but work stopped in 1998.

One group of people said:

'The system is too late, the city has already spread out, few people live near the centre, and growth is now in the edge cities.'

Another group said:

'The fares are too high, only rich suburban people can use them. The poor people depend on buses, so the money should be spent on improving bus transport used by the people in the centre, the poor.'

Norwich City Council is carrying out an extensive consultation study *before* it begins any major changes (**C**).

Extensive urban redevelopment in the 1960s and 1970s did not always bring long-term solutions. Now it is thought that regeneration of small urban areas is often more successful, especially when the people who live there are involved in finding the solution.

Liverpool HAT, or Liverpool Housing Action Trust, was set up by the Government in 1993 to manage 67 high-rise blocks on 35 sites right across Liverpool, from the inner city areas to overspill estates

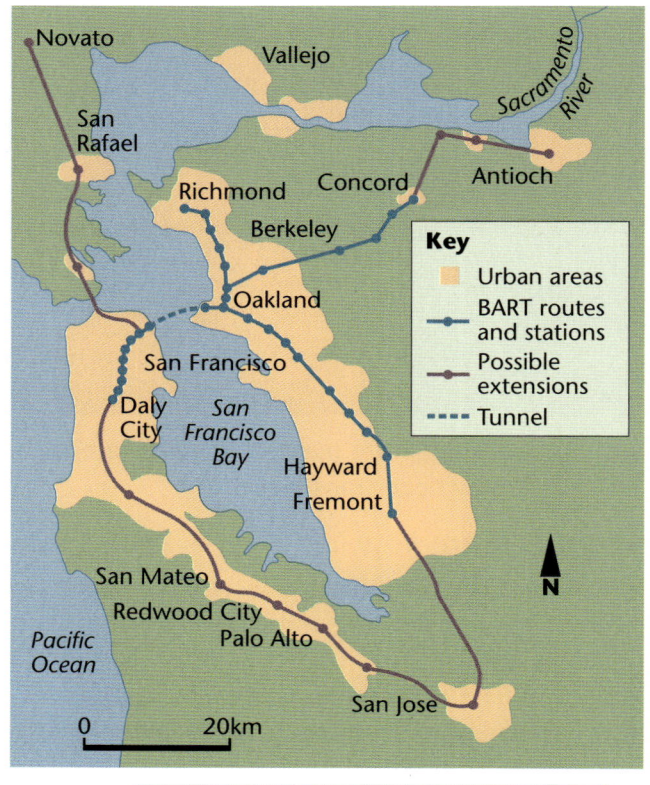

A – *San Francisco Bay Area Rapid Transit system (BART) needed agreement from many centres*

and suburbs. The aim is to regenerate each area, both in terms of housing and jobs, but HAT has to balance what the tenants want (through consultation), housing needs, the run-down state of each block, and the running costs. High-rise blocks cost twice as much as low-rise blocks to run. £300 million has been spent on redevelopment (changing) and refurbishment (doing up).

New technology may produce cheap new solutions in some areas. Internet CCTV is proving successful in improving the quality of life on one inner city housing estate in Hull (**D**).

3 **Changing city and town centres**

High-rise makeovers give inner cities a key to towering success

WAITING lists for three groups of 16-storey blocks in central Leeds, which were threatened with demolition less than 10 years ago, have grown to the stage where investment in security, shared heating and communal gardens has proved 'irresistible'.

Leeds has seen a growing move back into the city centre by home-buyers.

'People are gradually giving up the attitude of "tower block equals big sixties mistake",' said Richard Lewis, chairman of housing in Leeds, where a third of the 148 towers – from 5 to 25 storeys – are oversubscribed. 'There are still unpopular blocks which may be only half let. But there's much more potential than anyone would have thought just a few years ago.'

The 99 flats of Brignall Croft were painted in Leeds United colours -- blue and yellow – while a pastel-based livery on nearby blocks in Little London won a national paintwork award last year.

The Brignall Croft block will get energy-saving cladding and almost certainly a 24-hour security guard.

'Most people agree with paying that bit more, provided the charges only come in when the improvements have been finished,' said Betty Preston, a retired bus driver who lives in Brignall Croft. 'We're well aware of our advantages here, from the views across Leeds to the launderette they've installed in the block. And you do get a community feeling, with a community centre in Scargill Grange (the next-door tower) where a lot of bingo gets played.'

The scheme has been helped by a £200 000 Yorkshire Electricity grant for replacing outdated electric heating, and Leeds is looking for extra funds to extend block makeovers to outlying estates. Successful towers are already established, with entryphones linked to domestic TV sets helping both security and a sense of neighbourliness.

'The other key ingredient is the type of tenant,' said Mr Lewis, whose department has seen particular demand for blocks converted into sheltered housing for pensioners. 'We no longer make the mistakes of the days when my wife was first married and found herself stuck high up in a tower block with a 15-month-old, a 6-month old and a very big pram.'

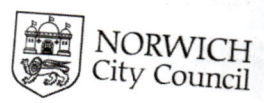

B – From the Guardian, 6 February 1999

NORWICH City Council   **NORFOLK COUNTY COUNCIL**

Talking Transport - Have Your Say

Norwich City Council and Norfolk County Council are consulting you on two major transport issues this Autumn and we want to know what you think!

Norwich is a fine city with a thriving economy, but the streets are already busy with traffic and things will get worse with traffic forecast to grow by 20% between now and 2011.

We want to do something about it because traffic jams are bad for everyone - businesses, shoppers, residents, commuters and tourists. We want to reduce road accidents and damage to historic buildings, improve air quality and safety for pedestrians and cyclists, reduce delays and congestion for public transport and motorists and improve parking enforcement.

So we want to know what you think about -

The City Centre Transport Plan
A 10 year vision for the City centre to create more space for pedestrians, cyclists, public transport and improve access to car parks by reducing through traffic.

On-Street Parking
The Road Traffic Act 1991 would allow us to improve and increase parking enforcement across Norwich and manage on-street parking spaces more effectively in the City centre.

All views must be received by Friday 10th November 2000.

Let us know what you think. Your views really do count so let's get talking transport!

City Centre Transport Plan

C – Norwich City Centre Transport Plan

Web camera scheme halves estate's crime

WEDNESDAY DECEMBER 27 2000

BY PAUL WILKINSON

AN EXPERIMENTAL security camera system that uses the Internet has helped police to halve crime on a once-notorious inner city estate.

Now the innovative closed-circuit television surveillance system is being considered by several other towns as a way of restoring normal life to urban streets, particularly after dark. The Thornton estate, close to the centre of Hull, once had a dark reputation: three prostitutes were murdered there in recent years and drug-related crime was endemic. But in the five months since the £400 000 scheme was introduced in July, reported offences have dropped by 45 per cent. It is the first time in Britain that a CCTV system using the Internet has been used to tackle crime.

A major plus factor with the scheme is that it does not involve digging up pavements to lay cables or ugly camera poles. As a result, the system is particularly appealing to historic areas anxious to preserve their heritage. Tiny cameras disguised as street lamps or hidden on buildings send digital pictures to a control centre by radio, laser or microwave transmissions. Operators can zoom in and track suspects using the exceptional clarity of the digital pictures to obtain clear identifications. Images can be emailed to police via the Internet.

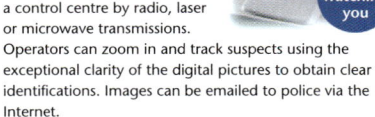

A resident's group, the Goodwin Resource Centre Association, representing the Thornton estate's 3500 population, worked out what form the high-tech system would take. 'The beauty of the system is that it is flexible and portable. We have cameras on roofs, in lifts, on street corners and both inside and outside buildings. We've put up 200 signs around the estate in the form of orange triangles to warn people that CCTV cameras are operating.'

In the past five months car crime dropped by 80 per cent, shop thefts by 69 per cent, house burglaries by 49 per cent and violent attacks by 30 per cent.

D – From The Times, 27 December 2000

Questions

1. Why should transport problems be tackled across a whole urban area rather than just in the centre? (A and C)

2. Why do people disagree about the building of the LA Metro Rail?

3. Use B. Why are the high rise makeovers a success?

4. Why are Norfolk County Council and Norwich City Council carrying out a consultation exercise together? What are they trying to achieve?

5. For a local transport, housing or development issue in your area, devise a leaflet or website page to encourage the involvement of local people.

6. How might the internet and new technology be used in the future to tackle inner city problems? (use D)

3.9 Manchester, a changing city

Greater Manchester has a population of 2.57 million people speaking 40 different languages in several distinct cultural communities. In addition, 7 million people live in the region and 20 million live within two hours' drive. More people are influenced by what happens in the centre than just those who live in the city.

A – Old Manchester

B – Moss Side estate, Manchester

How did Manchester grow?

The city grew around cotton manufacturing, and some buildings in the centre still reflect its industrial past. City centre housing was middle-class, and smaller terraced houses surrounded the inner city mills and factories. Slum clearance and redevelopment in the 1960s led to new estates and tower blocks (page 46). Redevelopment of the city centre in the 1970s gave Manchester, amongst other things, the Arndale Centre, a concrete retail site that led to the decline of nearby shops and the surrounding streets. Manchester, like other cities, suffered **counter-urbanization** as people moved away from the centre.

On Saturday 15 June 1996, an IRA bomb ripped through the city centre, causing at least £700 million damage and destroying the retail heart. By the end of the same year plans were under way to reshape a centre better than ever before.

How is the centre being rebuilt?

A new pedestrian street has integrated the Cathedral with the centre. Pedestrian ways link squares and shops giving almost a kilometre of traffic-free shopping. A new square, 240 trees, a park, the biggest Marks & Spencer in the world, a refurbished Corn Exchange, a heritage centre, a leisure retail development with IMAX cinema, and an eight-storey hotel have been added. Entertainment and leisure sites are flourishing in Manchester's old industrial areas and along the canals around the centre.

What does the city centre provide now?

In the city centre now there are shops, business and office sites, tourist facilities, restaurants, pubs and clubs, theatres, sports facilities, heritage and religious sites — and transport, because only a few people live in the centre.

Living in the city centre

Housing in the very centre is limited and very expensive. It is mostly young affluent professional people who live here, often in converted warehouses and old industrial buildings.

Close to the centre are two very different housing areas. The Miles Platting and Ancoats estates have 3000 council properties (houses, flats, maisonettes and sheltered accommodation) and 100 terraced private houses. There are ambitious plans to regenerate the distinctive parts of Ancoats, creating Britain's first urban village. The area suffers from all the usual problems of inner city life, for example:

3 Changing city and town centres

D – New Manchester

- drug dealing, high crime rate (three times the county average) – the derelict mill and factory buildings are used by drug users and other criminals, and considered unsafe and dangerous by local residents
- poor health (lower life expectancy than other parts of the city)
- low levels of employment and income
- 83.7 per cent of households depend on public transport.

The houses were improved in the early 1990s and are in good condition but they are hard to let and the area is losing population. City centres need to serve people now, and be sustainable. Manchester centre was rebuilt using mostly private funding, but where will the money come from for poor communities like Miles Platting and Ancoats?

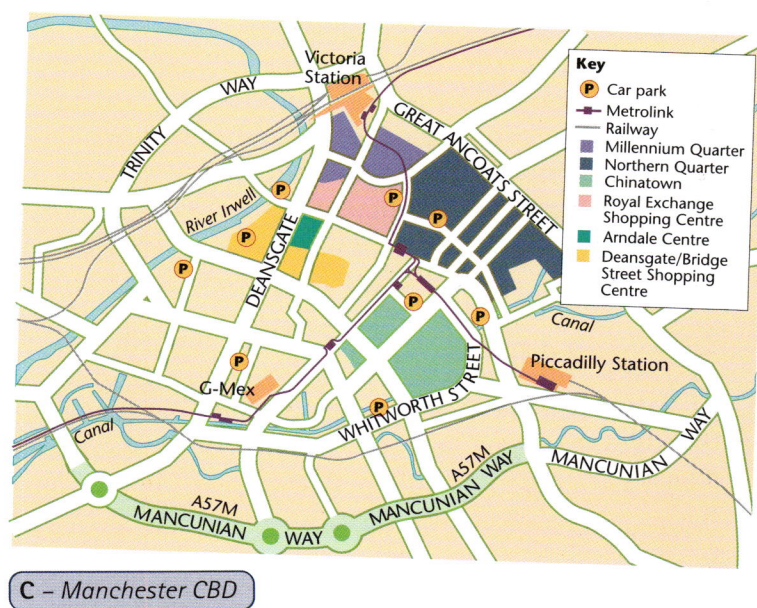

C – Manchester CBD

Key
- P Car park
- Metrolink
- Railway
- Millennium Quarter
- Northern Quarter
- Chinatown
- Royal Exchange Shopping Centre
- Arndale Centre
- Deansgate/Bridge Street Shopping Centre

Questions

1 Describe Manchester city centre before and after 1996. Why have so many trees and pedestrian areas been added? What is the centre like now? Use **C**, and the text. Refer to land use, transport routes and policy.

2 Suggest 2 ways in which local people could improve the quality of their lives on poor housing estates and attract private investement.

63

Managing Change in the Human Environment — **Changing city and town centres**

Exam practice questions

Mark schemes can be found on the book's website, at www.heinemann.co.uk/issuesmarkschemes

1. Use the information in A and B to answer this question.
   a) What is meant by 'high density of building'? (1)
   b) Describe transport in Tokyo (use A and B). (3)

A – High density of building in central Tokyo

B – 'Pushers' cramming people onto a train in Tokyo

2. Urban planning schemes do not meet the needs of everyone. Choose an example of *one* of the following:
   - urban transport
   - inner city redevelopment
   - inner city housing.

   Describe the main features and problems of the scheme. (8)

3. There are different types of urban planning developments, such as inner city redevelopment, changing transport systems, city centre retail development, and new towns.

   Choose *one* example of an urban planning development that you have studied. Describe its main features, and the benefits or disadvantages of the scheme. (8)

4. 'Sport may seem an unlikely catalyst for regeneration, but Arsenal Football Club is helping one community by putting money into a redevelopment scheme in a poor part of Islington. The scheme includes a 60 000-seater stadium, 1000 new homes, a doctor's surgery, 3500 new jobs, and investment in the area of £400 million plus. One-quarter of the housing will be low-price 'affordable' properties – a requirement of every major new urban scheme.'

   Use the information to explain who might support this proposal, and who might disagree with it? Give reasons for your answers. Describe the benefits or disadvantages of the scheme. (8)

MANAGING CHANGE IN THE HUMAN ENVIRONMENT

4 Pressure at the rural/urban fringe

How can changes and pressures to develop the rural/urban fringe be managed more efficiently in the UK and in the European Union?

Managing Change in the Human Environment

4.1 Why have changes occurred?

What is the rural/urban fringe?

The rural/urban fringe is the area between the heavily built-up town or city and the open countryside. In the UK there is no clear definition of 'rural' and 'urban', but planners talk about **greenfield sites** and **development envelopes**. A line is drawn around an urban area, whether a village or a city, and within that 'envelope' all sorts of building can take place. Outside that line is countryside or green fields where development is restricted. Where the line is drawn can cause controversy, as many people have conflicting opinions. Often it is very hard to see a clear division between the two areas, but this rural/urban fringe is changing (see B).

Why have changes taken place?

In the 19th century there was still a clear difference between urban and rural areas. In the rural areas most people worked in the countryside, and in towns people worked in factories or offices or in urban services. In the 20th century things began to change and city centres became less attractive and more expensive places to be, for people and for industry.

By the 1920s people could live in one place and travel to work by train or bus. Cities began to spread outwards and commuter towns grew around larger cities like London. From the 1960s, cars became cheaper and more people used them

A – The rural/urban fringe

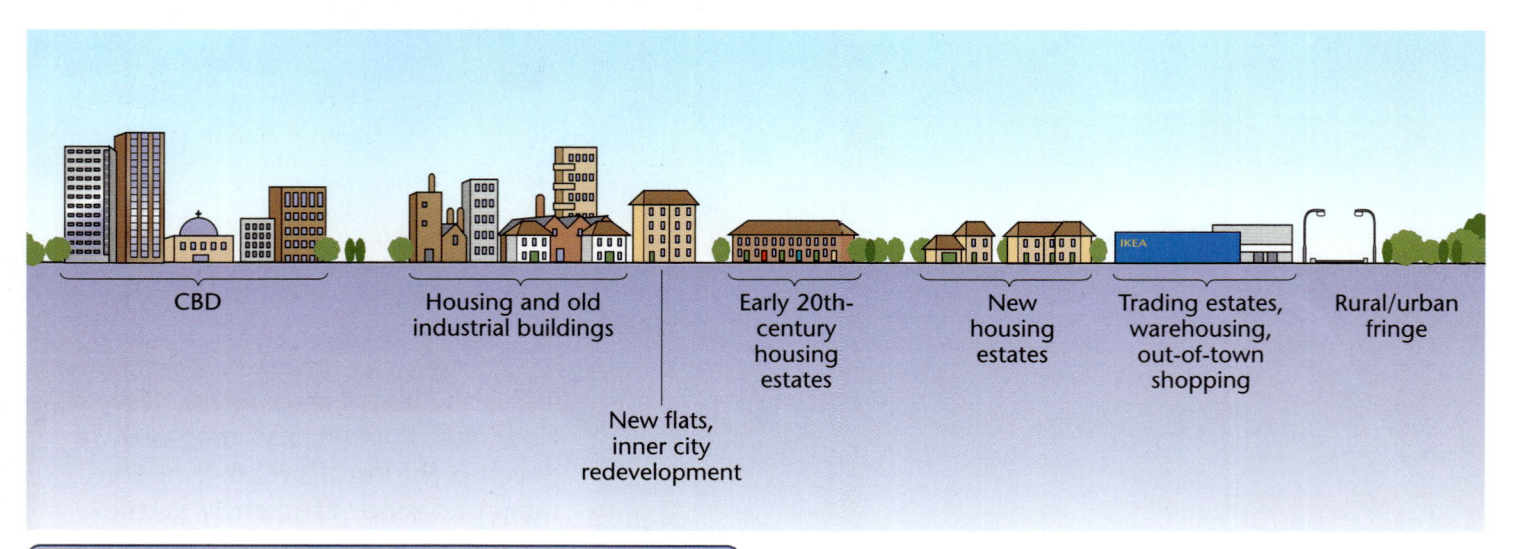

B – Cross-section of a city from the CBD to the rural/urban fringe

CBD | Housing and old industrial buildings | New flats, inner city redevelopment | Early 20th-century housing estates | New housing estates | Trading estates, warehousing, out-of-town shopping | Rural/urban fringe

4 Pressure at the rural/urban fringe

to get to work, choosing to live in a pleasant environment rather than a less attractive city centre (C). When people moved out of cities, other, often poorer, people moved in.

Industry also changed and new locations were found away from traditional areas inside the cities. Cheap land and easy access encouraged low-rise factories and warehouses on the city edges. These sprawled over large areas of land for the same land price as a small high-rise building in the city centre.

Heavy goods vehicles could bring in goods and distribute products more easily from the edge of urban areas than from inside the city. The industries that stayed in the middle were those that needed a central location.

In the 1980s and 1990s urban areas sprawled outwards rather than upwards. The divide between rural and urban areas now is less clear. This widening of the rural/urban fringe has become a source of great controversy. This has created discussion and, sometimes, conflict between local people, local authorities, governments and people who want to build there. Many people have benefited from the changes but much countryside has been lost.

Does transport affect the rural/urban fringe?

The massive increase in the use of cars has caused problems both for rural and urban areas. New roads tend to be outside cities, and the new roads built to reduce congestion and speed up traffic, like motorways, take up more land than old roads. The demand for roads increases, particularly for wide, fast roads like the M25, and more traffic is attracted to them which in turn increases the pressure on the rural/urban fringe for more shopping and industrial development.

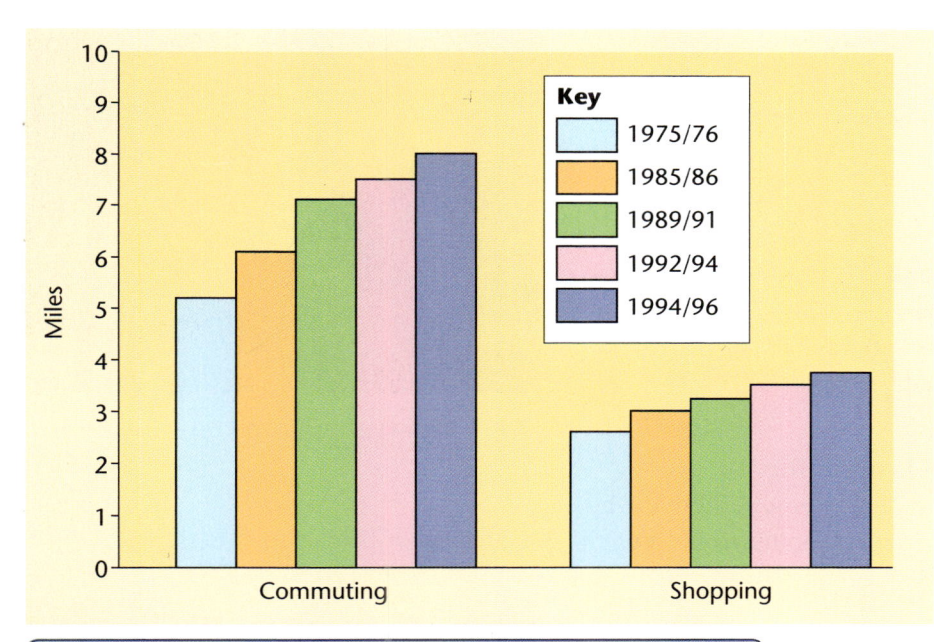

C – Average journey length for commuting and shopping, 1975–96

Questions

1. a) What is the rural/urban fringe?
   b) How might you recognize it? What are its characteristics? (B)

2. Describe five changes that have taken place in cities that have caused them to spread outwards.

3. Draw a sketch cross-section across a city from the middle to the edge to show how the size and shape of buildings changes as you travel outwards. Label a high-rise block in the middle, Victorian housing, etc.

4. How have changes in people's lifestyle changed the amount that we travel? (Refer to C.)

Managing Change in the Human Environment

4.2 What has happened to housing?

In the 1920s and 1930s people began to commute to work by train, bus and tram, and suburbs grew around the edge of all cities. Welwyn Garden City was one of the first cities built and designed to give people a better quality of life with semi-detached houses and gardens. Wide roads with verges, and trees and houses in curves and crescents, replaced the straight roads and blocks of the 19th-century city. Those people who were able to moved out from crowded central locations to a more peaceful life on the edge of cities.

After 1945, more estates were built in the fields on the city margins as house-building accelerated after the Second World War. A number of new towns, like Stevenage near London, were planned and built in the countryside so that green land was left around the cities.

In the 1960s and 1970s many inner cities were redeveloped. Slum areas were cleared and replaced by high-rise blocks of flats or maisonettes. Often people were rehoused in the cities but some who had the choice and the money to travel, moved out. By the 1970s and 1980s, a ring of suburban housing estates surrounded most towns and cities. House-building in the rural/urban fringe continued through the 1990s.

Villages on the edge of towns have been completely changed as a result of urban expansion. Some villages have been absorbed into suburbs as house-building has spread out from the urban area. Other villages have remained separate from the town but have changed in character. They change as different people move in, perhaps retired people or young families with children, and the 'incomers' may outnumber the original village inhabitants.

In the future, more houses than ever will be needed. The UK government estimated, in 1998, that the population would increase by 1.2 million by 2021, but that 4.3 million more households would be needed.

Why do we need more houses?

- More single people want to live on their own, either in flats or small houses.
- More people want to live in small family units and not stay with the larger family as many used to.
- More people are living longer, often staying in their own homes, on their own and living well into their eighties and nineties as life expectancy increases.

A – A 1950s housing estate

B – 1960s high-rise blocks

C – A changing village

4 Pressure at the rural/urban fringe

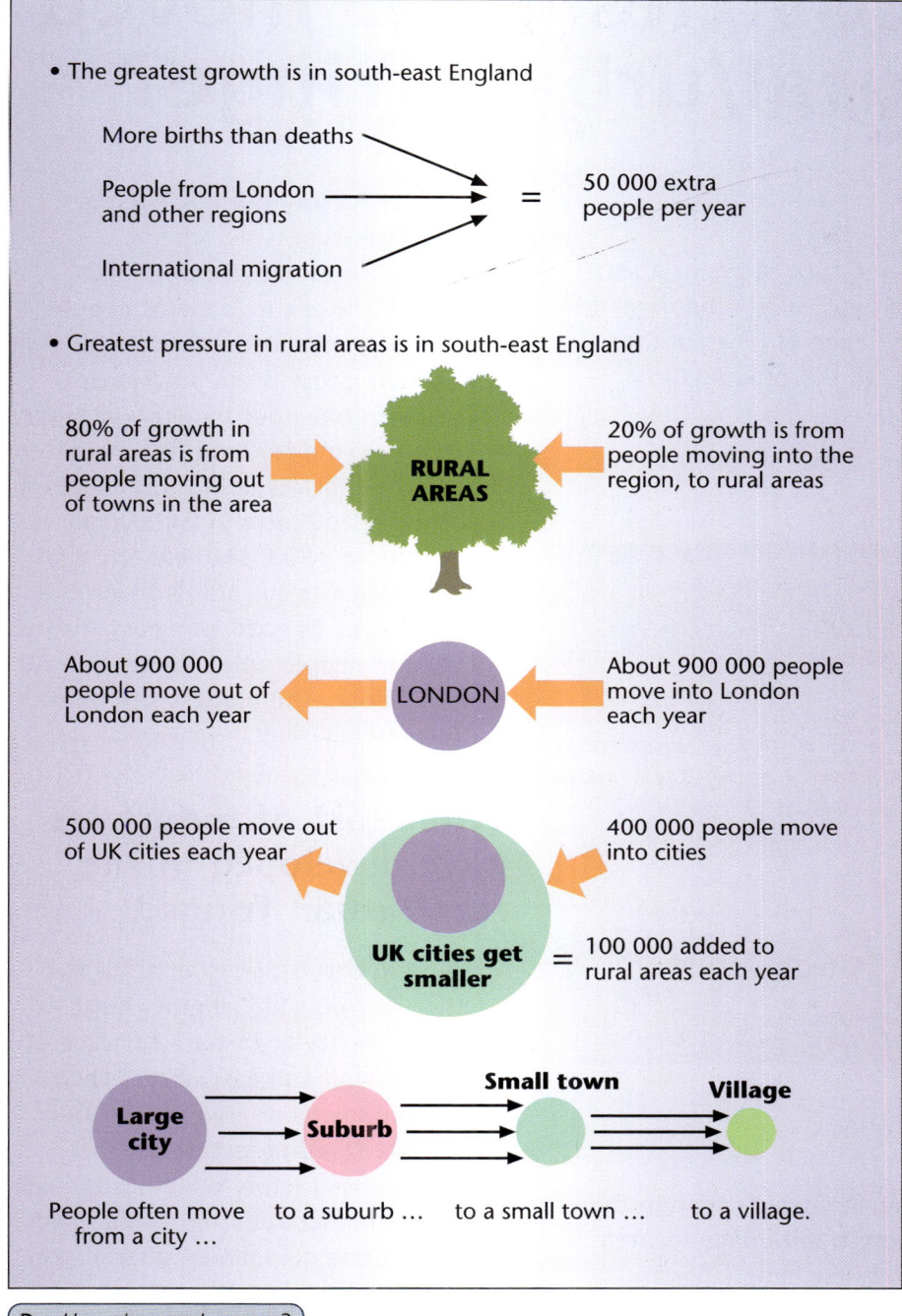

Why is the population increasing?
- People move here from other countries. In 1999 net migration into the UK was 185 000.
- People are living longer. Lower male death rates have increased the number of births over deaths.
- The rate of natural increase (more births than deaths) has risen.

Where is the greatest growth?
The greatest growth is in south-east England, which has an increase of more than 50 000 people a year (**D**), and this area has the biggest problems.

Where do people move to?
People are constantly moving house — about 5 million a year. The greatest flow of people from cities is from the suburbs to the countryside (see **D**). Most move within the local area, but about 15 per cent move to other regions.

For example, in the 1990s about 40 000 people left the conurbations in the Midlands and the North. Most of these people simply moved to the edges of the cities, and only a few (about 4000) migrated to the south.

Who are the people who move out?
Most of the people who move to rural areas are families, or wealthy or retired people, all looking for attractive houses and locations.

D – How do people move?

- The greatest growth is in south-east England
  - More births than deaths
  - People from London and other regions
  - International migration
  = 50 000 extra people per year

- Greatest pressure in rural areas is in south-east England

  - 80% of growth in rural areas is from people moving out of towns in the area → **RURAL AREAS** ← 20% of growth is from people moving into the region, to rural areas

  - About 900 000 people move out of London each year ← **LONDON** ← About 900 000 people move into London each year

  - 500 000 people move out of UK cities each year ← **UK cities get smaller** ← 400 000 people move into cities
  = 100 000 added to rural areas each year

  - Large city → Suburb → Small town → Village
  - People often move from a city … to a suburb … to a small town … to a village.

Questions

1 How did housing change:
- in the 1920s–1930s
- after 1945
- in the 1960s–1970s
- in the 1970s–1980s?
- How has it changed since 1990?

2 Why are more houses needed in the UK?

3 What are the biggest changes taking place in where people live? Devise your own diagram. Use **D**.

4 Suggest five reasons why people move from a city to a town to a rural area. Draw a labelled diagram to explain this movement.

5 Has the population changed in your area? Are people moving away, or moving into your area? Why? Is housing changing?

Managing Change in the Human Environment

4.3 What activities have moved to the rural/urban fringe?

How has retailing changed?

Out-of-town shopping sites — perhaps just one superstore, or a **retail park** with several stores — are now common near every urban area (A). All sorts of retail sites have sprung up on the edge of cities in the rural/urban fringe, and goods vary from food to DIY products to designer clothes.

Why are they there? Why did these stores move out of the city centres in the 1980s and 1990s?

A - *An edge-of-town retail park*

They all needed:
- cheap land — land at the urban edge is much cheaper than in the city centre where many of these shops were traditionally located
- a big site in order to build an extensive low-rise shop
- easy access for a large number of people arriving by car, and for frequent deliveries — 72 per cent of people have access to a car and use them to go shopping at any time of day or night
- big parking areas
- access to a large population of people who will come and buy the goods.

Because access and parking are so important, stores have tended to gather together on retail parks in order to share car parking and other services.

The higher the value of the product, or the more scarce the product, the further people will travel to buy it. Stores selling designer clothes, or factory outlets, cluster around peak access points like motorway junctions. The M25, for example, provides millions of people with easy access to the retail sites that have grown around the junctions. Retail parks have got bigger and bigger and the demand for land has increased. One of the first really big retail sites was the MetroCentre in Gateshead. It was begun in 1983, and was the first out-of-town site for many major chain stores. Access by road was easy for the 1.3 million people who lived within 30 minutes' drive. The biggest site in 2000 is Bluewater in Kent.

What sort of industries have developed in the rural/urban fringe?

The rural/urban fringe is an attractive location for industry, whether large or small, secondary or tertiary, because of the cheap land and easy access there. Even small towns of fewer than 5000 people have **trading estates** at the edge. Low-rise factory buildings provide cheap accommodation for small-scale manufacturing companies, distribution depots, etc. These trading estates are often planned and built by the local authority to attract industry and increase local employment. Some trading estates are extensive and include leisure facilities like cinemas, hotels and drive-through fast food outlets.

Science parks have developed in attractive rural fringe locations, near centres of skill and expertise, like a

4 Pressure at the rural/urban fringe

university. Most science parks have a low density of building, with 70 per cent or more of the land landscaped to blend into the rural environment. Cambridge Science Park was one of the first to be established, by Trinity College in 1970. It is landscaped with low-rise, low-density buildings on the edge of rural land but with easy access to the M11 and the M25. Chilworth Science Park is on the edge of Southampton, near the University, close to an area of high-value housing and the M27 and M3, and in the rural/urban fringe.

High-tech industries are said to be **footloose** because they do not have the traditional requirements of old industries. Small high-tech companies often choose semi-rural locations because the quality of life there is better than in the city. Many gather together in particular locations, like Silicon Valley in Central Scotland, or along the M4 and M11 out of London. Although the major attraction is the expertise of the local workforce, they are also in pleasant semi-rural locations. Often, the result is the extension of the rural/urban fringe.

B – Oxford Science Park

How have leisure activities grown in the rural/urban fringe?

Leisure and recreation activities are now very important to all age groups, because more people than ever before have cars, money, and the time to enjoy leisure activities (C). Some recreation facilities like leisure centres are still in cities but many are now on the edge of urban areas where there is easy access and cheap land. For some people, shopping is the most important leisure activity, but others just want the peace and quiet of open countryside where they can sit and relax.

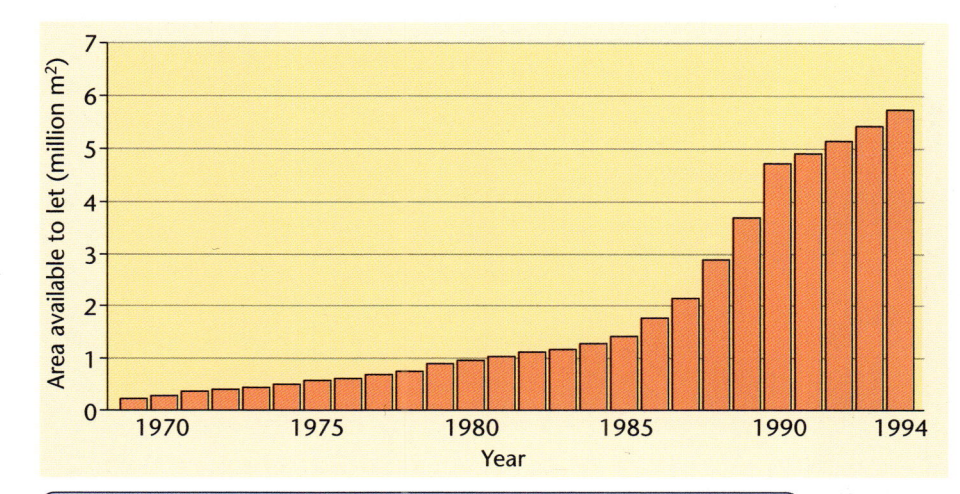

C – The increase in out-of-town retail floor space in the UK, 1969–94

Questions

1. a) Why has the pattern of retailing changed since the 1980s? Describe the changes in retail floor space shown in C.

2. a) Name your nearest retail park. How often do you go there?
   b) Make a list of the stores there. Are they national chain stores or local shops? You could try to find out how big they are (floorspace).

3. What problems have been created in the rural/urban fringe by out-of-town retailing? Use text and C.

4. Name five leisure and recreation facilities that you might see in the rural/urban fringe. What leisure facilities are there in your nearest rural/urban fringe area? Who uses them?

5. Suggest some reasons why industry may move to the urban/rural fringe from an inner city area.

Managing Change in the Human Environment

4.4 What are the consequences of pressure at the rural/urban fringe?

Developments at the rural/urban fringe trigger change in the neighbouring rural areas and in the centre of the urban area. There are positive and negative changes in both — some immediate like the building of hundreds of new houses, some gradual like the slow change in the character of a village. People have opinions about whether these changes are good or bad and what should happen in the future but opinions vary. How they vary will depend on all sorts of things, like where the people live, how long they have lived there, their age, how much money they have, and whether they are involved in the changes as residents, as visitors, or as planners trying to manage events.

Housing and the rural/urban fringe

Housing has probably had the biggest impact on the rural/urban fringe. Housing estates have been built around every urban area but they vary in character and style. The most popular housing for developers to build is easy-to-sell, high-value housing. Some estates are made up only of expensive, detached houses, a few per hectare, perhaps inside a secure wall with an entrance gate. Others are high-density compact housing with 30 or more houses to the hectare. Housing styles and patterns change too, but planners and builders do want estates to look attractive. In the 1960s and 1970s some unattractive estates were built at what was then the rural/urban fringe, with little character and all in much

The Village collection

Welcome to Nerrols Court
• CHEDDON FITZPAINE, TAUNTON •

Nerrols Court is an attractive village-style development in the parish of Cheddon Fitzpaine, on the outskirts of Taunton.

The location of Nerrols Court could hardly be more convenient, particularly with regards to shopping. The important county town of Taunton boasts familiar High Street names, complemented by many traditional stores and a thriving market. The Riverside Centre, a major out-of-town shopping complex close to junction 25 of the M5, has everything for a full day out – supermarkets, electrical and white goods retailers, theme pubs, fast-food outlets and recreational facilities such as ten-pin bowling and cinema.

The residents of Nerrols Court will also be very well connected. The development gives quick and easy access to the A358, A38 and M5, which is only a short distance away. And Taunton is on the London–Penzance mainline rail route enjoying good links with the North, Midlands, London, South Wales and rest of the South-West.

For many home-buyers, all these benefits will be reasons enough to make the move to Nerrols Court and a brand-new Beazer home. But for those who might need a little more persuasion, an improved quality of life could well be the deciding factor.

After all, within striking distance is some of Britain's most beautiful coast and countryside – the Quantock Hills, Exmoor National Park, and the pretty resorts, towns and villages of West Somerset. What more could you possibly ask for?

A – A new housing development on the rural/urban fringe

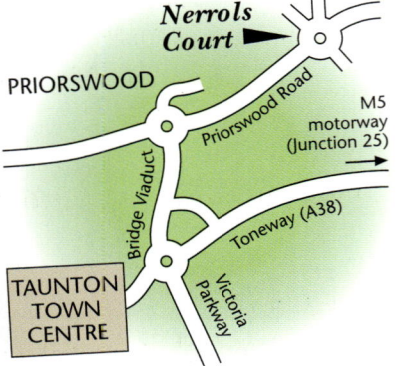

B – Development at Cheddon Fitzpaine, near Taunton

4 Pressure at the rural/urban fringe

What are the advantages for the people who move into these new houses?	What are the disadvantages for the people who move into rural/urban fringe housing estates?
• Attractive houses and gardens. • Garages (parking a car in some big cities like London is nearly impossible, or very expensive). • Peace and quiet and cleaner air compared with an inner city area. • Less crime and a feeling of greater security than in the city. • A good environment in which to bring up children. • Easy access to the countryside. • Easy access to major roads and transport routes. • Easy access to other out-of-town developments, like retail parks (see A and B).	• You need a car – rural buses tend to be expensive and infrequent. • Often there are few other facilities like doctors and schools, so you have to drive into the nearest town or large village. • Employment may be very limited in the local area, so people must travel every day. • Play areas for children may be very limited so sometimes children play in the road (some new high-density housing areas with brick roads mixed with pedestrian walks are a particular problem). • There is little for young people to do in many new housing estates in semi-rural locations, other than to drive to a pub, to an out-of-town cinema or back into the city.

the same style. Some of these estates have become the focus for the types of inner city problem that people were trying to avoid when they moved to them from the inner city.

The size of housing developments varies, from infilling the odd patch of land with three or four houses, to some of the biggest estates in Europe, like the Owlsmoor area in Camberley in Surrey, which was built in the 1970s and 1980s.

Suburbanization of villages

Villages near an urban area are likely to change. Villages used to be the focus of rural life and with close-knit communities, but are there many really rural settlements left today? Perhaps only 3–4 per cent of village people actually work in the countryside, and some of these people are plumbers, builders, etc. who work in both urban and rural places. Some villages have become tourist centres with gift shops or tea gardens. Sometimes houses in the more rural areas are bought as second homes by wealthy people from the cities. Some villages have very big retired populations and the younger people have had to move away to find work. The influx of hundreds, or even thousands, of newcomers, triggers more change. Does this matter?

How have villages changed to become like the suburbs to a city?

- There are lots more houses, in estates.
- In some villages there is infilling, with single houses built on odd patches of land between other houses, or in large gardens.
- Trees and green land have been replaced by buildings.
- The village shop is used just for convenience goods like milk, while the big weekly shop is done in nearby supermarkets.
- Other services, like community groups, are lost.
- The really small village schools close and children have to travel to larger schools in neighbouring villages or towns.
- People in the new houses all run cars, and these can become a hazard.

Questions

1. What sort of housing development has taken place in the rural/urban fringe? Give an example.
2. Explain at least five advantages and give disadvantages of living in the rural/urban fringe (use an example).
3. How may a village change if more housing is built there and it is suburbanized (use an example)?
4. Using B and an atlas, draw an annotated sketch map to show Taunton and Cheddon Fitzpaine and the features that would make this an attractive place to live.

4.5 What do people think about developments in the rural/urban fringe?

What do people think about industry?

People have very mixed views. Often, those who need work want industry in semi-rural areas, but people who have retired to these places do not want change. It also depends on the type of industry. For example, the application to gather together commercial plastics operations on one greenfield site on the urban fringe outside Newport (Isle of Wight) met with great local opposition, and the application was refused. In another case in the 1990s, a kitchen/bathroom company employing 5000 people in several different sites in Yorkshire wanted to bring all the scattered operations onto one site. The trading estate on the edge of Bradford was not big enough, but extensive negotiation took place with the planning authority and the company was allowed to expand into a greenfield area because the benefits were thought to be greater than the disadvantages.

There are *advantages* for local people and for the industries:

- Trading estates tend to be planned and constructed in an environmentally friendly way, with low-rise buildings in 'quiet' colours.
- Many of the rural/urban fringe industries are small-scale high-tech or service industries, so do not produce much pollution.
- Industries provide employment for rural areas where unemployment is often high.
- Several activities may gather together on one site, so the impact can be minimized.

There are also some *disadvantages*:

- Large areas of countryside may be lost.
- Buildings may be out of character with existing rural buildings.
- Traffic is likely to increase, both cars used by the workforce and customers, and lorries.
- There may be noise, and some pollution (of air, land or water).

How have retail parks affected the rural/urban fringe?

Food retailers and non-food retail sites at the rural/urban fringe can vary enormously in size and scale. The bigger the site the bigger the impact, because more stores mean more of everything, from daily deliveries to the number of shoppers. Large sites attract other services, like fast-food outlets, pubs or a multiplex cinema, so more land is engulfed by buildings, car parks and roads. Many people travel to work there too. Service industries, like retailing, employ large numbers of people, most of whom live in the wider urban area and so will have to travel to the site, probably by car. Many more people will work in other, support services like maintenance, security, etc.

Questions

1. Figure A includes extracts from the Bluewater website. Suggest five positive reasons to go there. What are the advantages of the site? How has it been landscaped? Why?

2. Read B. What are the problems of older retail sites like the MetroCentre?

3. Describe any industrial or retail developments taking place at the urban edge in your area. Try to suggest reasons for these developments. What are the benefits and disadvantages of these developments?

4 Pressure at the rural/urban fringe

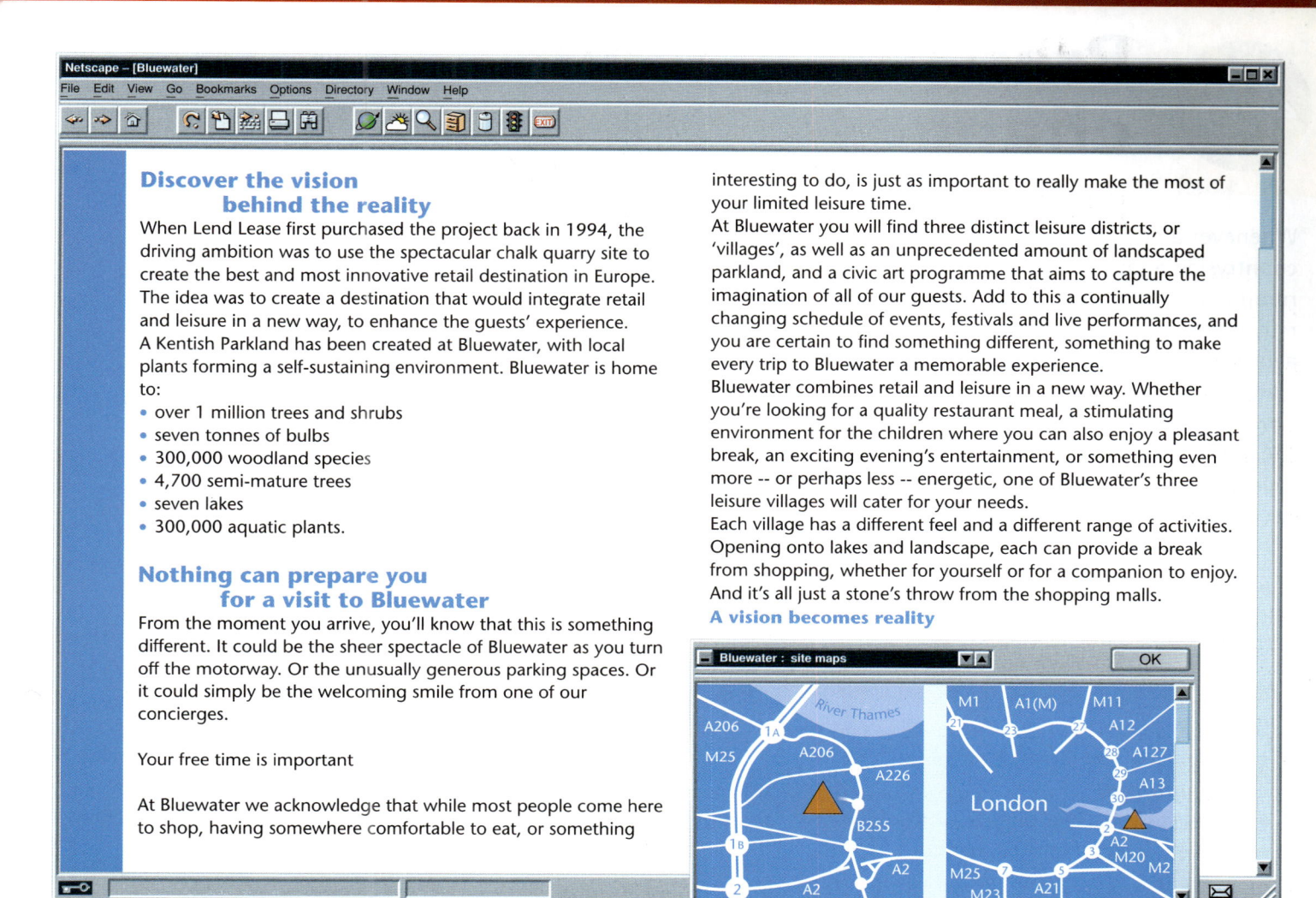

Discover the vision behind the reality

When Lend Lease first purchased the project back in 1994, the driving ambition was to use the spectacular chalk quarry site to create the best and most innovative retail destination in Europe. The idea was to create a destination that would integrate retail and leisure in a new way, to enhance the guests' experience.
A Kentish Parkland has been created at Bluewater, with local plants forming a self-sustaining environment. Bluewater is home to:
- over 1 million trees and shrubs
- seven tonnes of bulbs
- 300,000 woodland species
- 4,700 semi-mature trees
- seven lakes
- 300,000 aquatic plants.

Nothing can prepare you for a visit to Bluewater

From the moment you arrive, you'll know that this is something different. It could be the sheer spectacle of Bluewater as you turn off the motorway. Or the unusually generous parking spaces. Or it could simply be the welcoming smile from one of our concierges.

Your free time is important

At Bluewater we acknowledge that while most people come here to shop, having somewhere comfortable to eat, or something interesting to do, is just as important to really make the most of your limited leisure time.
At Bluewater you will find three distinct leisure districts, or 'villages', as well as an unprecedented amount of landscaped parkland, and a civic art programme that aims to capture the imagination of all of our guests. Add to this a continually changing schedule of events, festivals and live performances, and you are certain to find something different, something to make every trip to Bluewater a memorable experience.
Bluewater combines retail and leisure in a new way. Whether you're looking for a quality restaurant meal, a stimulating environment for the children where you can also enjoy a pleasant break, an exciting evening's entertainment, or something even more -- or perhaps less -- energetic, one of Bluewater's three leisure villages will cater for your needs.
Each village has a different feel and a different range of activities. Opening onto lakes and landscape, each can provide a break from shopping, whether for yourself or for a companion to enjoy. And it's all just a stone's throw from the shopping malls.

A vision becomes reality

A – Bluewater – the positive view

Road hell spoils dream site for family shopping

TODAY more than 100,000 people will crowd into the MetroCentre, Britain's largest out-of-town shopping centre on the edge of Gateshead, easily filling all the 12,000 parking spaces.
 Only a fifth of them – barely 20,000 – will have arrived by bus. By tonight the dual carriageway A1 alongside the half-mile long complex will be gridlocked as thousands attempt to leave – at the same time.
 'It can be hell,' said volunteers office worker Gary, as he headed for the car with his two children, aged eight and four, after an afternoon's shopping yesterday.
 'Once we got caught in a queue for almost one hour. It was very dangerous with traffic trying to get on to the main road. So now we come when it's quiet. OK, at the right time this place is very convenient. But it's been sad to see so many smaller shops in nearby town centres go to the wall as this centre has flourished.'
 Soon after the centre opened, the Department of Transport was forced to add another lane on part of the A1 to ease MetroCentre congestion. Now there is talk of more road 'improvements' to help traffic flow as the complex continues to grow in a piecemeal fashion.

B – From the Guardian, 15 February 1997

C – Bluewater shopping centre

75

Managing Change in the Human Environment

4.6 Pressure groups – urban changes

Whenever a city sprawls into the countryside and there are changes at the rural/urban fringe, somebody will object. It may be someone living locally, or miles away. People may object to the loss of countryside, the size or quantity of the new buildings, what they are used for, or the new roads. People may join together as a group to make their views known, becoming a **pressure group**. Sometimes several pressure groups may work together.

There are two different sorts of pressure group:

1 *Proactive groups* exist all the time and keep a watch on what is happening. For example:

- Friends of the Earth, a national organization
- local societies like the Isle of Wight Society which monitors changes in both rural and urban areas on the island
- small local clubs like a football club which will be aware of plans to put houses on recreation grounds, or sell off school playing fields, etc.

Conference rejects new homes plan

Government plans for 43 000 homes a year to be built in the south east have been opposed by a regional planning conference. A 39 030 vote at the South East Region Planning Conference (SERPLAN) on Monday – attended by council representatives covering the area from Essex to the Isle of Wight – rejected the proposals. Speaking after the meeting, Mr McEwan (Ongar county councillor) said house building on the scale proposed by the government would inevitably mean the loss of large areas of Essex countryside, while at the same time houses in the north and Midlands were standing empty or even being demolished.

Citizen *21 June 2000*

Bishop's Stortford (Hertfordshire), population 34,000, is a market town 2 miles from Stansted airport, near the M11. It has seen an increase in housing in the last 20 years as the airport has expanded. The A120 by-pass reduced some through traffic but there is still traffic congestion.
CAUSE, Campaign Against Unsustainable Stortford Expansion, is a pressure group to prevent any further large scale housing development which could have an adverse effect on the character of the town and reduce the quality of life for its residents.
CAUSE is a coordinating group for member organisations, – local residents associations e.g. Bishop's Park Residents Association, councils, Civic Society etc.
'Only strong and active opposition will halt Stortford's headlong expansion and prevent the town's roads and amenities from becoming further overburdened.' Quote from CAUSE website.
The 1991 County Structure Plan defined green land north of the town up to the A120 by-pass as land for major new housing development, 2,728 homes, partly to accommodate employees from the expanding airport.

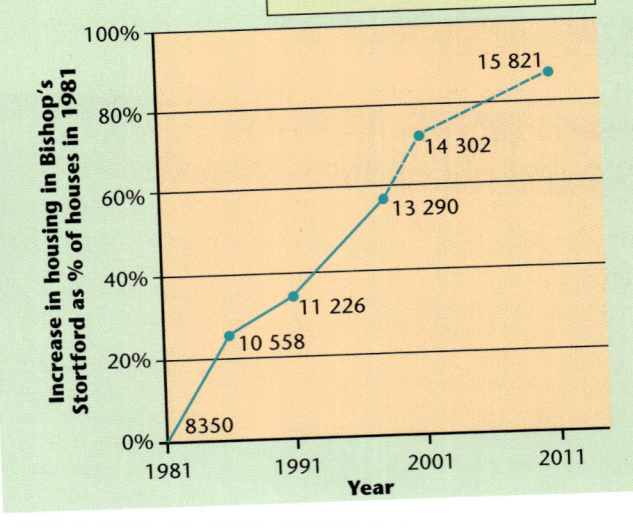

A – *One pressure group's campaign*

2 *Reactive groups* are set up when something happens that is a threat to the countryside, to the rural/urban fringe, or to the quality of life of residents. For example:
- a residents' association set up in opposition to house-building plans that will affect them
- road-building campaigners who object to the destruction of countryside and the construction of more roads.

A campaign by any one of these groups may go on for years. The campaign to stop a by-pass being built around Newbury in Berkshire lasted for nearly 20 years!

Pressure groups can persuade the government or a local authority to change its actions, but not everyone will agree with the views of a particular group. House-building generates most arguments. There are always two sides to any dispute: on one side are those who want to build the houses and who want to live there, and on the other are those who do not want any more houses. In the 1980s, such a person was labelled a **NIMBY** (from **N**ot **I**n **M**y **B**ack **Y**ard).

Urban change

Does development at the rural/urban fringe have an effect on the neighbouring urban area?

The simple answer to this question is, yes. Any change in where people live and how they live will have an effect on both old and new urban areas. Most people who move to the edge of a city come from a house closer to the city centre. They leave behind houses that other people may or may not want, and some inner city areas now have many empty houses. These areas may decline and become vandalized, with rising crime rates and many social problems.

Who is affected by the changes?

The people in inner city areas are often the elderly, the unemployed and young people who do not have the money to make the choice to move. Instead of a balanced population with people of all ages living in one community, there may be families and working people at the urban edges, and the old and the poor in the inner city. People who are working spend more money in local shops, etc. than the old and the unemployed, so more money goes into the newer housing areas than into the poorer communities.

Have some city centres changed?

The out-of-town shopping developments of the 1980s and 1990s have also affected inner city areas. In the 1960s and 1970s people bought their food in local shops, and other goods in the city centre. Shops in the central area need a large number of shoppers to provide enough trade if they are to survive. People choose where they will shop, and when they drive to the new retail parks on the urban fringe, the traditional areas decline. So shops close in the centre, fewer people visit the area and some inner city or neighbourhood shopping areas become places with boarded-up shops, litter, vandalism and muggings.

Today, 72 per cent of households have access to a car, but this still leaves 28 per cent without regular use of a car, and these people cannot travel to the newer retail sites. What will they do when the inner city shops close?

Questions

1 a) What is the difference between a proactive and a reactive pressure group?
  b) Design a leaflet to tell people why a pressure group object to a new housing estate or industry in your local urban fringe area.
2 a) Read the text in A. Would *you* allow the house-building to go ahead in Bishop's Stortford? Give five reasons for your answer.
  b) Name a town or city where you know that the urban edges are growing and the inner area is declining. What do you think will happen to the central area eventually?

Managing Change in the Human Environment

4.7 How can change at the rural/urban fringe be managed?

Have strategies to manage change been effective?

Planners, with local authorities and interested people, have been trying to manage change at the urban fringe since housing first began to spread rapidly into the countryside. Several alternative strategies have been tried over the years. These include:

- designating major areas of countryside as **green belt** (see pages 80–81)
- building whole **new towns**
- protecting some **environmentally sensitive areas** (see page 84)
- re-using inner city **brownfield sites**
- redeveloping **city centre**s (see page 85)
- encouraging development in some areas and banning it in others.

What influences how people manage rural and urban areas?

Policies change over the years as people, ideas and technology change. Some strategies for managing rural/urban areas are found to be effective while others cause conflict. What were people trying to achieve in the past? What are they trying to achieve now, and what are the influences on future planning?

When housing development and new town planning began after 1945, other things were important and priorities were different. Then, it was necessary to provide decent houses as quickly as possible. Now, the need is for different types of houses, both low-cost and high-cost, built by private developers. Industry and jobs have changed and people want to live in different places.

How government tries to control development

The government tries to manage change through **PPGs** – planning policy guidelines – and legislation. Councils use these PPGs to plan house-building and development for the future. The biggest problem is going to be how to fit in the 4 million more houses that the government thinks will be needed by 2016. Half of these could be on rural land. All policies have tried to avoid conflict and to balance the needs of individuals, but not all have been successful.

Super-villages and country towns

In the 1980s the demand for houses was rising and developers put forward several plans for small towns and villages, some within green belts but all with good transport links to a neighbouring urban area. One example in 1983 was the Tillingham Hall development, a small new town within 6km of the M25 between Basildon (8km away, itself an earlier new town), Brentwood and Upminster. The urban edge of London was only 7km away, so it was an ideal location. Many more proposals followed to build new, small settlements rather than to add more houses to existing villages, or make urban fringe housing estates bigger. So new **super-villages** grew in green belts around the rural/urban fringe.

In the late 1990s, Cambridge struggled with the problems of housing an influx of people who were attracted to the expanding high-tech industry there (the area is known as Silicon Fen because of the number of bio-tech, computer software and other science-related industries). The people working in these industries want a good quality of life, and houses. Cambridge Science Park continued to grow, but experts warned that the city was fast sinking under the pressure of the people flooding in. One development that is helping to relieve the city's housing problems is Cambourne, a new village 11km (7 miles) west of Cambridge (**A**).

4 Pressure at the rural/urban fringe

The site will contain three villages, Upper, Lower and Great Cambourne, based around village greens. Eventually, the development will provide 3300 homes and include a high street, two new schools, a business park, golf course, lakes and nature reserves.

The builders are unashamedly attempting to create a rural idyll. According to their brochure, 'small cottage-style homes will sit happily between pretty terraces and emanate outwards from the village centre into grander detached residences in the "unplanned" way of natural evolution.'

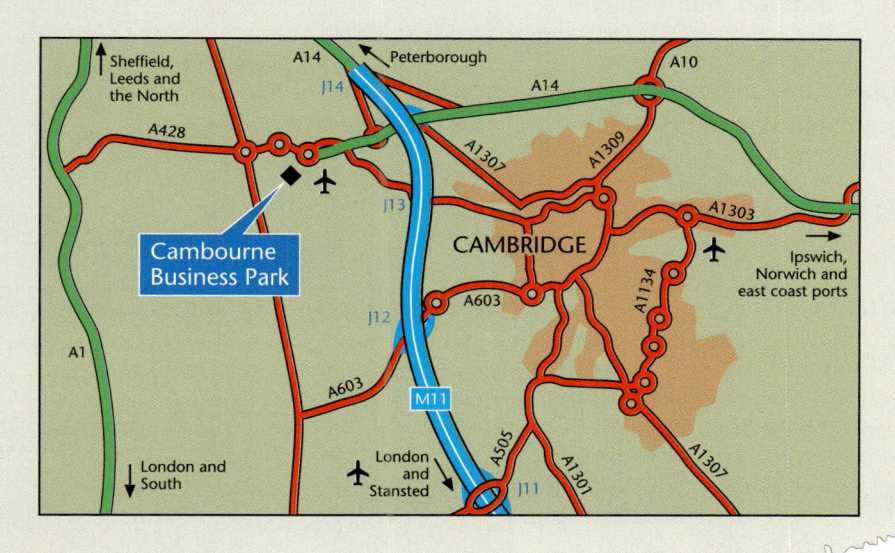

Cambourne could end up housing 8000 people, but even that may only be a drop in the ocean. Government forecasters say the area needs 100 000 –105 000 extra homes by 2015. And the population is expected to increase by 1% a year over the next 20 years. Regional planners have raised the possibility of another development of 10 000–20 000 homes about five miles to the north of Cambridge. Insiders believe Cambourne is a modest development compared with what's on the horizon.

The *Guardian*, 16 October 1999

A – *Cambourne, a new super-village*

Questions

1 a) What strategies have been used to try to manage change in the rural/urban fringe?
b) Why are planning policy guidelines necessary? Who proposes them, and who carries them out?
c) How many new homes will be needed in the UK by 2016?
d) Why and in what sort of location have 'super-villages' grown?

2 Do you think there are more advantages or disadvantages of new housing in a super-village?

3 Why is Cambourne being built? What will it be like? Draw an annotated sketch map to show the advantages of the location.

4.8 Green belts and new towns

Green belts

'*Green belt*' was a term created to describe a zone of countryside around a city within which building was tightly controlled. The first Green Belt Act was passed in 1938 when it was clear that countryside was being rapidly lost to housing. The main aims were:

- to check the spread of further urban development and stop the expansion of the rural/urban fringe
- to prevent towns merging
- to preserve the special character of towns.

Green belts also served to protect farmland.

By the mid-1980s another aim was to assist in urban regeneration. Some other developments besides farming have been allowed in greenfield sites, including recreation, mineral extraction, and housing (**B**).

The first green belt was a ring 25km wide around London, which included many towns (**C**). These towns were only allowed to develop by infilling between existing buildings, with no urban fringe growth.

The London green belt doubled in the 1980s, and green belts now cover approximately 11 per cent of Britain.

So are green belts a success or a failure?

Rural areas have been protected from urban sprawl, but there are problems:

- Development has jumped the green belt, not stopped.

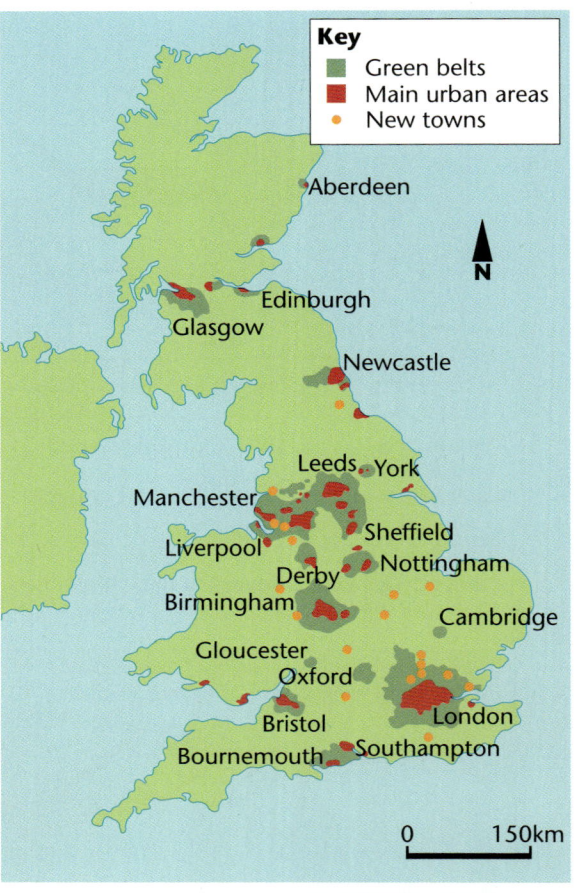

A – Green belts and new towns in the UK, 1995

B – Some uses of green belt land

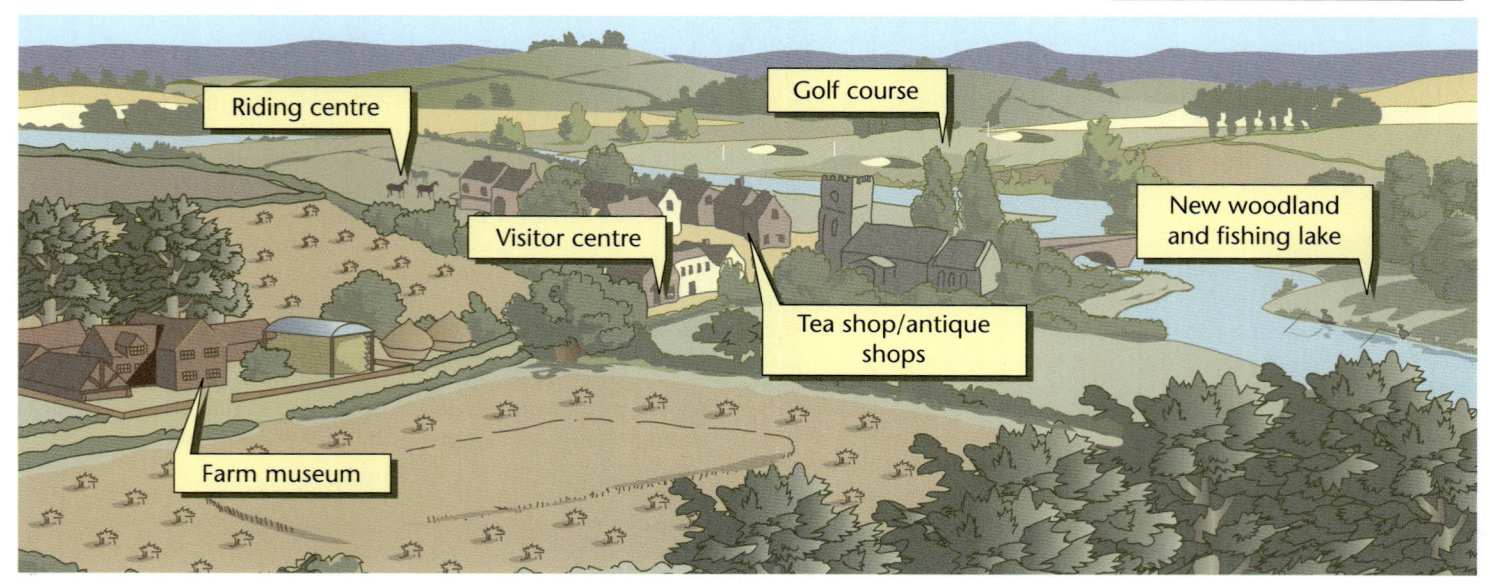

Labels: Riding centre; Visitor centre; Golf course; New woodland and fishing lake; Tea shop/antique shops; Farm museum

4 Pressure at the rural/urban fringe

- There is increased commuting as people travel long distances to work through the green belt.
- Planning regulations have been relaxed for things like the M25.
- House prices in London and elsewhere have been forced up because of the demand for houses.
- Planned new settlements are being built in the green belt because of the shortage of housing, particularly in the South East.
- Any building in the green belt encourages more. For example, the M25 encourages the demand for motorway service stations, distribution warehouses, hotel sites, shopping and leisure schemes.
- Redundant farm buildings can be converted to other uses like industry, which in turn encourages more building.

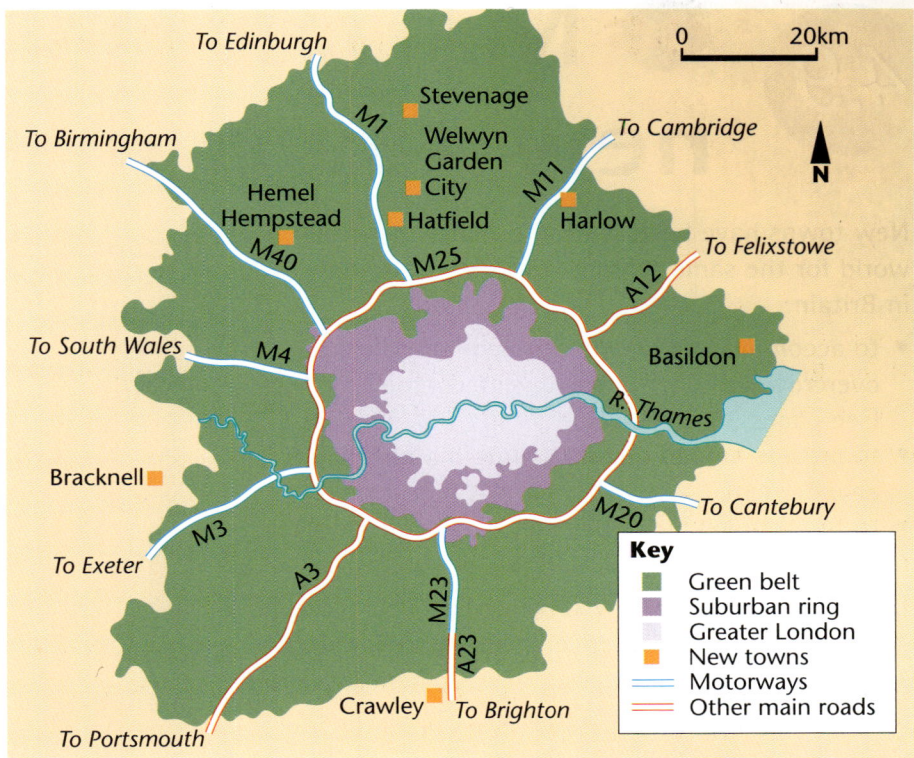

C – London's green belt and new towns

New towns

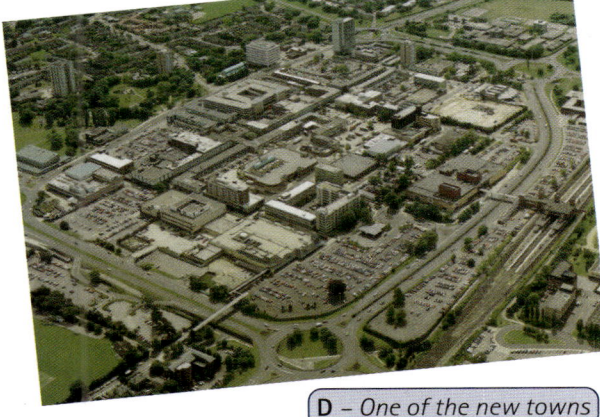

At the end of the Second World War, people in London were looking for a new way of life, so the Greater London Plan was drawn up to build eight new towns, each separated from London by a green belt and each with a population of 25 000–80 000. The New Town Act 1946 allowed the government to compulsorily purchase land for these new towns. It also allowed the expansion of 28 other settlements to take another 535 000 people out of London. It was hoped that they would provide a better quality of life and prevent existing cities spreading.

There are now 33 new towns in Britain successfully providing new homes for 1.3 million people. The first wave of new towns were close to London and when the new jobs ran out, people commuted back to London, so increasing traffic congestion. The second wave of new towns were built further out and have become areas of urban growth — but not without problems.

D – One of the new towns

Questions

1. a) When and why were green belts created?
   b) What can the land be used for?
   c) Look at B. How is this land used? Do you think this is appropriate, or not?
   d) Are green belts a success or a failure? Use your answer to (c) to help you.

2. a) Why were new towns built around London?
   b) Use C to make a list of the new towns around London. Find out more about them, e.g. Stevenage at: www.stevenage.gov.uk, Bracknell at: www.bracknellforest.gov.uk, or others at: www.englishpartnerships.co.uk.
   c) How many people live in new towns now?
   d) What were the advantages of new towns, and what are the problems now?

4.9 Marne-la-Vallée: a new town in France

New towns have been built in other parts of the world for the same reasons that they have been built in Britain:

- to accommodate people from conurbations or overcrowded urban areas in self-contained towns (see pages 38–39 Egypt).
- to provide a good quality of life in a pleasant environment
- to attract new industries and employment to an area.

Marne-la-Vallée is a new town of 250 000 people, 20km east of Paris in France. Planning began in the 1960s, as part of a pattern of development around Paris aimed at managing the rapid growth of the city. Green land was left in blocks between new towns, rather than in a circle around the city as it is around London.

Marne-la-Vallée is dependent on a rapid, efficient transport system that links with Paris and other parts of the country. The town is built along the RER

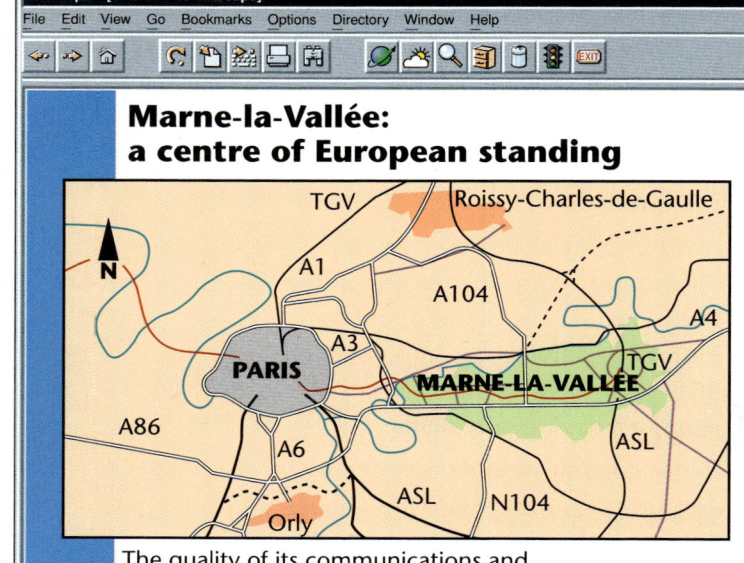

Marne-la-Vallée: a centre of European standing

The quality of its communications and telecommunications infrastructure, its strategic location within the Ile de France, within France as a whole and within Europe, the richness of its natural and urban spaces and its economic dynamism, have all earned Marne-la-Vallée a reputation as a centre of European standing. The growing number of foreign companies choosing one of Marne-la-Vallée's business parks as their base in France or as their regional base for the Ile de France seems to prove that this reputation is fully deserved.
EPAMarne/EPAFrance (public development authority of Marne-la-Vallée)
http://www.marne-la-vallee.com

A – Marne-la-Vallée: a European centre

B – Housing in Bailly, Marne-la-Vallée

4 Pressure at the rural/urban fringe

C – Land use in Marne-la-Vallée

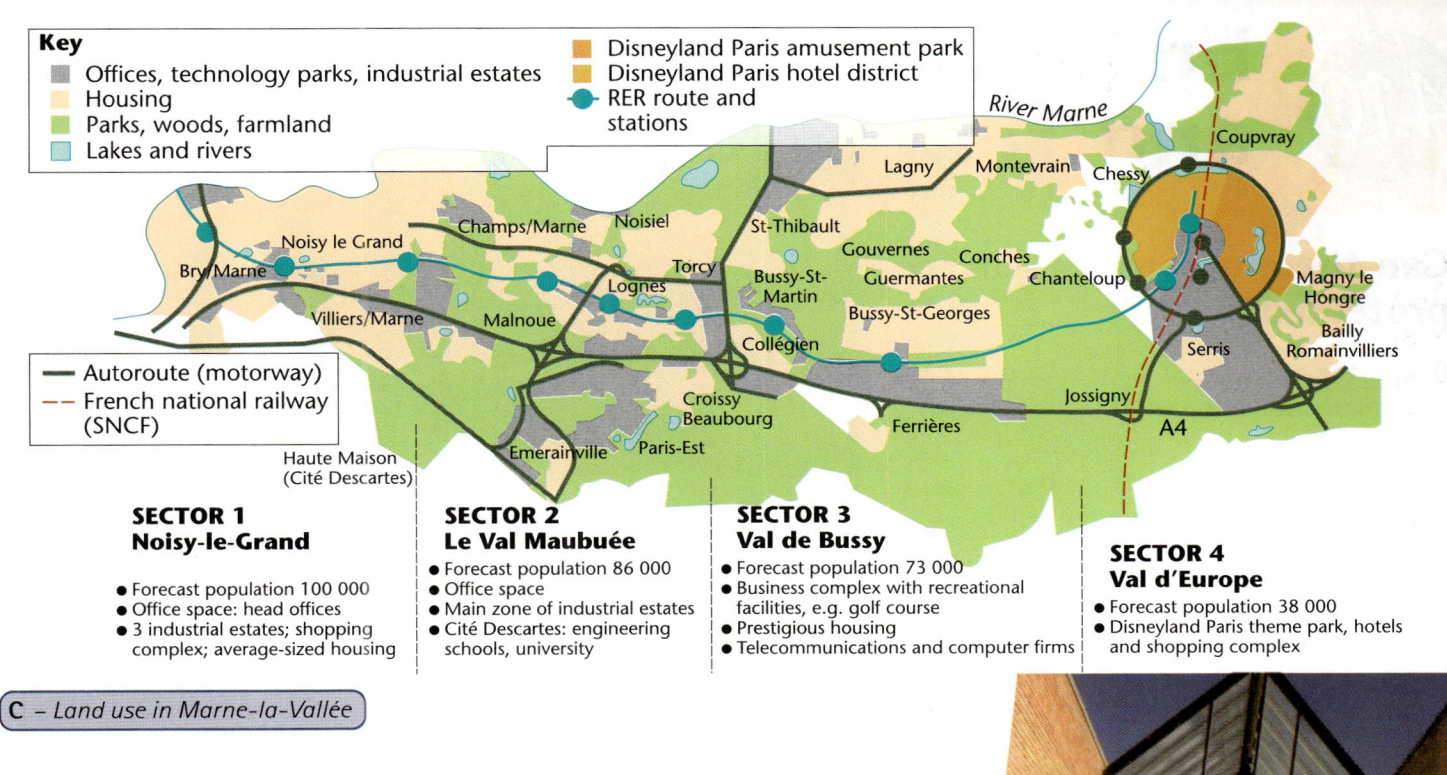

Key
- Offices, technology parks, industrial estates
- Housing
- Parks, woods, farmland
- Lakes and rivers
- Disneyland Paris amusement park
- Disneyland Paris hotel district
- RER route and stations
- Autoroute (motorway)
- French national railway (SNCF)

SECTOR 1 – Noisy-le-Grand
- Forecast population 100 000
- Office space: head offices
- 3 industrial estates; shopping complex; average-sized housing

SECTOR 2 – Le Val Maubuée
- Forecast population 86 000
- Office space
- Main zone of industrial estates
- Cité Descartes: engineering schools, university

SECTOR 3 – Val de Bussy
- Forecast population 73 000
- Business complex with recreational facilities, e.g. golf course
- Prestigious housing
- Telecommunications and computer firms

SECTOR 4 – Val d'Europe
- Forecast population 38 000
- Disneyland Paris theme park, hotels and shopping complex

(Regional Express Line), and has several stations. By road, it is only 15 minutes' drive from the centre of Paris along the A4 motorway. The town site is extensive and has been developed in four sectors, each with residential areas, office blocks and industrial estates, shops and leisure facilities, and open green spaces. Many of the industries are technology-based transnational companies. The Cité Descartes is Marne-la-Vallée's leading science park, begun in the 1980s and now covering 150 hectares. There are 2000 companies here, mostly working in ICT, several colleges, and 12 000 students. There are 60 000 jobs in the business zones, technology and science parks.

The population has grown rapidly from 100 000 in 1975, and many of the people who have moved into the area are young. Thirty-five per cent are aged 20–40. Only 9 per cent are over 60 years old, and the town continues to grow by 4000 people every year. Housing is a very important factor, and the new homes are attractive with easy access to extensive open spaces, including 4000 hectares of woodland and 35 lakes. At the eastern end is Val d'Europe, the huge Disneyland Paris theme park. Millions of people from all over Europe visit the park each year, travelling by means of the fast transport links.

Marne-la-Vallée has spread across a huge area along the River Marne, but it is not all high-density building. The extensive open areas are green, although they are not true countryside. Population in this development is planned to grow to over 300 000. What will be the impact on the surrounding rural area then?

D – Lycée Technique in Noisiel

Questions

1. Use C and text. Explain why an efficient transport system is so important to Marne-la-Vallée.

2. Marne-la-Vallée describes itself as 'high class, in a fine natural setting'. Use the text and photographs to write a brief description of the town using the headings:

   Location   Environment   Buildings   Employment.

3. Think about the number of people who travel to Disneyland Paris. What might be some of the benefits and costs to the region?

4. What might be the problems in 30 years' time when the 35 per cent of people who are now 20–40 will be aged 50–70?

4.10 Environmental protection and redevelopment

Can the environment be protected?

One of the key influences on the current UK environmental policy was the global Earth Summit conference in Rio de Janeiro in 1992, which looked at balancing development with care and protection of the environment. This resulted in Agenda 21. The aim was to provide **sustainable communities** which can develop in the present without damaging the future environment. Is it possible to build all the extra houses we need, and still protect the environment?

Some areas of countryside are protected because they are special ecosystems, like estuaries or meadowlands, and they can be made into areas of Special Scientific Interest (SSSIs). Although protected, such sites in the rural/urban fringe may be damaged by development.

A – An environment at risk

How important are brownfield sites?

Brownfield land is land that has been used for industry or housing, which is no longer needed. There is a lot of brownfield land in urban areas, so if all these sites were used, would there still be a housing problem? The suggestion is that 60 per cent of new housing should be built on brownfield sites by 2016, but not all sites are suitable. Some are old industrial and waste disposal sites carrying toxic chemicals. (A)

Cleaning a contaminated brownfield site is expensive. It is estimated that £2000–£8000 would be added to the cost of a new house in Birmingham if all the houses were built on cleaned brownfield sites. Some houses have been built on contaminated sites, which has led to serious pollution problems.

Most new houses are needed in the south, but most brownfield sites are in the north of England. The best sites in the south have already been used, so any remaining ones are likely to be very expensive to clean. Perhaps only 30 per cent of all new houses will be built on brownfield sites.

The Bluewater shopping and leisure scheme was begun in 1986 (see page 75) on an 81ha chalkpit brownfield site. The development was planned to be 40m below ground level, leaving the surrounding green belt unaffected. However, the area attracted further development and there are now plans for 20 000 new houses, which will have a huge impact on the rural/urban fringe.

Could redevelopment in city centres stop the drift to the rural/urban fringe?

If declining city centres were redeveloped, would more people move back to live there, and would fewer people drive out of the city to shop? Different places have dealt with the problem in various ways. For example:

- Housing schemes in cities, like Docklands in London, have led to an increase in the number of people living in the city centres.

4 Pressure at the rural/urban fringe

- *Tunbridge Wells* was faced with a 20 per cent drop in spending in shops in the town between 1980 and 2000, so it refashioned the town centre to make it more attractive, with a focus on leisure, e.g. with pavement cafés.

- The WestQuay development in *Southampton* (B) is described as 'regional shopping in the heart of the city'. It is like an undercover retail park but in the city centre (see pages 49 and 57).

Opening late September

Welcome to WestQuay
Regional shopping in the heart of Southampton

Welcome to WestQuay

WestQuay is the premier shopping destination for the South Coast region. The centre offers an unrivalled combination of fabulous brands in a superbly designed, spacious environment right in the heart of the city. With a wide range of fashion and lifestyle retailers, including a new John Lewis, Waitrose and a major Marks & Spencer store, many of WestQuay's stores are new to the region, including Sephora, Gap, H&M Hennes, Karen Millen, Jane Norman, Eisenegger, Tower Records, Kangol and Monserrat. These are complemented by stores such as Next, Habitat, Monsoon, Accessorize and the Discovery Store.

At WestQuay we understand it's the little things that can transform a simple day trip into a great day out. Ease of access, plenty of parking, friendly staff and quality catering. We are committed to providing the perfect environment for a relaxing, enjoyable and satisfying shopping trip.

The choice of catering options in our Food Terrace is second to none. Every possible taste is catered for, from a reviving pot of afternoon tea to a superb three course lunch in a wide selection of restaurants and coffee shops, such as Cafe Giardino, Bradwells, Costa Coffee, Thyme and Aroma. Great care has been taken to create a peaceful, spacious environment with superb views of the port and bustling city below. It is the ideal place to meet friends or just watch the world go by from one of the quiet seating areas provided.

Services
Our shopmobility service is located in the podium car park on the second floor and offers members a host of benefits, including easy hire of manual wheelchairs and electric scooters when you are visiting WestQuay. A shoppers escort service can also be arranged in advance.

'Abacus' is a professional, supervised in-centre crèche available seven days a week, for children between 3 months and 8 years and their parents/guardians. The Abacus team are highly qualified and are authority checked. Stringent security ensures parents can be contacted should it be necessary. You can choose to stay and play with your child or spend your time shopping. Our specially designed facilities offer crèche family fun, and birthday party facilities, with an emphasis on learning through play as well as total entertainment.

Ease of Access
There is extensive car parking in the city, including 4,000 new spaces in two car parks at WestQuay and a new public transport interchange to drop you at the centre's Arundel Circus entrance. You can take the free CityLink shuttle bus which operates between Southampton Central Station and WestQuay, buses run every 10 minutes during shopping hours – journey time is 7 minutes. The CityLoop service runs every 30 minutes and connects Southampton central station, the Coach station and Town Quay to the main shopping areas and leisure facilities in the city centre.

B – *WestQuay, Southampton*

Questions

1. Devise a letter to the local planning department listing five reasons why a particular site, such as heathland or an estuary, should be protected from development. If possible, refer to real locations.

2. What is a brownfield site? Can the UK's housing problem be solved by building on such sites?

3. a) Why might people move back into a city centre to live?
   b) What changes could be made to persuade people to stay in the city centre, rather than move out?

4. Look at B. What changes are being made to attract people into the centre of Southampton?

5. Suggest what could be done to improve the centre of your nearest city.

Managing Change in the Human Environment

Decision-making exercise

A new town for Hampshire — Micheldever Station

Recent government studies have suggested that nearly four million new homes will be needed by 2020, and nearly two million will be built in the countryside. Across Britain, up to 2589 square kilometres of green fields and woodlands will be destroyed by 2016.

Figure A shows some of the proposed new housing developments. Figure B gives the views of the Council for the Protection of Rural England, who believe that the 800 000 empty houses in England could be used.

Questions

1. Why might a local farmer and a local builder have conflicting views about the proposed development?
2. Why should farmland be protected against further development?
3. Identify five reasons why people might want to live in semi-rural areas.
4. Describe the main characteristics of the proposed new town of Micheldever Station.

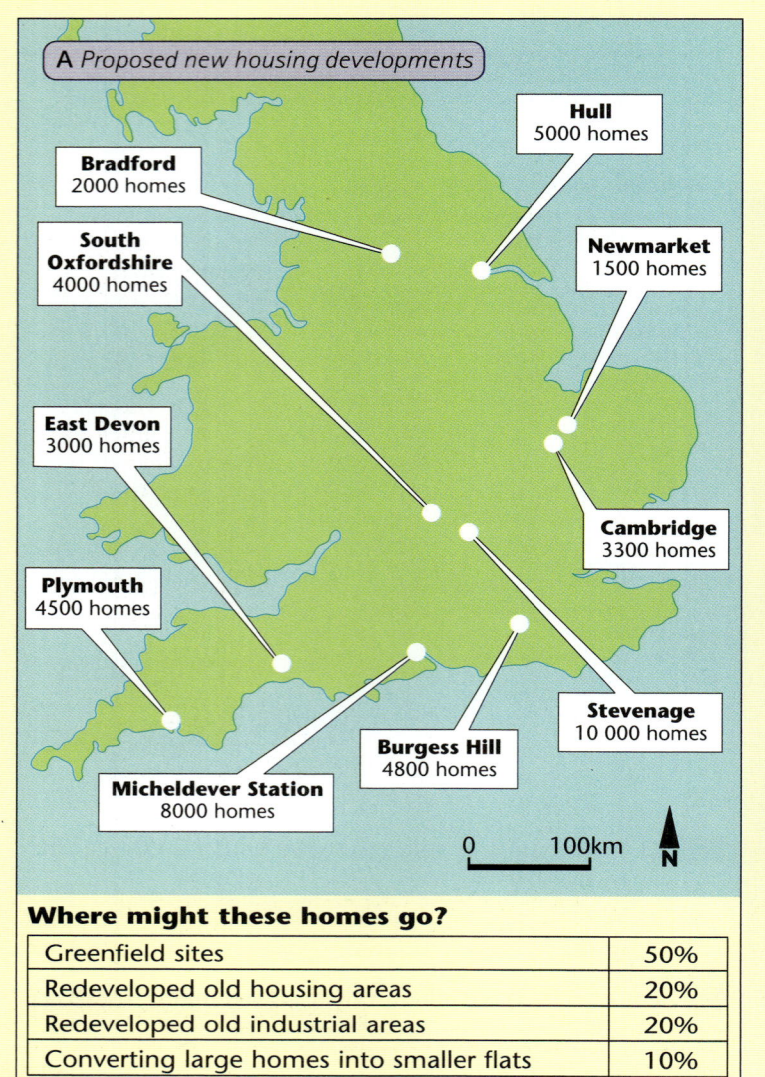

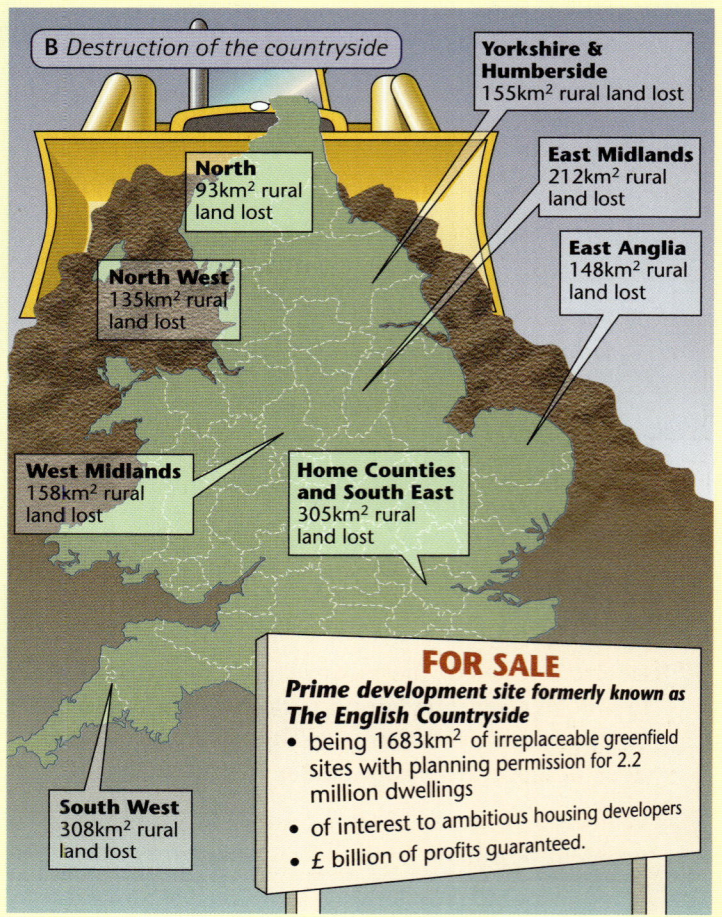

A *Proposed new housing developments*

- Bradford — 2000 homes
- Hull — 5000 homes
- South Oxfordshire — 4000 homes
- Newmarket — 1500 homes
- East Devon — 3000 homes
- Cambridge — 3300 homes
- Plymouth — 4500 homes
- Stevenage — 10 000 homes
- Burgess Hill — 4800 homes
- Micheldever Station — 8000 homes

B *Destruction of the countryside*

- Yorkshire & Humberside: 155km² rural land lost
- North: 93km² rural land lost
- East Midlands: 212km² rural land lost
- North West: 135km² rural land lost
- East Anglia: 148km² rural land lost
- West Midlands: 158km² rural land lost
- Home Counties and South East: 305km² rural land lost
- South West: 308km² rural land lost

FOR SALE
Prime development site formerly known as The English Countryside
- being 1683km² of irreplaceable greenfield sites with planning permission for 2.2 million dwellings
- of interest to ambitious housing developers
- £ billion of profits guaranteed.

Where might these homes go?

Greenfield sites	50%
Redeveloped old housing areas	20%
Redeveloped old industrial areas	20%
Converting large homes into smaller flats	10%

Pressure at the rural/urban fringe

5. Do you think the new town development at Micheldever Station should go ahead? Give reasons for your decision.

C *Micheldever Station: A possible layout*

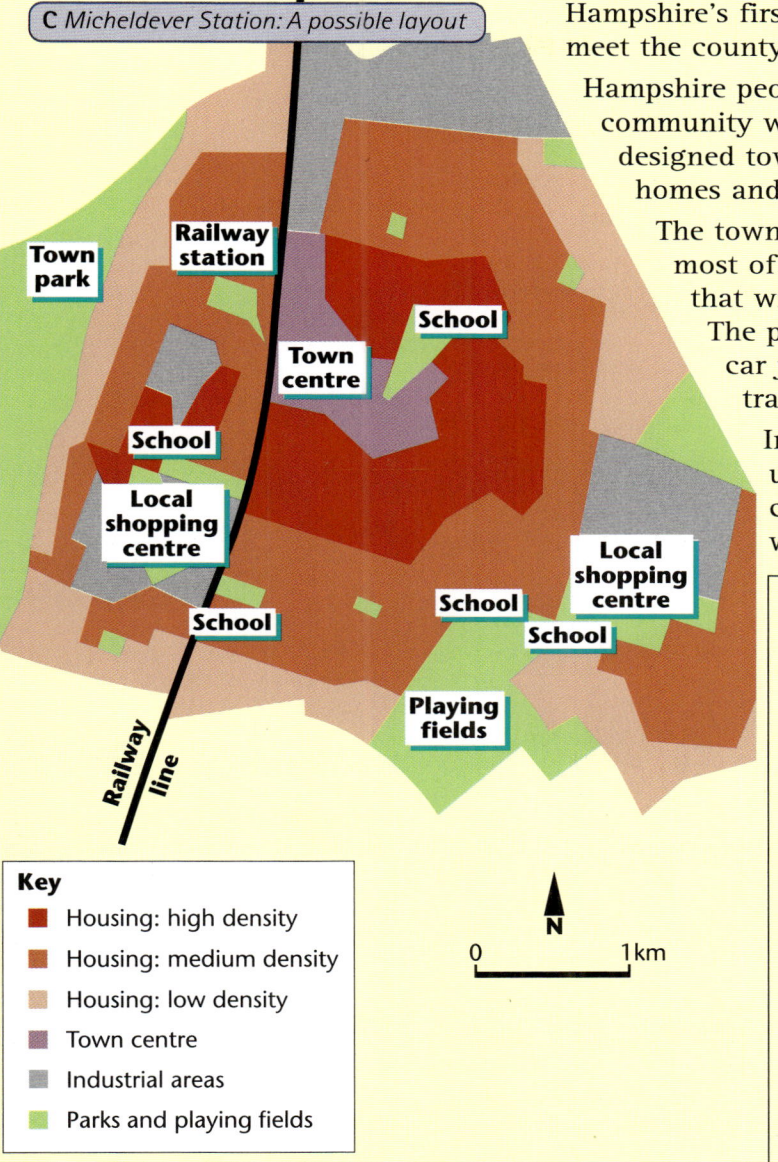

Key
- Housing: high density
- Housing: medium density
- Housing: low density
- Town centre
- Industrial areas
- Parks and playing fields

Hampshire's first new town for years is being promoted to help meet the county's fast growing housing needs.

Hampshire people who believe in the idea of a new community want to create a well-balanced, sensitively designed town at Micheldever Station, with high quality homes and a range of facilities.

The town will be of sufficient size to provide jobs for most of the working population and support facilities that will cut the need for residents to travel elsewhere. The plan also puts emphasis on the need to minimise car journeys and increase the use of public transport, including rail.

In the long term, the town will be able to provide up to 8000 homes without destroying its character. Careful environmental management will help to ensure this.

Five schools are planned, all with cycle routes. The secondary school will have sports and leisure facilities available to the community.

The town centre will have business, social, leisure and healthcare provision. It will be a lively and safe environment, with limited vehicle access and the needs of the disabled people fully catered for.

About 10600 new jobs are expected, both in the industrial estates and local services.

D *Some of the main features*

Managing Change in the Human Environment

Pressure at the rural/urban fringe

Exam practice questions

Mark schemes can be found on the book's website, at www.heinemann.co.uk/issuesmarkschemes

1. Study A. Using evidence from the photograph:
   a) State the land uses at A, B and C. (3)
   b) Describe the methods of transport in this area. (3)
   c) Suggest the advantages of this area for the developments at A, B and C. (6)
   d) Housing schemes on the rural/urban fringe do not meet everyone's needs. Describe the main features and problems of such a scheme. (8)

A

2. There are different types of planning development in the European Union, for example:
   - out-of-town shopping
   - new towns
   - green belts
   - new transport systems.

   Choose *one* example of a rural/urban planning development you have studied. Describe the main features of this development. (6)

MANAGING THE PHYSICAL ENVIRONMENT

5 Living with tectonic hazards

Many people live in areas affected by earthquakes and volcanoes. What are the causes of these events, and how can people learn to live with them?

Managing the Physical Environment

5.1 Earthquakes and volcanoes

The Earth is made up of several layers. The top layer is called the **crust** and is thought to be between 5km and 90km thick. Underneath this is the **mantle**, a mass of hotter molten rock which becomes denser and more solid towards the centre of the Earth. In the centre is the core, a dense mass of mainly solid rock (**A**).

The location of volcanoes and earthquakes

There is a definite pattern in the location of volcanic activity (**E**). The theory of plate tectonics suggests that the Earth is divided into seven large and twelve smaller crustal **plates** (**B**), which 'float' on the mantle rather like the cracked shell on a boiled egg.

There are two types of crustal plate: *continental* and *oceanic*. The places where the plates meet are called *plate margins*. In these areas the Earth is unstable, and volcanic activity or earthquakes are common. In some places the plates are being forced apart, and in other places they are being pushed together.

Types of plate margin

Destructive plate margins

Destructive plate margins are where plates are moving together and collide, destroying the edges of the plates. This happens at collision or subduction zones.

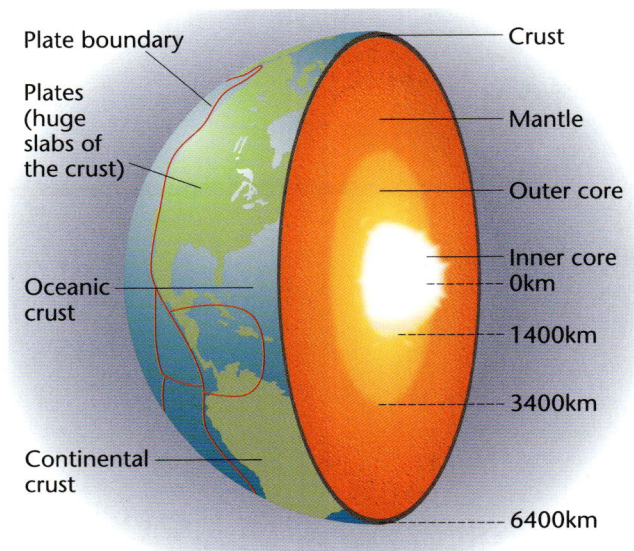

A – Cross-section through the Earth

- **Collision zones** occur where two continental plates collide and push together to form fold mountains. The Himalayas are being created in this way, as the plate carrying India collides with the Eurasian Plate.
- **Subduction zones** occur where an oceanic plate is moving towards a continental plate (**C**). The heavier oceanic plate sinks below the lighter

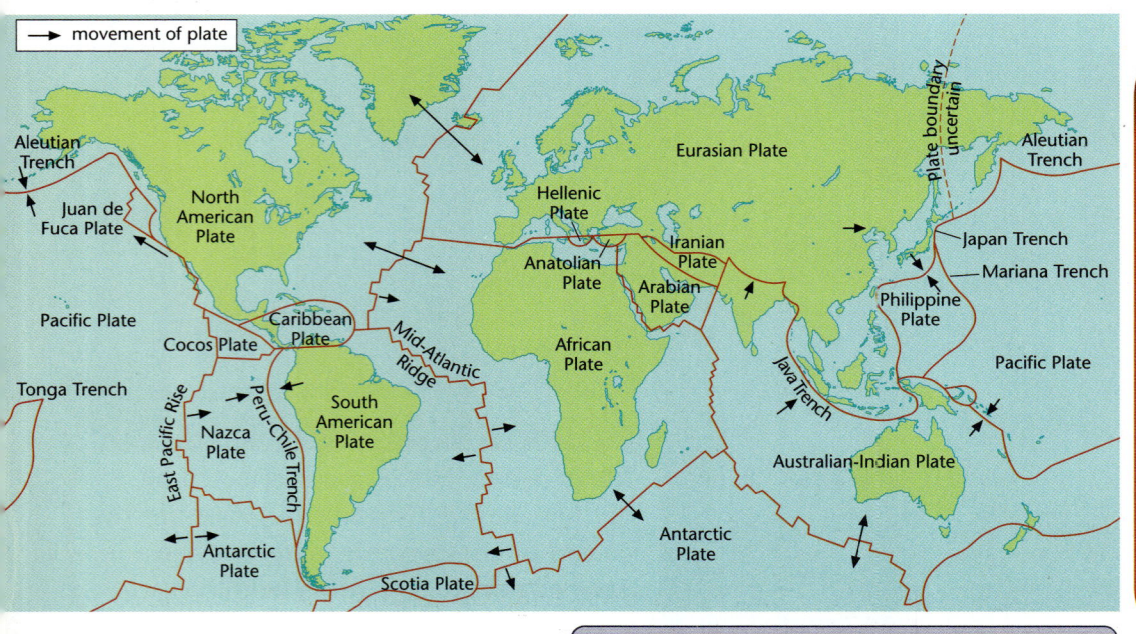

B – The Earth's major plates and plate boundaries

Factfile

Earthquakes
- occur in narrow belts
- can be found near all types of plate margin
- occur on land and at sea.

Volcanoes
- occur in long, narrow belts
- are found most frequently at destructive plate margins
- are most common around the Pacific 'Ring of Fire' and the western mountain chains in North and South America.

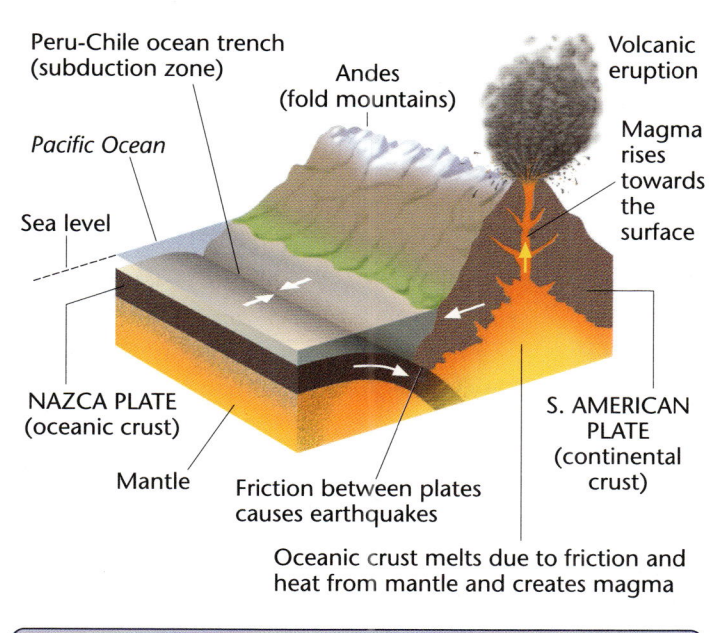

5 Living with tectonic hazards

C – The South American destructive margin: a subduction zone

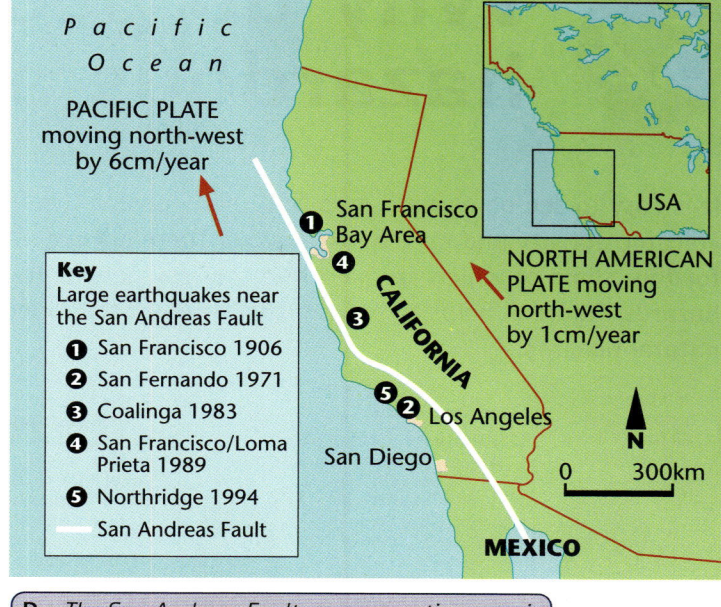

Labels: Peru-Chile ocean trench (subduction zone); Andes (fold mountains); Volcanic eruption; Pacific Ocean; Magma rises towards the surface; Sea level; NAZCA PLATE (oceanic crust); Mantle; Friction between plates causes earthquakes; S. AMERICAN PLATE (continental crust); Oceanic crust melts due to friction and heat from mantle and creates magma

D – The San Andreas Fault: a conservative margin

Labels: Pacific Ocean; PACIFIC PLATE moving north-west by 6cm/year; NORTH AMERICAN PLATE moving north-west by 1cm/year; San Francisco Bay Area; California; Los Angeles; San Diego; Mexico; USA

Key – Large earthquakes near the San Andreas Fault:
1. San Francisco 1906
2. San Fernando 1971
3. Coalinga 1983
4. San Francisco/Loma Prieta 1989
5. Northridge 1994
— San Andreas Fault

continental plate. As this happens the heat from the mantle and friction from contact between the plates melts the edge of the oceanic plate. The melting plate creates **magma** that rises to the surface to form volcanoes. At the same time friction between the two plates can trigger earthquakes.

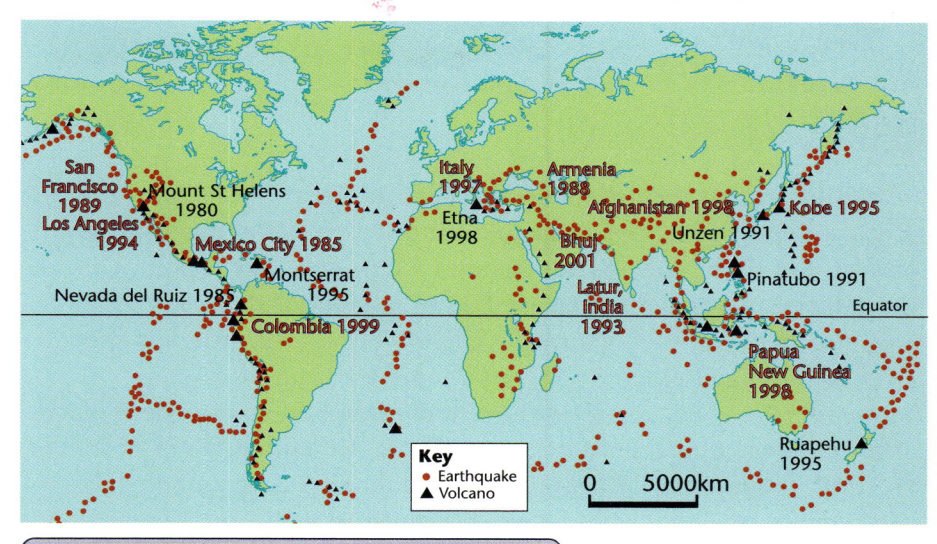

Constructive plate margins

Where two plates move away from each other, magma rises into the gap and cools, creating new rock. Examples are the Mid-Atlantic Ridge and the islands of Iceland and the Azores.

Conservative plate margins

Here, plates move alongside each other. In some areas the plates do not move smoothly past each other but 'stick' together. Pressure builds up until a sudden movement sends shockwaves through the Earth. In California (USA), the San Andreas Fault is the junction between the North American and Pacific Plates. Both plates are moving towards the north-west, but one is moving faster so tension builds up, resulting in earthquakes (**D**).

E – Volcanoes and earthquakes around the world

Notable labelled events: San Francisco 1989; Mount St Helens 1980; Los Angeles 1994; Mexico City 1985; Nevada del Ruiz 1985; Montserrat 1996; Colombia 1999; Italy 1997; Armenia 1988; Etna 1998; Afghanistan 1998; Bhuj 2001; Latur, India 1993; Kobe 1995; Unzen 1991; Pinatubo 1991; Papua New Guinea 1998; Ruapehu 1995

Key: ● Earthquake ▲ Volcano

Questions

1. Use Figures B and E to compare the location of earthquakes and volcanoes with the position of the global plate boundaries.

2. Copy out and complete the following table:

Type of plate margin		Example
Destructive	• Subduction zone	Nazca Plate/South American Plate
	• Collision zone	
Constructive		
Conservative		

3. Using an annotated diagram, explain how volcanoes are formed at destructive plate margins.

Managing the Physical Environment

5.2 Why do people live in hazardous areas?

It is easy to see on a world map that many people live in places where volcanic activity and earthquakes occur. There are a number of reasons for this, some of which are based on the way people perceive natural hazards. Figure **A** helps to explain the different reactions to living with natural hazards.

Fatalistic: If it happens, it happens, and it's all part of living in this area.

Acceptance: Hazards are a part of everyday life which we try to live with. We know hazards will happen, but continue to live in this area because it has so many advantages.

Adaptation: Events can be predicted and warnings given. The area has been made much safer with modern technology, so even if a disaster occurs few people will be affected.

A – Living with natural hazards

In MEDCs a great deal of money is spent on hazard prediction and preparation, and millions of people continue to live in places where hazards are likely, such as Los Angeles (USA) and Tokyo (Japan). In these places when a disaster occurs the number of deaths is usually low, but there is a high economic cost. In LEDCs, much less is spent on prediction and preparation, but people continue to live in vulnerable areas because they have few alternatives, and these places offer them the opportunity to earn a living. When a disaster occurs in an LEDC, the number of deaths is often higher, but economic costs lower. Few people will have insurance though, so disasters have more long term impact.

Benefits of living near unstable plate margins

Across the world millions of people live in unstable areas. This is because these areas offer particular economic advantages, including the following:

- *Good physical and economic opportunities:* although California (USA) is an earthquake zone it has an excellent climate, spectacular beaches and a wide range of job opportunities.
- *The opportunity for intensive agriculture:* where volcanic rocks have been broken down they produce very fertile soils rich in minerals, as on the slopes of the Taal volcano in the Philippines (**B**).
- *The opportunity for mineral extraction* a number of minerals can be found in volcanic areas including industrial minerals such as copper, manganese and sulphur, as well as precious stones. This provides jobs directly linked with mining and in associated industries.
- *The opportunity to generate energy:* geothermal energy can be generated using the temperature of the rocks underground. In Iceland this source of energy is used for heating houses, factories and public buildings (**C**).
- *The development of tourism:* volcanic activity often occurs in highland areas of spectacular scenery, such as Mt Fuji National Park in Japan. These areas attract millions of tourists who provide many job opportunities. After the Mount St Helens (USA) eruption in 1980, a visitor centre was opened which now attracts over a million people a year.

B – Volcanic soils are often used for intensive agriculture, as here around the Taal volcano in the Philippines

5 Living with tectonic hazards

C – Geothermal energy can be tapped in volcanic areas

Is California worth the risk?

Absolutely, say 30 million residents

There should be plenty to talk about this week at the annual conference of the Society for Risk Analysis. The 800 or so people who are expected to attend will gather in San Francisco. They will see a city of tumbled roadways and jolted buildings left by the recent earthquake. People are asking themselves: 'Is it crazy to live in this area?'

That question is never entirely out of mind in California. But now the painful memories of the Pretty Big One, as the locals are calling the recent quake, have lent a certain sharpness to the prospects of further shake-ups. Last week scientists were telling Californians that the state faces a 50% chance that another quake as strong as the recent one could happen 'at any time' during the next 30 years.

Even so, few are rushing to catch the next plane east. In Santa Cruz, near the epicentre of the quake, homeowners are wondering if they should rebuild on the fractured hillsides, where landslides may now become a problem. Many residents are nonetheless eager to rebuild. Californians are generally unworried by the threat.

'The Earth shakes and rolls under my feet', shrugs Wallace Stegner, a 40-year-old resident of Los Altos Hills. 'It's never particularly alarmed me.'

There is evidence that it takes repeated batterings to shake people's confidence. Natural disasters do not often occur in so predictable a manner. Mary Skipper is getting ready to replace her mobile home near Charleston (South Carolina), in a spot hit hard by Hurricane Hugo in September. 'I know this is a flood plain', she explains. 'But something like Hugo may never happen again for another 100 years.'

'Applied to San Francisco, it means that a second quake there in a year or two would have a much greater impact. We could expect to see a significant out-migration from California', says geologist Curtis C. Roseman. 'One quake doesn't do the job.'

To say that Californians have been willing to tolerate the risks arising from life on a fault line is not to say they have been indifferent to them. The recent quake was comparable in strength to the one in Armenia last December, which killed 25,000. 'A substantial help to the much lower death rate in California was that California was aware of the risk and made significant investments as a precaution', says M. Granger Morgan, head of the Department of Engineering and Public Policy at Carnegie-Mellon University. But after last week, earthquakes are going to be viewed as a much more persistent risk than they were before.

D – From *Time* magazine, 5 November 1989 (shortly after the 1989 earthquake)

Questions

1. Why might people in LEDCs take a more fatalistic view about natural hazards?

2. Use D to help you explain why living in hazardous areas might be 'worth the risk'

3. a) Why are tourists attracted to areas of volcanic activity?
   b) Complete a spider diagram like the one below, to describe the jobs that might be linked with the development of tourism.

TOURISM — Transport, Hotels

5.3 Earthquake activity

Most earthquakes result from sudden movement at destructive or conservative plate margins, where plates are moving towards or alongside each other. Pressure builds up until there is sudden movement resulting in a shockwave in the Earth's crust. The initial movement may last for only a few seconds but it can be followed by a series of **aftershocks** that may be felt over a period of many days.

How are earthquakes measured?

Earthquakes can be measured using the Richter scale or the Mercalli scale. The **Mercalli scale (A)** measures the amount of surface shaking, and describes its likely effects. The **Richter scale (B)** measures the magnitude, or energy released, on a scale of 1 to 10. It is a logarithmic scale, so an earthquake measuring 4.0 on the Richter scale is ten times stronger than one that measures 3.0.

The effects of earthquakes

Primary effects are the immediate effects caused directly by the earthquake. This includes death, injury, and damage to buildings and infrastructure.

Secondary effects are indirect effects, including fires and any further damage. They also include death due to disease, lack of food, water, shelter and medical facilities. Economic effects might include job losses and the loss of communication networks.

Why do earthquakes affect areas in different ways?

The effects of selected earthquakes in the 1990s are shown in **C**. This shows that earthquakes of the same magnitude can have very different effects. There are several reasons for this:

- *Distance* – from the epicentre.
- *Type of land* – the Mexico City earthquake (1985) was made worse because the city is built on a clay bed which amplified the shockwaves.

Definitions

*An **earthquake** is a shaking of the Earth's crust generated by sudden movement. The point where the shockwave starts is known as the **focus**. The point on the Earth's surface above this is the **epicentre**.*

1. Not really felt
2. Felt by people sitting down
3. Hanging objects swing
4. Shaking is like the passing of heavy lorries
5. Liquids spill, doors swing open
6. Windows break, furniture moves
7. Difficult to stand, loose bricks and roofing tiles fall
8. Walls collapse, branches broken from trees
9. Underground pipes break, cracks appear in ground
10. Buildings collapse, landslides occur
11. Rail tracks bend, many buildings totally destroyed
12. Virtually total damage

A – The Mercalli scale

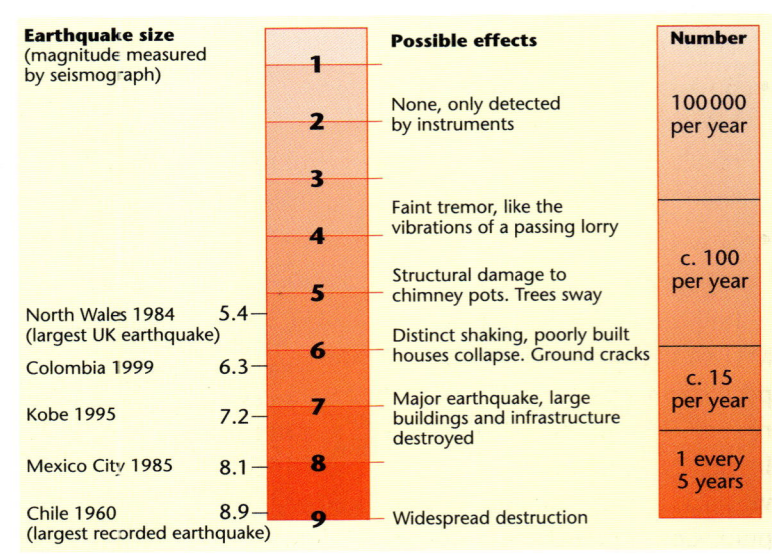

Earthquake size (magnitude measured by seismograph)		Possible effects	Number
	1	None, only detected by instruments	100 000 per year
	2		
	3	Faint tremor, like the vibrations of a passing lorry	c. 100 per year
	4		
North Wales 1984 5.4 (largest UK earthquake)	5	Structural damage to chimney pots. Trees sway	
Colombia 1999 6.3	6	Distinct shaking, poorly built houses collapse. Ground cracks	c. 15 per year
Kobe 1995 7.2	7	Major earthquake, large buildings and infrastructure destroyed	
Mexico City 1985 8.1	8		1 every 5 years
Chile 1960 8.9 (largest recorded earthquake)	9	Widespread destruction	

B – The Richter scale

5 Living with tectonic hazards

- *When the earthquake happens* – in an urban area, if an earthquake happens at night, fewer people will be on the streets. If an earthquake happens in winter, the secondary impacts on homeless people are greater, especially in LEDCs.
- *How well-prepared an area is* – if buildings have been constructed to withstand earthquakes and the population are prepared, the effects will be reduced.

Preparing for earthquakes

Earthquakes cannot really be predicted accurately, although it is possible to identify the areas most at risk by studying past earthquake events. The Earth is monitored constantly for any signs of movement which might suggest that an earthquake is likely.

In order to be prepared:

- People who live in earthquake-prone areas can be educated in what to do in the event of an earthquake. Japan has a disaster day on 1 September, to remind the people how vulnerable they are. Rescue drills are practised and children have lessons in school about how to respond in the event of an earthquake.
- Buildings and transport structures can be built to withstand earthquakes by reinforcing them with steel or building them on large rubber shock-absorbers.
- Services such as gas, water and electricity can be laid in more flexible pipes to stop them breaking so easily.

MEDCs are more able to afford the prediction and preparation techniques that reduce the number of deaths and injuries. In LEDCs, few buildings are constructed to withstand earthquakes, and services are poor. Consequently the number of deaths and injuries is often greater.

Disasters take their toll across the globe

The following is a chronology of the world's major earthquakes that have killed more than 1,000 people in recent years.

17 Aug 99:	Turkey, 7.4 on Richter scale. About 15,600 people were killed in the country's worst natural disaster in 60 years.
25 Jan 99:	Colombia, 6.3 on Richter scale. Colombia's central coffee-growing region shattered with at least 1,170 people dead.
17 July 98:	Papua New Guinea, 7.1 on Richter scale. Undersea earthquake created three waves that struck the coast and wiped out villages. At least 2,100 dead
30 May 98:	Afghanistan, 6.9 on Richter scale. Up to 4,000 people killed and 50 villages destroyed in Takhar province.
4 Feb 98:	Afghanistan, 6.1 on Richter scale. 4,500 killed when the Rustaq district of Takhar province was hit.
10 May 97:	Iran, 7.1 on Richter scale. 1,560 people killed and 2,810 injured in rural areas of eastern Iran. The quake levelled 11 villages.
28 Feb 97:	Iran, 5.5 on Richter scale. 1,000 people dead and 2,000 injured in north-west Iran.
28 May 95:	Russia, 7.5 on Richter scale. The country's worst earthquake killed 1,989 people in the Far East oil-producing town of Neftegorsk.
16 Jan 95:	Japan, 7.2 on Richter scale. 6,430 people killed after a strong earthquake ripped through central Japan near Kobe.
30 Sept 93:	India, 6.4 on Richter scale. Thousands killed and 36 villages destroyed after a series of earthquakes rocked western and southern India.
21 June 90:	Iran, 7.7 on Richter scale. 35,000 dead, 100,000 injured, 500,000 homeless. The worst recorded disaster in Iran.

C – From The Times, 22 September 1999

Questions

1. What is meant by:
   a) the primary effects and
   b) the secondary effects of natural disasters?
2. Describe three factors that can affect the impact of earthquakes.
3. What is the difference between *prediction* and *preparation*?
4. Using C, copy and complete the following table, putting the earthquakes in order of magnitude:

Magnitude	Location/Date	Effects
7.7	Iran/June 1990	35 000 dead, 100 000 injured, 500 000 homeless

Managing the Physical Environment

5.4 The Kobe earthquake — January 1995

On 16 January 1995 an earthquake measuring 7.2 on the Richter scale devastated the Japanese city of Kobe. The earthquake struck at 5.46 a.m. and the initial shock lasted only 20 seconds. The epicentre was on Awaji Island in Osaka Bay, close to the major cities of Kobe and Osaka (**A**). After the initial earthquake there were more than 600 aftershocks.

The affected area is in southern Japan on a narrow strip of land between Osaka Bay and the Rokko Mountains. This coastal plain is a transport corridor used by motorways and the 'bullet train' to move people and goods along the southern coast of Japan. Kobe is a major industrial city of nearly 1.5 million people, and a port responsible for 30 per cent of Japan's trade. The area also has an international airport.

Effects of the earthquake

Figure **B** describes one couple's experience of the earthquake, and illustrates some of the immediate effects. Other short-term effects included the following:

- There were approximately 6000 deaths and 35 000 injuries.
- Nearly 200 000 buildings were destroyed, including 170 000 houses; in the Central Business District nearly 80 per cent of all buildings were damaged, many beyond repair.

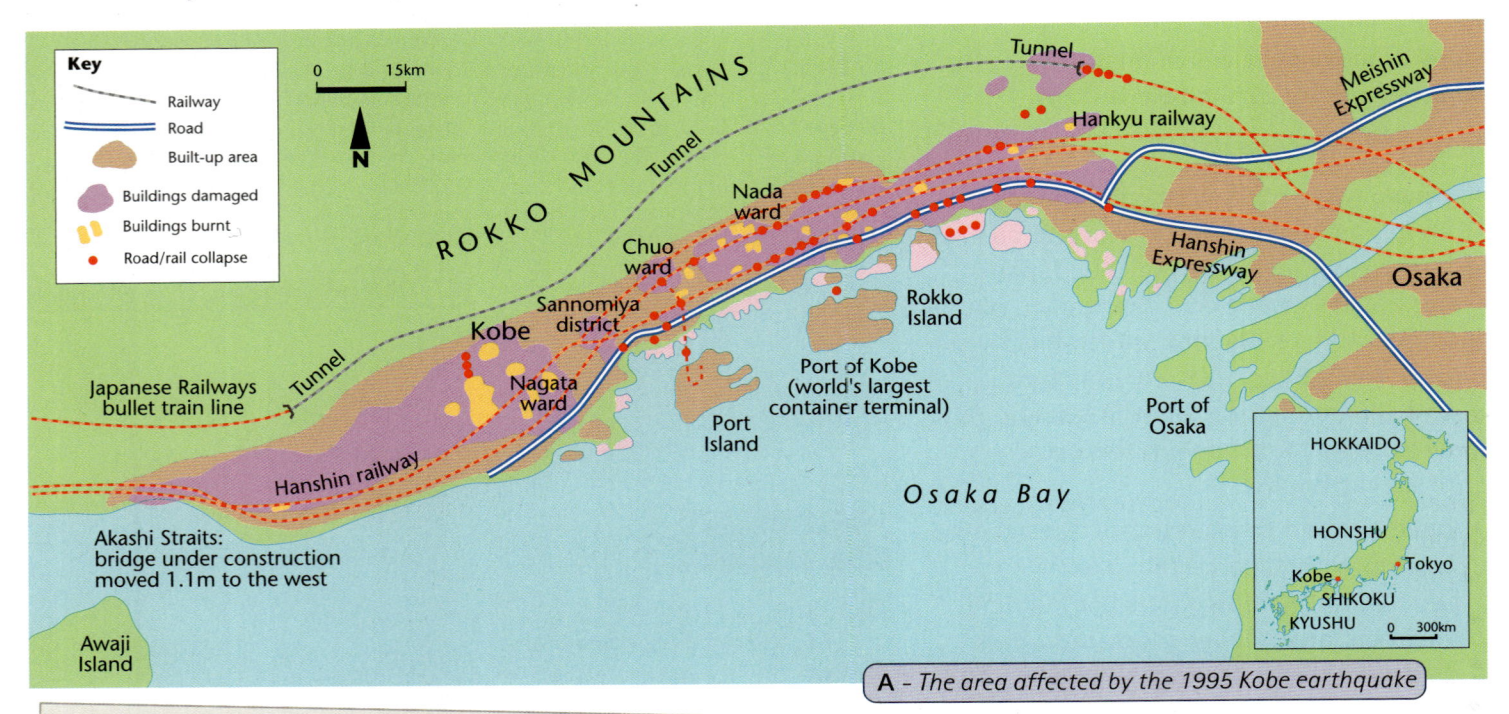

A - The area affected by the 1995 Kobe earthquake

Tom Robb and his wife Naoko were woken by the quake at their home near Kobe. 'The house started to rock like we were on a boat. We looked at the clock and saw it was early in the morning and thought, what is this? Then the house shook like crazy. It felt like it was shaking for a long time,' said Mrs Robb.

The couple's three-storey detached concrete house escaped damage but Mrs Robb said that, according to television reports, many wooden houses in Osaka had collapsed. Several aftershocks later rocked the city.

'No damage was done but we both got really scared. We have never experienced anything like this in our whole lives.'

Mrs Robb said she was still awaiting news of her sister, who lives in the centre of Kobe.

'We saw on TV that the train station and supermarket next to her house had completely burnt down but we haven't been able to contact her. The trains aren't running because of derailments and the roads are jammed. People are being warned not to travel because there are huge cracks in the road and many buildings are about to fall down.'

B - From the *Guardian*, 18 January 1995

- Over 300 000 people were evacuated from their homes and had to live in temporary accommodation such as schools and community centres.
- The Hanshin Expressway collapsed in several sections (**C**) and a 130km section of rail track had to close.
- Supplies of gas, water and electricity were disrupted.
- Damaged gas mains caused over 300 fires.
- Over 250 000 telephone lines were damaged.
- The ports of Kobe and Ashiya were severely damaged.

Some of the longer-term effects included:

- Many people moved away from the area, and some were too afraid to return.
- A number of high-rise buildings were so badly damaged that they had to be demolished (62 in Kobe out of 269).
- Some companies, including Mitsubishi and Panasonic, were forced to close, with the loss of over 20 000 jobs.
- Many new jobs were created in the construction industry as the area was rebuilt – reconstruction costs were estimated at $120 billion.
- Social services claimed that there were hundreds of deaths through suicide, or as a result of neglect as people in temporary accommodation failed to look after themselves.

C - The collapsed Hanshin Expressway

Rebuilding the area

The Kobe earthquake not only destroyed a major industrial area, it also badly affected people's confidence, because they thought a rich country such as Japan could predict and be well prepared for such an event.

Since the disaster, the government has put in place new measures which should ensure that the effects of any future earthquakes are less significant. These include:

- re-zoning the city with more open space and wider roads
- constructing stronger buildings with flexible frames
- using more fire-resistant building materials
- making sure all new buildings are built on the most solid ground
- increasing the amount of monitoring equipment along the southern coast.

Eighteen months after the earthquake, much of the area was back to normal, with new roads and railways and all the infrastructure repaired. Thousands of new buildings have been constructed – the disaster was seen as an opportunity to build new shopping centres and industrial areas (**D**).

D - Kobe, 18 months after the earthquake

Questions

1. Using an atlas and **B** on page 90, explain why earthquakes happen in this area.
2. Why was it fortunate that the earthquake happened so early in the morning?
3. Write a brief news report describing the immediate effects of the earthquake.
4. How did the Kobe earthquake affect communications in the area?
5. Explain how the new measures might reduce the effects of future earthquakes.

Managing the Physical Environment

5.5 The Colombian earthquake – January 1999

In January 1999 an earthquake measuring 6.3 on the Richter scale occurred in western Colombia (**A**). The epicentre of the earthquake was near the city of Armenia, in the coffee-growing region of the country. Nearly 2000 people were killed as a direct result of the earthquake, and thousands more were injured. Many nearby towns and villages were affected by landslides, and in Bogota, the Colombian capital, buildings swayed as a result of aftershocks.

Other effects of the earthquake

- More than 180 000 of the 250 000 residents of the city of Armenia lost their homes (**B**).
- Water and electricity services were cut off.
- Many roads were destroyed and communication links badly damaged.
- Hospitals were damaged, making it difficult for emergency services to cope with the injured.
- The entire fleet of fire service vehicles in Armenia was destroyed.
- There were outbreaks of disease due to bodies not being collected and people having to drink contaminated water.

A – *Location of the Colombian earthquake, 1999*

After the earthquake

Two days after the earthquake, Armenia's mayor called for international help, asking for food, medicines and blankets. Hospitals reported a lack of antibiotics to treat the growing threat of disease, and suggested that people were dying because of a shortage of basic medicines. One local resident said: 'Hell has come to Colombia. There is no way to measure the scale of this disaster. We are a poor country and it will take many years to get over this tragedy.'

B – *Devastation in Armenia*

5 Living with tectonic hazards

Why were the effects of the earthquake so great?

- Many of the buildings were poorly built, trapping residents inside when they collapsed.
- People were not expecting an earthquake in this area and were unsure of what to do.
- The emergency services were not trained and equipped to deal with an earthquake.
- This is a poor area, and many people were without clean water for days, increasing the risk of disease.
- Many people found themselves living on the streets or in very basic temporary accommodation.
- Most of the local industry was destroyed and many people lost their source of income.

12 seconds of terror that cost 2000 lives

It took just 12 terrifying seconds, but in that brief eternity more than 2000 people were crushed to death in Colombia's worst earthquake this century.

The powerful tremor devoured whole towns and brought multi-storey homes and offices crashing to the ground. Two-thirds of the city of Armenia, high in the Andes, was demolished; some 700 buildings destroyed, and 180 000 residents left homeless. Hundreds of bodies were still trapped in the debris last night as rescuers clawed for survivors. In one 10-storey apartment building an estimated 560 people were killed. Rescue officials estimated that 2000 may have died in Armenia alone, with the disaster zone spanning 20 towns and villages in five provinces across the west of the country. Civil defence officials said at least 550 were confirmed dead and 2700 more injured, with the toll rising by the hour as corpses were pulled from the shattered concrete and tangled metal.

Pedro Maria Londono, 46, and the rest of his four-member family were miraculously saved when every room but the one they were in was destroyed. 'In 12 seconds I lost what took 20 years to build.' said Londono.

But amid the despair there was joy. Locals cheered in the streets of down-town Armenia as a Red Cross team rescued three men trapped for 13 hours in the rubble of a wrecked four-storey building. The men had been drinking coffee in a pawn shop and saved themselves by ducking between a large safe and the wall just before the floors above them collapsed.

The injured were being evacuated by air to Bogota, Medellin and Cali, and by road to nearby Manizales. Without refrigerator trucks to store the hundreds of rotting corpses, there were fears epidemics could break out.

Stunned residents in Colombia's coffee belt chose to wait out the night around bonfires rather than venture back into their crumpled homes. The earthquake, which measured six on the Richter scale, started 20 miles below the Earth's crust and rattled buildings as far away as the capital Bogota, 140 miles away from the epicentre.

C – *From the Daily Express, 27 January 1999*

Questions

1. Using **B** and **C**, describe the immediate effects of the earthquake on Armenia.
2. Why was the damage to fire service vehicles so devastating?
3. Describe the secondary effects of the earthquake.
4. Why will it 'take many years to get over this tragedy'?
5. Why do LEDCs often need international help after a natural disaster?

Managing the Physical Environment

5.6 Volcanic activity

There are more than 600 active volcanoes in the world, more than half of which encircle the Pacific Ocean – this area is known as the Pacific 'Ring of Fire' (**A**). Volcanic eruptions happen when molten rock and ash from the mantle reach the Earth's surface. Most volcanoes occur at plate margins where the Earth's crust is unstable. However, some are found in places where the Earth's crust is thin and magma escapes to the surface. These are known as **'hot spots'** (**B**).

Evidence of past volcanic activity can be seen in the form of geysers and hot springs where water is superheated by the high temperature of the rocks underground. One famous **geyser** is 'Old Faithful' in the Yellowstone National Park (USA) which regularly ejects steam about every 40 minutes.

Volcanic eruptions can produce a number of features, including:

- volcanic cones, which are made up of layers of **lava** and ash laid down by a number of eruptions over time – these are often called composite cones
- lava flows, which can cool quickly and form a steep cone, or travel large distances before finally cooling into a mass of relatively flat igneous rock

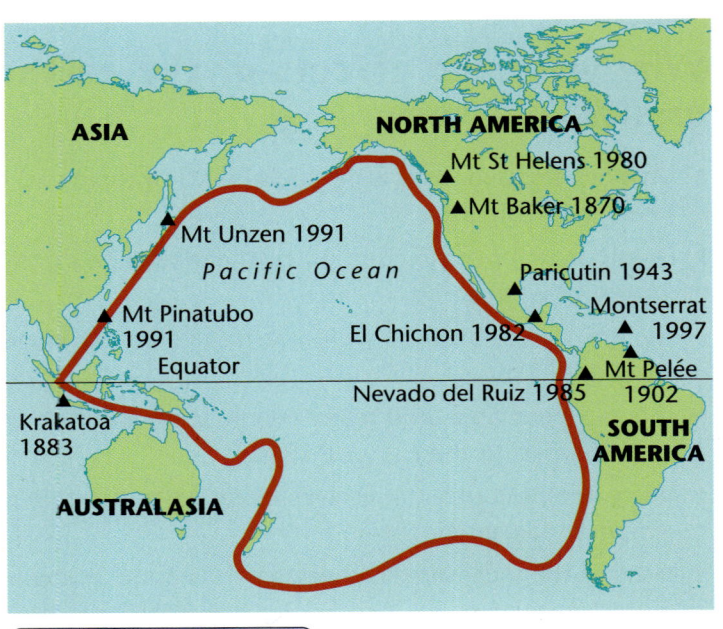

A – The Pacific Ring of Fire

- ash falls, which can cover vast areas of land and cause buildings to catch fire
- pyroclastics, which are materials erupted from a volcano – they can include cinders, ash, pumice, and clouds of superheated gas known as nuées ardentes
- toxic gas clouds, which can poison or suffocate people and animals
- mudflows, caused by meltwater mixing with volcanic ash – also known as lahars.

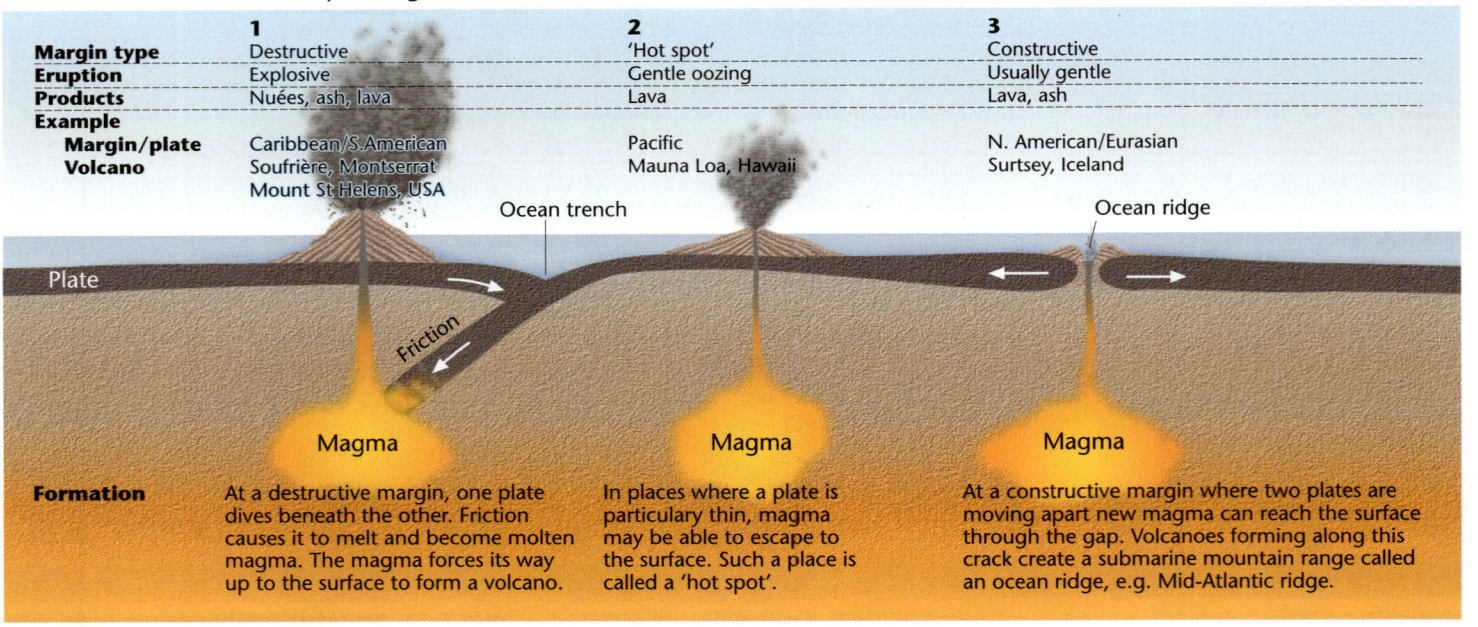

	1	2	3
Margin type	Destructive	'Hot spot'	Constructive
Eruption	Explosive	Gentle oozing	Usually gentle
Products	Nuées, ash, lava	Lava	Lava, ash
Example			
Margin/plate	Caribbean/S.American	Pacific	N. American/Eurasian
Volcano	Soufrière, Montserrat, Mount St Helens, USA	Mauna Loa, Hawaii	Surtsey, Iceland
Formation	At a destructive margin, one plate dives beneath the other. Friction causes it to melt and become molten magma. The magma forces its way up to the surface to form a volcano.	In places where a plate is particulary thin, magma may be able to escape to the surface. Such a place is called a 'hot spot'.	At a constructive margin where two plates are moving apart new magma can reach the surface through the gap. Volcanoes forming along this crack create a submarine mountain range called an ocean ridge, e.g. Mid-Atlantic ridge.

B – Different types of volcano

5 Living with tectonic hazards

What is the volcanic hazard?

The actual lava flow from a volcanic eruption rarely causes many deaths. The effects of ash, gas and mudflows are far more significant. When a gas cloud blew out from Mont Pelée (on Martinique in the Caribbean) in 1902, 30 000 people were suffocated within minutes. In the Nevada del Ruiz (Colombia) eruption of 1985, almost the entire population of Armero (more than 20 000 people) were killed by mudflows which engulfed the town (**C**).

So why do people live near volcanoes?

There are many economic benefits of living near areas of volcanic activity, for example:
- rich fertile soils weathered from volcanic rock
- the opportunity to produce **geothermal energy** from the high temperatures underground
- a wide range of minerals and precious stones can be found in areas of volcanic activity
- the opportunity for the development of tourism.

Can volcanic eruptions be predicted?

It is not possible to prevent volcanoes from erupting, and it is difficult to monitor more than a small number of eruptions each year. However, some measures can be taken that help to predict likely eruptions and limit the effects of actual eruptions.

Prediction

Scientists study any changes in the Earth's surface that might give clues to possible volcanic eruptions. Before many eruptions a number of things may occur, including:
- a number of small earth tremors
- bulging, or cracks, appearing in the side of a volcano
- an increase in the ground temperature, with ice and snow melting in mountain areas
- a number of small ash eruptions
- changes in the make-up of gases and chemical emissions from the crater.

Many of these events can be detected by sensitive instruments, or by satellite technology. Early warning of a likely eruption can then be given.

Limiting the effects of volcanic eruptions

The key to reducing the effects of volcanic eruptions is to make sure that people do not live in the most vulnerable areas. Hazard zoning maps can help by identifying the areas most likely to be affected, and making people aware of the dangers. Many MEDCs now have evacuation procedures in place, and emergency services are trained to deal with the impact of a volcanic eruption. In LEDCs, monitoring and preparation are often less well developed, and consequently the human costs of an eruption are greater.

C – *Volcano victim trapped by debris after the eruption of Nevado del Ruiz in Colombia in 1985*

Questions

1. Briefly explain how volcanoes are created at:
   a) destructive plate margins
   b) constructive plate margins
   c) 'hot spots'.
2. 'The volcanic hazard is not just lava.' Explain this statement.
3. Explain the importance of prediction and preparation in protecting people from volcanic activity.
4. Why do people live in places where volcanic eruptions are likely?

Managing the Physical Environment

5.7 Eruption of Mount St Helens – 18 May 1980

Mount St Helens (2950m) is located in the sparsely populated Cascade Mountains in north-west USA (**B**). For 123 years it was an inactive volcano, but on 18 May 1980 the most powerful global eruption for 60 years occurred.

What caused the Mount St Helens eruption?

Like so many volcanic eruptions, this one was caused by magma rising at the point where an oceanic plate, the Juan de Fuca Plate, descends under the continental North American Plate (**A**). The resulting friction creates heat which changes the destroyed oceanic crust into magma. Over time the build-up becomes so great that it forces its way to the Earth's surface.

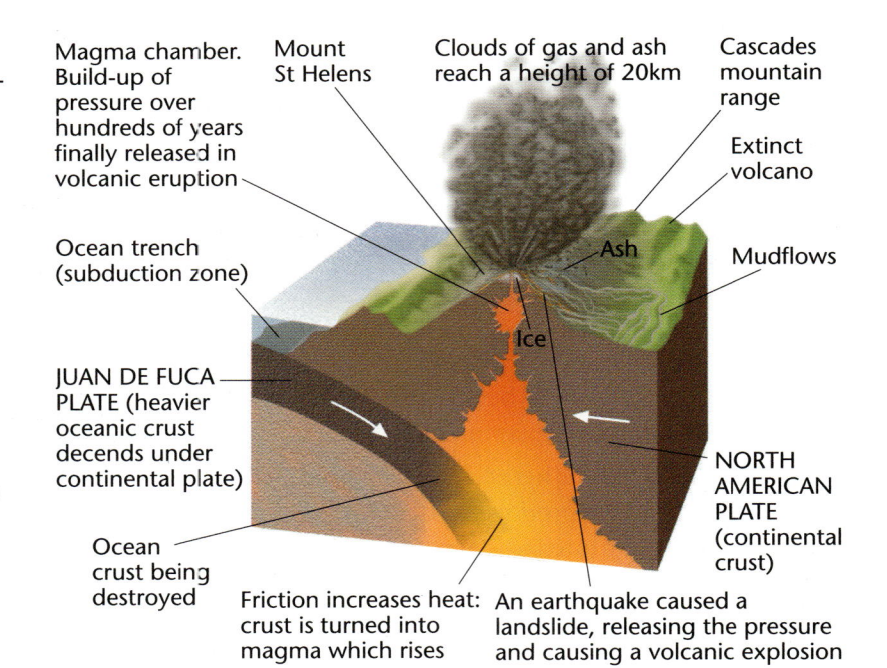

Labels on diagram A: Magma chamber. Build-up of pressure over hundreds of years finally released in volcanic eruption; Mount St Helens; Clouds of gas and ash reach a height of 20km; Cascades mountain range; Extinct volcano; Ocean trench (subduction zone); Ash; Mudflows; Ice; JUAN DE FUCA PLATE (heavier oceanic crust decends under continental plate); NORTH AMERICAN PLATE (continental crust); Ocean crust being destroyed; Friction increases heat: crust is turned into magma which rises; An earthquake caused a landslide, releasing the pressure and causing a volcanic explosion

A – Causes of the eruption

Build-up to the 1980 eruption

20 March	The volcano 'awakes' at 3.47 p.m. with an earthquake of 4.0 on the Richter scale.
25 March	47 small earthquakes in 12 hours.
27 March	Small explosion forms a new crater 70m across.
30 March	Steam ejected.
1 April	Ground shakes – possible movement of magma and gas. Roads around the volcano are closed as tourists are attracted by the event.
12 April	A bulge 100m high and 2km in diameter appears on the north side of the volcano.
13 April – 17 May	Small-scale activity continues. The bulge grows 1.5m a day, indicating a build-up of magma. Snow and ice melt on the mountain and local farm animals behave strangely.
18 May	An earthquake at 8.32 a.m., 5.1 on the Richter scale, causes the bulge to slide forwards. A landslide of rock, ice and soil moves north at 250km/h, suddenly releasing the pressure. A vast explosion results sending a cloud of gas and volcanic ash into the air, devastating the area north of the volcano.
By early June	Ash has blown right around the world. Mount St Helens is reduced in height by 400m.

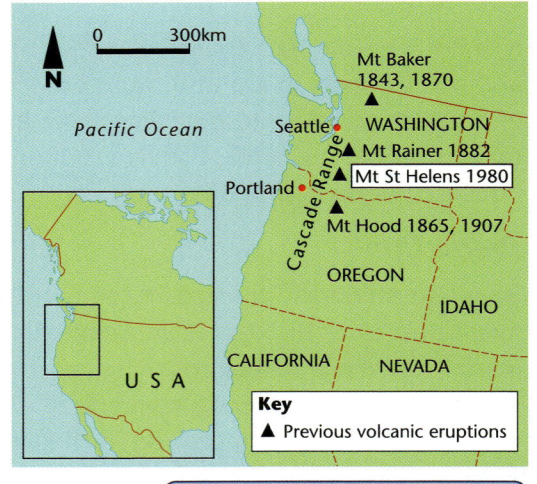

Map B shows: Pacific Ocean; Seattle; Portland; WASHINGTON; OREGON; IDAHO; CALIFORNIA; NEVADA; USA; Cascade Range; Mt Baker 1843, 1870; Mt Rainer 1882; Mt St Helens 1980; Mt Hood 1865, 1907. Key: ▲ Previous volcanic eruptions. Scale 0–300km.

B – Location of Mount St Helens

Effects of the eruption on human activities

- *People:* Because of the monitoring of the volcano and warnings given, most people were evacuated to a safe distance. Even so, 63 people died, most from the poisonous gases from the eruption.

- **Landscape:** All vegetation for a distance of 21km to the north of the volcano was flattened.
- **Farming:** The volcanic deposits eventually increased soil fertility, but in the short term crops and livestock were lost.
- **Forestry:** Huge areas to the north were flattened. The loggers' livelihood was devastated, but some 10 million trees were later replanted.
- **Communications:** Navigation on the Columbia River was disrupted. Flooding washed away road and railway bridges.
- **Fishing:** Lava flows and ash clogged channels and raised water temperatures. Many fish died.
- **Tourism:** Media interest both during and after the eruption brought tourists to the area. In 1993 a tourist centre was opened at Mount St Helens, and now attracts over 1 million visitors a year.

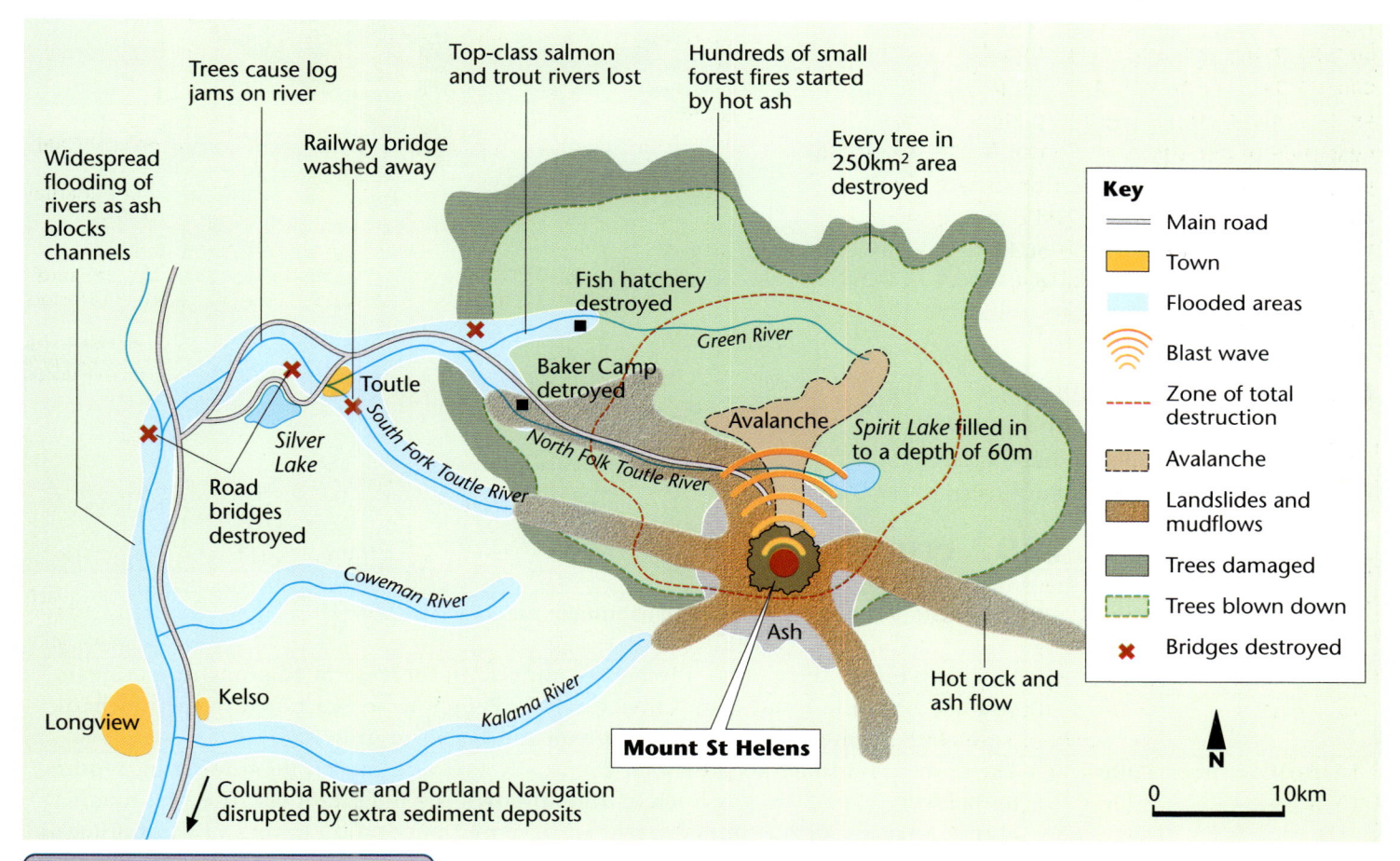

C – Mount St Helens after the eruption

D – Effects of the eruption on the area

Questions

1. Describe and explain the causes of the eruption.
2. Why were only a small number of people killed by such a large eruption?
3. List four effects of the eruption on human activities.
4. Use D to describe the effects of the eruption on the physical landscape.
5. 'The Mount St Helens eruption has brought some economic advantages.' Explain this statement.

Managing the Physical Environment

5.8 The Soufrière Hills eruption – Montserrat 1997

Montserrat is one of a number of islands in the Caribbean that have been formed by volcanic activity. It is located on a destructive plate margin where the Atlantic and Caribbean Plates move together, forming a string of volcanic islands known as an **island arc** (B). The Soufrière Hills are at the southern end of the island of Montserrat. Chance's Peak (A) had been dormant for more than 400 years before 1997. The area was described in a guidebook in 1991 as:
'... one of the most perfect ecosystems in the world, an inactive volcano and sulphur spring where tropical plants grow in abundance.'

The weathered volcanic rock in the area provided excellent fertile soil for agriculture, and before 1997 many of the island's 11 000 inhabitants farmed the area or lived in the nearby capital of Plymouth.

By the end of 1997 more than half of the population had left the island, and with farms and industry destroyed, those remaining faced an uncertain future.

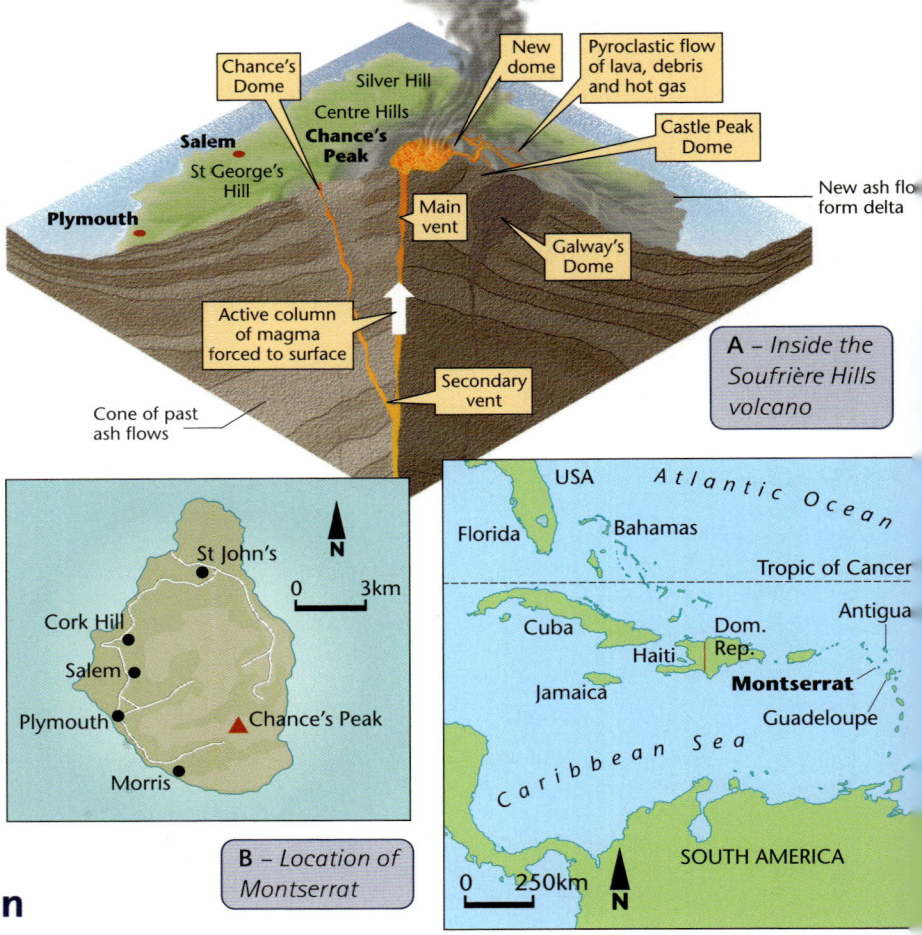

A – Inside the Soufrière Hills volcano

B – Location of Montserrat

Build-up to the 1997 eruption

January 1992 – July 1994	Scientists noticed small-scale earthquake activity.
July–August 1995	People living in the capital, Plymouth, noticed an increase in sulphur fumes. Steam and ash began to erupt from Chance's Peak. People were evacuated to the northern 'safe zone'. Domes on the side of the volcano began to grow (A).
May–September 1996	The domes continued to grow and eventually pressure caused them to erupt, sending pyroclastic flows (ash, gas, rock and mud) down the mountain (C). The first magma eruption occurred. Ash plumes resulted in more than 50 000 tonnes of ash falling on southern Montserrat.
October 1996 – May 1997	Smaller pyroclastic flows continued and there were a number of landslides. Some people who had been evacuated began to return, against the advice of scientists.
June–July 1997	There was continued dome growth until late June when the eruption peaked, with pyroclastic flows of 5 million cubic metres covering an area of 4 km^2. These flows overran settlements, killing 23 people and destroying 150 houses. The danger zone was extended, with more people being moved to the northern part of the island (D).
August 1997	A pyroclastic flow (C) destroyed what was left of Plymouth. The danger zone was extended to the far north of the island.

5 Living with tectonic hazards

C – Pyroclastic flows near Plymouth, 1997

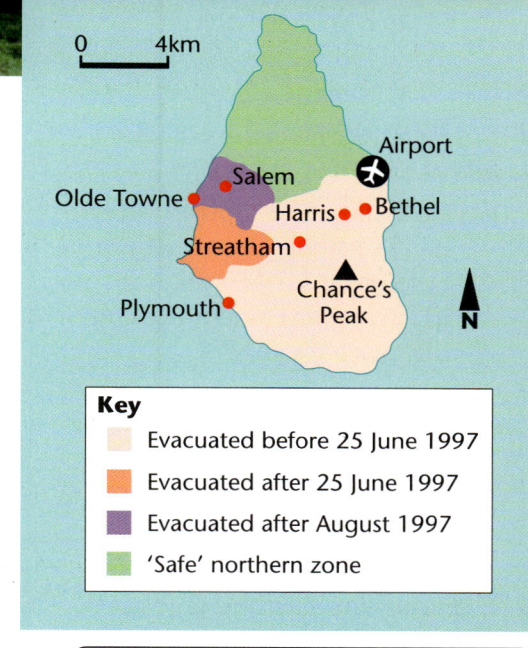

D – Evacuation areas in Montserrat 1997

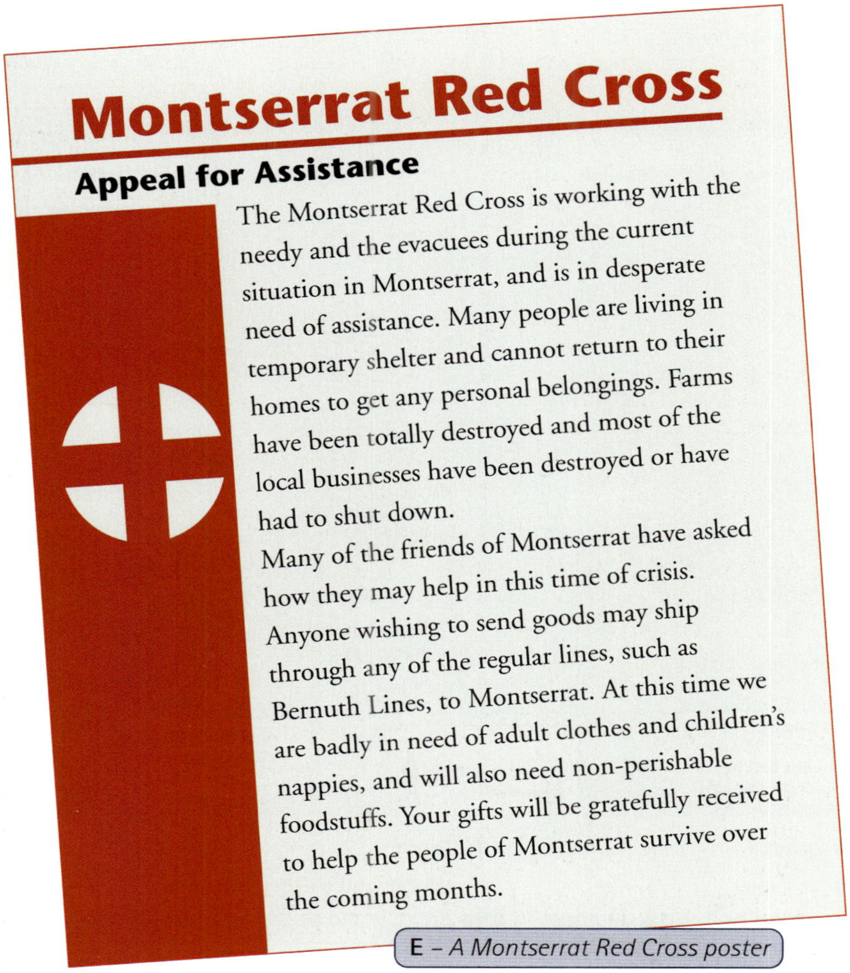

Key:
- Evacuated before 25 June 1997
- Evacuated after 25 June 1997
- Evacuated after August 1997
- 'Safe' northern zone

Montserrat Red Cross

Appeal for Assistance

The Montserrat Red Cross is working with the needy and the evacuees during the current situation in Montserrat, and is in desperate need of assistance. Many people are living in temporary shelter and cannot return to their homes to get any personal belongings. Farms have been totally destroyed and most of the local businesses have been destroyed or have had to shut down.

Many of the friends of Montserrat have asked how they may help in this time of crisis. Anyone wishing to send goods may ship through any of the regular lines, such as Bernuth Lines, to Montserrat. At this time we are badly in need of adult clothes and children's nappies, and will also need non-perishable foodstuffs. Your gifts will be gratefully received to help the people of Montserrat survive over the coming months.

E – A Montserrat Red Cross poster

Questions

1. Briefly describe the events between 1992 and 1997.
2. Why were so few people killed by the Montserrat eruptions?
3. Why did so many people leave the island?
4. Use E to explain why aid agencies are important to LEDCs following natural disasters.

Managing the Physical Environment — **Living** with **tectonic hazards**

Exam practice questions

Mark schemes can be found on the book's website, at www.heinemann.co.uk/issuesmarkschemes

1 Study A (San Francisco Earthquake 1989).
   a) What is meant by the term *epicentre*? (1)
   b) State one example of damage caused by the earthquake. (1)
   c) Explain briefly the causes of an earthquake. (4)
   d) How might people in San Francisco have been affected by the earthquake? (4)
   e) San Francisco has many tall buildings. Suggest why so few of these were damaged by the earthquake. (4)

2 Study B (Montserrat volcano 1997).
   a) How did the eruption affect:
      i) the numbers of people living on Montserrat
      ii) transport on the island
      iii) people's jobs? (3 × 2)
   b) After the eruption, some people moved to the north of the island. Describe two problems for the people now living there. (2)

3 Explain why earthquakes and volcanoes only occur in certain parts of the world. (6)

4 Use examples to explain why people live in areas that are subject to volcanoes and earthquakes. (6)

5 'You cannot prevent volcanoes and earthquakes, but you can prepare for them.' Explain this statement. (6)

6 Use examples to explain why volcanoes and earthquakes often have a more damaging effect in LEDCs. (6)

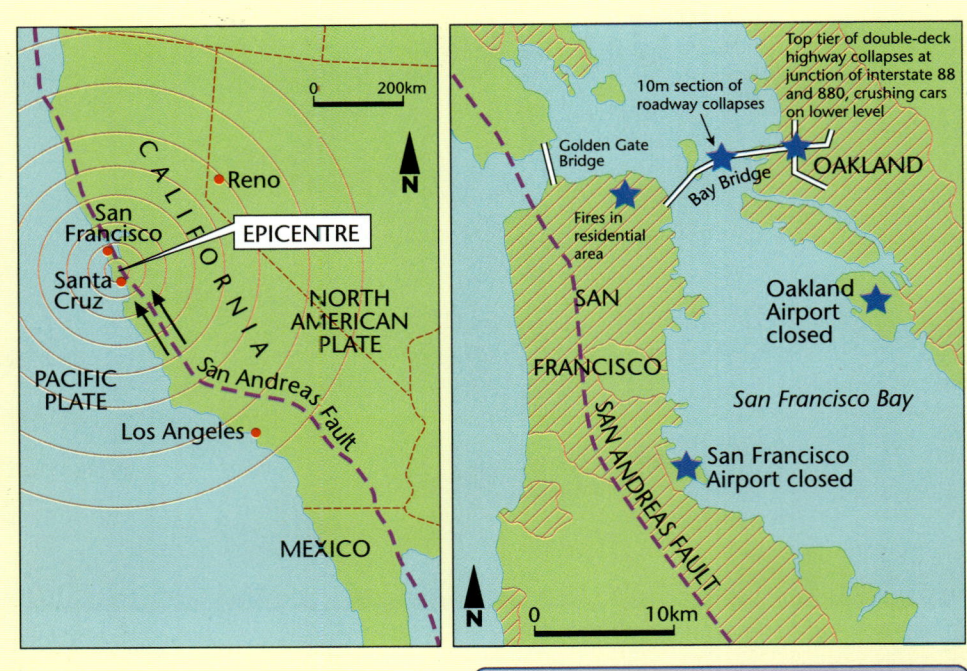

A – The earthquake in San Francisco in 1989

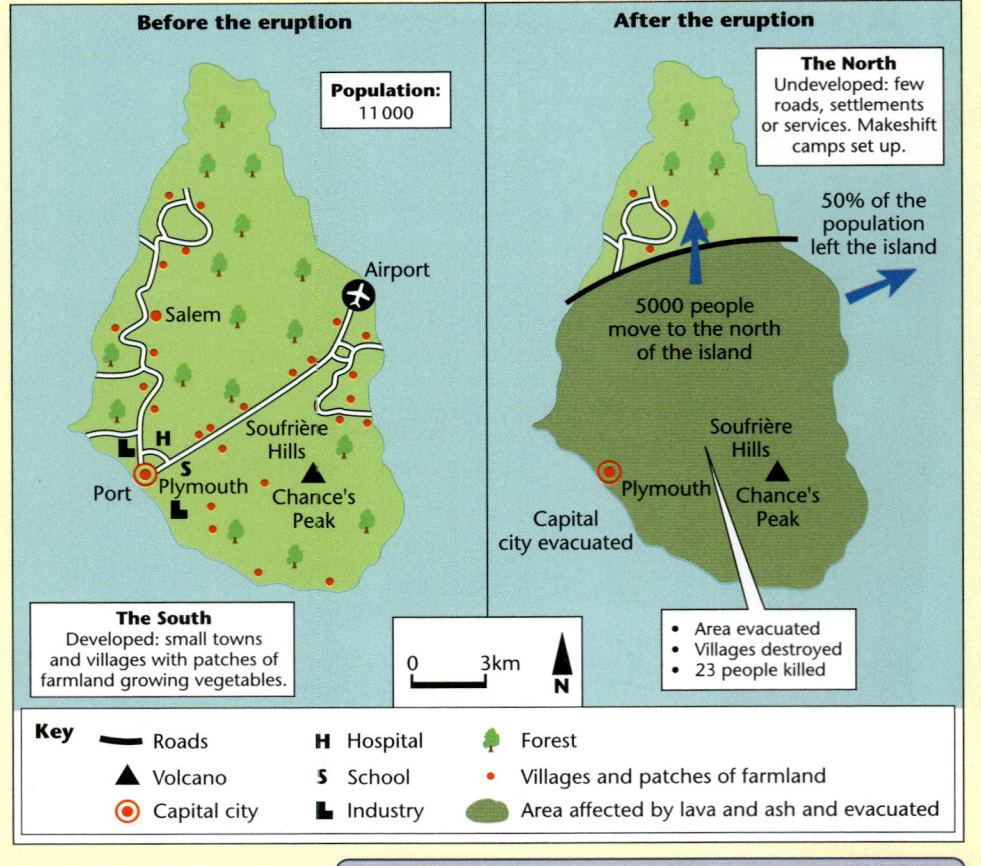

B – The eruption of Chance's Peak on Montserrat in 1997

MANAGING THE PHYSICAL ENVIRONMENT

6 Weather hazards

Many people live in areas affected by storms and floods. What are the causes of these events, and why do their impacts vary?

Managing the Physical Environment

6.1 The climate of the British Isles

The **climate** of the British Isles can be described as:
- *maritime* — because it is affected by ocean currents that bring higher rainfall to the west and moderate the temperature
- *moist* — because **precipitation** is reliable all year and is never exceptionally low
- *temperate* — because temperatures at sea-level are rarely extreme.

Figure **A** divides the British Isles into four areas, each having a distinctive character based on its precipitation and rainfall.

A – Summary of the climate of the British Isles

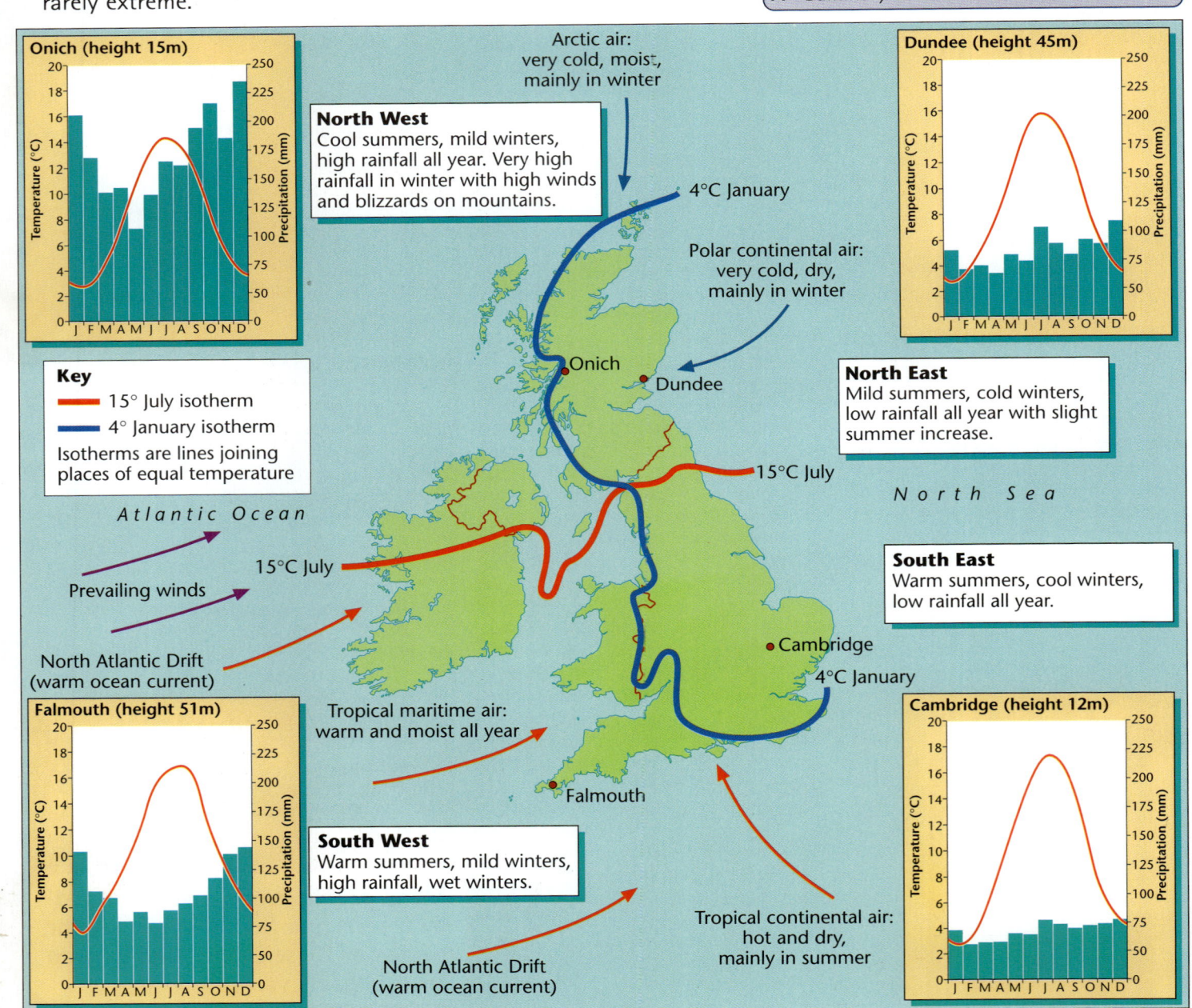

Onich (height 15m)

North West
Cool summers, mild winters, high rainfall all year. Very high rainfall in winter with high winds and blizzards on mountains.

Arctic air: very cold, moist, mainly in winter

4°C January

Polar continental air: very cold, dry, mainly in winter

Dundee (height 45m)

Key
— 15° July isotherm
— 4° January isotherm
Isotherms are lines joining places of equal temperature

North East
Mild summers, cold winters, low rainfall all year with slight summer increase.

Atlantic Ocean

15°C July

North Sea

Prevailing winds

15°C July

North Atlantic Drift (warm ocean current)

Tropical maritime air: warm and moist all year

South East
Warm summers, cool winters, low rainfall all year.

Cambridge
4°C January

Falmouth (height 51m)

Falmouth

South West
Warm summers, mild winters, high rainfall, wet winters.

North Atlantic Drift (warm ocean current)

Tropical continental air: hot and dry, mainly in summer

Cambridge (height 12m)

6 Weather hazards

Microclimates

A microclimate is where the climate of a small area is different from that in the surrounding area. This is quite common:

- in coastal areas where ocean currents and winds affect a local region and where south-facing places can be slightly warmer
- in urban areas where buildings store heat and release it slowly, raising the **temperature**. Rows of tall buildings can also change wind patterns and create shade.

Figure **B** describes how the climate of a central urban area can be different from that in the surrounding suburbs.

Britain's weather: why a city has its own climate
Urban jungles...

The city of Bath was the site of the first study of the climate of an urban area. The study was undertaken by two geographers, William Balchin and Norman Pye, and was published in 1947. Over the next two decades many similar studies were carried out around the country.

Probably the biggest and most detailed of these was conducted by Tony Chandler in London between 1958 and 1964. The fact that human beings have succeeded in modifying the climate of urban areas has long been known. Built-up areas alter some weather elements directly, such as wind, temperature and humidity, whereas other elements are affected indirectly, including snow-cover, visibility, fog frequency and sunshine. More controversially, some researchers claim measurable changes in rainfall.

Even in Britain, city centres have on rare occasions been more than 10°C (18°F) warmer than the outer suburbs. These large differences are likely to occur around sunrise. Increased rainfall is more likely to occur in large conurbations in tropical regions. There are comparatively few occasions during the year when the higher temperature of the air in British cities is sufficient to trigger those rising currents of air – thermals – which in turn produce rain-clouds. Even when they do occur, the wind at cloud level is sufficient to carry the clouds beyond the city boundary before any rain falls.

B – From the Daily Telegraph, 19 August 2000

Questions

1 a) Construct a table to compare the following features at the four weather stations in A:
- lowest temperature
- highest temperature
- temperature range
- amount of rainfall in wettest month
- amount of rainfall in driest month.

b) Which place would you expect to have:
- the highest number of wet days
- the most sunshine hours each year?

Explain your answers.

2 a) What is a microclimate?

b) Use B to describe how the climate in an urban area might be different from that in surrounding areas.

6.2 Weather systems

The **weather** can be shown using a weather map, called a synoptic chart, or using a satellite image. **Synoptic charts** use symbols to show the pattern of air pressure and general conditions recorded at weather stations (**A**). Satellite images are photographs taken from space (**B**) and they show the pattern of clouds. Weather forecasters gather information from synoptic charts and satellite images over a period of time and use them to predict what might happen in the future.

The British Isles are affected by two types of weather system: a low-pressure system, known as a **depression**, and a high-pressure system, known as an **anticyclone**.

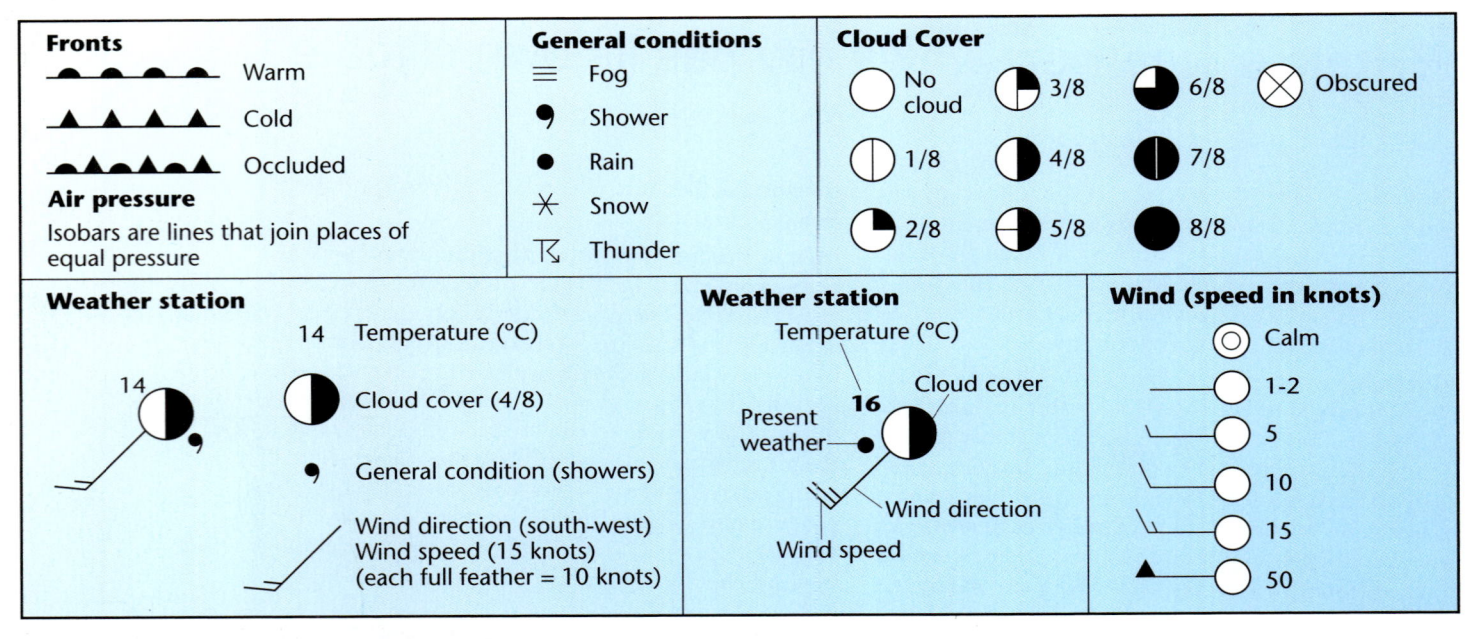

Fronts		General conditions		Cloud Cover							
⌒⌒⌒	Warm	≡	Fog	○	No cloud	◐	3/8	◕	6/8	⊗	Obscured
▲▲▲	Cold	9	Shower	◔	1/8	◐	4/8	◕	7/8		
⌒▲⌒▲	Occluded	●	Rain	◔	2/8	◐	5/8	●	8/8		

Air pressure
Isobars are lines that join places of equal pressure

General conditions: ✶ Snow, ⚡ Thunder

Weather station

- 14 Temperature (°C)
- Cloud cover (4/8)
- General condition (showers)
- Wind direction (south-west)
- Wind speed (15 knots) (each full feather = 10 knots)

Weather station

- Temperature (°C)
- Cloud cover
- Present weather
- Wind direction
- Wind speed

Wind (speed in knots)

- ⊙ Calm
- 1-2
- 5
- 10
- 15
- 50

A – Weather symbols and a weather station

B – Satellite image of a depression

Factfile

- *All air is under pressure.*
- *Average air pressure at sea-level is 1013 millibars (mb).*
- *Air moves from an area of high pressure to one of low pressure.*
- *An **isobar** is a line on a synoptic chart joining places of equal air pressure.*
- *The closer isobars are together, the stronger the wind.*
- *A **weather front** is the leading edge of a block of air.*

6 Weather hazards

Depressions (low-pressure systems)

Depressions develop over the North Atlantic Ocean where warm moist air from the south meets cold polar air from the north (C). The boundary where these two air masses meet is called a *front*. The warm front is the leading edge of a block of warmer air. Behind it comes the cold front, the leading edge of a block of colder air. Winds in a depression blow anticlockwise in the northern hemisphere, getting stronger as they move towards the low-pressure centre. At the front the warmer air is forced to rise above the cooler air and condensation occurs, often causing clouds and frontal rain. Where the cold front catches up with the warm front it is known as an *occluded front*. Because depressions are made up of air masses of different temperatures, the weather can be very unsettled, with strong winds and heavy rainfall (D).

C – Features of a depression

The passage of a depression

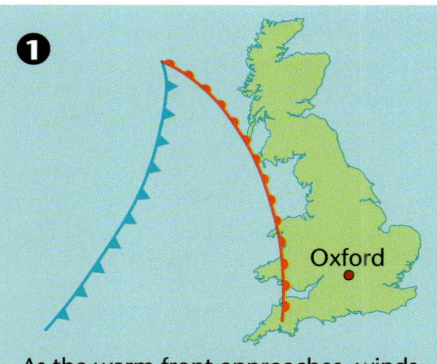

① As the warm front approaches, winds increase from the south west and clouds begin to form. When the warm front passes, the temperature rises and winds increase. Clouds are dense and rain falls steadily.

② Oxford is now in the warm sector and temperatures are slightly higher. Winds decrease. Skies are clearer with some broken cloud and light drizzle. Strong winds blow from the south-west.

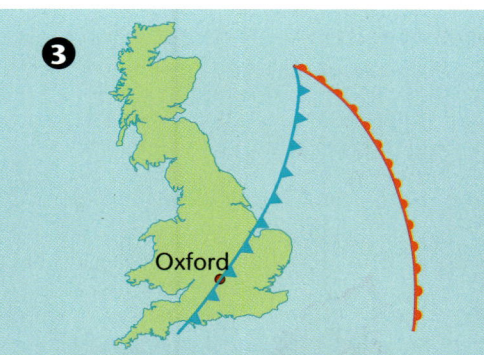

③ As the cold front approaches, the temperature falls. Dense clouds begin to appear and heavy rain falls, accompanied by thunder and lightning. Strong winds blow in from the north-west.

D – The passage of a depression across Oxford

Questions

1 Describe the weather conditions at the following weather stations:

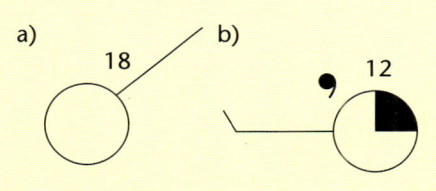

a) 18

b) 12

2 Look at E.
   a) Name the features at A, B and C.
   b) Describe the weather conditions at weather stations D and E.
   c) How is the weather in London likely to change in the next 24 hours?

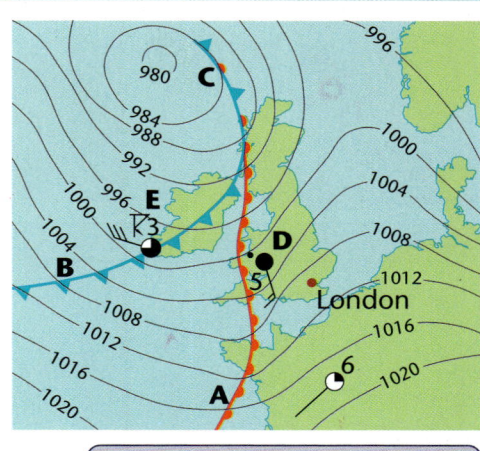

E – Synoptic chart for a winter day

Managing the Physical Environment

6.3 Anticyclones: high-pressure systems

Anticyclones are areas of high pressure where air is descending so the weather is stable with clear skies and little or no wind. In the northern hemisphere the air drifts outwards from the anticyclone in a clockwise direction (**C**).

In the summer an anticyclone brings long periods of hot weather with clear skies and gentle breezes (**A–B**). In extreme cases this can cause a summer heatwave and problems of drought, as it did in the British Isles in 1995 when there was virtually no rain for the whole of August.

In the winter, the clear skies can produce warm, sunny days, but at night temperatures fall rapidly and frosts are likely.

A – Typical summer anticyclonic conditions

B – Satellite image of an anticyclone over the British Isles

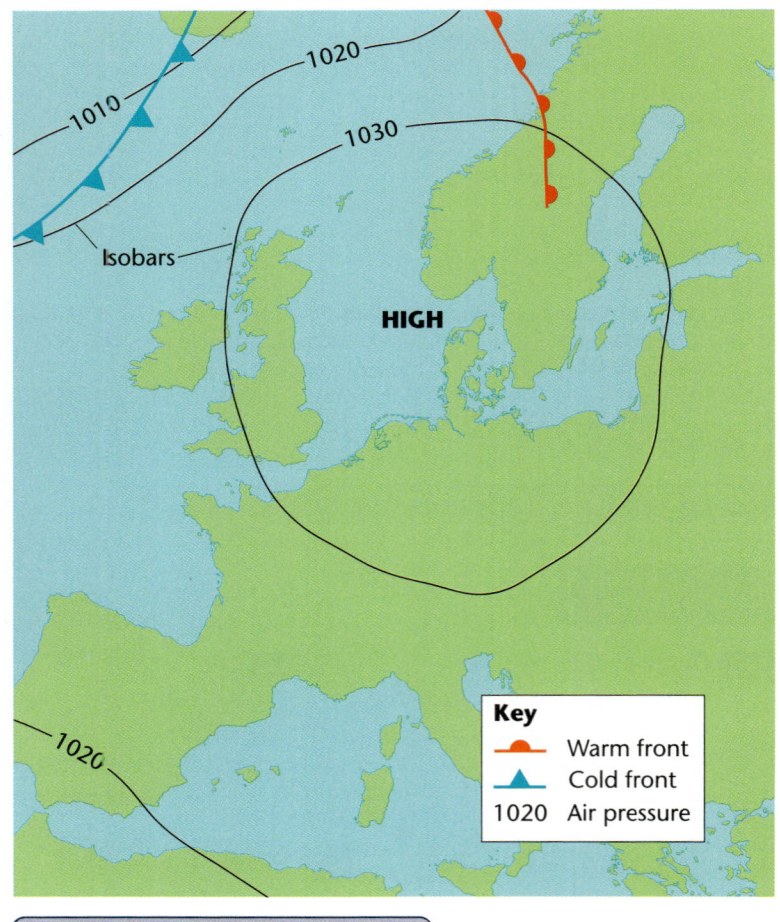

C – Synoptic chart for an anticyclone

Key
- Warm front
- Cold front
- 1020 Air pressure

6 Weather hazards

Newspaper weather reports

Newspapers use different symbols to describe the conditions of the weather. These are often in colour and are more visual. Figure **D** is an example of a newspaper weather report.

Situation at noon today

Low P will fill as it drifts south-east. High A will intensify and transfer northwards.

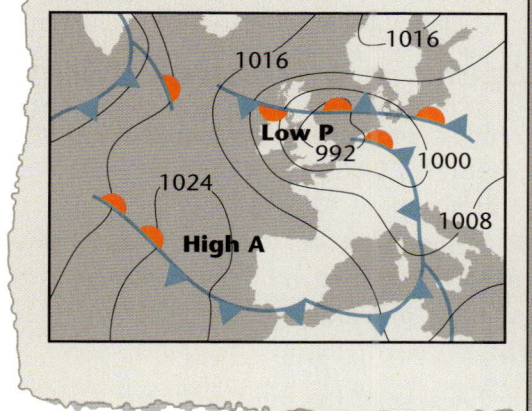

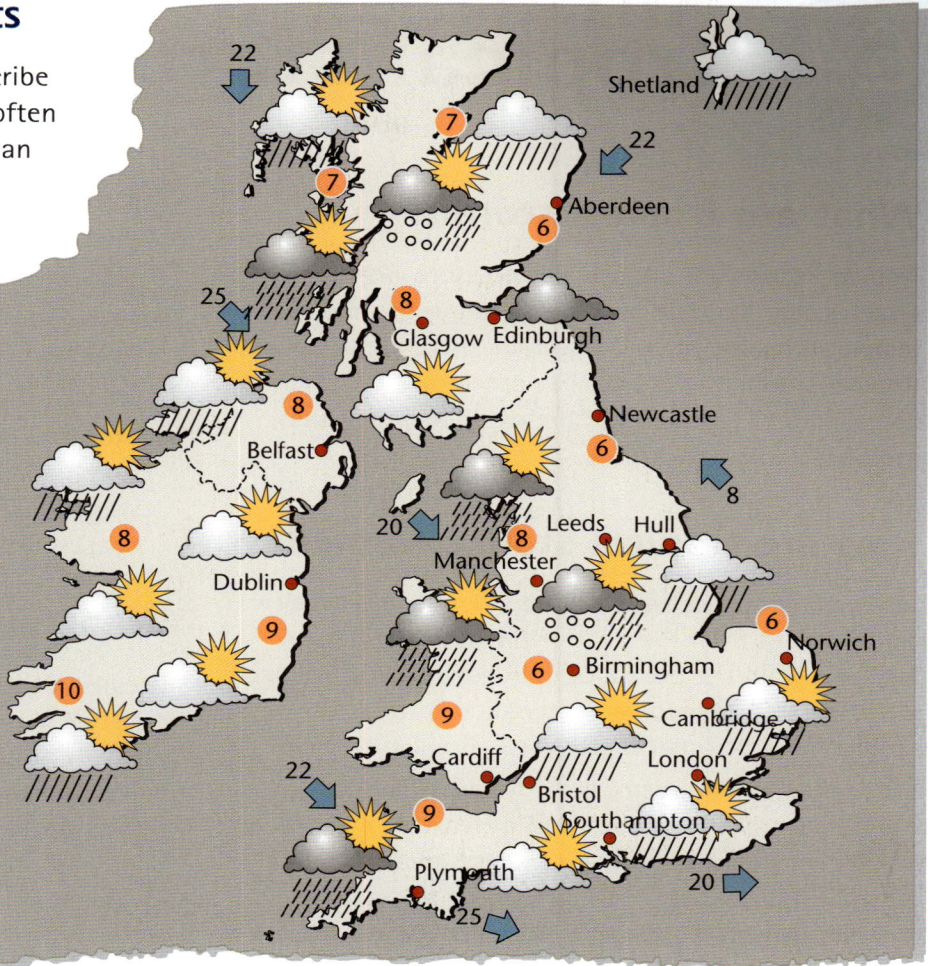

D – A newspaper weather map

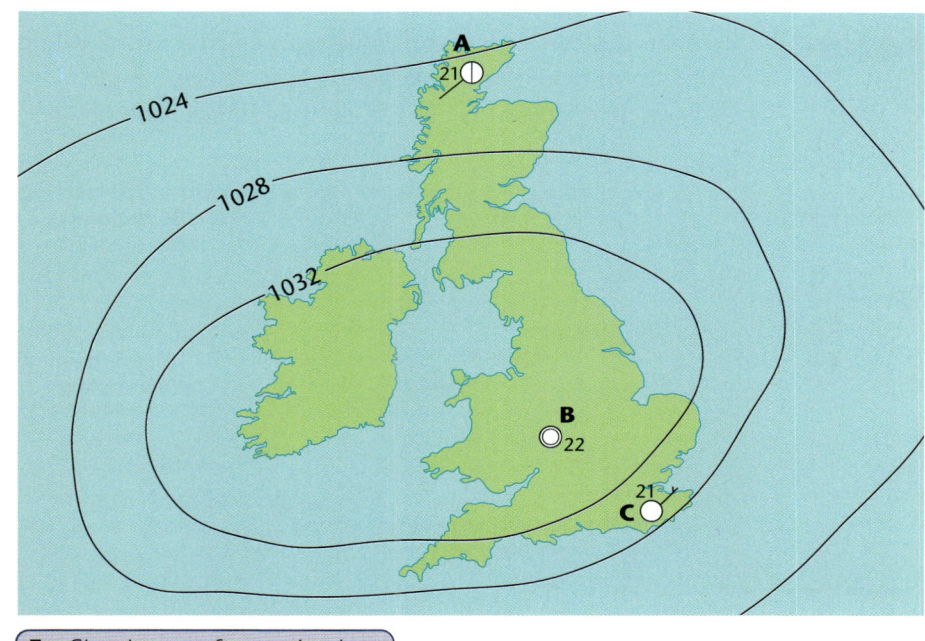

E – Sketch map of an anticyclone

Questions

1 Look at E.
  a) i) Describe the conditions at weather stations A, B and C.
     ii) Why is there unlikely to be any rainfall?
  b) Describe and explain the weather associated with an anticyclone:
     i) in summer
     ii) in winter.

2 Using D:
  a) Describe the weather in:
     • north-west Scotland
     • East Anglia (Norwich/Cambridge area).
  b) Why do newspapers not use the official weather chart symbols?

6.4 Tropical storms

What are tropical storms?

Tropical storms are intense low-pressure weather systems that build up near the Equator where ocean temperatures are high. On average there are about 60 tropical storms each year. They are known by different names in different parts of the world as **hurricanes**, **cyclones** and **typhoons** (**A**).

How are tropical storms formed?

Tropical storms contain massive amounts of energy which comes from the heat of the atmosphere and moisture from the ocean. Certain conditions have been identified as common characteristics in the development of tropical storms:

- ocean temperatures of more than 27°C
- warm-water ocean depths of at least 70m
- high levels of heat causing violent updrafts of air
- high levels of humidity
- major winds all blowing in the same direction.

These characteristics tend to occur at certain times of the year, usually in late summer or early autumn.

What is the tropical storm hazard?

- *Strong winds* Winds reaching 200km/h are quite common. These winds can tear up vegetation and push over electricity pylons. Buildings may be damaged, and in poorer areas whole towns can be devastated.
- *Heavy rainfall* Heavy rainfall can rapidly increase river levels and cause flooding. On steeper slopes there is the risk of landslides.
- *Storm surges* The low pressure means that sea-level is very high. The strong winds create huge waves, which push towards coastal areas causing extensive coastal flooding.

What happens in a tropical storm?

Because of the high temperatures, massive amounts of moisture are evaporated from the ocean and this rises rapidly into the atmosphere. When this warmer air meets cooler air at high altitude, it condenses to form clouds. As the warmer air rises, more air is sucked in to take its place and this provides the source of energy for the storm (**B**).

The storm spirals because of the rotation of the Earth. The air is thrown outwards from the centre, while the eye remains calm as warmer air descends (**B**). The general wind pattern moves the storm towards land where it often does most damage in coastal areas. When the storm begins to move across land its source of energy (the ocean) is cut off, so it begins to lose power.

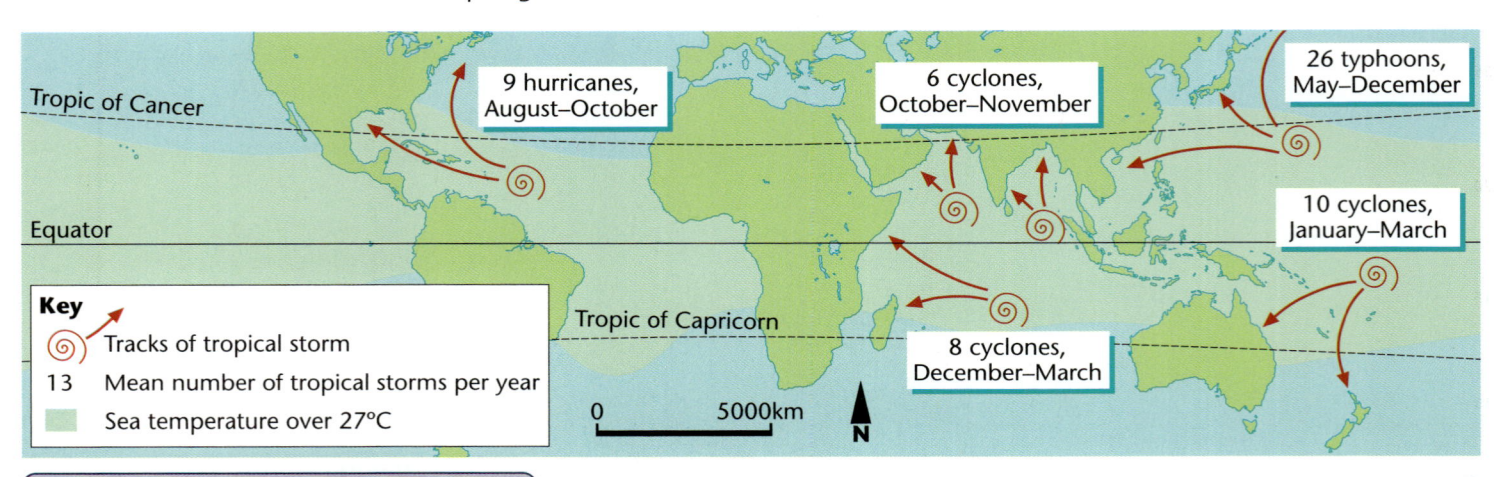

Key
- Tracks of tropical storm
- 13 Mean number of tropical storms per year
- Sea temperature over 27°C

- 9 hurricanes, August–October
- 6 cyclones, October–November
- 26 typhoons, May–December
- 10 cyclones, January–March
- 8 cyclones, December–March

A – *Location and frequency of tropical storms*

6 Weather hazards

Can tropical storms be predicted?

Because tropical storms are a regular event and occur within particular areas, it is possible to predict and prepare for them. Warning systems can monitor storm developments and try to forecast the strength and direction of movement. This is done in several ways:

- There is constant satellite monitoring by the National Hurricane Center in Florida (USA), which identifies the formation of storms and tracks their path and strength.
- Colorado State University (USA) and University College (London) constantly monitor ocean temperatures and the global climate to see when tropical storm conditions are developing.

Despite modern scientific methods, prediction is not easy because the strength and direction of a tropical storm can change quickly. More money is being spent on improving early warning systems, evacuation plans and flood defence schemes.

Although tropical storms affect both MEDCs and LEDCs, often the poorer countries do not have the money and technology to predict or prepare for them.

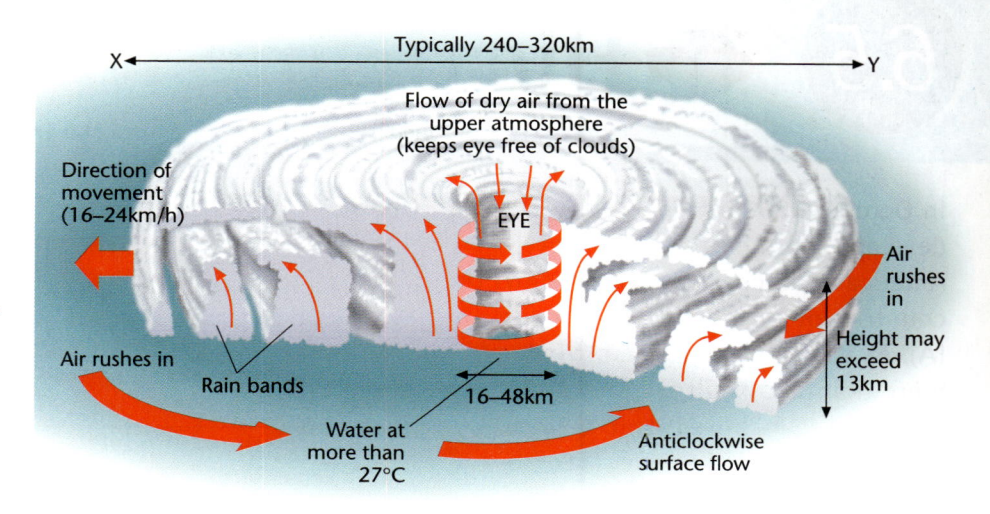

B – Development of a tropical storm

Questions

Hurricane Andrew developed in the Atlantic Ocean in August 1992. Its path was monitored for 10 days as it moved towards the USA. The table gives the position of the eye of the storm.

August	Latitude	Longitude
18	14°N	54°W
19	17°N	56°W
20	20°N	59°W
21	22°N	62°W
22	24°N	65°W
23	24°N	72°W
24	24°N	78°W
25	26°N	85°W
26	28°N	91°W
27	32°N	92°W

1 On a copy of C:
 a) Plot the path of the hurricane, using the co-ordinates given.
 b) Shade in an area equal to one grid-square's width on either side of the path – this is the area of possible damage.
 c) Describe the path of the hurricane.
 d) Explain why the hurricane began to die down after 27 August.

2 Why is predicting tropical storms difficult?

3 Why is it important to try to predict tropical storms?

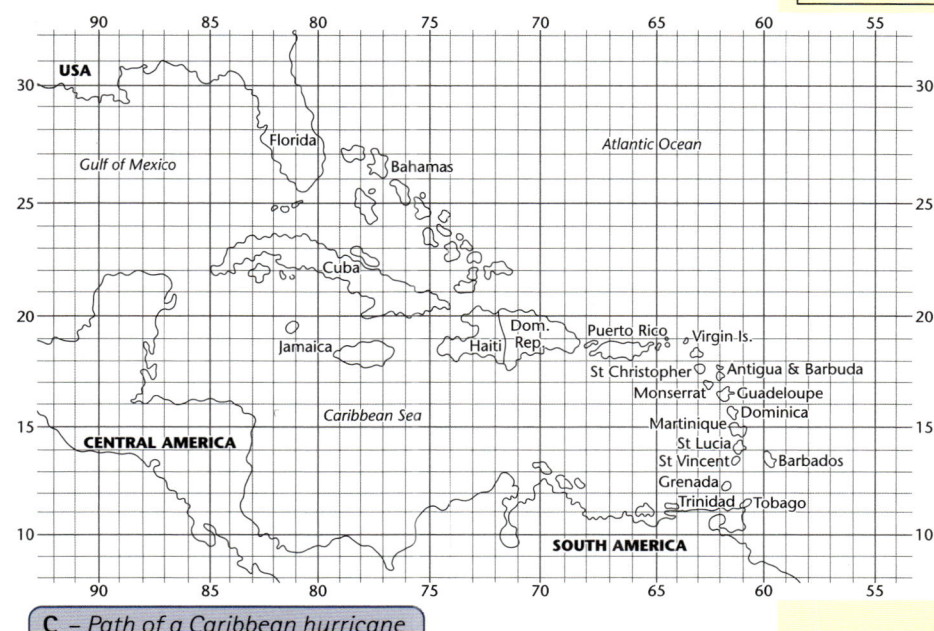

C – Path of a Caribbean hurricane

Managing the Physical Environment

6.5 cs Hurricane Mitch, 1998

In October 1998 a tropical storm developed to the east of Central America and began moving towards the countries of Nicaragua and Honduras (A). As it reached the coast, winds of more than 280 km/h were recorded, and torrential rain caused large areas to be flooded. Roads and bridges were washed away, and in some areas complete villages were destroyed as winds tore down the poor-quality buildings. As rain continued to fall, large areas of land quickly flooded. On steeper slopes, flash floods and mudslides buried some areas under thousands of tonnes of mud, rocks and vegetation.

The day after the hurricane, rivers in the area were ten times their normal width, and it was reported that half a million people had lost their homes, many having to be evacuated to safe areas (C).

Factfile

	Honduras	Nicaragua	Comparison with UK
Population 1998 (million)	6.3	4.8	58.6
Human Development Index (HDI)*	.57	.53	.93
Gross National Product ($ per capita)	600	380	18 700
Adult literacy (%)	73	66	99
Population/doctor	1266	2039	300

* The **Human Development Index** takes into account income, health and education. The highest possible figure is 1.0.

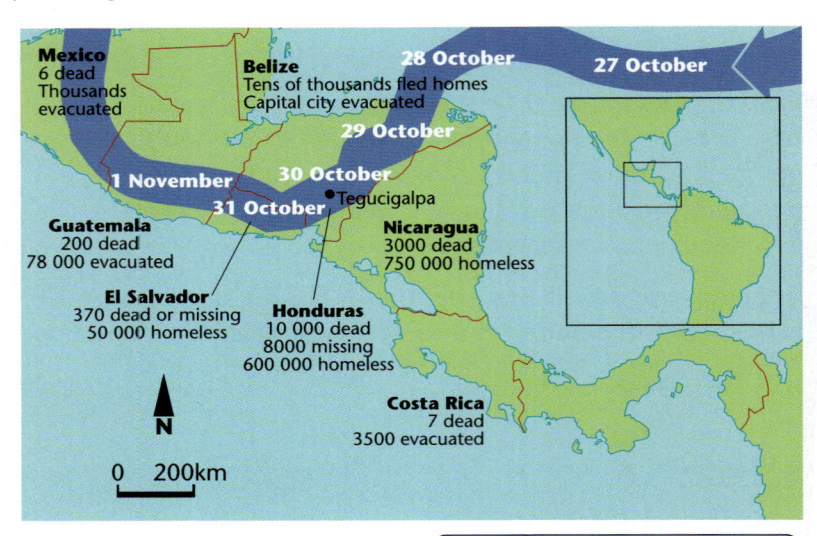

A – The path of Hurricane Mitch

The impacts of Hurricane Mitch

Honduras

- Final death toll over 17 000.
- Many towns completely destroyed.
- Schools, roads, bridges and power lines lost.
- Over 70 per cent of the year's crops ruined, leading to food shortages.
- Around 600 000 people forced to live in makeshift shelters.

Nicaragua

- Death toll nearly 3000.
- 20 per cent of the population made homeless.
- All main roads out of the capital city destroyed.
- 20 per cent of all farms ruined.

Could the impacts have been reduced?

Honduras and Nicaragua are two of the poorest countries in Central America, and they do not have the money or technology to prepare for hurricanes. However, some people have suggested that the disaster was made worse because:

- many towns had no proper storm drains
- homes were poorly constructed
- villages were built on steep hills or unstable slopes
- deforestation may have left slopes bare, increasing the possibility of landslides.

6 Weather hazards

C – Evacuation of people following the hurricane

Questions

1 Natural disasters have *primary* or immediate effects, and *secondary* or longer-term effects.
  a) Describe the primary and secondary effects of Hurricane Mitch.
  b) Use **B** to explain why the secondary effects might be more significant in LEDCs.

2 How might human actions have made the disaster worse?

Mud havoc hampers rescue
From David Adams in Managua

AS RESCUERS searched yesterday for more victims of Central America's worst storm, the relief effort in Nicaragua and Honduras was severely hampered because collapsed roads and bridges effectively paralysed transport.

Both countries, where an estimated 7000 people died as a result of Hurricane Mitch, have small airforces with only half a dozen helicopters shuttling to and from the disaster areas to bring in emergency supplies and rescue stranded villagers. The authorities fear outbreaks of cholera and malaria, and planned to burn victims' bodies yesterday to cut the risk of disease. 'We are trying to organize delivery of food and medical supplies to worst-hit areas,' said Pedro Joaquin Chamorro, the Nicaraguan Defence Minister. 'But there are so many towns and villages cut off that we don't have the physical capacity to deliver all that is needed. It's the worst calamity this country has ever suffered. The whole country is a shambles.'

The heavy rains washed away roads to the cities of Leon and Chinandega in the north-west, as well as hundreds of small towns and hamlets. Señor Chamorro said it would take at least a week for army construction teams to repair the roads and replace destroyed bridges.

Hundreds of towns and villages have been without food and drinking water for several days. Thousands made homeless have begun walking along country roads trying to reach larger towns in search of food and medicine.

In northern Honduras, large banana plantations which provide one of the country's largest export crops, were virtually wiped out.

In Nicaragua, the Pan American Highway, the main road north from Managua, the capital, was crowded with people trying to leave the disaster area on foot. Others went in the opposite direction, searching for relatives.

B – From The Times, 4 November 1998

6.6 Rebuilding Nicaragua after Hurricane Mitch

After Hurricane Mitch, much of Nicaragua was devastated (**A**) and the country had a number of emergency needs because of:

- the *threat of disease* as a result of damage to the water supply system
- *food and medicine shortages* because crops had been destroyed and medical reserves used up
- *damage to the infrastructure* because roads and bridges had been destroyed
- *homelessness* caused by the destruction of thousands of homes.

Short-term aid was given to Nicaragua to deal with the initial problems of food and medical shortages.

Much of the longer-term aid was provided by the World Bank, the world's largest source of development assistance. The World Bank was set up in 1947 to provide aid to developing countries in the form of loans and technical assistance. Its aim is to reduce poverty and give people the opportunity to improve their living standards.

Figure **A** describes some of the impacts of the hurricane and the ways in which the World Bank responded.

Rebuilding Nicaragua after Hurricane Mitch

Hurricane Mitch was the most destructive hurricane of the past 200 years. It left 2 million homeless and caused an estimated $10 billion of damage. The United Nations World Food Programme estimates Hurricane Mitch has set back development in Central America by at least ten years.

Although many countries in Central America were affected, Nicaragua was amongst those most badly hit. While Hurricane Mitch did not remain headline news for long, its effects are still being felt today. Initial emergency aid is extremely important in the short term, but long-term help is also needed. In Nicaragua, the storm destroyed everything from homes and power lines to roads and schools. The motorway linking Honduras, Nicaragua and Costa Rica was crushed and villages surrounding it were destroyed.

'Life came to a complete stop. Initially, children couldn't get to school, people couldn't go to the market or anywhere else, and trade came to a standstill.' (Nicolette Bowyer, the World Bank's country officer for Nicaragua)

Rebuilding the roads

In the months that followed Hurricane Mitch, a $25 million World Bank-supported project was introduced to help rebuild the roads. This was one of a number of World Bank projects to rebuild schools, health clinics, roads and bridges. The World Bank also provided money for environmental management and protection against the effects of future natural disasters.

The road project created new jobs and new ways of doing business in the country. The World Bank encouraged workers to form teams and set up their own small businesses to repair the roads. These teams then competed against one another to get the work done.

After six months of hard work the roads were rebuilt.

Rebuilding the schools

Meanwhile, another aspect of rebuilding Nicaragua was the need to rebuild schools, train teachers and provide school books after countless schools were destroyed by the storms. In Nicaragua, many of the school books used today will have been made available with money from the World Bank. 'The World Bank has financed the purchase of nearly 4.7 million textbooks and 4.3 million workbooks distributed to nearly 850 000 primary school students in Nicaragua.' (Robin Horn, who manages the World Bank's Basic Education Programme)

Raising the standards of education is a crucial part of reducing poverty in Nicaragua, where over one-fifth of the population (10 years or older) cannot read or write. The World Bank granted a $52.5 million loan to help increase the numbers of children who can go to school. The new project gives money to areas that have previously been neglected. The project will also fund training for teachers, set up school libraries and nursery schools, and repair buildings that were damaged by Hurricane Mitch.

A – Rebuilding a country

Hurricane Georges, 1998

In September 1998, Hurricane Georges swept through the northern Caribbean, before moving towards the USA and finally dying out over the southern states of the USA (C). The newspaper article in (D) describes the effects of the hurricane as it moved across the less economically developed Caribbean islands towards the USA.

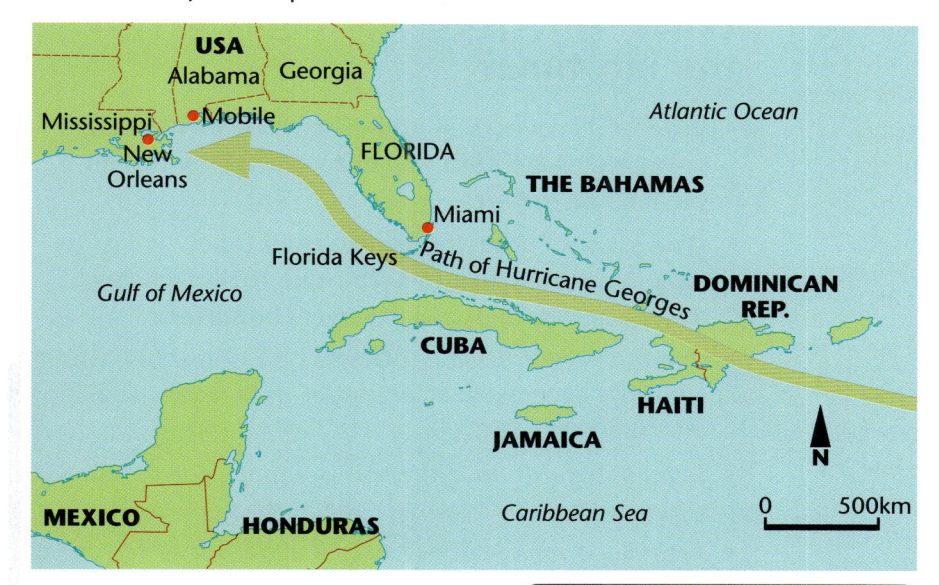

B – Damage caused by Hurricane Georges

C – The path of Hurricane Georges

Millions take to the road as storm sweeps north towards USA
Giles Whittel writes from Houston

AFTER decades of near misses, New Orleans found itself the prime target of Hurricane Georges yesterday.

Officials ordered large-scale evacuations, with 1.5 million inhabitants asked to leave … The Red Cross was prepared with dozens of shelters to house up to 35 000 left temporarily homeless by the storm. It was southern Louisiana's fourth weather-related evacuation order in a month … No casualties were reported in Florida, in contrast to the death toll of more than 300 in the Dominican Republic. But Hurricane Georges still destroyed entire mobile home parks and left furniture and boats strewn across main roads.

Coast evacuated as Hurricane Georges hits Florida

HURRICANE Georges barrelled deep into the Gulf of Mexico yesterday, leaving a trail of sunken houseboats, twisted trees and tangled power lines in the Florida Keys.

Last night the storm, which had left over 300 people dead as it tore across the Caribbean, forced the evacuation of coastal areas in Alabama and [Mississippi] …

A hurricane watch was issued for more than 425 miles of coastline, from Florida to [Mississippi] …

No deaths were reported in Florida, where 1.4m people were ordered to evacuate … The worst-hit areas remained Haiti and the Dominican Republic … More than 80% of food crops in the impoverished countries have been wiped out by the hurricane in the past week. More than 100 000 people have been left homeless in the Dominican Republic alone …

D – From The Times, 28 September 1998

Storm hit town…
from David Adams in the Dominican Republic

Almost a week after Hurricane Georges ripped through this tropical port city on the south coast of the Dominican Republic, leaving five dead and thousands homeless, its 300 000 residents are still waiting for assistance.

As in much of the south of the country, where at least 200 people were killed by Georges and scores are missing, San Pedro remains without electricity or running water.

"As the days go by the situation is getting worse. The city is totally destroyed," said Marie Jimenez, the head of the city council.

Hurricane debris lies in piles beside city streets, but no one seems to be collecting it. In the Plaza Duarte, the city's once shady, palm-lined central square, trees lie where they fell. Across the street, neon shops signs dangle perilously over the pavement.

Food and bottled water are scarce and prices have almost doubled for many items. The hurricane damaged 34 000 homes in the city – about 80 percent of dwellings. Schools are still closed and are not likely to reopen soon, since many classrooms have been occupied by homeless families. The city's only hospital can barely function on a faulty generator, and Senor Jimenez fears the outbreak of diseases on an epidemic scale.

Questions

1. What problems did Nicaragua have after Hurricane Mitch? Why was short-term aid needed?
2. Describe the main projects that were used to rebuild Nicaragua. Explain the importance of these projects to Nicaragua.
3. Use the articles in D to explain why tropical storms can have different effects on MEDCs and LEDCs.

6.7 The hydrological cycle

Hydrology is the study of water. The **hydrological** or **water cycle** is the circulation of water between stores (oceans and lakes), the atmosphere and the land. This can be seen in **A**.

The hydrological cycle can be seen as a natural system which recycles water. At the small scale the amount of water being stored or moving around the system varies according to the climate. During a period of heavy rainfall, water levels in lakes and rivers may increase, whereas during dry periods more water is held in the atmosphere and the level of water in lakes and rivers goes down. At the global scale these factors should even themselves out over time, so water is a sustainable resource.

There are many ways that the natural water cycle can be interfered with, by changing the levels of storage, rates of flow and use of water. Some of these can be seen in **B**.

Hydrographs

Hydrographs show the relationship between rainfall and the flow of water in a river basin (**C**). After heavy rainfall some of the water will find its way into a river. If the land is very steep, rainfall may move into a river quickly, but if the land is gently sloping this may take more time. The time it takes for rainfall to reach a river is called the lag time.

What other factors might affect the lag time?

- *Vegetation cover* If an area is covered with trees or grass, water will take longer to reach a river than if the land were bare.
- *Type of rock* **Porous** rocks, like chalk, allow water to soak in slowly, while **impermeable** rocks like clay allow water to flow quickly over the surface.
- *Compaction of the soil* If the soil is compacted, water will flow over the surface rather than slowly soaking into the ground.
- *Level of saturation* If the soil is already saturated, water is likely to flow over the surface.
- *Artificial drains* Artificial drains allow water to reach streams and rivers quickly.
- *Type of surface* Rain falling on grass will soak in slowly, whereas on concrete or tarmac it flows quickly over the surface.

A – The hydrological cycle

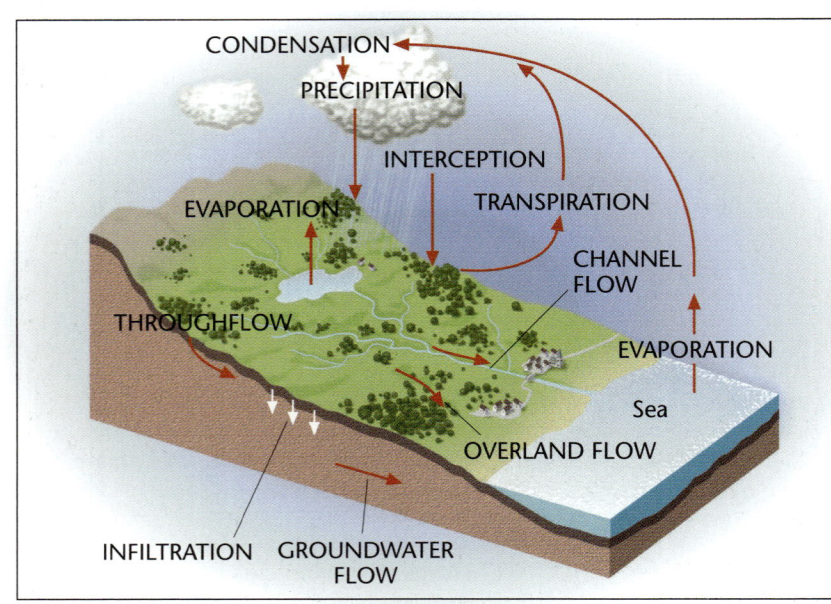

Channel flow	Movement of water in streams and rivers.
Condensation	Water vapour turning into water droplets.
Evaporation	Water turning into water vapour.
Groundwater flow	Movement of water underground through rocks.
Infiltration	Seeping of water into the soil.
Interception	Collection of water by vegetation.
Overland flow	Flow of water over the Earth's surface.
Precipitation	All water that falls to Earth.
Throughflow	Movement of water through the soil.
Transpiration	Loss of moisture from plants.

6 Weather hazards

B – The human water cycle

C – A hydrograph

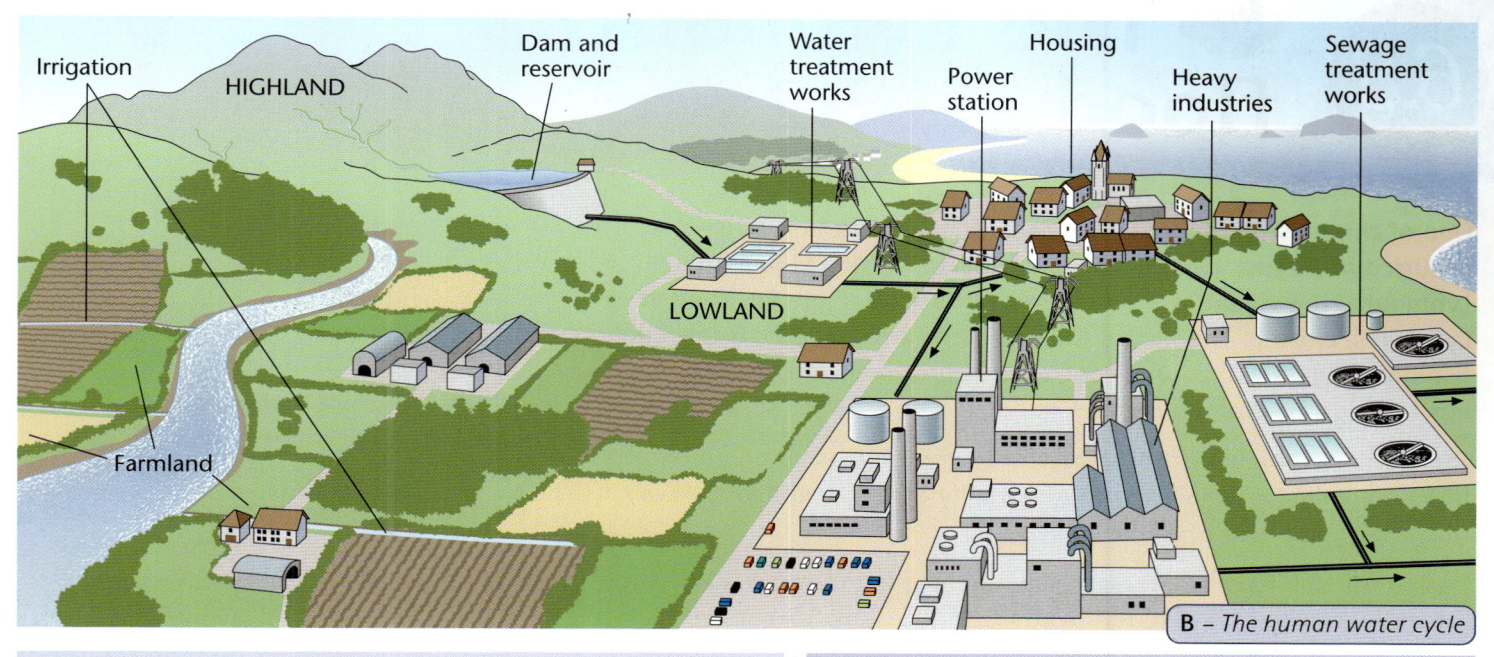

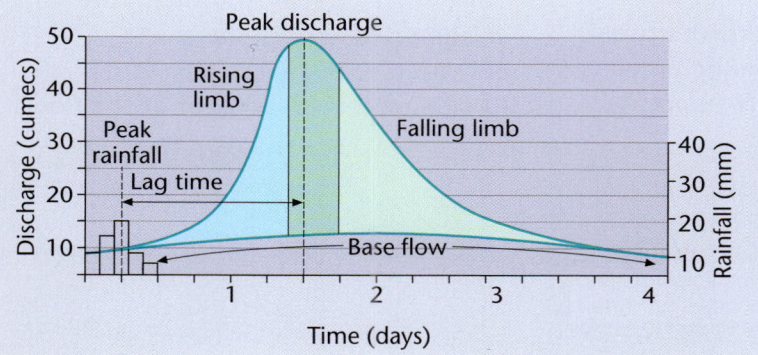

Base flow — Normal flow of the river.
Cumecs — Cubic metres per second.
Discharge — The amount of water in the river.
Falling limb — Decreasing water in the river.
Lag time — Time between the highest rainfall and the highest (peak) discharge.
Rising limb — Increasing water in the river.

How can urbanization change the natural flow of rivers?

- Vegetation is replaced with tarmac and concrete.
- Artificial drains are put in, replacing natural streams.
- Rivers are straightened and road drains are fed into them.
- Artificial banks are built alongside rivers, stopping them from flooding.
- Streams are made to flow through pipes underground.

Questions

1. Describe and explain the ways that the natural water cycle can be changed by human development.

2. Use the following data to draw a hydrograph for a British river over 12 days. Mark the discharge figure in the centre of each day.

Day	1	2	3	4	5	6	7	8	9	10	11	12
Precipitation (mm)	0	10	20	10	0	0	25	20	10	0	0	0
Discharge (cumecs)	20	30	35	50	60	55	60	80	90	70	60	40

a) i) Mark on your graph the two storms.
   ii) Mark and label the lag times for each storm.
   iii) Mark on the rising and falling limbs.
b) Give two reasons why the discharge was higher after the second storm.
c) If the normal flow of the river is 40 cumecs, and the banks of the river are only high enough to cope with a discharge of 70 cumecs, what happened after the second storm?
d) Why might hydrographs be useful in managing rivers?

3. a) How might urbanization increase the risks of flooding?
   b) What could be done to reduce flood risks in urban areas?

Managing the Physical Environment

6.8 The Lynmouth flood, 1952

One of the most dramatic river floods ever to affect the British Isles occurred in August 1952 in the north Devon fishing village of Lynmouth. The village is built at the confluence of the East and West Lyn rivers, close to the Bristol Channel. It had developed as a small fishing village and a tourist centre for holidaymakers exploring the north Devon coastal areas and Exmoor.

There were a number of reasons why Lynmouth was vulnerable to flooding, including the physical geography of the area and the way that the village had been developed (B).

During August 1952 there was exceptionally high rainfall (C) and the ground became saturated. Rainwater began to flow across the surface of the land directly into the river, turning it into a torrent of fast-flowing water and mud. The water was channelled into the narrow valley and the force was so great that large boulders and uprooted trees were pushed down the valley. This material became trapped behind the small bridges across the valley, creating artificial 'dams'. Eventually the bridges gave way under the pressure, sending a wave of water, mud and boulders down the valley at more than 30km/h. Estimates suggest that the height of this water was nearly 15m, and as it moved through the village on its way to the sea it destroyed nearly everything in its path (D). Figure E is an account of the flood.

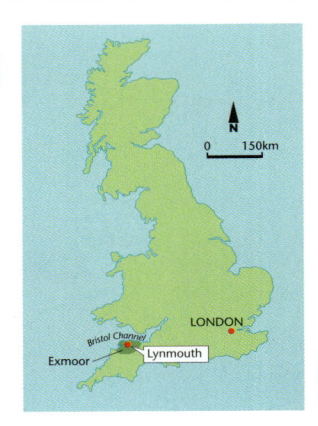

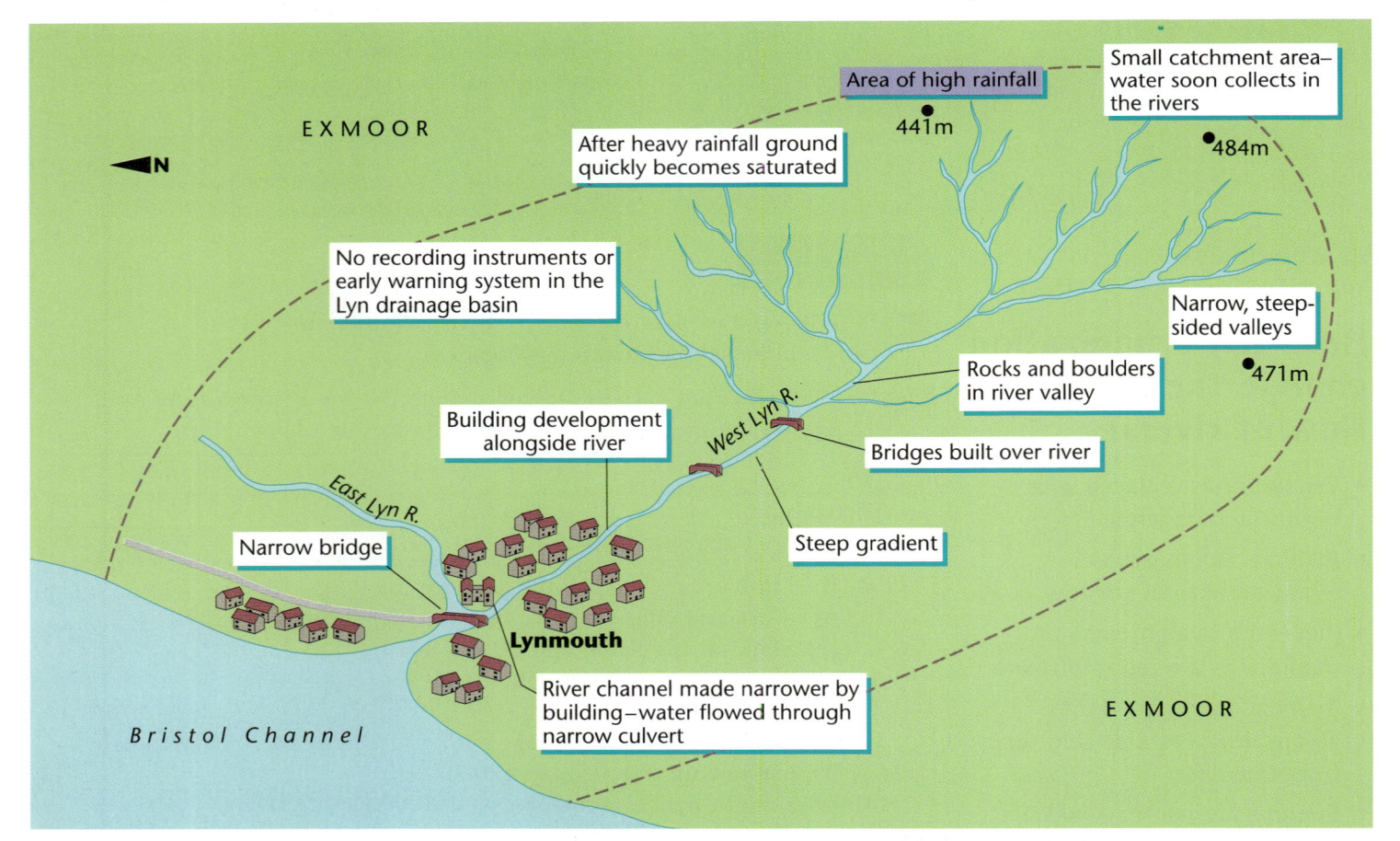

A – Location of Lynmouth

B – Why Lynmouth was vulnerable to flooding

6 Weather hazards

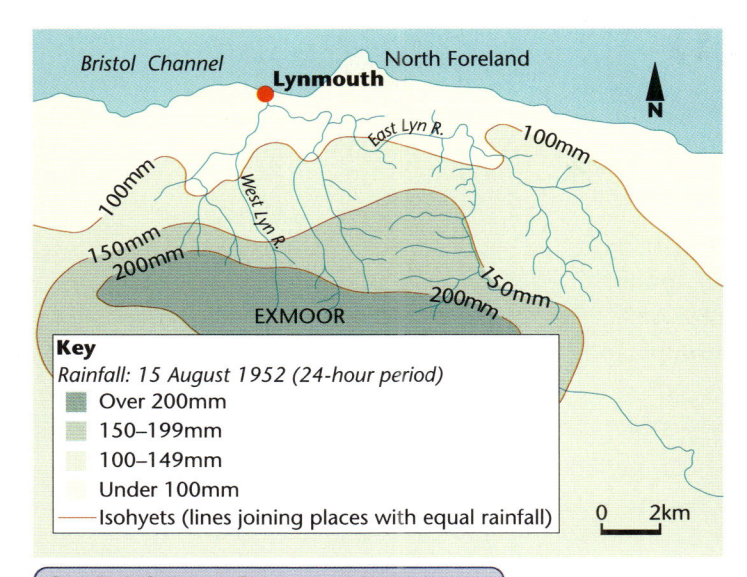

C – Rainfall over Exmoor, 15 August 1952

D – Devastation in Lynmouth

Managing the River Lyn after the flood

After the flood the rebuilding of the village was carried out in conjunction with a local flood action plan. The aim of the plan was to make sure the area could cope with exceptional levels of heavy rainfall and that such a disaster would never happen again. Today, Lynmouth looks very different (**F**), and since the flood of 1952 it has managed to cope with many periods of heavy rainfall without serious effects.

'It had rained constantly for nearly three weeks and the level of water in the river was already high. On the 15th August we had more rain in one day than I had ever known. I was told later that it was one of the heaviest falls of rain ever recorded in 24 hours. In the evening the level of the river began to rise rapidly – it was thought that the bridges up the valley had collapsed. Trees and boulders were sweeping through the high street and smashing everything in their path. The water rose so quickly that houses filled up within minutes and people had no time to get out of their homes and get to higher land. From the higher land you could see lights in the cottages going out as the water rose and could only imagine the horror of the people trapped inside. At 1.20 a.m. a violent roar was heard above the general noise -- in the morning it was realized that it must have been the time when all the main buildings collapsed and were swept out to sea...'

E – Adapted from The Sunday Times, 31 August 1997

F – Lynmouth in the 21st century

Questions

1. Explain why the causes of the flood are described as both 'natural' and 'human'.

2. *Either:* 'The Lynmouth flood killed 34 people and destroyed 90 homes. More than 130 cars were swept out to sea.' Using this as an opening statement, write a description of the flood. *Or:* Use **D** and **E** to help you describe the impacts of the flood.

3. After the flood: the height of the river banks was increased; the bridges were bigger; the river was straightened; land on the river banks was left undeveloped. Explain how these measures might reduce the risk of flooding in future.

Managing the Physical Environment

6.9 Flooding in Bangladesh

Bangladesh (A) is affected by two types of flood:

- *River floods*, which happen every year, depositing millions of tonnes of fine silt at the mouth of the rivers and creating large areas of fertile agricultural land. These floods are linked to the general pattern of rainfall and melting snow in the Himalayas.
- *Coastal floods*, which are created by cyclones that build up in the Indian Ocean and move towards the Bay of Bengal. Water is funnelled towards Bangladesh and a **storm surge** develops. This may reach 7m in height, flooding large areas of land (B).

Although physical factors increase the risk of flooding, there are also a number of human influences (C).

Flood protection

While it is impossible to prevent flooding in Bangladesh, several measures have been introduced as part of the Flood Action Plan, a scheme financed by the **World Bank** in 1990. This included a number of points for action:

- *Introducing flood warning systems* — using weather satellites to warn people about cyclones and possible floods.
- *Improving urban flood protection* — installing embankments and pumps in urban areas, protecting housing, hospitals and transport networks.
- *Building embankments alongside rivers* — so that as floodwaters rise they do not flood adjacent land.
- *Constructing flood shelters (killas)* — concrete shelters built on stilts above the ground to provide safety against winds and floodwater.
- *Protecting the coastal areas* — building a coastal barrier to protect lowlands from the effect of a storm surge.

How well has the flood action plan worked?

Not all of the proposals are in place and, at £100m a year, maintenance costs are very high for one of the world's poorest countries.

A – Location of Bangladesh

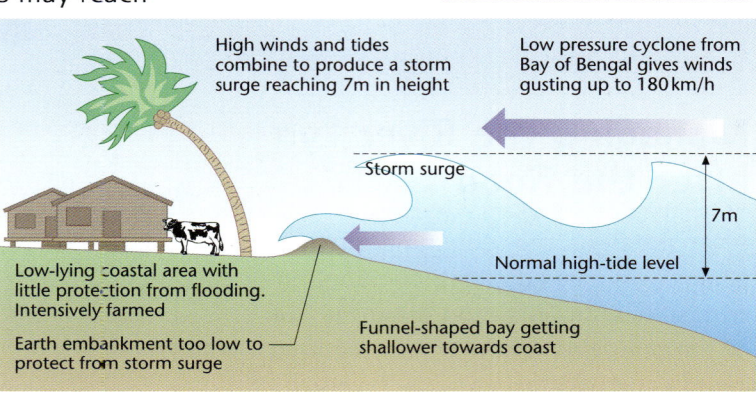

B – Effect of a storm surge on Bangladesh

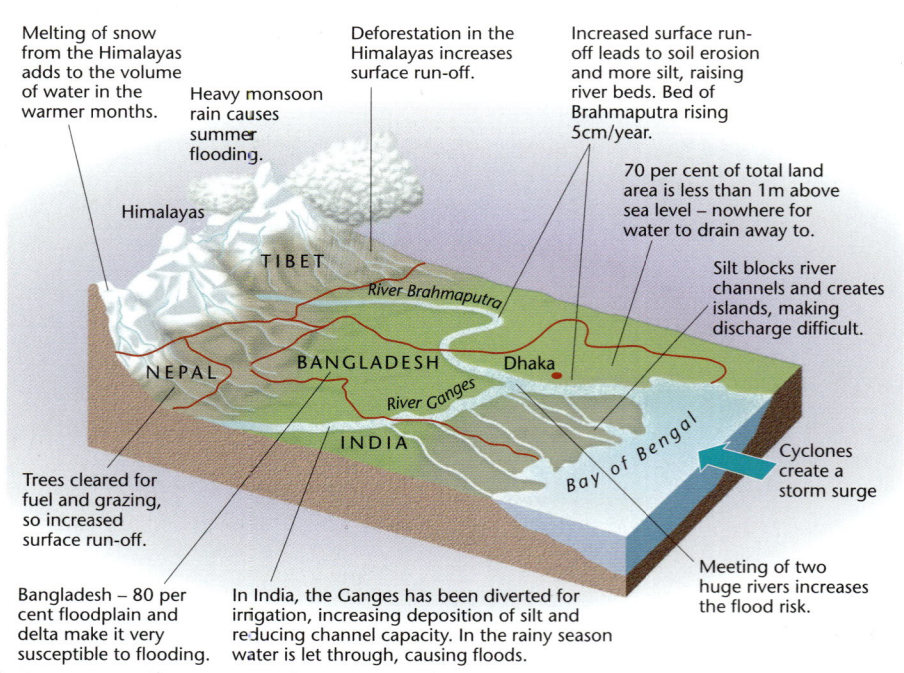

High winds and tides combine to produce a storm surge reaching 7m in height

Low pressure cyclone from Bay of Bengal gives winds gusting up to 180 km/h

Storm surge

Normal high-tide level

Low-lying coastal area with little protection from flooding. Intensively farmed

Earth embankment too low to protect from storm surge

Funnel-shaped bay getting shallower towards coast

C – Causes of flooding in Bangladesh

Melting of snow from the Himalayas adds to the volume of water in the warmer months.

Heavy monsoon rain causes summer flooding.

Deforestation in the Himalayas increases surface run-off.

Increased surface run-off leads to soil erosion and more silt, raising river beds. Bed of Brahmaputra rising 5cm/year.

70 per cent of total land area is less than 1m above sea level – nowhere for water to drain away to.

Silt blocks river channels and creates islands, making discharge difficult.

Trees cleared for fuel and grazing, so increased surface run-off.

Bangladesh – 80 per cent floodplain and delta make it very susceptible to flooding.

In India, the Ganges has been diverted for irrigation, increasing deposition of silt and reducing channel capacity. In the rainy season water is let through, causing floods.

Cyclones create a storm surge

Meeting of two huge rivers increases the flood risk.

Advantages
- The flood embankment in Dhaka appears to be reducing the effects of flooding in the city.
- The flood warning system gives some people time to prepare.
- People are more educated about what to do in the event of a flood.
- A number of shelters have been built.
- The building of embankments has created jobs.

Disadvantages
- Pumping systems do not always separate floodwater from sewage, creating problems of disease.
- Embankments create pools of stagnant water which attract mosquitoes and can lead to disease.
- Stopping water from going into one area can create flood problems elsewhere.
- The pattern of flooding has changed, and this affects the farming and fishing communities.

Managing flooding in Bangladesh is difficult and expensive, and with a growing population and the possible rise in sea-level due to global warming, the challenge is immense.

D – *People caught up in the floods*

April 1991
The cyclone has brought devastation to a region where it is difficult to make a living at the best of times. Winds of more than 225km/h and waves more than 7m in height swept over the coastal lowlands. People clung to buildings and trees, but the wind was too strong for them to hang on for long. It is estimated that nearly 200 000 people and half a million cattle have drowned. When the floods eventually subside the people will be faced with food shortages and problems of contaminated water. Thousands of hectares of crops have been lost and the fishing industry has been destroyed. Communications will take months to repair.

August 1998
The flooding has lasted nearly three months and more than half of the country is affected. At one stage, the capital city, Dhaka, was under 2m of water, and power supplies and the sewerage system collapsed. It is estimated that more than a thousand people have died, mainly from dysentery and snake bites. When the floodwater subsides there will be a massive shortage of food because the entire stock of rice has been destroyed and more than 100 000 cattle drowned.

E – *Newspaper reports on the recent floods*

Questions

1 a) Use the following data to draw a climate graph for Bangladesh:

Month	J	F	M	A	M	J	J	A	S	O	N	D
Temperature (°C)	22	24	28	32	32	30	29	30	30	29	25	24
Rainfall (mm)	10	25	40	50	140	290	320	330	250	120	40	5

b) In which months of the year are river levels likely to be highest?

2 Why do so many people live in areas that are prone to flooding in Bangladesh?

3 Draw a table like the one below and complete it by identifying the physical and human causes of flooding.

Physical	Human

4 Use D and E to describe the effects of flooding.

5 'Flood protection measures often create as many problems as they solve.' Use examples to explain this statement.

Managing the Physical Environment

6.10 The autumn 2000 floods in the British Isles

Between October and December 2000, the British Isles were affected by a series of depressions moving in from the Atlantic Ocean. This can be seen on **B**. These depressions brought strong winds and record rainfall to many areas (**A** and **C**). Several **tornadoes** were reported along the south coast, and in some areas large trees were blown down and bridges damaged.

Weather station	October 2000 total (mm)	Previous record (mm)	Records began
Linton-on-Ouse (North Yorks)	134.6	129.8 (1960)	1958
Bracknell (Berks)	177.8	170.9 (1987)	1962
Valley (Anglesey, North Wales)	209.2	192.5 (1987)	1941
Herstmonceux (East Sussex)	291.0	224.0 (1987)	1976

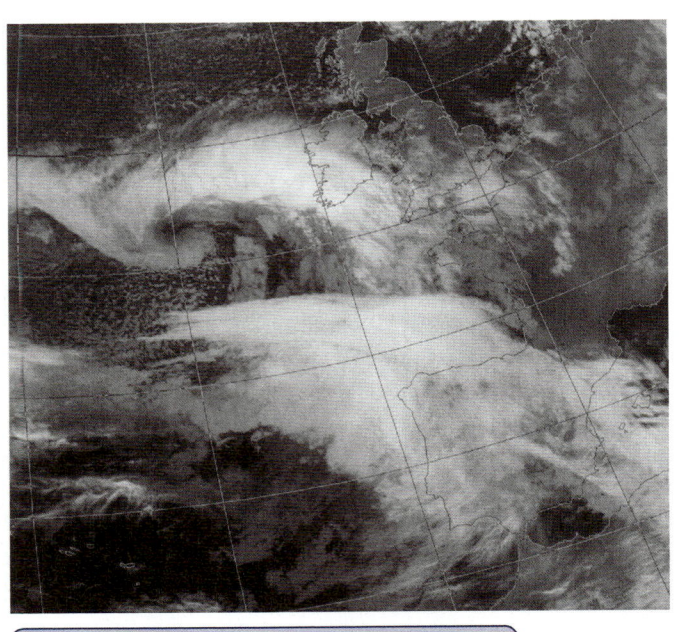

A – Record rainfall figures

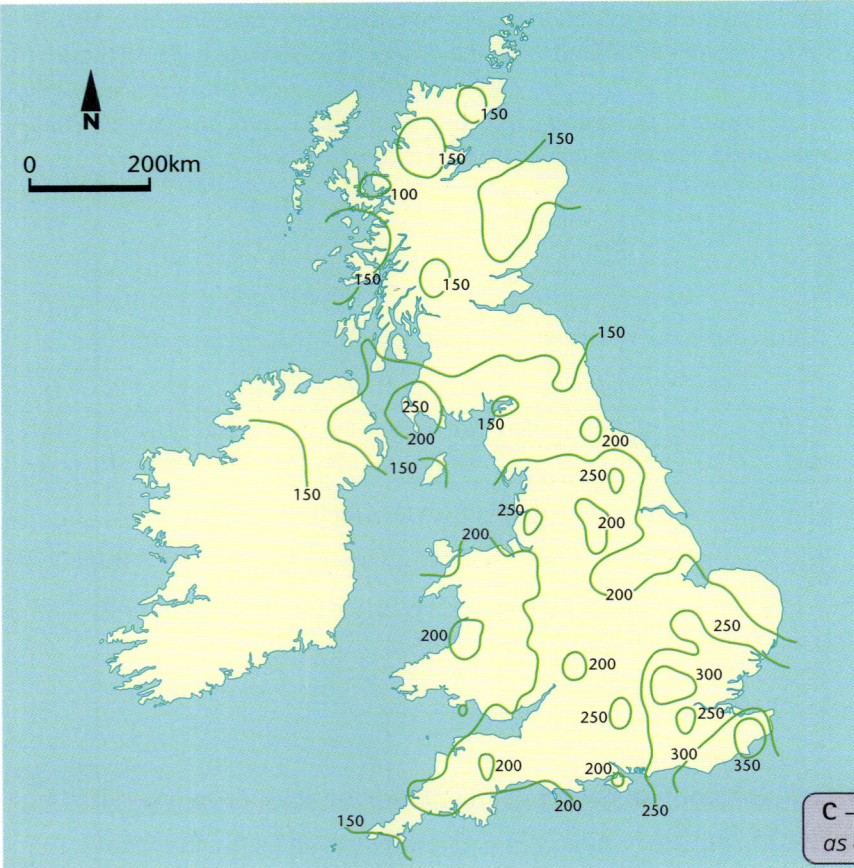

B – Satellite image of the approaching storm

The following is a weather report for 5th November:

'Heavy rain will begin falling in Cornwall, Devon and parts of Wales this morning, spreading to the rest of southern England and the Midlands by this evening. By late afternoon between 25 and 50mm of rainfall will have fallen in many parts of the country. In the worst-hit areas water levels will rise rapidly, particularly where the ground is already saturated. The heavy rain will be accompanied by gale-force winds reaching 60mph in exposed areas. Some structural damage is expected.'

C – Precipitation in October 2000 as a percentage of the average

6 Weather hazards

Has development increased the risks of flooding?

It has been suggested that development and poor planning decisions are to blame for the increased risk of flooding. This is because:

- in the last 30 years, 2 million houses have been built on floodplains
- many rivers have been straightened so that they no longer meander across meadows and marshes when water levels are high
- in urban areas, hard surfaces and drains mean that rainfall moves into the water system more quickly
- insufficient money has been spent on flood defence schemes.

D – Flood-affected areas in the UK, 5 November 2000

Map annotations:
- Scotland remains largely unaffected by the weather.
- Severe flooding in York has left the city almost cut off. Hundreds of homes have been evacuated near the rivers Ouse and Derwent.
- There are weather warnings to motorists throughout Lancashire, Cheshire and Merseyside.
- Much of the Vale of York is also under water and transport has been hit badly throughout the area. Parts of Selby are without electricity.
- The Lower Dee Valley area is at risk of severe flood warning.
- There are flood warnings around Cambridge.
- Six severe flood warnings are in place on the River Severn between Bewdley and Gloucester.
- Flooding is expected in Bath, and flood warnings still apply on the River Avon.
- Flood warnings remain in force on Somerset's four main rivers.
- The A29 to Bognor Regis remains closed due to flooding.
- The rivers Cuckmere and Rother in East Sussex, and Tiese and Rother in Kent, are under flood warnings.

E – Floods at Bewdley on the River Severn, right, and the centre of Uckfield

F – From the Sunday Mirror, 5 November 2000

As the fresh wave of storms sweeps in from the West, we will get the whole of November's rain … in just two days

THE Roman city of York miraculously escaped serious flooding by just two inches yesterday as water levels reached their highest levels since 1625.

In the Severn Valley, people have become like astronomers, searching the skies for the first signs of the coming storm.

It will first dump its rain on the Welsh mountains 100 miles to the north. Depending on its severity, fresh torrents of water will pour into the valley, boosting the flood to even more critical levels, forcing thousands more out of their homes.

In the little village of Holly Green, once a place of fragrant lanes but where now stinking water laps against cottage doors, one resident said, 'It was the suddenness that was the most terrible thing. One moment the water was a trickle under the door, the next it was climbing the walls. I marked it with a pencil. It was going up six inches an hour at its peak. The river has a power that astounds you – it's gouged out a completely new course for itself.'

Driving across the Severn plain is like visiting the aftermath of an Indian monsoon.

Questions

1. What does C suggest about the amount and pattern of rainfall in October 2000?

2. Use D, E and F to describe the effects of the floods.

3. Explain why development may have increased the risk of flooding.

Managing the Physical Environment

6.11 River management — the Mississippi, USA

At nearly 4000km long, the Mississippi River is one of the longest rivers in the world. Its source is near the Canadian border, and on its way to the Gulf of Mexico it flows through ten states. In total its drainage basin covers nearly 40 per cent of the USA, with many large cities along its route (**B**).

The Mississippi is one of the busiest inland waterways in the world. From its delta in the south, large ships can reach 200km inland. Convoys of barges are towed from this point throughout the river system as far as the northern industrial areas. New Orleans (**A**), near the Mississippi delta, is one of the busiest ports in the USA, and a wide range of agricultural and industrial goods pass through it.

The Mississippi has always flooded and it is this that has given the area its massive **floodplain** of deposited silt which creates fertile agricultural land. The river used to flow between natural **levées** (banks) which protected areas from flooding except in very wet periods. Over the years there have been a number of floods including a major flood, in 1973. Because of the risk of flooding a range of engineering schemes have been put in place to try to control the river:

- Over 300 dams have been built to control the water.
- Increases in the height and strength of the levées — at St Louis they are over 15m high and they run alongside the river for nearly 20km.

A – New Orleans, a major US port

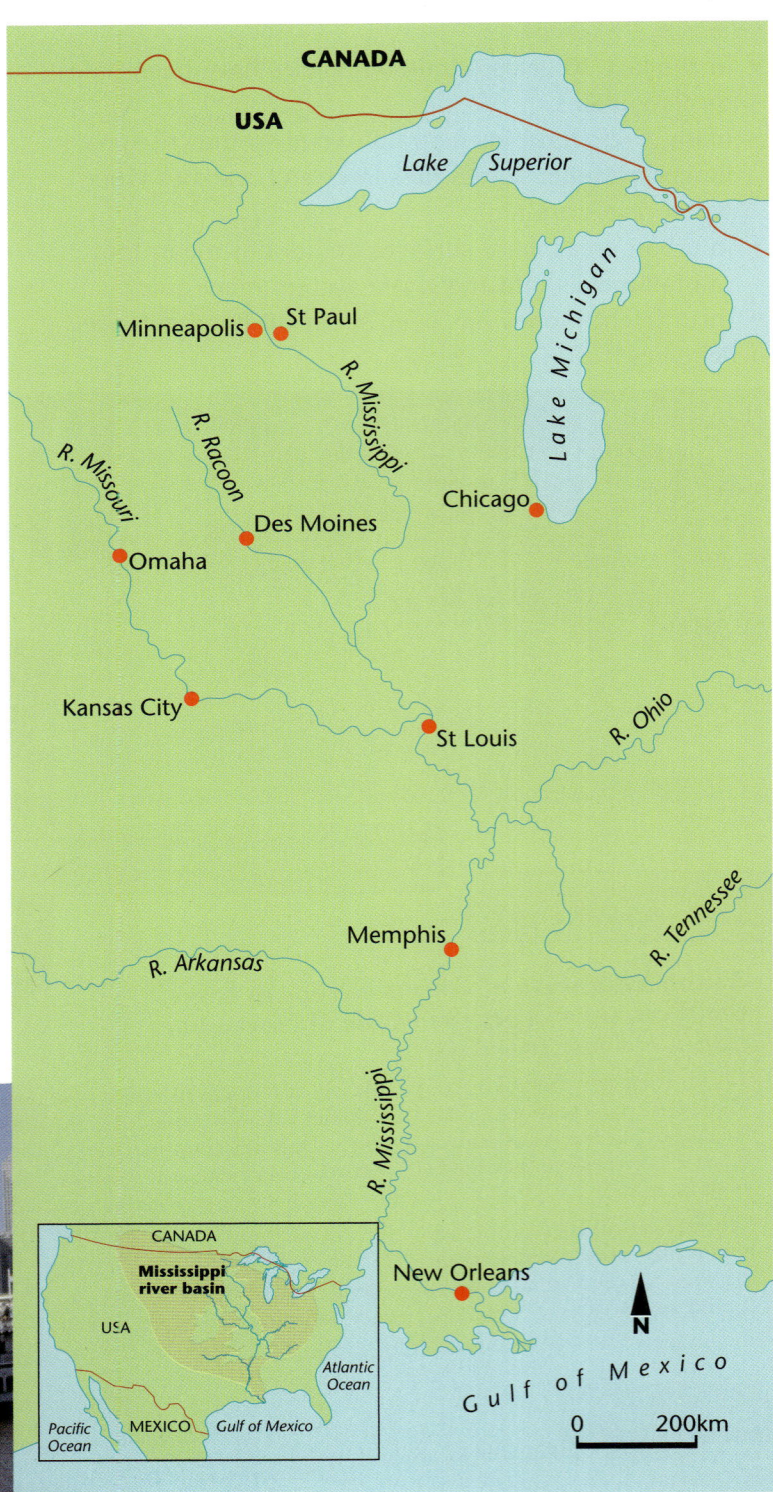

B – The Mississippi River

- New levées built to prevent the river from spilling onto the floodplain.
- Storage reservoirs created to hold excess water.
- **Dykes** constructed to control the flow of the river.
- Sections of the river straightened by cutting through meanders to increase the flow of the river.
- Parts of the river lined with concrete slabs to increase the rate of flow and reduce erosion of the river banks.

For 20 years after the floods of 1973 these schemes appeared to have been effective in reducing the flood risk — until 1993!

The 1993 floods

Heavy rainfall in April and May saturated the ground and when the rainfall continued throughout June and July it caused flash floods. By mid-July the level of the river had reached an all-time high and the levées began to collapse under the pressure of the water. The river spread across the floodplain to a width of more than 20km (**C**). Nearly 30 million sandbags were used to try to protect areas from flooding.

The effects of the flood
- Forty-eight people were killed.
- Floodwater covered an area larger than the British Isles, stretching from Memphis in the south to Minneapolis in the north.
- Around 70 000 people were evacuated from their homes.
- More than $2 billion worth of crops were lost.
- The river was closed to traffic for two months.
- Some towns never recovered. They were abandoned and rebuilt on higher land.

There were different opinions about the cause of the floods. These are summed up here:

'Rain causes floods, heavy rain causes big floods.'
An army engineer suggesting that it was mainly unusually high rainfall that caused the floods

'People cause floods by river engineering.'
Friends of the Earth, St Louis

Environmentalists argued that the engineering controls designed to reduce the risk of flooding may have made things worse by:

- shortening the river and making it flow more quickly, increasing erosion of the levées
- speeding up the flow of the water and increasing pressure on the river banks
- changing the flow of the river, which made the floods the worst ever recorded, although the volume of water in the river was less than during previous floods.

C – *The 1993 floods*

Questions

1. Why is the Mississippi naturally subject to flooding?
2. Write a paragraph describing:
   a) the physical causes of the floods in 1993
   b) how human changes might have increased the risk of flooding.
3. What were:
   a) the short-term impacts of the flood?
   b) the long-term impacts of the flood?

Managing the Physical Environment — Weather hazards

Exam practice questions

Mark schemes can be found on the book's website, at www.heinemann.co.uk/issuesmarkschemes

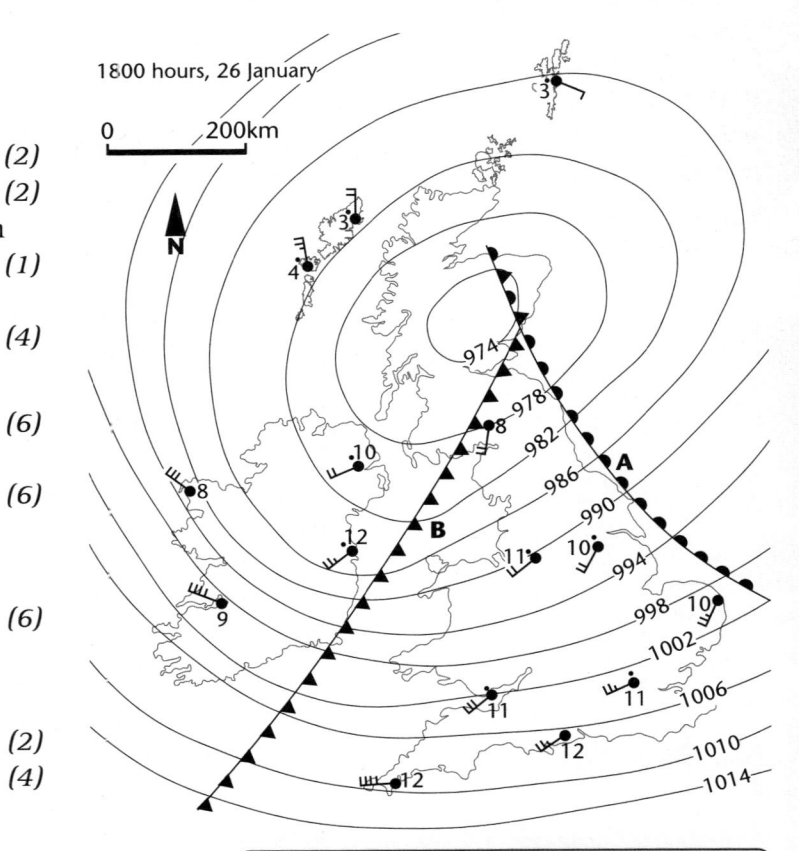

1. a) Study A showing a weather map for the British Isles in winter.
    i) Draw the correct weather symbols for 'rain shower' and 'fog'. (2)
    ii) Name the features found at A and B. (2)
    iii) What is the name of the weather system shown on the map? (1)
   b) Describe the weather associated with the system shown on the map. (4)

2. a) What conditions are associated with the development of hurricanes? (6)
   b) What are the hazards associated with hurricanes? (6)

3. Using examples you have studied, describe and explain the physical and human causes of floods. (6)

4. Read B, about the flood crisis in Bangladesh in 1999.
   a) What caused the floods? (2)
   b) Describe the effects of the floods. (4)
   c) Describe and explain the sorts of international help the Bangladesh government asked for. (6)
   d) Why might the long-term effects of the floods be significant? (4)

5. Using examples you have studied, explain why some areas of the world are more badly affected by natural disasters than others. (8)

A – A weather map for the British Isles in winter

1800 hours, 26 January

Britain has given £21m to the relief effort in Bangladesh following the recent floods. The money will go towards food relief and agricultural rehabilitation projects. The floods in Bangladesh were caused by exceptional monsoons, and over 20 million people have been badly affected. Many people have had to leave their homes and land during the floods, living in overcrowded shelters and camps. Food prices have also risen.

The Government of Bangladesh have described the floods as an 'economic disaster'. They recognize that the current rice crop will fall significantly below needs, and that the cost of damage to agriculture, roads and public buildings will be enormous. Bangladesh cannot meet the needs from its own resources and has asked for rapid international assistance. The immediate priority is for humanitarian relief: food, shelter, clean drinking water and healthcare. The main agricultural priority has been the distribution of rice seedlings, vegetable seeds and additional help to clear and plough fields.

The effect on the country's infrastructure has been extreme. Over 1000km of national roads have been damaged, 420km of road embankments and 100 bridges have been damaged or destroyed. Railways have been submerged. River embankments, culverts and irrigation channels need rebuilding, and tube wells and sanitation facilities have been ruined.

B – Bangladesh flood crisis

MANAGING THE PHYSICAL ENVIRONMENT

7 Water and food supply

> Many people suffer as a result of poor water and food supplies. What can be done to ensure adequate supplies of food and water?

Managing the Physical Environment

7.1 The causes of poor food supplies

The reasons for poor food supplies are both physical and human. *Poverty* and *drought* are the biggest problems. Millions of poor people have died during droughts when richer people have bought food, moved away, or used technology to find more water. Between 1983 and 1985 at least 500 000 people died from starvation in Ethiopia, but in the drought in England in 1995 nobody died from a lack of food or water.

What are the causes of poor food supplies?

- *Poverty* means that in times of drought people cannot buy food to stay alive and may have to eat their animals or seeds that should be kept for the next season's crop. Poor farmers find it hard to borrow money to get over temporary difficulties.
- *Lack of available land* affects millions of people in rural areas. Three-quarters of the people who lack food work on the land. People need enough land to grow their own food, but population growth puts more pressure on the land.
- *Commercial farming* and the growth of cash crops (**A**) have reduced food production in many places. Food crops used to be grown on the best land, but now this is often used for **commercial (cash) crops** such as cotton or flowers.
- *War and civil conflict* frequently disrupt farming. People are prevented from working the land and from planting or harvesting their crops.
- *Poor transportation* is a cause of poor food supplies in some places. Poor infrastructure may mean that food fails to reach remote areas. This can be a particular problem in times of drought.
- *Lack of advice, support* and **appropriate technology** in rural areas may result in low crop yields.
- *Expensive seeds or fertilizer* may reduce the amount of food a poor farmer can grow.
- *Overworked land* leads to **soil degradation** (a decline in fertility), especially during a drought.
- *Soil erosion*, caused by over use of the land, leads to the loss of millions of tonnes of fertile topsoil each year in places as far apart as China, East Africa and the UK.
- *Overgrazing*, caused by too many animals on the land and the consequent loss of the vegetation cover, leaves the ground bare, so soil is blown or washed away.
- *Pollution* from agricultural chemicals and salt build up in irrigated areas reduce the soil quality.
- *Drought*, caused by too little rain, unreliable rainfall, and the mismanagement of land and water supplies, probably causes most hunger and deaths each year (**B** and **C**).

A – *Cash crops are grown for export, often at the expense of local food crops*

Problems of unreliable rainfall

Much of India is a drought area for at least part of the year. Rainfall is unreliable, and people depend on the monsoon rains that fall between June and September. Moist winds blow over the land from the Bay of Bengal and the Indian Ocean, usually bringing torrential rain. This enables 700 million people to grow food to eat and to sell. But if the rains are late, people run out of food. In 1987 the rains were six weeks late, and millions of people were forced to leave the land and head for the cities in order to find food.

Droughts develop slowly, but they can be the cause of many thousands of deaths in LEDCs. Farmers learn to live with unreliable water supplies, but if there is so little rain that cereals do not grow, famine follows.

7 Water and food supply

Kenya's Masai left in wilderness of dying cattle and red tape

Rains too late and aid too little for herdsmen to survive

Drought has already killed most of the Masai herders' cattle. Now the weakened remainder are dying in the chill of belated rains

'By day we kept them standing, but at night the cows lay down and died'

B – Headlines from the Guardian, 25 November 2000

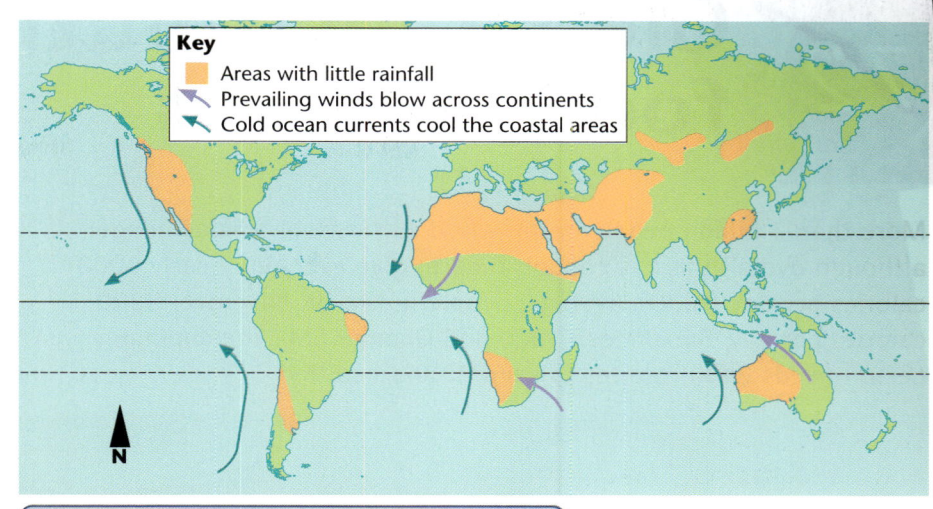

C – Areas in the world that have too little rainfall

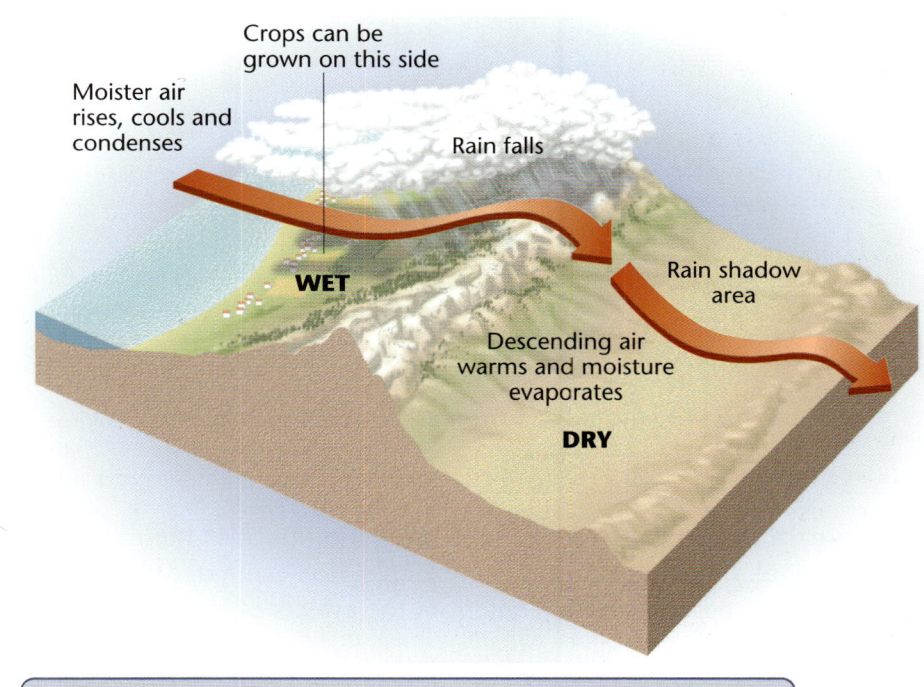

D – Some places suffer drought because they are in a rain shadow area

Why do some places get so little precipitation?

- Moist winds blowing over mountains bring rainfall on one side but leave a dry rain shadow area on the other (D).
- Air blowing across a continent gradually loses moisture and becomes drier.
- Anticyclones (high pressure systems) create sinking air which is warmed, so moisture evaporates giving dry air.
- Changes in rainfall patterns can cause seasonal rains to be late, or the amount of rain to be below average.

Questions

1. Describe and explain four causes of poor food supply.
2. Explain why the monsoon rains are so important to India.
3. Why do some places get so little rainfall?
4. What is a cash crop? Why do LEDCs grow cash crops?
5. Why are the effects of drought less significant in MEDCs?

133

Global distribution of food supplies

More than 1 billion people in the world suffer from serious hunger, although overall there is enough food to give everyone nearly 3000 calories per day (A). On average, people in the UK have over 3300 calories per day, Bangladesh 1900 and Ghana 1500. The average person needs 2400 calories to keep fit and healthy.

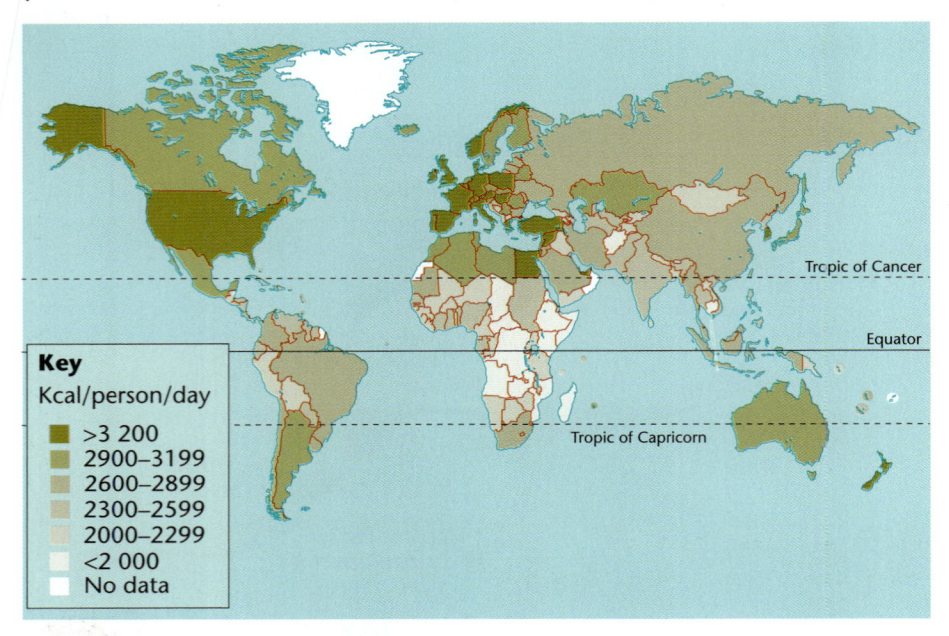

A – Global distribution of food supplies

Key Kcal/person/day
- >3 200
- 2900–3199
- 2600–2899
- 2300–2599
- 2000–2299
- <2 000
- No data

Undernutrition (too little food) and **malnutrition** (lack of the right kinds of food) are widespread in many LEDCs. It is estimated that around 24 000 people die *each day* from the effects of hunger.

Nutrition is usually described in terms of calories. People can survive on about 1500 calories a day, but quality in the diet — vitamins, minerals and proteins, for example — is also important. Children, especially those under 5 years, suffer the effects of malnutrition and starvation more quickly than adults. Malnutrition can develop gradually as food supplies diminish, or rapidly where a disaster wipes out crops.

Poverty and hunger go together. Across the continents, approximately 40 per cent of those who are hungry are **subsistence farmers** and their families, 40 per cent are tenant farmers or landless agricultural workers and their families, and 20 per cent live in urban slums. Many of those in urban slums in LEDCs migrated there because they could not get enough food in the rural areas. There are also hungry people in urban MEDCs, including possibly as many as 30 million US citizens. Those who are most likely to go hungry are children, pregnant women, families of single parents, and the unemployed. Eighty per cent of hungry children actually live in countries where there is sufficient food in total to feed everybody.

The negative food loop – a downward spiral

Many of the rural hungry are farmers who try to grow enough food to eat, with some to store and a little to sell. If a farmer cannot produce enough, a negative downward spiral follows (C). Malnourished people are less able to work effectively and they farm less well, producing less food. People with little to sell get poorer nutrition and can grow less.

Where are the hungry people?

A lack of food is most common in countries across South-east Asia, India, the Middle East, Africa and South America, like a hunger belt around the world. Possibly half the world's hungry people live in just a few countries: India, Bangladesh, Pakistan, Indonesia and Nigeria. One-third of the children in Africa south of the Sahara are malnourished. The population of Africa has risen by over 50 per cent since 1950, but food production by less than 40 per cent. The Food and Agricultural Organization (FAO) estimated that in 2000, 30 per cent of the 60 million people in the world who are most in need of urgent food assistance lived in East Africa, where around 18 million were affected by serious food shortages (C and D):

- *Eritrea* – 1.5 million people displaced by war and unable to grow crops, with 300 000 suffering from drought.
- *Ethiopia* – the number receiving food assistance was 6 million.
- *Somalia* – 750 000 need food assistance.
- *Kenya* – 4.4 million need food help because of drought.
- *Sudan* – civil conflict and drought leave 2.9 million in need of food.
- *Tanzania* – late and unreliable rainfall prevents 800 000 people from growing sufficient food.
- *Uganda* – drought in the north-east and civil conflict in the west mean that food supplies are precarious.

B – Hunger in East Africa, 2000

People in West Africa, central and southern Africa are similarly affected. In other parts of the world, 25 million people need food help in Asia, 7 million in the Near East, 1 million in Central America (mostly as a result of Hurricane Mitch) and 1 million in Eastern Europe. Each year about 30 countries need emergency food aid.

C – The negative food loop – a downward spiral

The effects of malnutrition?

- *Kwashiorkor* is caused by a lack of protein, and leads to swollen hands and legs and a bloated stomach, tiredness and lack of growth (E). It is common in areas of malnutrition.
- *Marasmus* is caused by a severe lack of food. It results in diarrhoea, wasting, and low immunity to other diseases.
- *Anaemia* is caused by a lack of iron and makes people extremely tired. Subsistence farmers with anaemia may become less productive.
- *Blindness* resulting from a lack of vitamin A affects 250 000 children a year. It can be prevented by eating fruit and vegetables.

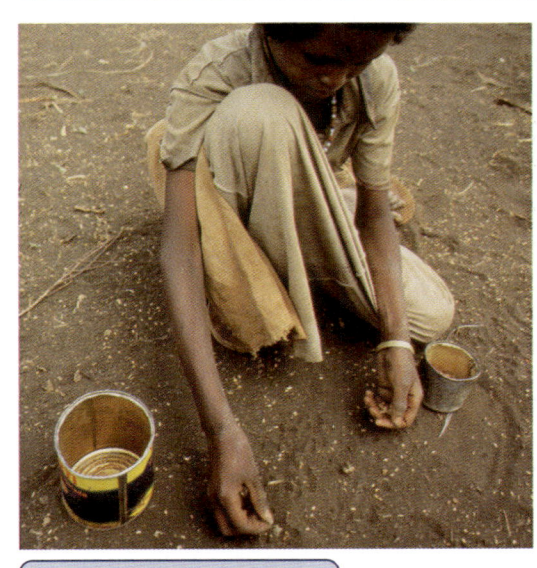

D – The meaning of famine

E – Kwashiorkor – a result of malnutrition

Questions

1. Name three countries which average:
   - more than 3200 calories per day
   - less than 2600 calories per day.

2. a) Between which latitudes do most hungry people live?
   b) In which continents do most hungry people live?

3. 'During times of drought only the poor go hungry.' Explain this statement.

4. a) What is malnutrition?
   b) What are the effects of malnutrition?

5. On an outline map of East Africa, suggest the major reasons and impacts of food shortages in 2000.

Managing the Physical Environment

7.3 Drought and desertification

The term 'desertification' was first used in 1949 to describe the way that semi-arid areas appeared to be developing into deserts in some parts of the world. At the 1977 United Nations, Environmental World Conference, desertification was defined as 'a reduction in the biological productivity of the land, which leads to desert-like conditions'. Following the droughts in the African **Sahel** in the 1980s, where lack of rainfall (**C**) killed much of the natural vegetation, the term 'desertification' was increasingly used.

The causes of desertification vary, but it is generally accepted that it results from a combination of natural processes and human activity.

Definitions

Drought — *a lack of rainfall over a long period of time.*

Desertification — *the spread of desert-like conditions into semi-arid regions.*

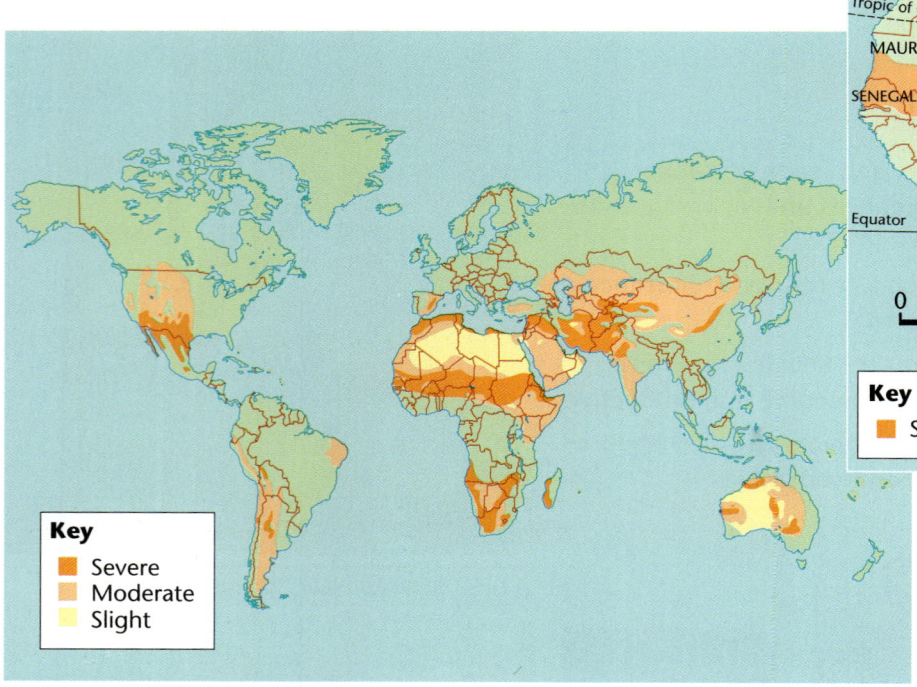

B – The Sahel region

A – Areas at risk of desertification

Who is affected by desertification?

Nearly 1 billion people are affected by desertification. In the poorer parts of the world it has increased the problems of food shortages and led to the spread of famine. This has been particularly apparent in the sub-Saharan area of North Africa known as the Sahel (**B**). However, desertification is a global problem. Desertification is also a problem in many MEDCs, with the western USA, parts of Australia and southern Europe being increasingly vulnerable (**A**).

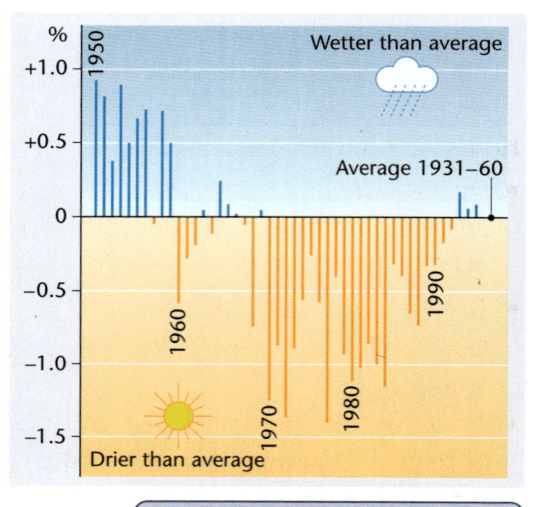

C – Pattern of rainfall in the Sahel

7 Water and food supply

DROUGHT IN AFRICA

LACK OF RAINFALL has brought drought to large parts of central and northern Africa. In Chad more than 3000 people have died in the past three months in what is believed to be the worst drought this century. In Mali nearly 2 million people are at risk and infant mortality rates are increasing as disease takes a hold. Cattle losses in Mauritania have reached over 60% and Niger expects to lose half of its food crops – so long-term prospects are poor. It is estimated that up to 2 million people are at risk of food shortages in Burkina Faso. In eastern Africa both Ethiopia and Sudan are suffering from poor harvests and more than 6 million people in Ethiopia are at risk of famine. Levels of disease are increasing rapidly in overcrowded relief camps where many children have already died.

D – Consequences of drought in the Sahel region, 1986

Why did the people of Yatenga ask for help?

Because Oxfam listens
We listened to the people of Yatenga in Burkina Faso. The land they depended on for survival was turning to desert. Oxfam heard about a local method of putting lines of stones across a slope to stop water running away and preserving topsoil. This is called bunding.

Because Oxfam trains
Training people to build stone lines across slopes improved the soil and slowed down the loss of water. This improved farming and meant that more land could be used and food production increased.

Because Oxfam stays
This project has now been in operation for 12 years and today Yatenga is criss-crossed with lines of stones. Oxfam has taught local people how to cultivate trees and other plants. As well as providing food, fuel and animal fodder, the roots of the plants help to bind the soil, keeping it in place.

E – Tackling the problem: building a stone wall in Burkina Faso

The Sahel

The Sahel is a semi-arid region to the south of the Sahara Desert (B). Total annual rainfall is low and there is a dry period each year. Long-term rainfall is variable, and since the 1970s rainfall totals have often been below average, causing drought and famine (D).

Causes of desertification

Natural processes

- *Climate change:* Since 1960 rainfall totals have been below the long-term average for eight in every ten years (C).
- *Loss of vegetation:* As rainfall declines there is a reduction in natural vegetation. This leaves the land open to erosion and the loss of topsoil.

Human activity

- *Overgrazing:* In some areas animals have stripped vegetation away, leaving areas of bare soil.
- *Overcultivation* The land is overused and becomes exhausted and less fertile.
- *Deforestation:* The cutting-down of trees for firewood has removed the protective cover of vegetation and left the land open to erosion.

Questions

1 a) Use the following to construct a climate graph for Timbuktu in Mali:

	J	F	M	A	M	J	J	A	S	O	N	D
Precipitation (mm)	3	3	3	3	5	23	80	80	38	3	2	2
Temperature (°C)	22	24	28	32	34	35	32	30	32	31	28	23

b) Describe the climate of Timbuktu and explain why the area is vulnerable to drought.

2 Explain the links between rainfall, drought and famine.

3 Why might overgrazing during wetter periods cause problems in the Sahel during drier periods?

4 Describe and explain how the Oxfam programme in Burkina Faso (E) is making people less vulnerable to drought.

5 'It was once thought that the Sahara Desert was advancing by between 5 and 10km a year, but the use of modern satellite photography suggests that deserts expand and contract in relation to rainfall.' Explain this statement.

Managing the Physical Environment

7.4 Water, water everywhere?

Water is one of the most important natural resources and is vital for all living things. People can survive for long periods with limited food, but for only a few days without water. Nearly 50 per cent of the world's people lack access to safe water (**A**). In many parts of the world, getting enough water for drinking, cooking and washing is a constant problem, and finding water for crops and animals is an added pressure. Even when water is available it may be many miles away or be polluted and lead to health problems (**B**).

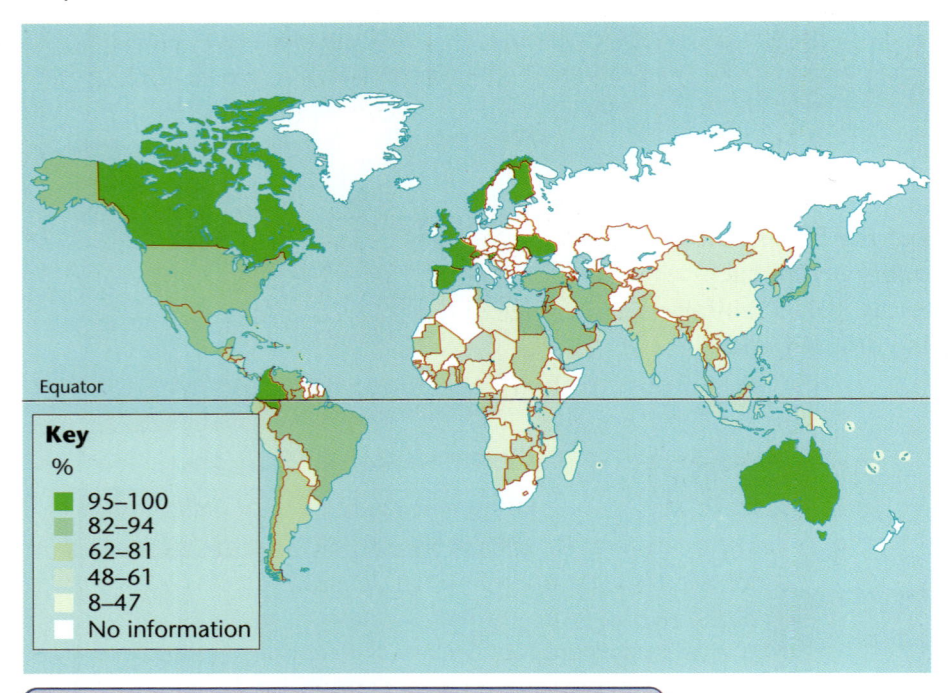

Key %
- 95–100
- 82–94
- 62–81
- 48–61
- 8–47
- No information

A – *Global percentage of people with access to safe water*

Rachel Anton lives in the Tabora region of Tanzania. She is 18 years old and is pictured here with her baby Laurent Julius, who is 7 months old. Rachel spends an average of 5 hours per day collecting water from this small puddle – her only water source.

'I have walked a long way, but this is the nearest source. I am hoping to fill four buckets of water for drinking and cooking. We get frequent stomach problems because of the water. I would be happier if there was water near my home – and healthier.'

B – *Rachel's story*

Rural/urban differences in LEDCs

In rural parts of **LEDC**s, rivers and lakes are often the only source of drinking water, but they can also be used by animals, or be polluted by industrial chemicals or sewage (**C**).

Levels of access to safe water are often higher in urban areas in LEDCs because it is easier to organize supplies where a lot of people live close to each other (**D**). However, the continued growth of urban areas is putting increasing pressure on water supplies. During the 1980s (which was the United Nations' 'International Drinking Water Supply and Sanitation Decade'), 80 per cent more urban dwellers were reported to have gained access to safe water and 50 per cent to a waste disposal (sewerage) system. But because of the rise in urban populations, the

C – *This cow has been drinking from chemically polluted water* number of those without safe water remains the same, and those without **sanitation** rose by 70 million. The growing demand for water in urban areas is putting enormous pressure on water resources in many developing cities. The observations by WaterAid set out in E illustrate some of the problems.

Many of the poorest urban dwellers in LEDCs buy bottled water, which is very expensive, or have to boil water which means added fuel costs. If they cannot afford this they are forced to use unsafe drinking water which can carry serious health risks.

Country	Safe water		Sanitation	
	Urban	Rural	Urban	Rural
Bolivia	77	15	55	13
Ecuador	75	37	75	34
Mozambique	44	17	61	11
Pakistan	99	35	40	8

D – Percentage of people with access to safe water and sanitation in selected countries

CITIES RUNNING DRY

China:
Between 1983 and 1990, the number of cities in China that were short of water rose from 100 to 300; those with a serious water problem from 40 to 100. By the year 2002, Beijing will suffer a daily water shortfall of 500 000m³.

Mexico:
Mexico City, having over-pumped the Mexico Valley aquifer, is now forced to pump its water supply a distance of 180km and up 1000m from the Cutzamala River, at much higher cost. The city faces the problem of exhausting its water supply by the year 2002.

Indonesia:
Jakarta has so depleted its underground aquifers that seawater has seeped 15km inland, making the supply saline (salty). Investments in pipelines to bring water from other sources are expected to top $1 billion.

E – Observations from WaterAid

F – Collecting clean water from a hole in the sand, Uganda

Questions

1 a) Draw a bar chart to show the differences in access to safe water between urban and rural areas for the countries shown in D.
b) Describe and explain these differences.

2 Use figures B and C to explain the problems of water supply.

3 Read the following statement about a family in Uganda, in Africa.

Haufaruna-Sebuliba is 16 years old. He lives in Nakalanga Village in Uganda. His family grow a small amount of coffee as a cash crop. Sebuliba has a protected spring in his village and therefore has access to safe water now. People in the village tell us that since they've had clean water they are saving money on visits to the doctor and chemist. It costs between 500 and 1000 Shillings for medicine for sickness and diarrhoea. Before the clean water was available, parents were spending this in an attempt to cure their sick children. Clean water means good health which in turn leads to improved wealth.

Explain how clean water improves both health and wealth.

7.5 The effects of contaminated water

Nearly half the diseases suffered by people globally are related to contaminated water supplies or poor sewerage systems. Today, water-related diseases are confined largely to the poorer parts of the world. Clean water and effective sewerage systems in MEDCs have eradicated many of the problems of water-borne diseases, and enabled a much healthier lifestyle.

In many LEDCs, untreated water is used for drinking, while sewage is emptied into rivers and even on to the street. Consequently many people suffer from diarrhoeal and parasitic diseases. Children suffer most — the World Health Organization (WHO) estimates that over 3 million children a year die as a result of diarrhoea, and many people who are sick are so weakened that they cannot lead productive lives.

The United Nations (UN) designated the 1980s as the 'Water Decade'. The aim was that by 1990 everyone would have access to safe water. This aim was not achieved — in 1990 1.3 billion people were still without access to safe water, and 1.9 billion without effective sanitation.

Water-related diseases

Water-related diseases are usually classified as follows:

- *Water-borne diseases* are caused by organisms that survive in water, and are passed on to people when infected water is drunk. They include *cholera* and *typhoid*.
- *Water-based diseases* occur where water provides the habitat for parasites and insects. Parasitic diseases are spread by small worms or larvae which are ingested (eaten or drunk), or which burrow their way under the skin. Examples are *Guinea worm* and *Schistosomiasis (bilharzia)*, commonly found in Africa. Water provides the habitat for many insects which then pass on disease by biting people. Mosquitoes breed in water and may transmit *malaria* and *yellow fever*. The number of reported malaria cases fell up to the mid-1980s, but there were major outbreaks in the early 1990s, particularly in South America and Africa (**A**). Estimates claim that 30 per cent of children in Africa are infected, and India has over 15 million sufferers. In Brazil alone, the number of infected people rose from 50 000 in 1970 to over half a million in 1995.
- *Water-washed diseases* Disease can be passed on through poor hygiene, for example if hands are not washed in clean water. Examples are diarrhoeal diseases and skin and eye infections.

Cholera

Cholera is an acute diarrhoeal disease which can kill in hours. The bacteria are passed on through drinking contaminated water. Infected people quickly become dehydrated and unless rehydration treatment is given quickly, death can be rapid. The root causes of cholera are poverty, overcrowding and lack of education.

Where people are forced to drink contaminated water and live in overcrowed conditions, the disease can spread rapidly. There were major outbreaks of the disease in the early 1990s, particularly in South America and Africa (**B**).

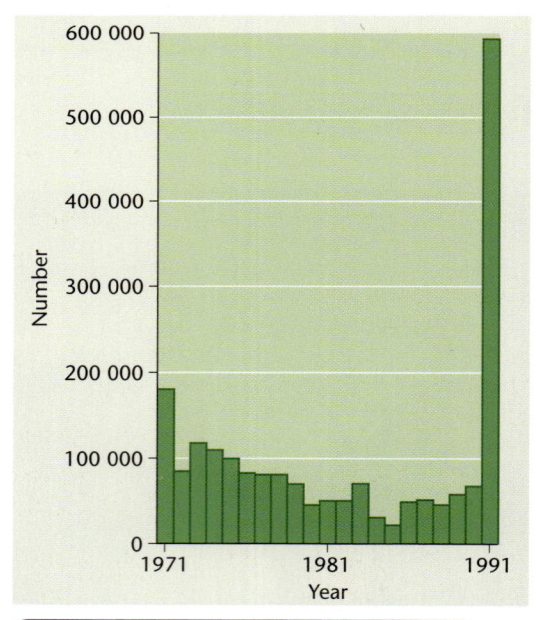

A – *Worldwide cases of malaria, 1971–91*

	Infections	Deaths
Africa	153 367	13 998
Asia	49 791	1 286
Europe	316	9
North America	26	0
South America	391 220	4 002

B – *Cholera in 1993*

7 Water and food supply

The Thames Water Marunda Project in Jakarta

In 1930, the population of Jakarta, the capital city of Indonesia, was 530 000. Today it is estimated to be 11 million. Like many urban centres in the developing world, the city attracts people from other parts of the country seeking work and a better quality of life. However, Jakarta's rapid growth presents an enormous headache for city planners as they struggle to provide the necessary services. As the city continues to grow, Jakarta's water company has only managed to provide half the population with piped water. Many other people rely on water from wells. This water has to be boiled to kill off any harmful bacteria. Diarrhoea caused by drinking polluted water is responsible for 20 per cent of the deaths of children under 5 in the city.

In the north of the city, land is actually sinking as Jakarta's groundwater supply is over-used by people. Houses on low-lying land have to be rebuilt every few years to keep them above sea-level. Meanwhile, seawater is seeping into the land, polluting the remaining groundwater.

C – A squatter settlement in Jakarta

Problems in Marunda

The problems of water supply are particularly difficult for the people who live in Jakarta's squatter settlements, like Marunda in north-east Jakarta (**C**). It lacks even the most basic services, including a reliable, clean water supply. In the past, the women here had to queue to collect water from standpipes, or they had to buy water from private street vendors, which could cost more than 30 times the price of piped water. For the poorest families, these costs could be devastating. Marunda residents also faced serious health risks as sewage and other domestic waste was not flushed away.

Investment from abroad

The Jakarta authorities asked private water companies to get involved and in 1999 Thames Water, a British company, began a £60 000 project to bring piped water to the people of Marunda.

From the start, Thames Water has understood the need to involve local people in the construction and maintenance of the project. This way, the project could be better suited to local needs and could gain the trust and support of Marunda's residents. As a result, 2000 local people have been working on the project alongside 10 staff from Thames Water UK.

A pipe-dream come true?

By July 2000, the project was finished and 1600 houses in Marunda were connected to Jakarta's main water supply. This enabled 12 000 residents to have water piped directly into their homes. Residents can now receive water at a third of the price that they used to pay. Savings on water enable families to spend more money on other basic needs. Improved sanitation has already brought health benefits as it reduces the risk of disease.

'The water, clear and cool like crystal, is now flowing from every tap. Now what we hoped for has been fulfilled; washing, drinking, everything clean.'
Marunda resident, May 2000

Questions

1. Explain what is meant by:
   - water-borne disease
   - water-based disease
   - water-washed disease.
2. Explain why disease often helps to keep people poor.
3. What effect has the Thames Water project had on the people of Marunda?

7.6 Alternative strategies to improve food and water supplies

The goal of the 1996 World Food Summit was to reduce the number of undernourished people to half the present level by 2015. Better seeds and a reliable water supply would help.

The Gene Revolution – changing plants

During the 1960s there was a huge increase in crop yields with the use of chemical fertilizers, insecticides and new varieties of plants. Between 1967 and 1992 the world rice harvest doubled, and in Indonesia the crop tripled to 48 million tonnes. Rice is the least internationally traded cereal and the one most eaten by small farmers, so increasing the yield can benefit a lot of people. Rice plants were bred that:

- had strong stalks to carry an increased number of grains
- had a growing season of 110 days instead of 160 days, giving two or three harvests a year.
- were resistant to a range of diseases and insects
- were short-stemmed (to reduce rain and wind damage).

Recent advances in **biotechnology** and **genetic engineering** offer the possibility of more dramatic changes in crop growing, but will they benefit farmers in LEDCs?

Plants could produce more, but they will need **intensive farming**. Genetically modified (GM) seeds will cost more, they may need more (possibly scarce) water resources, and may need to be grown as single crops in huge fields, using machinery and more chemicals. This type of farming may not be appropriate to traditional or subsistence farming practices. A high proportion (64 per cent) of people in India farm the land and do not want to be reliant on biotechnology corporations and cannot afford increased technology. Farmers there are setting up their own seed banks to preserve existing crop varieties, and are voicing their concerns about the possible impacts of more scientific farming.

A – Most people in Egypt live close to the River Nile

Water resource planning in Egypt – a national development

The River Nile flows for 6825km between Lake Victoria and the Mediterranean Sea, draining 10 per cent of Africa. For thousands of years the annual Nile floods supplied water and rich silt to the riverside lands and the delta in Egypt. People lived on each side of the river, on a densely populated irrigated strip of land surrounded by desert (**A**).

In the 1960s the Aswan High Dam was built to manage the flooding and to provide hydro-electric power (HEP) for the developing nation. The HEP provides one-third of Egypt's electricity. The dam is 4km wide, 100m high and almost 1km thick. The resulting Lake Nasser is 600km long and is the second largest artificial lake in the world.

Egypt's agriculture was transformed. By the mid-1980s the area used for crop growing had doubled and all-year-round **irrigation** enabled two crops to be grown each year. Today, nearly all of Egypt's farmland is irrigated.

7 Water and food supply

In the mid-1980s, droughts in Ethiopia led to very low water levels in Lake Nasser and the lower Nile basin, and some environmental problems became apparent (**B**). In Egypt the pessimistic view is that people are now more likely to contract diseases, live with polluted water, grow less food and eat less protein. The population is still increasing and there are more mouths to feed.

Could different water supplies be used?

In 1997 Egypt was planning to build a new valley of the Nile, linking up a series of oases using underground aquifers. People could then live away from the Nile. However, the costs of such a scheme are huge, and it is likely to cause a fall in water levels.

What could affect the water supply in the future?

The Nile Basin is now suffering from a water deficit. Ethiopia, which supplies 80 per cent of the Nile water, Sudan and Egypt are most concerned with Nile water. Ethiopia is planning to dam the river to irrigate its drought areas where increased food supplies are desperately needed. Populations in Sudan and Ethiopia are growing more rapidly than in Egypt. If water is restricted, Egypt will suffer environmental, social and economic damage. Agreements between the nations have been made in the past but there is often conflict between them.

Other countries in the region – Burundi, Rwanda, Tanzania, Congo, Kenya and Uganda, for example – could also have an influence on the water flow in the river.

Advantages of the Aswan dam

* Flooding is controlled and managed.
* Irrigated land has increased.
* Crop yields have increased, with double cropping.
* Cash crops – sugarcane, cotton, vegetables – have increased, bringing in more money.
* Tourism along the river has increased – a major source of jobs and income.
* There is all-year river navigation.
* Fishing, recreation and tourism are also possible on Lake Nasser.
* HEP helped industry to develop.
* More towns and villages have electricity.

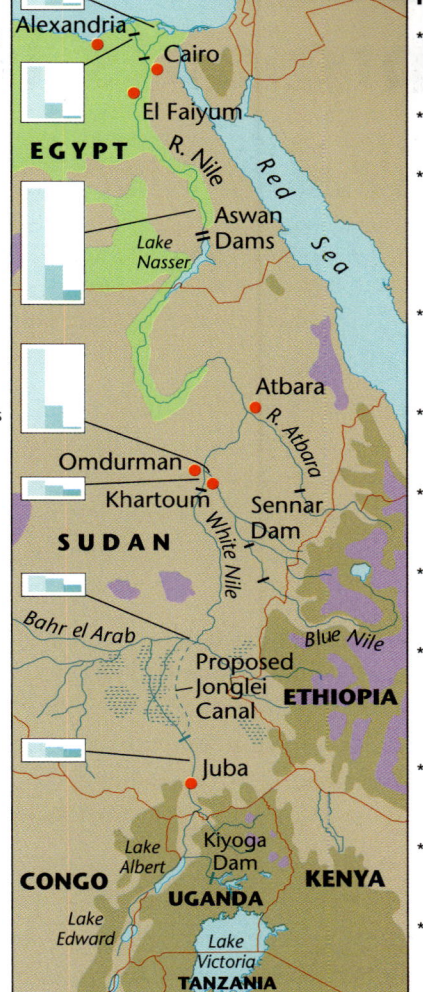

Problems resulting from the Aswan Dam

* Fertile silt is no longer spread over the land.
* Chemical fertilizers are needed.
* Water is shallow and slow-moving – bilharzia (from river snails) and other diseases have increased.
* Fertilizers, pesticides, herbicides, domestic and industrial waste pollute the river water.
* Polluted water flows into the Mediterranean Sea.
* Salt from irrigation water collects and crop yields fall.
* Delta sand bars, deprived of silt, are eroding away.
* Lagoons behind the sand bars used for fishing (a good source of protein), are disappearing.
* Low-lying Egypt may flood as sea-levels rise and the delta erodes.
* In Lake Nasser, fish and silt are trapped behind the dam.
* Lake Nasser is surrounded by desert – 2m of water evaporate from the entire surface every year (which increases the concentration of salt in the water).

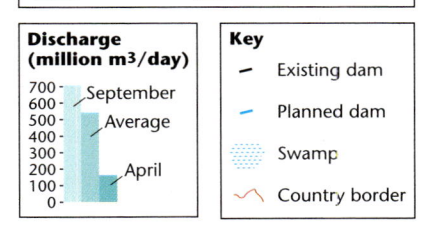

B – The flow of the River Nile is carefully controlled

Questions

1. a) What changes to crops took place in the 1960s?
   b) Globally, who could be helped most by the 'Gene Revolution'?
2. Suggest five things that you think might help subsistence farmers.
3. a) Give three reasons why Nile water is so important to Egypt.
   b) What are the advantages and disadvantages of the Aswan Dam?
   c) Suggest three reasons why conflict over water may happen in the future in the Nile Basin.

Managing the Physical Environment

7.7 Sustainable food and water projects in LEDCs

Sustainable farming in Thailand

Chiang Thaidee lives in Surin, a dry, infertile area of eastern Thailand (**A**). This region is flat and treeless, and even if there is enough rain it is only possible to grow one rice crop a year. During the dry season the ground is baked hard.

Chiang bought 1ha of land with money he had saved. He started work on his land by digging a large pond. He decided not to hire a tractor, because he did not want to get into debt, so he dug the pond by hand over several years. At first the pond would not hold water through the dry season, but by lining it with animal manure and lime, it gradually became sealed.

This barren plot of land has gradually become an oasis of water, trees and animals. There are now 12 ponds covering almost half the land. Mango, lemon, coconut, banana and other fruit trees grow around the ponds. Herbs and shrubs have been planted underneath the trees. Besides providing food the fruit is a valuable source of income. Chiang also grows and sells seedlings to other farmers as a way of earning more money.

The ponds are full of fish, which provide high-protein food throughout the year (**C**). Chiang has set up breeding ponds, and sells fish from these to other farmers. Chickens and ducks roam freely around the farm. They help by eating termites and other pests, provide fertilizer for the trees and plants, and food for the fish. Chiang buys young chickens which are fattened for a month before being sold at a profit. He also raises pigs, and harvests mushrooms.

Apart from selling his produce, Chiang has a small kitchen garden. Here the family grow vegetables for their own use. This saves money and they also know that the vegetables they eat have not been sprayed with chemicals.

Chiang's hard work has built a sustainable farm, one that sets an example to other farmers in the region. Using farming methods that do not harm the environment, he has provided his family with an adequate diet and income, giving them greater security (**B**).

A – Surin in Thailand

Activity	Income (£)
Fruit	1538
Fish	1154
Chickens	738
Pigs	415
Fruit tree seedlings	115
Mushrooms	46

B – Chiang's farm income

C – Fish pond in Thailand

WaterAid

WaterAid is a specialist development charity based in the UK. Its aim is to help poor people in Africa and Asia to achieve sustainable improvements in their quality of life by improving the domestic water supply and building sewerage systems.

The Hitosa water supply project – Ethiopia

Hitosa is a district of Ethiopia, in north-east Africa (**D**). It has a population of nearly 200 000 and is approximately 160km south-east of Addis Ababa, Ethiopia's capital city. Most people in the area live in rural settlements and rely on agriculture for a living.

Why Hitosa had a water problem

Although Hitosa is not a drought area, the rivers that were its source of drinking and washing water do not flow near the settlements, which are spread out across the fertile plains. This meant that women had to spend several hours each day fetching water, and it was constantly in short supply. In the 1960s a tanker used to bring water and sell it to local people, but this was expensive and did not last long. A pipeline scheme developed in the 1970s worked for a short time but fell into disrepair because technical help was not available to keep it going.

Hitosa's new water scheme

Since 1996 more than 60 000 people living in 31 communities have been provided with water through a gravity supply system (**E**). Water runs from two springs in the mountains and passes through 140km of pipeline to 122 distribution points and more than 300 individual buildings. This was a joint scheme, with the government responsible for design and construction, WaterAid providing most of the money, and local communities contributing labour. The system is simple to run and is managed by local community representatives who employ people to operate the service. Water charges are low enough for people to afford the water, while at the same time covering all of the running and repair costs.

The scheme is the largest water supply project in Ethiopia and is being extended to serve a total of more than 70 000 people by 2008. It is already improving people's living standards. The time saved in not having to collect water is being used to improve farming methods and to make products that can be sold in local markets.

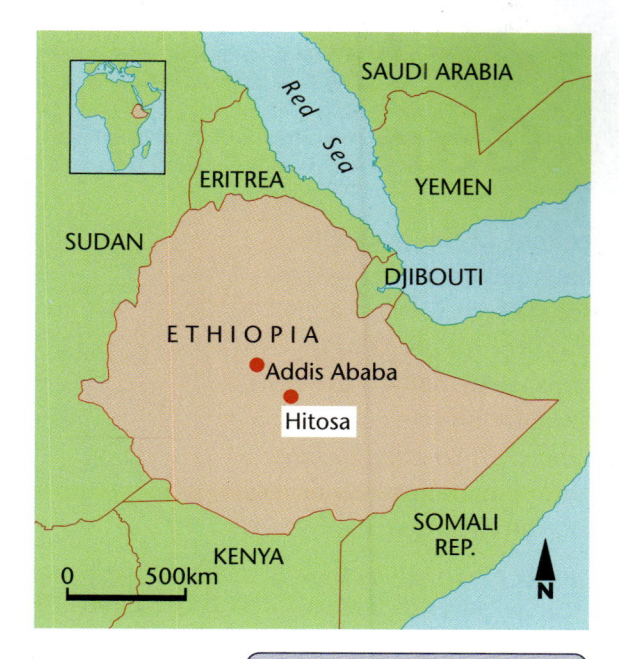

D – *Hitosa district in Ethiopia*

E – *Clean water for the people of Hitosa*

Questions

1. a) Explain how Chiang Thaidee developed his farm.
   b) How has it improved his family's quality of life?
2. a) Why is a reliable and cheap source of water so important to the people of Hitosa?
   b) How has the water supply project improved living standards in the area?
3. Why are both of these described as 'sustainable' projects?

Managing the Physical Environment

7.8 Managing the River Ganga, India

Nearly 70 per cent of the available water in India is polluted, and water-borne diseases such as cholera and typhoid account for 80 per cent of health problems. Less than 40 per cent of the rural population has access to a safe water supply, while only 29 per cent of the total population has access to good sanitation facilities.

The quotations in **A** are taken from a travel book, *Slowly Down the Ganges*, about a boat journey along the River Ganga. The Ganga basin drains around 25 per cent of India's land area and provides a quarter of its water resources. It is home to approximately 20 per cent of India's people, and has many large riverside settlements (**B**). The streams feeding the river rise in north-west India and Nepal, and any human actions in these areas can affect the river further downstream. With a rapidly increasing population and growing industrial development, the area has increasing levels of pollution.

'A map of the town showed fourteen sewage disposal points on the banks of the river, one of them next door to the drinking water pumping station.'

'I noticed a fire by the river bank and said to local people that it was a nice fire. A man replied, "Yes, it's a woman." Then I noticed that the foreshore was littered with half-burnt skulls and bones.'

'Now the walls began to exude a dampness and the smell of sewage as it trickled down between the houses to the river. Here it was not difficult to understand why this area had one of the highest rates of infant mortality in the whole country.'

'There were cows everywhere and the ground was slippery with their excrement, most of it being washed into the river.'

A – *Adapted from* Slowly Down the Ganges *by Eric Newby*

Sources of pollution

- *Urban waste* — human sewage and household waste account for a large proportion of the pollution in the Ganga. Only 30 per cent of the people in the area are connected to a sewerage system, and the remainder of any waste goes straight into the river.

- *Industrial waste* — water is drawn from the river to be used in a range of heavy industries found in the riverside industrial towns. Waste water from tanneries, chemical works, textile mills and agricultural processing plants is released into the river.

- *Agricultural chemicals* — pesticides and insecticides find their way into the river as run-off from the intensively farmed riverside farms.

- *Religious practices* – local Hindus purify themselves by bathing in the River Ganga at Varanasi (**C**). Hundreds of cremations take place on the river banks each day, and half-burnt bodies find their way into the river. With the increasing price of firewood it is not uncommon for bodies simply to be weighted down and thrown into the river.

B – *The Ganga basin*

7 Water and food supply

The Ganga Action Plan

In 1986 the Indian government launched the Ganga Action Plan. The Plan aims to improve the water quality of the river by:

- installing sewage treatment plants in the largest riverside settlements
- providing low-cost sanitation facilities and bathing areas
- building electric-powered crematoria to reduce the number of bodies being burnt on the river banks
- putting flesh-eating turtles in the river to clear up the body remains
- monitoring river quality to ensure that water quality constantly improves
- educating local people in the need for separation of sewage and household waste.

Is it working?

Water quality has improved in many of the riverside towns, and the level of sewage in bathing areas has decreased. Increasing numbers of people are connected to sewage treatment plants. A local Environmental Education Centre has been developed in the Varanasi area. It is running programmes with schools and local villages that promote activities to reduce river pollution. It is hoped that this will improve the quality of the river water and reduce levels of disease.

C – *Bathing in the Ganga at Varanasi*

Poisoned water in the delta of death

Two million people living by the Ganges river are dying slowly from the effects of arsenic in wells, writes **Julian West**

IN THE lush paddy fields of the Ganges delta, at least 2 million people are being slowly poisoned by drinking water. A further 66 million are at risk.

The killer is arsenic, which in some cases has been found in concentrations exceeding the internationally recognised 'safe' limited by more than 500 times.

Throughout the neat, mud-hut villages of the Ganges delta, villagers bear the signs of arsenic poisoning – gangrene and horrific skin cancers.

Hundreds are believed to have died since doctors identified the disease in 1984, although no one knows the exact number.

Experts are still researching the cause, but most believe it was created by the millions of tube wells sunk throughout India in the 1960s.

In Bangladesh, there are an estimated 3 million tube wells. But in erasing famine and providing year-round crops, the wells in the Ganges delta unleashed a killer. The region's arsenic is in the bedrock. By pumping hundreds of thousands of gallons to irrigate crops, the rock dried out and released arsenic in deadly amounts into the water table.

Three water-purifying plants are being built, and two pipeline projects, are planned. Wells are being replaced with deeper tube wells that it is hoped will by-pass the arsenic-contaminated layer of rock, and help resolve the problem.

D – *From the* Sunday Telegraph, *29 March 1998*

Questions

1. Describe the sources of pollution in the River Ganga.
2. Explain how the Ganga Action Plan will improve water quality and raise living standards.
3. Read D.
   a) Explain the causes of water pollution.
   b) Describe the effects of the pollution.
   c) What is being done to solve the problem?

Managing the Physical Environment

7.9 Water management in the western USA

The Colorado River and its tributaries flow through seven states before reaching the Gulf of California (**B**). It flows through a semi-desert landscape where rainfall is low and temperatures extreme.

The original reason for managing the river was to control its flow and prevent flooding. To achieve this the Hoover Dam was constructed in 1935 (**A**). Since that time more than 20 more dams have been built along the river, and the Colorado is now one of the most managed rivers in the world. It is used for domestic and industrial water supplies, irrigation for agriculture, and electricity generation. So much water is taken out of the river that for much of the year it enters the Gulf of California as a mere trickle.

The growing demand for water

The demand for water has grown so rapidly that each state is given a water quota which is controlled by the US Bureau of Reclamation. There are a number of reasons for the increase in demand.

- *The growth of tourism* Since 1940, Las Vegas has developed into the gambling centre of the USA. It has a major tourism industry, attracting over 7 million visitors a year. The area has a number of large hotels and conference centres with a full range of leisure facilities including watersports and golf courses.
- *The growth of 'sunbelt' cities.* Phoenix, the capital of Arizona, has become the USA's seventh biggest conurbation, with over 5 million people. The growth of high-tech industries encouraged by cheap land and property, has attracted thousands of people to the area. Phoenix is increasingly referred to as a 'tech oasis', with large developments of new houses, many with swimming pools and large gardens.
- *Agricultural development* With high temperatures all year round and the increasing demand for food and agricultural raw materials, the western USA is ideally located for agricultural development. In the last 50 years there have been increasing levels of investment in irrigation and sprinkler systems (see page 131), to allow semi-desert areas to be used for agriculture.

A – The Hoover Dam

B – The Colorado river basin

The Central Valley Project, California

The problem
California has a seasonal pattern of rainfall and a distinct dry period in the summer. More rain falls in the north but much of the most suitable agricultural land is in the south. Consequently, in order to make good use of the land, irrigation is needed.

The project
The government decided to build a number of dams and reservoirs (C). This allows water to be stored and then transported along aqueducts. A network of canals takes water to the drier areas and makes intensive agriculture possible. The Central Valley is now used to grow a wide variety of crops, including fruit, vegetables and cotton. Beef cattle are also reared on the irrigated grasslands. This agribusiness supplies the markets of the large urban areas with foodstuffs.

The costs of the project
Although the project has turned a semi-desert landscape into one of the most agriculturally productive areas in the USA, there have been considerable economic and environmental costs.

- The original cost of the engineering projects has made the real cost of water one of the highest in the world.
- The silting-up of reservoirs reduces their capacity, and they are increasingly expensive to maintain.
- Salinity increases as water evaporates leaving behind salts which have to be washed out if the land is to remain fertile.
- Both plant and animal life are being poisoned by increasing salinity in some areas and nature reserves are being damaged.

C – Water control in the Central Valley, California

Questions

1 a) Use the following data to construct a climate graph for Yuma in Arizona:

	J	F	M	A	M	J	J	A	S	O	N	D
Av. temp. (°C): Daily max.	22	25	29	34	39	44	47	46	44	37	28	22
Daily min.	3	6	9	13	18	23	29	28	23	16	8	3
Av. rainfall (mm)	13	8	13	5	1	0	8	14	7	7	8	11

b) What is the average annual rainfall for Yuma?
c) Why is the climate in Arizona described as 'semi-desert'?

2 Why has the demand for water increased in the western USA?

3 Describe and explain two advantages and two disadvantages of the Colorado management scheme.

4 a) What is meant by 'agribusiness'?
b) What advantages does California have for agriculture?
c) Describe and explain two economic and two environmental costs of the Central Valley Project.

Managing the Physical Environment — Water and food supply

Exam practice questions

Mark schemes can be found on the book's website, at www.heinemann.co.uk/issuesmarkschemes

1 Study A.
   a) Which country has:
      i) the lowest food consumption
      ii) the highest food consumption? (2)
   b) i) Copy and complete the following table putting the countries in rank order according to food intake. (3)

Country	GNP/capita ($)	Food intake (calories/day)
Bangladesh	240	2 019
UK	18 700	3 317
Somali Rep.	120	1 499
Rwanda	180	1 821
USA	26 980	3 732
Brazil	3 640	2 848

A – GNP/capita ($) and food intake per day for six countries

Rank	Food intake	GNP
1	USA 3317	18 700
2		
3		
4		
5		
6	Somali Rep. 1499	120

   ii) Fill in the GNP for each country. (3)
   c) What does your table suggest about the relationship between food intake and GNP? (3)

2 a) Describe the pattern shown in B. (4)
   b) Explain how poor water supply or lack of sanitation may affect people's lives. (4)
   c) Using one or more examples, describe and explain how water supplies could be improved in LEDCs. (6)

Key
%
- 95–100
- 72–94
- 56–71
- 32–55
- 6–31
- No information

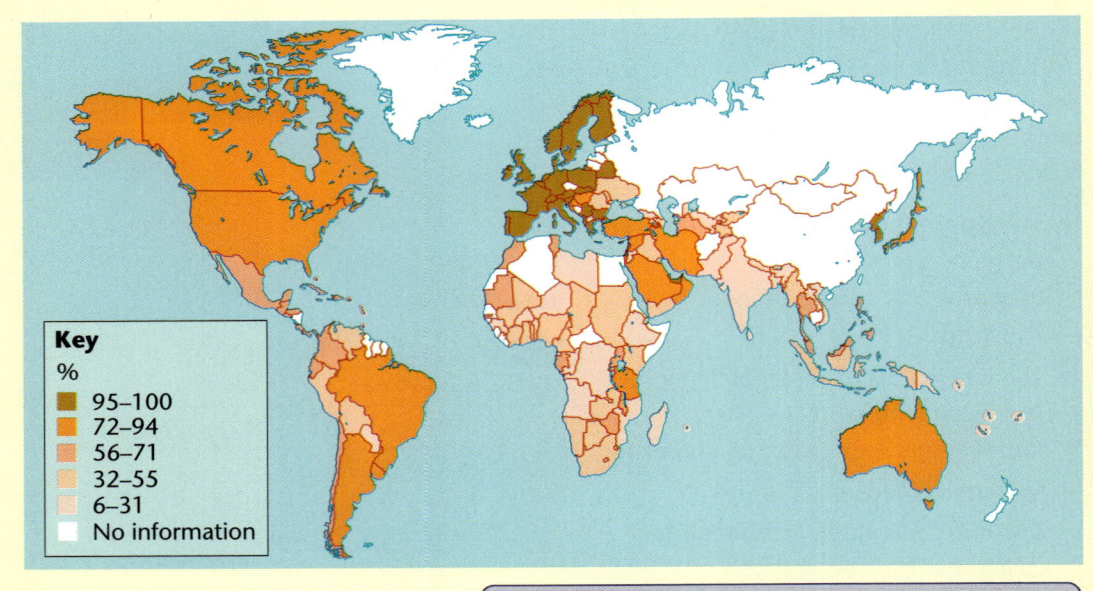

B – Percentage of population with access to sanitation

3 a) Describe two causes of hunger. (4)
   b) How can a lack of food affect people's health? (4)
   c) Use examples to describe the ways that agricultural production can be increased in LEDCs. (6)

4 a) Describe a water management scheme in an MEDC. (4)
   b) Explain the advantages and disadvantages of your chosen scheme. (6)

MANAGING THE PHYSICAL ENVIRONMENT

8 Pressures on the physical environment

> Some of the world's most spectacular natural landscapes have been shaped by physical processes over thousands of years. Are today's recreational demands putting these landscapes under increasing pressure?

Managing the Physical Environment

8.1 What makes natural landscapes attractive?

The coastline is the most important location for tourism, with more than 60 per cent of all holidays in the UK being in coastal areas. An area with good-quality beaches and spectacular scenery is attractive to holidaymakers. This was partly the reason for the development of the coastal resorts along the south coast of England, together with the higher number of sunshine hours and nearness to large urban areas. In the last 40 years the number of people taking their holidays abroad has increased, particularly to coastal areas like the Mediterranean (**A**) or Florida (USA). People are prepared to travel further afield in order to guarantee better weather.

Not all coastlines are seen as attractive. Some may be the site for heavy industries or be badly polluted, while others are too rocky, or very remote. Important features for people who want a coastal holiday are the availability and quality of the beaches. Holiday resorts spend a great deal of money preserving and protecting their beaches because they are an important resource. If beach quality is allowed to decline, people will go elsewhere and the local economy will suffer.

In areas where the natural environment attracts visitors it is often the environment itself that provides the basis for the local economy. Because of this there may be conflicts between preserving the environment and using it to develop the local economy.

A – Part of the Mediterranean coastline

There are many other natural environments that attract people. This may be because of the nature of the environment and the scenery, or because the environment offers opportunities for particular activities such as skiing or climbing.

Other physical environments that attract people include:
- upland areas of moorland with steep gorges and waterfalls
- mountain areas with high peaks and steep valleys
- areas with rivers and lakes
- areas with spectacular scenery, like the Grand Canyon in the USA (**B**)
- places with rare animal and plant life, such as tropical rainforests or savanna grasslands
- wilderness areas of unusual physical landscape, such as Alaska or Antarctica
- places where there is current volcanic activity.

B – The Grand Canyon, USA

National parks

National parks have some of the most spectacular scenery in the world. The first national parks in England and Wales were set up in 1951 in order to 'protect areas of great natural beauty' and to 'promote the enjoyment of recreational activity'. Since that time the number of visitors to the parks has risen dramatically — the most popular parks attract more than 20 million visitors a year. (C)

Reasons for growth in the number of visitors include:

- an increase in car ownership
- an increase in the length of paid holidays
- changes to working patterns resulting in an increase in leisure time
- greater affluence, which has given people more money to spend on holidays and day trips
- the development of new roads and motorways, increasing levels of access
- raised awareness of the beauty of the countryside and the recreational opportunities it can offer
- an increasing proportion of retired people.

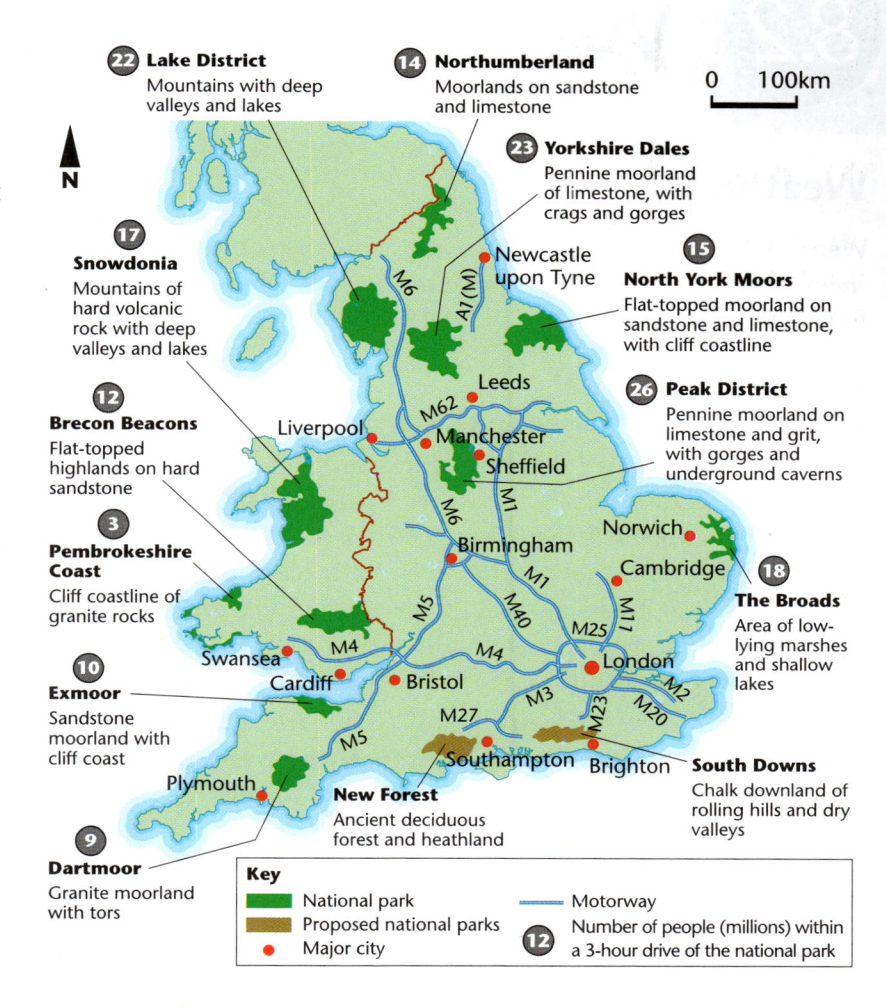

22 Lake District Mountains with deep valleys and lakes

14 Northumberland Moorlands on sandstone and limestone

23 Yorkshire Dales Pennine moorland of limestone, with crags and gorges

17 Snowdonia Mountains of hard volcanic rock with deep valleys and lakes

15 North York Moors Flat-topped moorland on sandstone and limestone, with cliff coastline

12 Brecon Beacons Flat-topped highlands on hard sandstone

26 Peak District Pennine moorland on limestone and grit, with gorges and underground caverns

3 Pembrokeshire Coast Cliff coastline of granite rocks

18 The Broads Area of low-lying marshes and shallow lakes

10 Exmoor Sandstone moorland with cliff coast

South Downs Chalk downland of rolling hills and dry valleys

New Forest Ancient deciduous forest and heathland

9 Dartmoor Granite moorland with tors

Key
- National park
- Proposed national parks
- Major city
- Motorway
- **12** Number of people (millions) within a 3-hour drive of the national park

C – Location and characteristics of national parks in England and Wales

Questions

1. Why are coastal areas still the most important location for tourism?
2. Describe the landscape in photographs A and B, and explain how it might attract visitors.
3. Why might there be a conflict between 'preserving the environment' and 'using the environment to develop the local economy'?
4. a) How many national parks are there in England and Wales?
   b) Which two parks have the most people within a three-hour drive?
   c) Identify four national parks that have different physical characteristics.
      i) Name each of the parks.
      ii) Briefly describe its location and characteristics.
   d) Why is it likely that the number of visitors to national parks will continue to increase?

Managing the Physical Environment

8.2 Weathering and erosion

Weathering

Weathering is the initial process in the breakdown of rocks. It can be divided into three main types: physical, chemical and biological.

Physical weathering

This is the action of temperature and rainfall on rocks.

- *Freeze–thaw.* Water gets into cracks in rocks and when temperatures fall, the water freezes. As it freezes, it expands and pushes the rock apart. This continual **freeze–thaw action** eventually leads to pieces of rock breaking away (frost-shattering). This type of weathering is common in highland areas where large quantities of frost-shattered material, called scree, are found at the base of steep slopes (**A**).

- *Wetting–drying.* In coastal areas where there are clay cliffs, the constant wetting and drying out of the rocks causes deep cracks to appear. Eventually the cliff begins to break down and material is washed away by the sea.

- *Changes in temperature.* Rocks are heated by the sun and expand during the day. At night, as temperatures fall, the rocks contract. This continual expansion and contraction causes cracks to appear and the rock begins to break down, often in surface layers (**B**). This is called *exfoliation* and is common in hot desert areas where daily differences in temperature can be great.

Chemical weathering

Chemical weathering is the breakdown of rocks by chemical reaction, usually involving rainwater. All rainwater contains weak acids, and these acids attack the rock. Limestone is particularly vulnerable as it is dissolved by rainwater. Many old limestone buildings need constant repair because of chemical weathering (**C**).

Biological weathering

Biological weathering is the breakdown of rocks by the action of plant roots or by animals. As the roots of plants grow, they force their way into cracks in rocks and this eventually forces the rock apart.

Definitions

Weathering — the breaking of rocks by the action of the weather, chemicals or plants.

Erosion — the wearing down or removal of material by water, ice or wind.

A – Scree results from freeze–thaw weathering

B – Exfoliation in a hot desert

C – A statue that has been damaged by chemical weathering

8 Pressures on the physical environment

The formation of limestone scenery

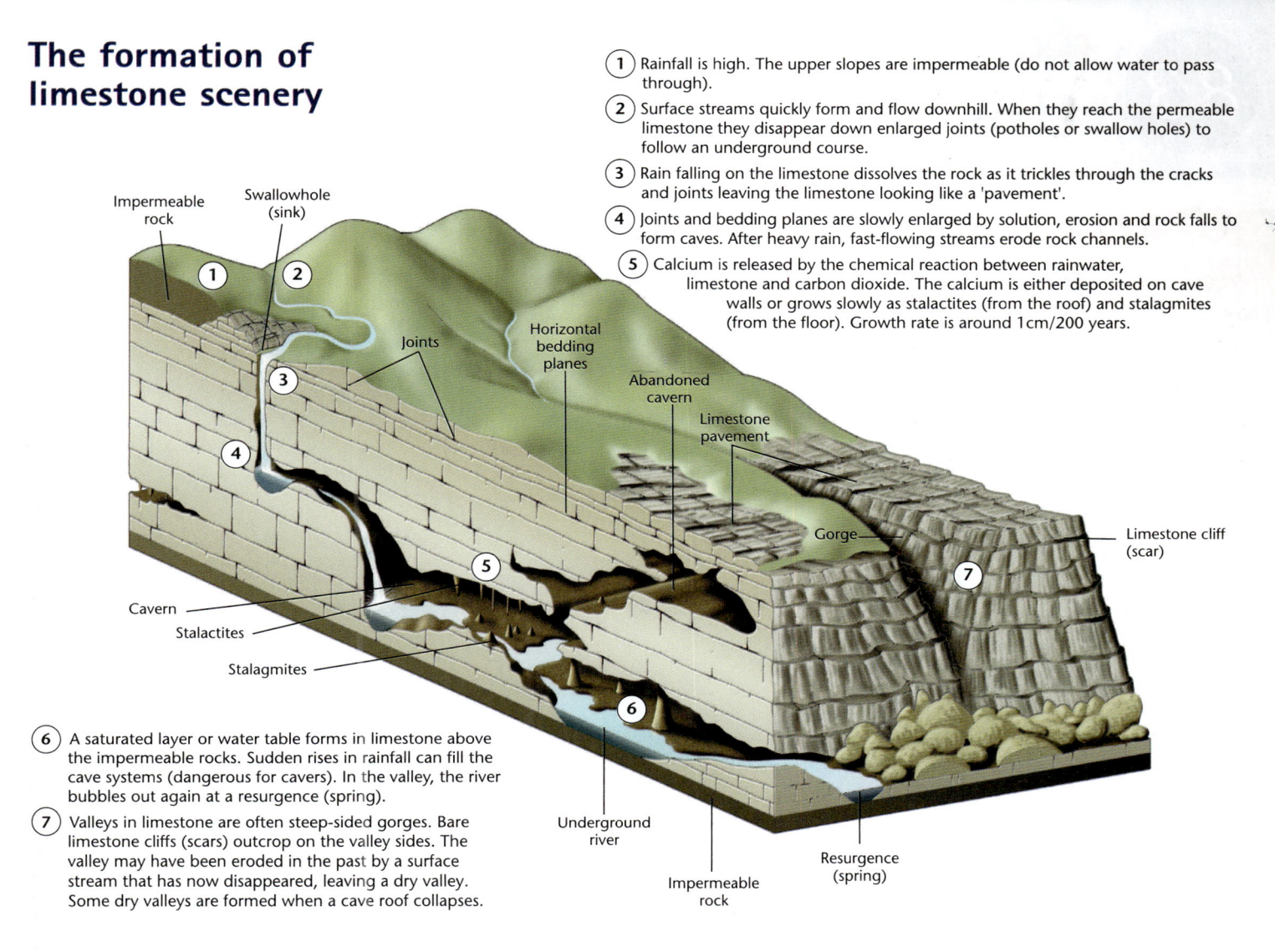

1. Rainfall is high. The upper slopes are impermeable (do not allow water to pass through).
2. Surface streams quickly form and flow downhill. When they reach the permeable limestone they disappear down enlarged joints (potholes or swallow holes) to follow an underground course.
3. Rain falling on the limestone dissolves the rock as it trickles through the cracks and joints leaving the limestone looking like a 'pavement'.
4. Joints and bedding planes are slowly enlarged by solution, erosion and rock falls to form caves. After heavy rain, fast-flowing streams erode rock channels.
5. Calcium is released by the chemical reaction between rainwater, limestone and carbon dioxide. The calcium is either deposited on cave walls or grows slowly as stalactites (from the roof) and stalagmites (from the floor). Growth rate is around 1cm/200 years.
6. A saturated layer or water table forms in limestone above the impermeable rocks. Sudden rises in rainfall can fill the cave systems (dangerous for cavers). In the valley, the river bubbles out again at a resurgence (spring).
7. Valleys in limestone are often steep-sided gorges. Bare limestone cliffs (scars) outcrop on the valley sides. The valley may have been eroded in the past by a surface stream that has now disappeared, leaving a dry valley. Some dry valleys are formed when a cave roof collapses.

Erosion

Rocks can be worn down and carried away (transported) by the action of water, ice or wind. The eroded material is eventually deposited to form new landscape features.

There are four main processes of erosion:

- **Attrition** — rocks collide as they are transported and are worn into smoother, rounded stones.
- **Abrasion/corrasion** — material rubs against river banks or valley sides as it is transported, or is hurled at cliffs by the sea. This acts like sandpaper on the landscape, gradually wearing it away.
- **Corrosion** — some rocks, like limestone and chalk, are dissolved by the natural acids in water and are carried away in suspension.
- **Hydraulic action** — river banks or cliffs can be worn away by the sheer force of water hitting them, or blasted apart as air is forced into cracks.

Questions

1. Why is freeze–thaw weathering more common in highland areas?
2. Why is exfoliation more common in desert areas?
3. Why is the rate of chemical weathering often greater in industrial areas?
4. What is the difference between *weathering* and *erosion*?
5. Describe the processes and features associated with weathering and erosion in limestone scenery.

Managing the Physical Environment

8.3 CS Coastal environments – the Wessex coast

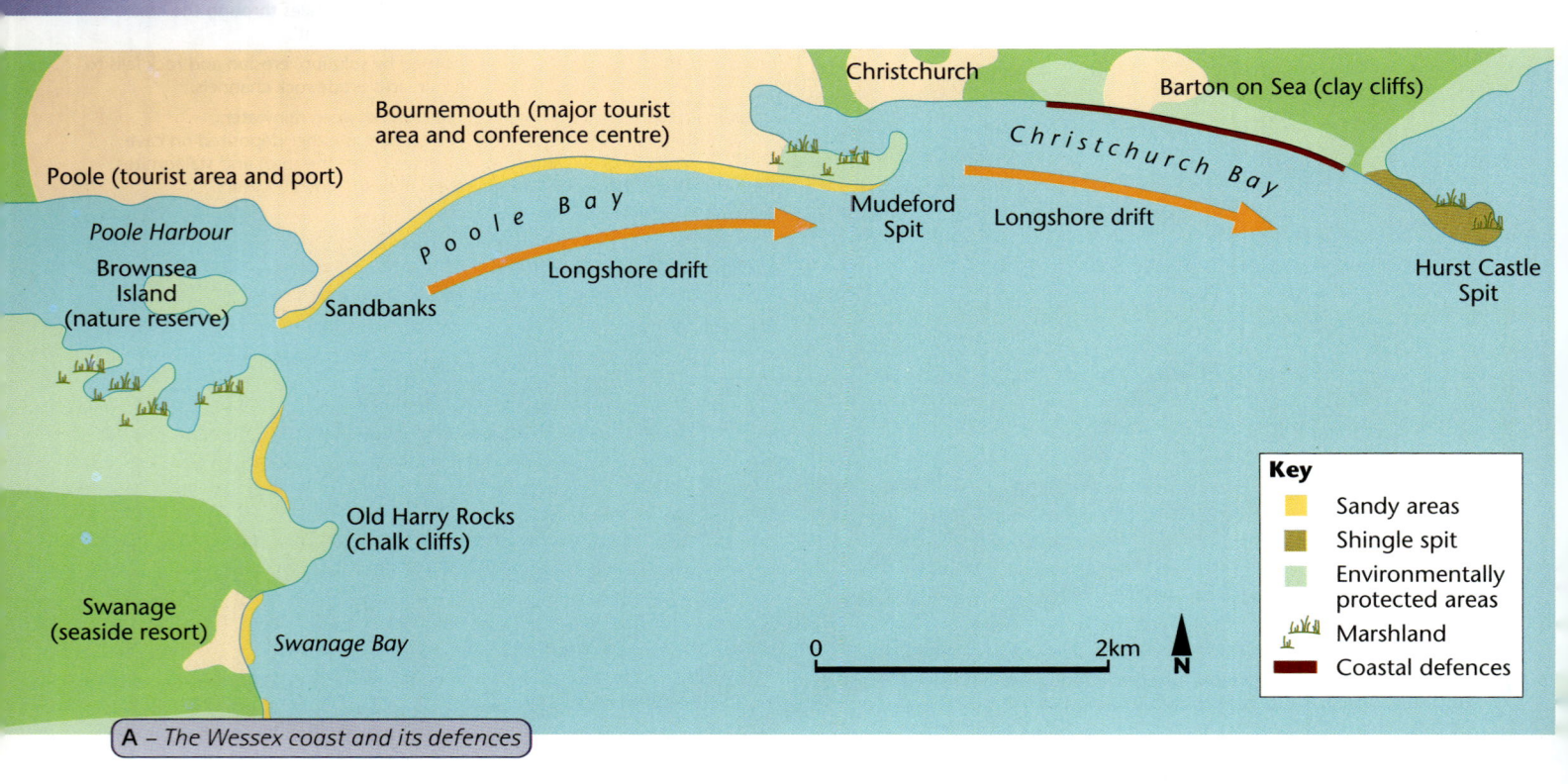

A – The Wessex coast and its defences

Coastal erosion

There are four main processes of erosion along the coast:

- *hydraulic action* — cliffs broken down by the waves forcing water or air into cracks in rock surfaces
- *corrasion* — waves hurling material against the cliff
- *attrition* — rock fragments rubbing against each other and being worn down
- *corrosion (solution)* — cliffs slowly being dissolved by seawater.

B – The erosion of a chalk headland

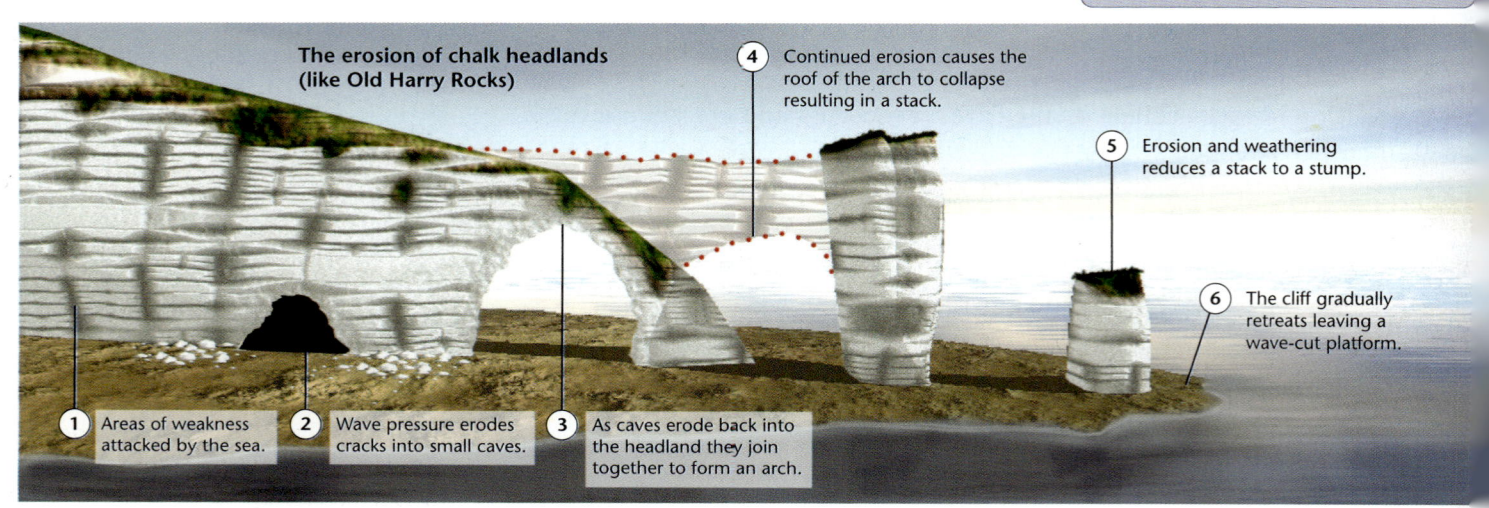

The erosion of chalk headlands (like Old Harry Rocks)

1. Areas of weakness attacked by the sea.
2. Wave pressure erodes cracks into small caves.
3. As caves erode back into the headland they join together to form an arch.
4. Continued erosion causes the roof of the arch to collapse resulting in a stack.
5. Erosion and weathering reduces a stack to a stump.
6. The cliff gradually retreats leaving a wave-cut platform.

8 Pressures on the physical environment

The movement of material by longshore drift

When waves approach a beach at an angle, the *swash* pushes material up the beach at the same angle. The *backwash* carries the material directly down the slope of the beach. In this way material moves along the coast in the process of longshore drift (C).

Key
- 1–6 Movement of pebbles along the beach
- swash
- Direction of longshore drift
- backwash

Waves approach at an angle
Backwash is always at right-angles
Direction of the longshore drift
Groynes built to slow movement of material and protect the beach

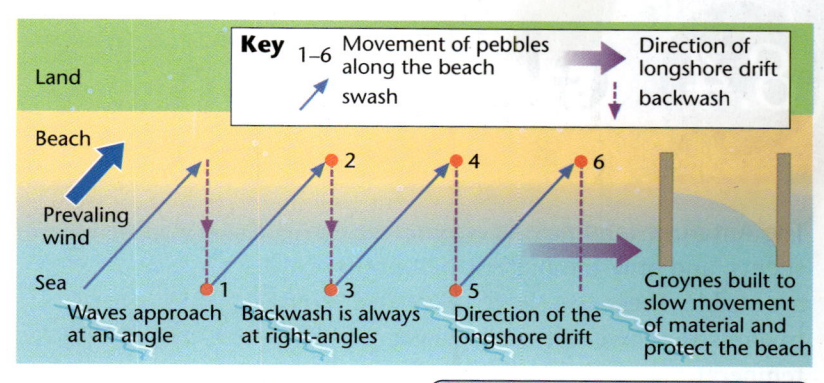

C – The process of longshore drift

Coastal deposition

In some coastal areas, material is deposited to create new landforms. *Spits* are formed where longshore drift moves large amounts of material along a coast until the coastline changes direction. At this point the material is deposited and it gradually builds up into a spit (D). The end of the spit is usually curved as a result of strong ocean currents pushing material towards the land.

River depositing silt
Longshore drift
Groynes
Storm waves curve the end of the spit

Key
- Saltmarsh/mudflats
- Shingle spit
- Marsh

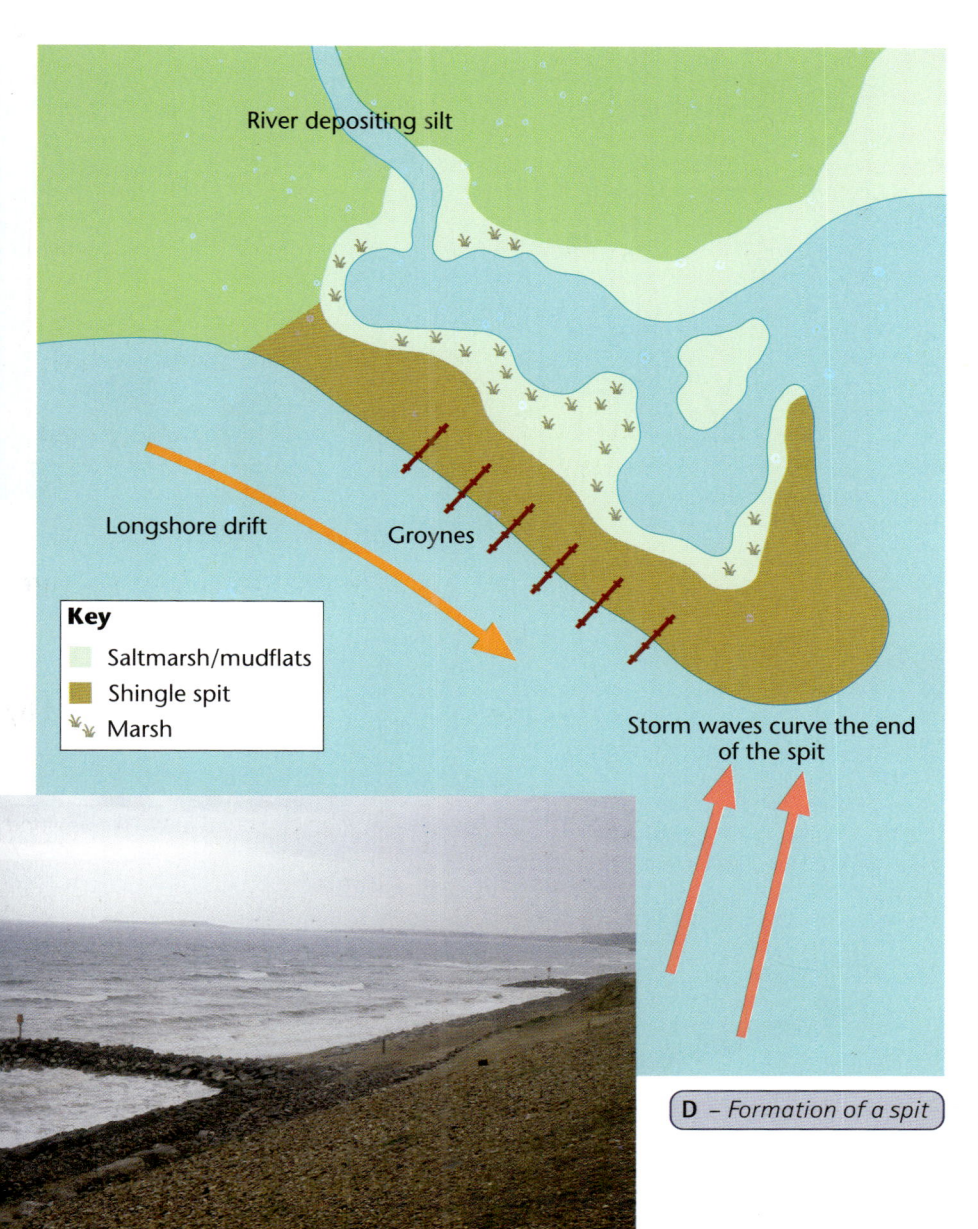

D – Formation of a spit

E – Groynes on the coast at Barton-on-Sea

Questions

1. Use **B** to describe and explain the formation of caves, arches and stacks.

2. a) What is the name given to the movement of material along a coast?
   b) Use an annotated diagram to explain this movement.
   c) Why are groynes (**E**) built in coastal areas?

3. Use **D** to describe and explain the formation of a spit.

4. Why might clay cliffs erode more quickly than chalk cliffs?

5. Why are coastal areas like the Wessex coast (**A**) popular with tourists?

Managing the Physical Environment

8.4 Glaciation

The Antarctic landmass is covered by ice-sheets, and only the highest mountain peaks are visible. These ice-sheets (**A**) move slowly towards the lower latitudes where temperatures are higher. Here the ice melts and large chunks break off and float away as icebergs. Scientists believe that ice-sheets both in the north and south polar regions are becoming smaller, and this could be evidence to suggest that global temperatures are rising. The other places that have permanent ice are high mountain areas where temperatures are very low all year round. Ice has collected in hollows on mountainsides and built up over thousands of years (**B**). As more ice collected, it was pushed down the valley as a **valley glacier** (**C**). At lower altitudes, where temperatures are higher, the ice melts and the resulting water flows down the valley as a river.

If temperatures increase, the glacier will melt and the whole of the valley is then drained only by the river. However, the glacier leaves

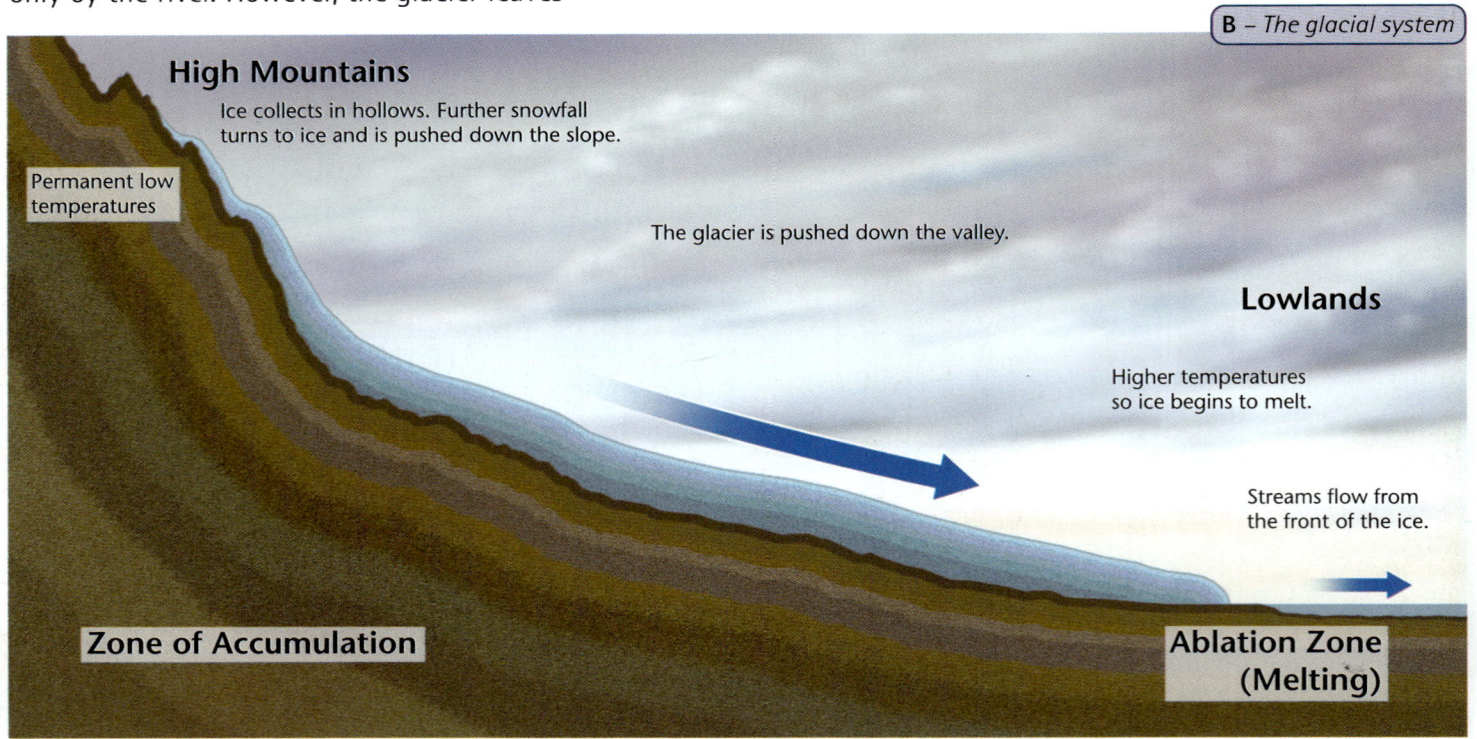

A – *An ice-sheet in Antarctica*

B – *The glacial system*

High Mountains
Ice collects in hollows. Further snowfall turns to ice and is pushed down the slope.

Permanent low temperatures

The glacier is pushed down the valley.

Lowlands

Higher temperatures so ice begins to melt.

Streams flow from the front of the ice.

Zone of Accumulation

Ablation Zone (Melting)

behind clear evidence to show that the valley was once glaciated. The ice was very powerful and it eroded away the sides and base of the valley — tell-tale signs of glacial erosion.

In Britain today there are no areas with permanent ice. Even the highest mountains only have snow and ice on them for a few months each year. However, 30 000 years ago the temperature was much lower and consequently much of Britain was covered in ice. The ice has gone but many of the features it produced remain, especially in highland areas.

C – A valley glacier

The effects of ice on a valley

Comparing a river valley with a valley that was once occupied by a glacier, it is possible to see the effects of glacial erosion (D). The river valley has a narrow base and is generally V-shaped with gently sloping sides. In contrast, the glacial valley has a very wide base and steep sides. The river here is insignificant in relation to the size of the valley, and could not have worn away all the land. As the ice pushed its way down a valley towards the lower land, it eroded both the sides and the base of the valley. When the ice melted, it left behind a massive U-shaped valley with straight sides.

Questions

1. Describe the features of the valley glacier in C.
2. a) Draw a sketch of:
      i) a river valley
      ii) a glaciated valley.
   b) Add notes to describe the main features of each valley.

D – A river valley (left) and a glacial valley (right)

Managing the Physical Environment

8.5 Glaciation – erosion

How does a glacier erode?

There are three main processes of glacial erosion:

- *Abrasion* – material carried by the glacier acts like coarse sandpaper, eroding away the sides and base of the valley.
- *Plucking* – ice freezes to the rock and as the ice moves down the valley it pulls the rock apart.
- *Meltwater erosion* – water flowing under the ice carries material that erodes the bedrock.

Features of highland erosion

Figure **A** shows how glaciers can erode hollows in mountainsides. As these hollows are enlarged, the land between them becomes sharper and the peaks narrower. The name given to these hollows is *corrie*, *cwm* or *cirque*. Where two corries are eroded on either side of a mountain, the sharp ridge between them is called an *arête*.

If a mountain peak is eroded on all sides, what is left is a very steep mountain peak with sharp edges, called a *pyramidal peak* (**B**).

During glaciation
- Weathered material (scree) falls on top of glacier
- Freeze–thaw helps to break up headwall
- Ice is forced down the valley under its own weight
- Rock fragments in the ice erode the hollow

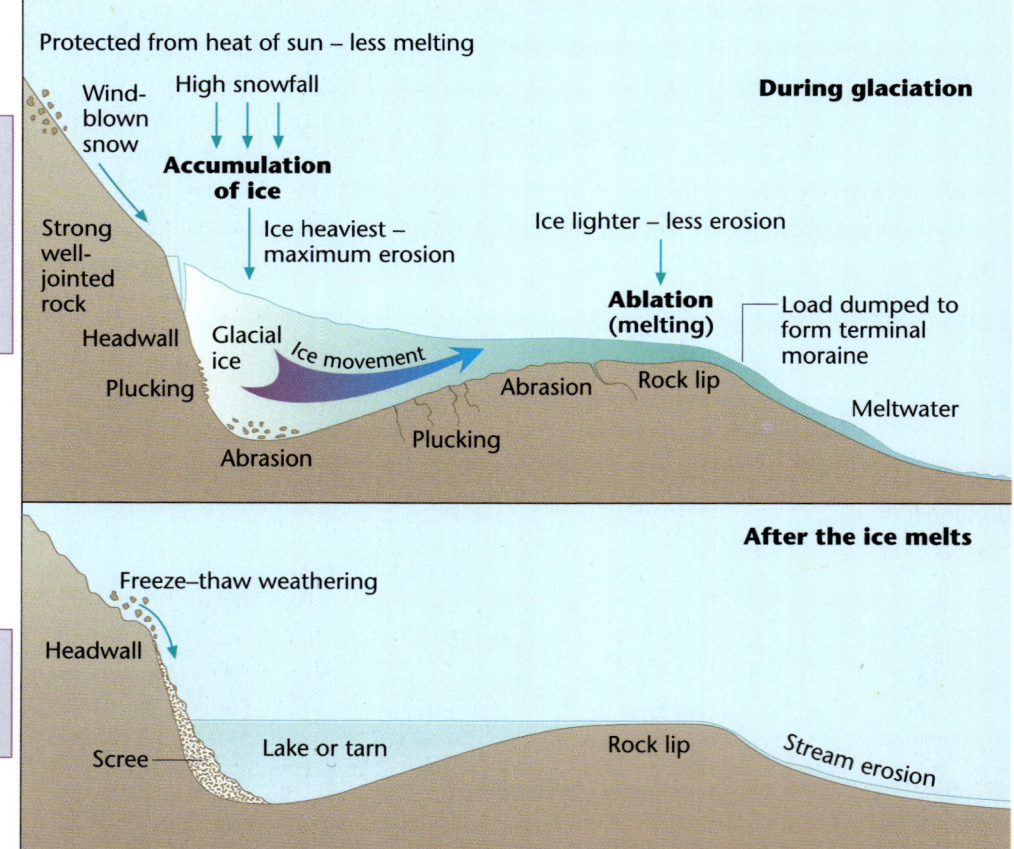

After the ice melts
- A steep headwall remains
- A lake fills the eroded hollow
- A smooth rock lip is visible

During glaciation

Protected from heat of sun – less melting
Wind-blown snow
High snowfall
Accumulation of ice
Strong well-jointed rock
Ice heaviest – maximum erosion
Ice lighter – less erosion
Headwall
Glacial ice
Ice movement
Ablation (melting)
Load dumped to form terminal moraine
Plucking
Abrasion
Rock lip
Meltwater
Abrasion
Plucking

After the ice melts

Freeze–thaw weathering
Headwall
Scree
Lake or tarn
Rock lip
Stream erosion

A – *The formation of a corrie*

Valley features

Further down the valley a number of erosional features can be identified. The shape of the valley itself is important. Glacial valleys are usually deep U-shaped troughs with steep sides (**d**, page 159). Because the main valley was eroded downwards so much, smaller valleys joining it were left hanging well above it. The streams from these hanging valleys now fall down the side of the main valley as waterfalls (**C**).

In the base of many glacial valleys, deep hollows were eroded. When the ice melted, these hollows filled with water to form long, narrow lakes, called *ribbon lakes*.

B – A pyramidal peak: the Matterhorn in the Alps

D – From the *Daily Express*, 13 January 2001

LIFE'S A FREEZE

THE JOSTEDALSBREEN glacier is the largest on the European continent, covering an area of 487km². Thousands of visitors take part in organised walks across various branches of the ice, including the Nigard Valley glacier, or simply enjoy the view from the informative Glacier Cathedral centre.

Plenty of options are available to suit different budgets or time constraints, from easy two-hour outings to all-day hikes, along with crash courses in ice-climbing.

Norway's fjordland provides excellent opportunities for rewarding outdoor activities. The place feels like a big kids' playground, with outdoor adventures set against captivating scenic backdrops – genuinely jaw-dropping vistas of still, blue fjords, neatly lined with pastel-coloured wooden boathouses – all in the shadow of jagged mountain tops.

C – A hanging valley

Questions

1. Describe the main features of glacial erosion.
2. Use an annotated sketch to describe and explain the formation and features of highland erosion.
3. Use **C** and **D** to explain why glacial landscapes attract visitors.

8.6 Glaciation – deposition

How does a glacier transport material?

Material carried by ice is called *moraine* and can vary in size from large boulders to fine clay. Rock fragments falling from the valley sides are transported as *lateral* (edge) *moraine*. If two glaciers join, a *medial* (middle) *moraine* is formed.

Glacial deposition

When a glacier begins to melt, the material it has been carrying is deposited. There are many different depositional features (**B**):

- *Boulder clay* — a layer of unsorted stones, clay and sand deposited as the ice retreats (melts).
- *Lateral and medial moraines* — ridges of material deposited at the edges or in the middle of the valley.
- *Erratics* — large boulders deposited as the ice melts, often hundreds of kilometres from where they originated (**A**).

A – An erratic

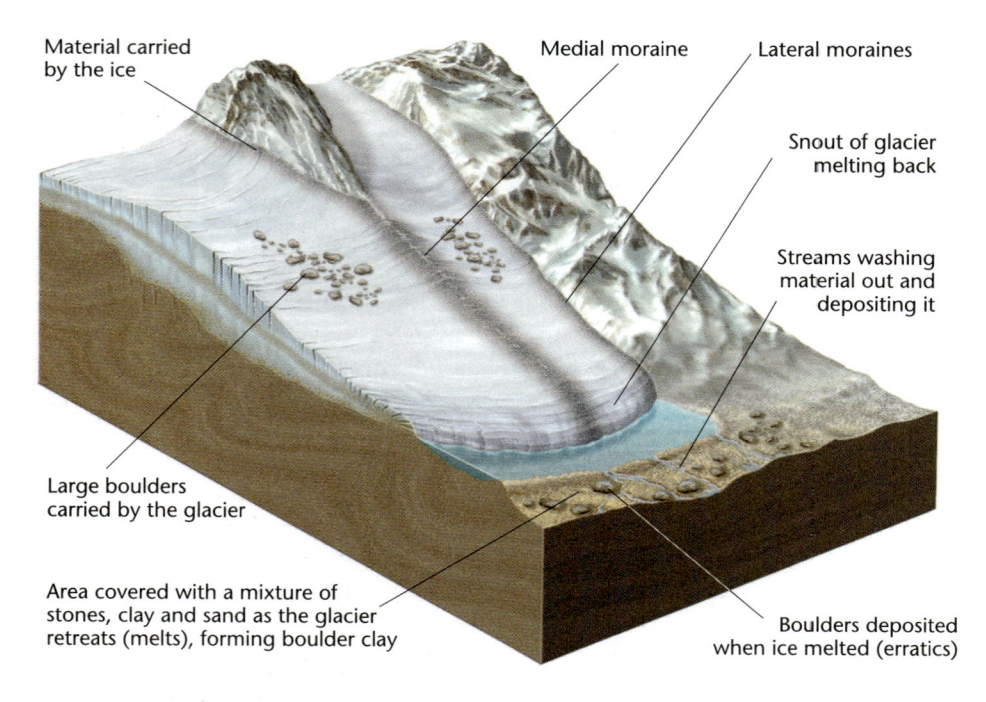

B – Features of deposition

8 Pressures on the physical environment

How a landscape is changed by glaciation

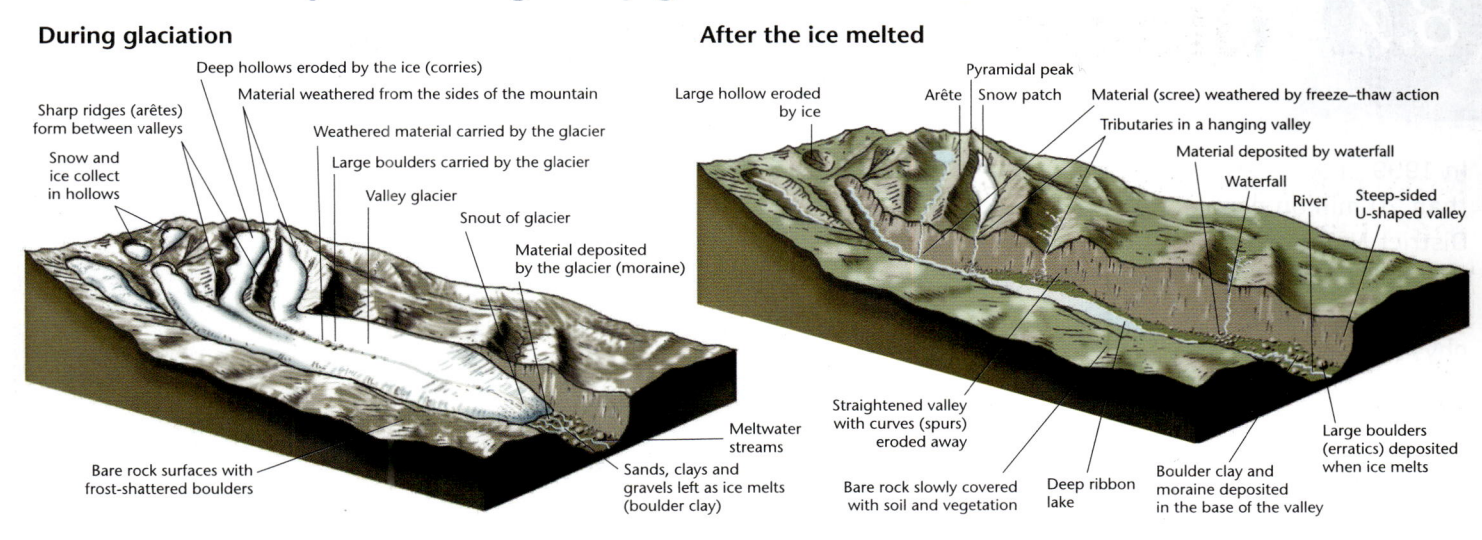

During glaciation

- Deep hollows eroded by the ice (corries)
- Material weathered from the sides of the mountain
- Sharp ridges (arêtes) form between valleys
- Weathered material carried by the glacier
- Snow and ice collect in hollows
- Large boulders carried by the glacier
- Valley glacier
- Snout of glacier
- Material deposited by the glacier (moraine)
- Bare rock surfaces with frost-shattered boulders
- Meltwater streams
- Sands, clays and gravels left as ice melts (boulder clay)

After the ice melted

- Pyramidal peak
- Arête
- Snow patch
- Large hollow eroded by ice
- Material (scree) weathered by freeze–thaw action
- Tributaries in a hanging valley
- Material deposited by waterfall
- Waterfall
- River
- Steep-sided U-shaped valley
- Straightened valley with curves (spurs) eroded away
- Bare rock slowly covered with soil and vegetation
- Deep ribbon lake
- Boulder clay and moraine deposited in the base of the valley
- Large boulders (erratics) deposited when ice melts

C – OS map extract 1:50 000 scale showing part of the Lake District

Questions

Study **C**.

1. Locate and describe three features on the map which might suggest that the area has been affected by glaciation.

2. Use map evidence to identify five factors suggesting that this area is used by visitors.

3. Explain how the physical geography of the area affects communications.

© Crown Copyright

Managing the Physical Environment

8.7 CS The Lake District National Park

In 1999, it was estimated that more than 20 million people visited the Lake District National Park (A). They visited the area largely because of the spectacular scenery and wide range of physical environments which offer both peaceful holidays and the opportunity for activity breaks. The qualities that attract visitors also encourage people to buy holiday homes in the area or even retire there.

The area has a resident population of over 40 000 people. Some of these people live in scattered settlements and isolated farms in the valleys, but most live in the major settlements on the edge of the lakes. Keswick, with a population of approximately 5000, is the largest settlement.

The Lake District National Park has many special qualities including:

- a number of different physical landscapes, including coastal areas, mountains with fast-flowing streams, and steep-sided, lake-filled valleys (C)
- a wide range of ecosystems including both freshwater and saltwater habitats, deciduous woodland, heathland and a variety of grassland communities — in some higher parts there are rare alpine communities, with mosses and lichens on north-facing slopes
- over 100 **Sites of Special Scientific Interest (SSSIs)** and a number of national nature reserves
- over 3000km of public footpaths and bridleways giving access to all but the most remote areas of the national park (B)
- a number of small, semi-rural settlements which have many attractive buildings with historical links

A – The Lake District National Park

B – Mountains in the Lake District

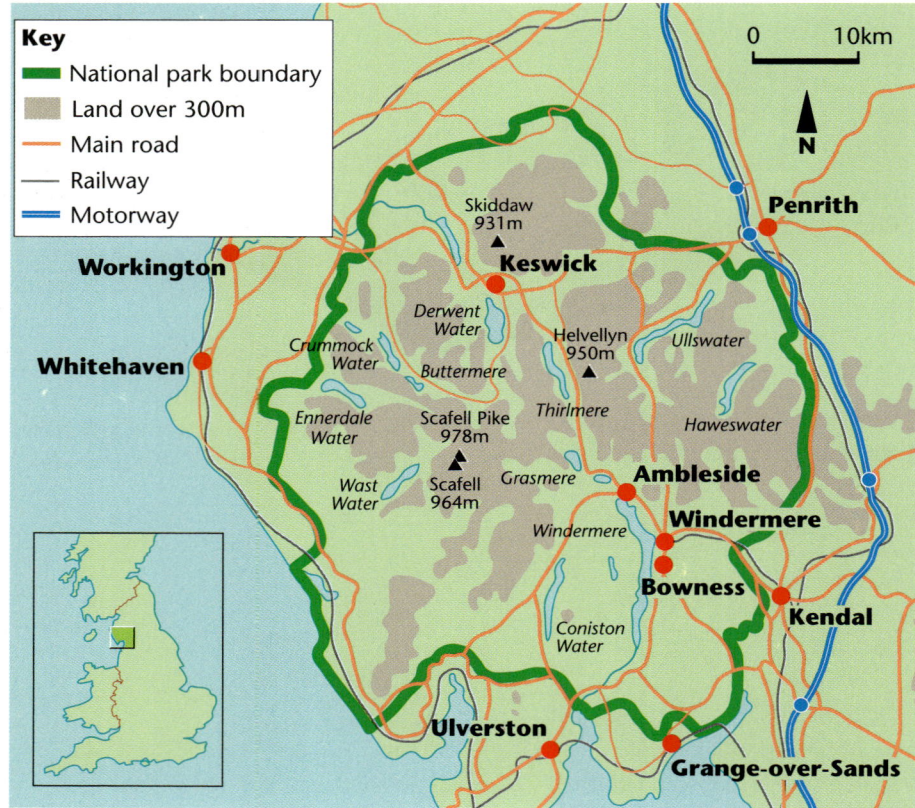

C – Ullswater from Crowbarrow Park, Cumbria

8 Pressures on the physical environment

- the opportunity for a range of leisure pursuits including walking, horse-riding, climbing and watersports activities.

The importance of tourism to the area

Tourism is very important to the local economy. The majority of the working population is employed either directly in tourism-based activities or in jobs that are linked to tourism (D). In Keswick and Windermere over 50 per cent of the working population is employed in hotels, catering or other tourism-related activities (compared with 6 per cent nationally). However, many of these jobs are seasonal or part-time and this can mean that average yearly incomes are low.

D – Tourism is vital to the residents of the Lake District

Factfile

THE LAKE DISTRICT NATIONAL PARK

Population: 42 239

Housing:
Dwellings   22 930
16% of all dwellings were second homes/holiday homes
Source: 1991 Census data

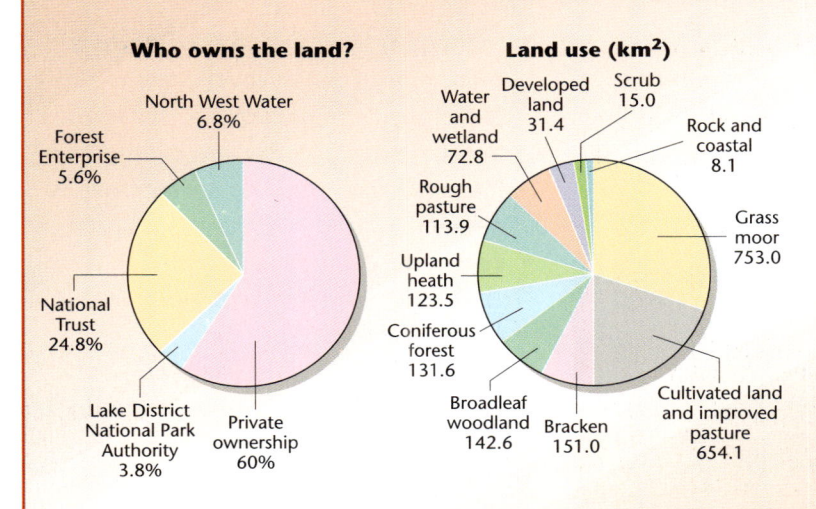

Who owns the land?
- North West Water 6.8%
- Forest Enterprise 5.6%
- National Trust 24.8%
- Lake District National Park Authority 3.8%
- Private ownership 60%

Land use (km²)
- Water and wetland 72.8
- Developed land 31.4
- Scrub 15.0
- Rock and coastal 8.1
- Grass moor 753.0
- Cultivated land and improved pasture 654.1
- Bracken 151.0
- Broadleaf woodland 142.6
- Coniferous forest 131.6
- Upland heath 123.5
- Rough pasture 113.9

Highest mountains
- Scafell Pike   978m
- Scafell   964m
- Helvellyn   950m
- Skiddaw   931m

Deepest lakes
- Wast Water   74m
- Windermere   62m
- Ullswater   61m

Percentage of residents working in different sectors of employment:

Agriculture, Forestry, Fishing	9.90
Energy/Water/Mining	4.70
Manufacturing	9.00
Construction	7.80
Retailing/Transport/Catering	37.50
Service industries	29.60
Other	1.50

Source: 1991 Census data; Cumbria County Council

Tourism Facts (1994):
- Number of day visitors   10 million (est.)
- Number of staying visitors   12 million (est.)
- 90% of visitors travelled to the area by car
- Average money spent by visitors per day:
  — day visitors   £10.80
  — staying visitors £33.82
- Most popular areas:
  1 Windermere/Bowness
  2 Keswick
  3 Ambleside
- Major problems identified by visitors:
  1 Overcrowding
  2 Traffic congestion
  3 Parking

E

Managing the Physical Environment

8.8 Managing visitors in the Lake District

The two main purposes of the Lake District National Park Authority are:
1 the conservation of the national park
2 the promotion of opportunities for the understanding and enjoyment of the national park.

Because the area is home to more than 40 000 residents, there is also a duty to look after the economic and social well-being of the local community. Since many local people rely on the tourist industry for employment, this might suggest that the area should have more visitor-related development. However, there is concern that increasing use of the area by visitors, and continued visitor development, are putting too much pressure on the area. In 1997 the Lake District National Park Authority made it clear in its management plan that the priority was 'to create a balance between the needs of local people and visitors while preserving the natural beauty of the area'.

What pressures does the area face?

- With over 20 million visitors a year, parts of the area become congested and there are serious traffic and parking problems during the summer.
- Many visitors take walks into the hills and this leads to problems of erosion on the more popular footpaths (A). A survey in 1999 calculated that it would cost nearly £5 million to repair the most damaged footpaths.
- Some areas become very overcrowded during the summer months, especially the lakeside towns and villages.
- In many towns, shops selling local goods have been replaced by gift shops and cafés which do not serve the needs of local people.
- One in six houses in the Lake District is either a second home or a holiday cottage. This demand pushes up property prices so that local people cannot afford to buy homes.
- In winter most holiday homes are empty, and some villages are losing their sense of community.
- Employment is often seasonal and dominated by the tourist industry. (In September 1997 at the Windermere Job Centre, 130 out of 142 vacancies were based on tourism.) Many jobs are therefore part-time and wages are low.

A - *Footpath erosion in the Lake District*

How is the Lake District National Park Authority responding to these pressures?

Some measures to deal with the pressures include:
- improving drainage in areas of footpath erosion and repairing footpaths sympathetically using natural materials
- resting some footpaths and directing people away from the busiest areas
- setting aside 'quiet areas' where activities are restricted, in order to preserve the peace of the area
- protecting some highland areas from excessive traffic by making them 'walk-in only' areas
- managing the lakes according to a hierarchy of usage levels, from 'developed' to 'natural' — Haweswater and Ennerdale Water are examples of 'natural' lakes, and no surface use is allowed
- zoning of developed lakes so that activities can only take place within a specified zone
- increasing parking areas along the A591, the main north–south route through the lakes
- banning heavy lorries except where they have business in the area
- encouraging the development of local crafts and skills and the manufacture of local products
- having stricter planning regulations for turning local buildings into tourist amenities.

8 Pressures on the physical environment

Honeypot sites

Some areas attract a large number of people because of their attractive scenery, leisure facilities or historical interest. These areas are often referred to as **honeypot sites** because they attract people like 'bees around a honeypot'. The challenge in these areas is to manage the pressures that thousands of visitors create, while trying to preserve the special nature of the area.

An example of a honeypot in the Lake District National Park is Lake Windermere (**B**), which attracts thousands of visitors, especially in the summer months when the lakeside towns become very crowded.

In this area:
- the increasing number of cars and coaches puts pressure on the limited number of roads and causes severe congestion in the summer months
- the lakeside towns become overcrowded, with people parking their cars in any available place as car parks are full
- there are increasing problems of pollution (litter, traffic, noise) and vandalism
- pressure is growing for further tourist development (caravan sites/holiday homes)
- there is increasing demand on the lake from a variety of users, including ferry boats, water-skiiers, powerboats, fishermen and windsailors.

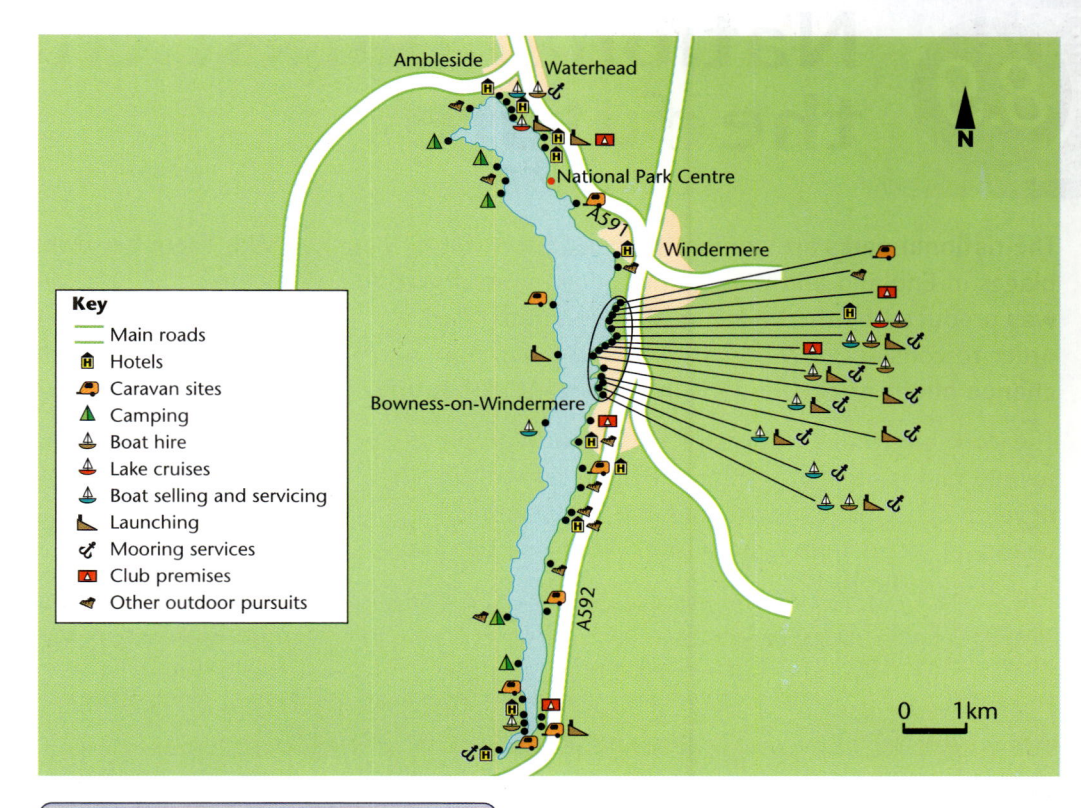

B – Recreational use of Lake Windermere

Questions
These questions refer to the information on pages 164–167.

1 In a survey carried out in 1994, a number of people were asked why they were visiting the Lake District. Figure **C** below shows the top seven answers.

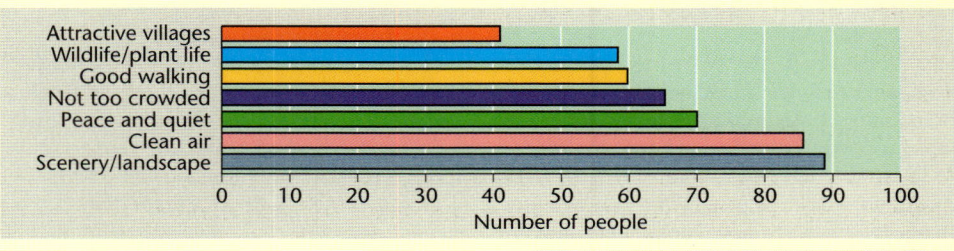

C – Why people visit the Lake District

a) Write a paragraph to describe how the physical environment attracts visitors to the Lake District.
b) For what other reasons might people visit the area?
c) People have said that the growing numbers of visitors are 'spoiling the very environment people come to see'. Explain what is meant by this statement.

2 a) Choose three ways that the Lake District National Park are being managed, and explain how they might reduce some of the pressures.
b) The Park Authority would like to remove powerboat activities from all of the lakes. Do you think that this is a good idea? Give reasons for your answer.

3 Why might conflicts between different groups of people (e.g. farmers, shopkeepers, walkers, water-skiers) develop in the area?

8.9 National parks: choices for the future

The national parks are among the most beautiful places in England and Wales. The following information was produced by the Yorkshire Dales National Park in order to consider how agricultural and industrial change might affect the look of the area in the future.

The Yorkshire Dales National Park is nearly all privately owned and is mostly farmland. Recent agricultural developments have meant that the landscape is changing faster than ever before. What will the area look like in the future?

- Will there be fewer farm buildings and drystone walls?
- Could the area be turned into a farming museum for tourists?
- Will the land be used more for leisure activities like horse-riding, hiking and shooting?
- Will forestry consist of blocks of fast-growing conifer trees rather than traditional broad-leaved forests?

Figure **A** gives an impression of what the landscape could look like in 30–40 years' time.

A – Options for the future?

The farming option
This landscape is geared to food production. With access to the latest technology and breeding techniques, larger farms could still make a profit by buying out the smaller farms to create big livestock ranches. The flowery meadows would be intensified and the grass taken mainly for silage. Large sheds and wire fences would replace walls and field barns. Broad-leaved woodlands would die as a result of stock damage and extensive conifer woodlands would be over planted. Some heather moorland would convert to grassland due to over-grazing.

The environmental option
Here no public money would be available to help farmers continue to farm livestock, and maintain traditional landscape features. Farmers would be helped by conservation agencies and would have access to a pool of labour to help with landscape maintenance work. Farmers could also supplement their income from farm-based tourism. There would be more heather moorland and flowery meadows than today. Broad-leaved woodlands, walls and field barns would be well looked after.

The natural option
If the whole area was deliberately taken out of private ownership and set aside for wildlife, or if farm support was withdrawn and much land was abandoned, a wild, forested landscape would develop. Since there would be no farming, visitors could wander where they wished, except in special wildlife reserves. In time even the barns and the farm buildings would be overgrown. A few people would find employment providing outdoor recreation.

Questions

1. Describe the characteristics of each of the three options for the future (A)

2. a) Which of the landscapes do you think is the best option for the future? Explain your answer.
   b) Are there any negative aspects to your choice?

8 **Pressures on the physical environment**

Figure **B** shows part of the Yorkshire Dales National Park.

B – *Ordnance Survey 1:50 000 map extract showing part of the Yorkshire Dales National Park*

Questions

1 a) Name the symbols found at the following grid references: a) 933720 b) 979646.
   b) State two ways that height is shown on the map.

2 In which direction does Malham Tarn (8966) lie from Arncliffe (9371)?

3 Describe the physical characteristics of the area in grid square 9570.

4 Malham Tarn is a local honeypot site. Use map evidence to suggest why people might be attracted to this area.

5 Use map evidence to suggest that the area on the map is heavily used by visitors.

6 Explain why traffic congestion might be a problem in the area shown on the map.

169

Managing the Physical Environment

8.10 cs National parks in the USA

Yellowstone was the world's first national park (**A**), set up in 1872 to protect the area against the expansion of industry. Since then over 50 national parks have been established to protect a range of different environments across the USA. The parks are managed by the National Parks Service, whose aims are:
- to protect areas of outstanding scenery and wildlife
- to provide areas of recreation for both American citizens and visitors from abroad.

The increasing use of national parks

The growth of car ownership and leisure time has led to a significant increase in the number of visitors to national parks. The six most popular parks account for well over 50 per cent of all visits (**B**), and it is in these parks that there are particular problems of overcrowding. There is also the added problem of 'honeypot' pressure within these parks as thousands of people visit the most scenic areas.

Pressures on the parks

- There is traffic congestion in the most popular areas, and the increased risk of traffic accidents.
- When car parks are full, people park illegally on verges, blocking roads and damaging vegetation.
- Increasing levels of pollution are caused by traffic, litter and noise.
- Wildlife, including bears and deer, are disturbed. Animals are put in danger by people feeding them or leaving litter, which they eat.
- Wilderness areas are damaged by hikers and campers who cut wood and build fires.
- Overuse of hiking trails can cause problems of erosion. Off-road vehicles can add to this problem.
- The development of hotels and other tourist facilities changes the land use.

A – Old Faithful, Yellowstone National Park

1	Great Smoky Mountains	9.1 million
2	Grand Canyon	4.8 million
3	Yosemite	4.2 million
4	Yellowstone	3.8 million
5	Arcadia	3.1 million
6	Rocky Mountains	3.0 million

B – Number of visitors to the top six national parks, 1999

Managing visitor pressure

The National Parks Service has put several schemes in place to manage visitor pressure in the busiest areas. These include:
- traffic management schemes to restrict traffic in the busiest areas, particularly at bank holidays and weekends
- the use of shuttle buses so that cars can be left at key points and people shown around by bus
- restricting visitor numbers by controlling routes in some areas
- encouraging the wider use of the popular parks in order to reduce the pressures on honeypot areas
- encouraging the use of the less well-known parks in order to take pressure away from the most popular parks
- education programmes to inform people about the fragile nature of the environments, and the dangers of overuse
- control of building developments inside the parks.

8 Pressures on the physical environment

Yosemite National Park

Yosemite National Park is a wilderness of evergreen forests and alpine meadows, on California's eastern flank (C). The landscape is a spectacular mixture of soaring mountains, plunging waterfalls and deep valleys. Within the park the Yosemite Valley is the main honeypot area. Visitors are attracted by the granite scenery and the Merced River which flows through the valley.

Pressures on the Yosemite Valley:

- more than 1 million vehicles each year
- the problem of parking in the valley
- the continual development of tourism facilities
- the increasing numbers of people wanting to camp in the area.

The following advice is given to visitors:

- Leave your car outside the park — use the tour buses.
- Limit the use of fires — do not cut down vegetation.
- Camp away from fragile vegetation.
- Bury waste — do all washing at least 30m away from streams.
- Do not build walls or damage the landscape.
- Take your rubbish home.
- Do not feed the wild animals.

C – *Location of Yosemite National Park, California*

D – *Yosemite National Park*

Questions

1. Why has the number of visitors to national parks increased?

2. a) State three ways in which the increase in visitor numbers is putting pressure on the parks.
   b) Explain how three of the ways suggested for managing visitor pressure might reduce the pressure in some areas.

3. Describe the attractions of the Yosemite National Park.

4. Why does the Yosemite National Park give advice to visitors?

171

Managing the Physical Environment

Decision–making exercise

Oasis Holiday Village, Cumbria

In 1995 a company put forward plans to build a holiday village in the Lake District. The location of this proposed development was just outside the national park boundary, 6km west of Penrith (A).

Local people had conflicting views on the proposal. Some considered that the jobs created would outweigh any problems, while others felt that such a large development would bring with it all sorts of pollution and congestion problems. A number of views expressed at the time are shown here.

After thorough consultation it was decided that the scheme should go ahead, and the Oasis Holiday Village opened in 1998.

Study the information about the development carefully before answering the questions.

Questions

1. Suggest why this area was chosen by the developers.
2. Use B to help you explain why people describe this area as a 'unique and special environment'.
3. Describe and explain the concerns that people had about the development.
4. Explain how the development might benefit the local economy.
5. Do you think the decision to allow this development to go ahead was correct? Explain your answer.

A – Location of the Oasis Holiday Village

A £100 million 'Oasis' holiday village is planned in an area of unspoilt countryside, and will create 1500 jobs.

The project, between the A66 and the A6 trunk roads, will include artificial lakes and an indoor waterworld. A range of sporting activities are planned and accommodation will be in lodges and villas.

The managing director said 'The village is for family holidays, and we have planned with environmental concerns very much in mind'.

Key
- National park boundary
- County boundary
- Motorway
- Roads
- Built-up areas
- Lakes

Pressures on the physical environment

B – The local environment

Major economic benefits will result from the construction and operation of the Oasis Holiday Village. Around 800 jobs will result from the construction phase, a large number of these will involve local people.

During the operation of the holiday village, the local area will benefit by:
- the extra wages for local people being spent on local goods and services
- spending on local goods and services by the company
- holiday makers spending money in the area.

The holiday village will require 700 permanent staff, of which two thirds will be full-time. Guests will have the opportunity to purchase foods and crafts produced in the Lake District, further increasing business.

Adapted from *Oasis Village Newsletter*, July 1995

Some of the objections to the development were:

'The Cumbria Wildlife Trust objects to this development because it will have an adverse impact on local animals, including squirrels, badgers and a variety of birds. The disturbance during construction will last two years and during this time many animals will move away, perhaps never to return.'

'We would like this development to stop for the following reasons:
- the scheme is too large and does not fit in with the environment
- it may cause water shortages for local people
- the noise, waste and light pollution is unacceptable
- this development may change the whole forest ecosystem.' (from the Whinfell Forest Action Committee)

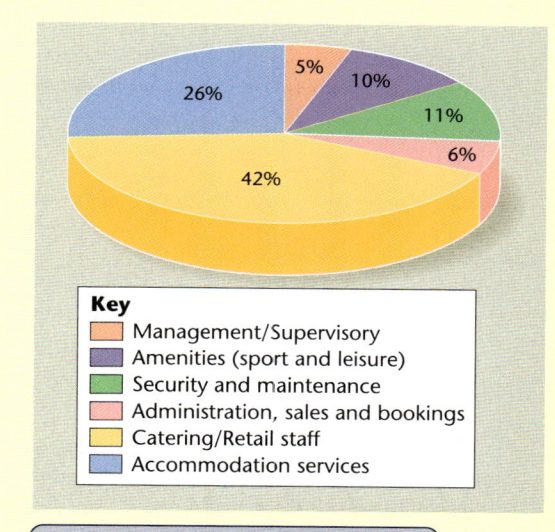

Key
- Management/Supervisory — 5%
- Amenities (sport and leisure) — 10%
- Security and maintenance — 11%
- Administration, sales and bookings — 6%
- Catering/Retail staff — 42%
- Accommodation services — 26%

C – Oasis Village employee statistics

Managing the Physical Environment — **Pressures on the physical environment**

Exam practice questions

Mark schemes can be found on the book's website, at www.heinemann.co.uk/issuesmarkschemes

1. a) What is meant by:
   i) weathering
   ii) erosion? (4)

   b) Study A.
   i) What are the features marked A and B? (2)

   ii) Feature C is a pyramidal peak. Complete the following paragraph to explain how it was formed. Choose the correct words from the box below.

   Ice builds up in hollows on hillsides. As the ice flows out of the hollow, erosion by plucking and _____ makes the hollow bigger to form a _____ with a steep back wall. Where several corries form back to back, a steep pyramidal peak is formed. The peak is sharpened by freeze–thaw _____ . (3)

   - weathering
   - corrie
   - deposition
   - abrasion
   - hanging valley
   - moraine

   c) Explain how weathering and erosion have changed a landscape you have studied. (6)

2. a) Using the information in B:
   i) State two problems of overuse. (2)
   ii) Which type of tourist may trespass *and* cause road congestion? (1)
   iii) Which two types of tourist may trespass *and* cause erosion? (2)
   iv) How many types of tourist may cause erosion? (1)

   b) What is a *honeypot site*? (2)

   c) i) Explain how natural environments can be damaged by overuse. (6)
   ii) Describe some of the ways that the damage can be reduced. (6)

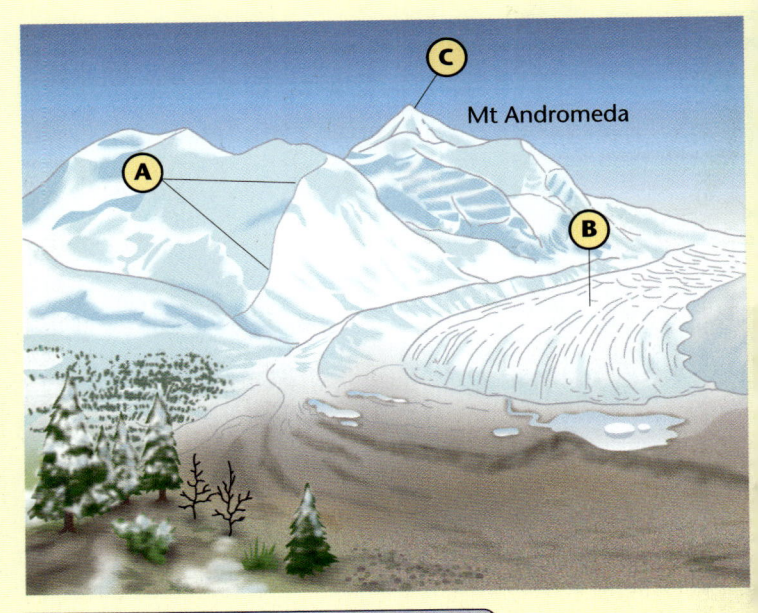

A – Mount Andromeda and the Athabasca Glacier in the Rocky Mountains, Canada

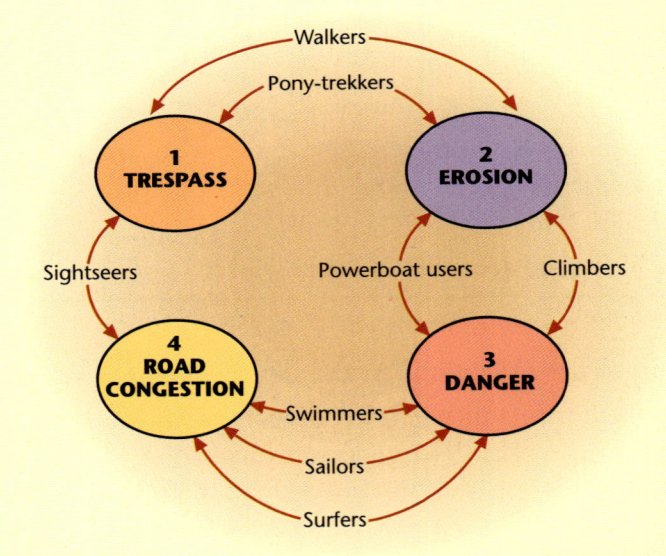

B – Tourist problems in an area

Key
1, 2, 3, 4 problems of overuse
→ types of tourist who cause problems
Trespass means entering land without the owner's permission.

MANAGING ECONOMIC DEVELOPMENT

9 Contrasting levels of development

Contrasting living standards exist between and within countries. How can development strategies be used to improve disadvantaged areas?

Managing Economic Development

9.1 Contrasts in development

Development refers to the way that a country's economy grows. All countries are developing — 50 years ago few people in the UK could afford to own a car, and yet today most families own at least one. This is a measure of how wealth has increased and technology has made manufactured goods relatively less expensive.

In the UK, average incomes are high and most people have access to good social facilities such as education and healthcare. This is not the case in all parts of the world. Some countries are wealthier than the UK, while in others many people live in extreme poverty with only basic facilities.

Countries are often described as being *more economically developed countries (MEDCs)* or *less economically developed countries (LEDCs)*. These terms divide the world into two parts: the highly developed 'North' and the developing 'South'. What this does not do is take into account the differences between countries. For example, using the simple North/South map, both Bangladesh and Brazil are identified as LEDCs, yet the average income in Brazil is approximately 15 times that of Bangladesh!

To give a more useful idea about development, more detailed information is required. One of the most commonly used statistics is **Gross National Product (GNP)/capita** (or GNP per person). This is the value of all the goods and services produced by a country in a year, divided by its population, and the resulting figure is usually given in US dollars ($). If GNP figures are included on the basic North/South map, a more detailed picture can be seen (**B**). This map illustrates the differences between North and South, but also shows that there are big differences within those areas (look, for example, at the difference between Africa and South America).

	MEDCs	LEDCs
Average wealth	Most have an average of more than $10 000 a year.	Most are under $3000 a year. There is a big gap between rich and poor.
Work	The majority of the working population are employed in service industries.	In the poorest countries most people work in primary industry, many as subsistence farmers.
Energy	High levels of consumption, both industrially and domestically.	Low levels of energy use with heavy use of primary fuels (wood/animal dung) in rural areas.
Housing	High standards of housing with high percentage of basic facilities (water/power/sanitation).	Many people living in poor-quality housing with few facilities.
Healthcare	Good access to doctors and a network of hospitals offering efficient treatment.	Few doctors, particularly in rural areas. Hospital facilities often expensive, treatment is at a basic level for most people.
Education	Compulsory education and high levels of literacy. Availability of higher education and training.	Access to education variable — often very poor in rural areas. Levels of literacy often vary between males/females.

A – General differences between MEDCs and LEDCs

Gross National Product was used by the United Nations to compare levels of development up until 1990. Then it was realized that although it is a useful statistic, it hides many important factors because:

- it is an average figure and there may be big differences within a country
- it does not always take into account the value of the informal sector of employment, or subsistence farming, so income figures may not be accurate

9 Contrasting levels of development

- it does not say much about general living conditions in a country or how much is actually spent on things like healthcare and education.

In order to get a better overall picture of development, a number of other criteria can be used. These should include both economic and social factors (C).

B – World development based on GNP/capita (US$)

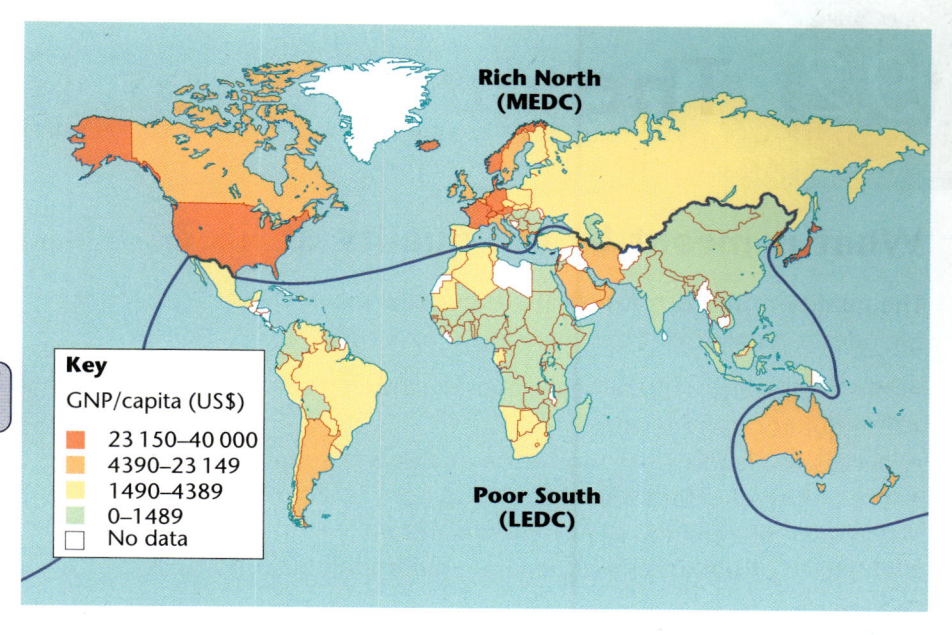

Key
GNP/capita (US$)
- 23 150–40 000
- 4390–23 149
- 1490–4389
- 0–1489
- No data

Rich North (MEDC)
Poor South (LEDC)

C – Measures of world development, 1997

Status	Country	GNP ($)	Birth rate	Death rate	Life expectancy	Infant mortality	Adult male literacy (%)	Adult female literacy (%)	People/doctor	Access to sanitation (%)	Access to safe water (%)	Energy use	Employment structure		
													Primary	Secondary	Tertiary
High-income countries (MEDCs)	Japan	39 640	10	7	80	4	99	99	608	95	85	3856	7	32	58
	USA	26 980	15	9	76	7.3	98	98	421	90	85	7819	3	24	70
	France	24 990	13	9	78	5	99	99	344	100	96	4042	6	28	63
	UK	18 700	13	11	77	6.2	99	99	611	100	96	3772	3	24	70
Middle-income countries (NICs)	Brazil	3640	22	7	67	48	83	83	844	92	73	718	25	25	50
	Mexico	3370	27	5	72	34	92	87	615	87	70	1561	23	29	48
Low-income countries (LEDCs)	Egypt	790	29	8	64	62	64	39	1316	84	68	600	40	19	41
	India	340	29	10	59	75	65	38	2459	63	29	248	61	14	25
	Kenya	280	38	12	54	62	86	70	21 970	49	43	110	78	9	13
	Bangladesh	240	31	11	58	77	49	26	12 884	83	30	64	60	15	25

*NICS = newly industrialised countries

Definitions

Infant mortality – the number of deaths per 1000 live births.
Adult literacy rate – the percentage of adults who can read and write.
People/doctor – the number of people for each doctor.
Access to safe water/sanitation the percentage of the population that has access to safe water/sanitation.
Energy use – the kg oil equivalent/person/year.
Employment structure – the percentage of the working population employed in the three main industrial areas
- **Primary:** industry associated with natural resources (mining, fishing, farming, forestry).
- **Secondary:** industry associated with manufacturing. This can either be finished products or parts of products.
- **Tertiary:** services industry (shops, garages, education, tourism, healthcare, etc.).

Questions

1. Why might using GNP to compare countries not always be useful?
2. Construct a scattergraph to see if there is a link between 'People per doctor' and 'Life expectancy'.
3. Suggest three other types of information that might be useful to compare countries. Explain your choices.

Managing Economic Development

9.2 The quality of life

What is meant by the quality of life?

The quality of life is not just about average income but includes a number of other factors, for example:

- the availability of healthcare and education
- the quality of housing
- access to clean water, sanitation and power supply
- the ability to afford a proper diet
- the level of personal security and safety
- the level of pollution and general environmental conditions.

In 1990, the United Nations realized that measuring development by using only GNP did not take many of these factors into consideration. It therefore devised the Human Development Index (HDI).

What is the Human Development Index?

The Human Development Index is described as a measure of social welfare, because it takes into account both social and economic factors. It uses the following data to construct an index:

- life expectancy
- school enrolment and attainment (literacy rates/years in school)
- the 'real' GNP per person — not just the amount of money but what it will actually buy in that country.

Top five countries, 1997		Bottom five countries, 1997	
Canada	.960	Mali	.229
France	.946	Burkina Faso	.221
Norway	.943	Niger	.206
United States	.942	Rwanda	.187
Iceland	.942	Sierra Leone	.176
UK =	0.92	World average =	.76

A – A comparison of living standards

Each of these variables is ranked from 0 to 1, with the poorest at 0 and the best at 1. So a country with very high life expectancy will have a figure close to 1. The HDI is the average of the three scores: the higher the number, the more economically and socially developed the country. (A, B)

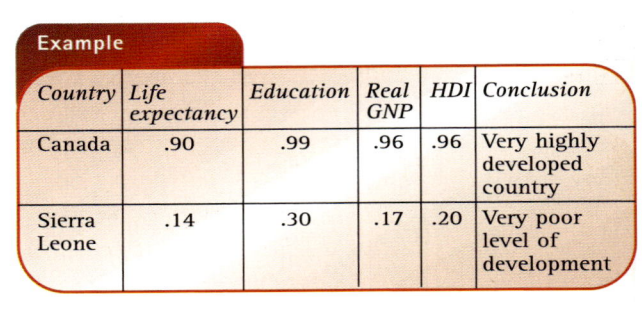

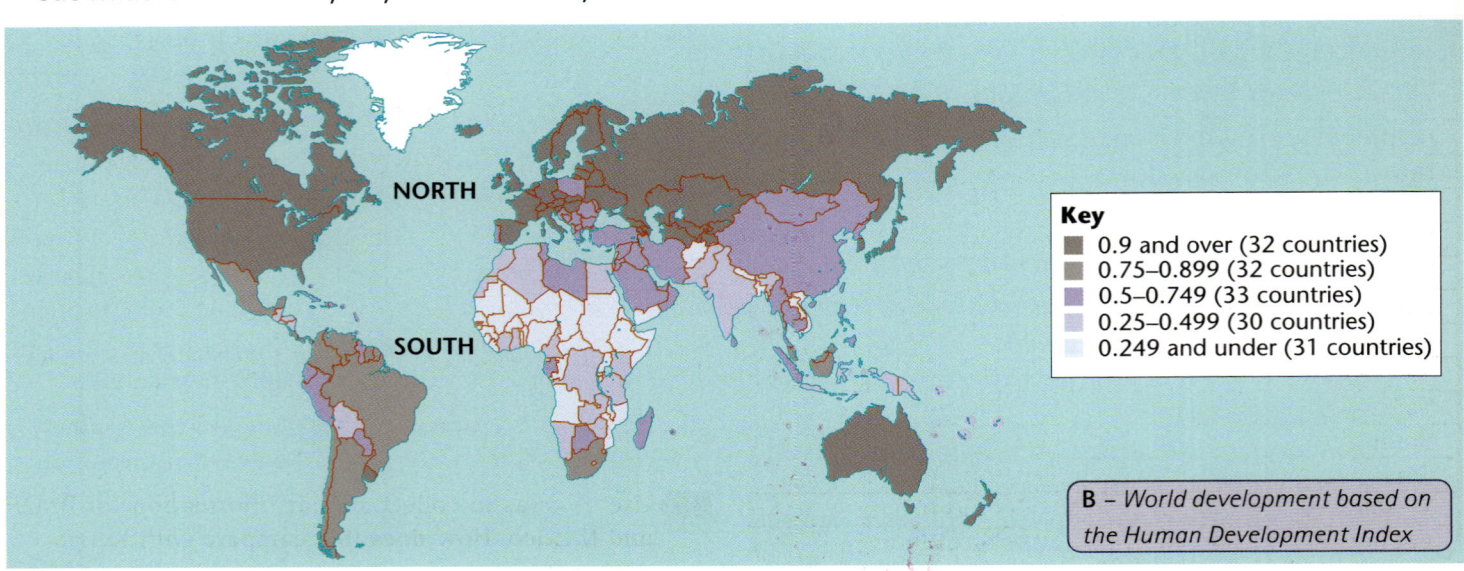

Example

Country	Life expectancy	Education	Real GNP	HDI	Conclusion
Canada	.90	.99	.96	.96	Very highly developed country
Sierra Leone	.14	.30	.17	.20	Very poor level of development

Key
- 0.9 and over (32 countries)
- 0.75–0.899 (32 countries)
- 0.5–0.749 (33 countries)
- 0.25–0.499 (30 countries)
- 0.249 and under (31 countries)

B – World development based on the Human Development Index

Comparing levels of development

Database: Kenya — an LEDC

Kenya is a tropical country on the eastern side of Africa. The land to the north is dry, while the eastern coastal zone bordering the Indian Ocean is more fertile. The main industries are agriculture (notably coffee and tea production) and tourism, which is growing rapidly. The country has high population growth which is putting pressure on per capita growth.

Birth rate	38/1000
Death rate	12/1000
Infant mortality	62/1000
Life expectancy	54 years
GNP ($)	$280
Labour force in agriculture	75%
Urban population	27%
Adult literacy	78%
People/doctor	21 970
Safe water	49%
Sanitation	43%
Cars	14/1000 people
Telephones	9/1000 people
Energy use	110kg oil/person

Database: Japan — an MEDC

Japan is located off the South-east Asian coast. It is a mountainous country with fertile coastal plains. It is one of the world's biggest producers of high-tech electronic products and motor cars. Most people live in modern, highly developed urban areas which are located in coastal areas.

Birth rate	10/1000
Death rate	7/1000
Infant mortality	4/1000
Life expectancy	80 years
GNP ($)	$39 640
Labour force in agriculture	7%
Urban population	78%
Adult literacy	99%
People/doctor	608
Safe water	95%
Sanitation	85%
Cars	520/1000 people
Telephones	487/1000 people
Energy use	3856kg oil/person

The Human Development Report 1997

The Human Development Report (1997) looked at 175 countries and made observations about the progress that had been made in reducing global poverty. It reported that since 1960:

- poverty had been reduced in almost all countries
- child death rates in LEDCs had been cut by more than half
- malnutrition rates had declined by one-third
- the proportion of children attending primary school had increased from 50 per cent to 75 per cent

At the same time it stated that:

- 1.3 billion people were living on less than $1 a day
- the income of a number of countries had decreased over the past 10 years
- 1 billion people could not read or write
- 840 million people were malnourished
- 1.2 billion people lacked access to safe water
- 30 per cent of the population in the least developed countries (mostly in Africa) were not expected to survive to the age of 40
- half a million women in LEDCs died each year in childbirth.

Questions

1. The HDI is a *composite* index (made up of more than one measurement of development). Why is this more useful than looking at a single measure?

2. Compare and comment on the pattern of HDI figures in African and South American countries (B).

3. 'The Human Development Report offers some hope for the future.' What do you think of this view?

4. Select five pieces of data from the databases which might be most useful in comparing Kenya and Japan. What does your chosen data suggest about the comparative levels of development?

5. Use an atlas to collect similar information for Brazil and Mexico. How does this compare with Kenya and Japan?

9.3 Contrasting living standards

Brazil

Development data such as GNP ($) or the Human Development Index (HDI) give an impression about a country's general level of development. Although this is useful when comparing countries, it often hides the fact that there might be significant differences within a country. In LEDCs, this is particularly true. In rural areas people are often poorer and have fewer opportunities whereas in urban areas access to jobs and services is better. Even within urban areas there are significant differences, with some people living in large, expensive housing with modern facilities, while other people live in overcrowded slums.

Figure A identifies some of the economic and social differences that exist in Brazil, a rapidly developing middle-income country in South America.

A – Brazil

Region	Urban population %	% employed in agriculture locally	Adult literacy %	% of Brazil's industrial employment	% of Brazil's energy use	Share of national income %
North	52	22	52	3	2	4
North East	49	24	42	12	12	11
South East	86	9	89	66	70	65
South	59	21	70	15	13	17
Centre-West	57	22	57	4	3	3

(Approximate data, - 1996)

North
Tropical rainforest area which is remote and inhospitable. The government has given financial assistance to develop agriculture and mining.

North East
Brazil's dry zone has regular problems of drought. Most large settlements and industry are found near the coast. Communications are poor and away from the coast it is mainly agricultural.

Centre-West
Except for the industrial and commercial area of Brasilia, the area is mainly agricultural. It is remote, with poor communications.

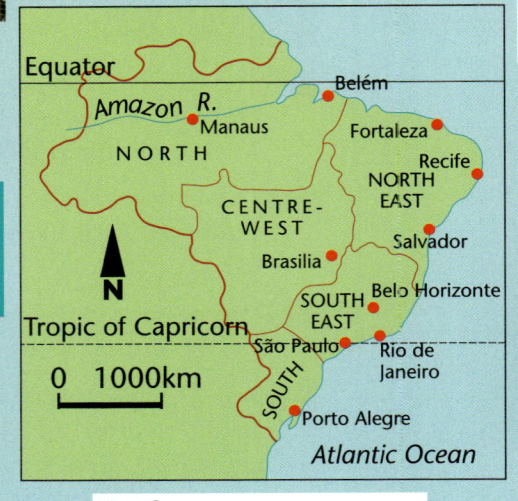

South
Recent industrial development on the coast with growing urban areas.

South East
The industrial heartland of Brazil, with many manufacturing and service industries. Large cities and coastal ports provide jobs, good communications and infrastructure.

9 Contrasting levels of development

CS Oil-rich countries — the Middle East

Oil is one of the world's most important sources of energy and at present most countries could not manage without it. It is only found in a few places in the world and many oil-producing countries use all the oil they are able to produce. A small number of countries in the Middle East have been able to sell large amounts of oil in recent years because they produce far more than they need (C). These countries are able to control nearly one-quarter of the world's trade in oil, and estimates suggest that they have approximately 40 per cent of all remaining reserves.

The wealth produced through selling oil has enabled some of these countries to develop rapidly, building new cities, communication networks, and large areas of housing with schools and hospitals. (B)

Few countries have changed as much as Kuwait and Saudi Arabia in the last 50 years. Kuwait was described as 'a small and sleepy mud-walled trading and fishing port' before the discovery of oil, while in the 1950s most of Saudi Arabia's people were desert nomads. Both of these countries have developed major oil-refining and petrochemical industries and today they have highly developed economic and social facilities. Most of the population live in modern cities, their children go to school, and living standards are high. However, some people have regrets about such rapid development and feel that it has put pressure on traditional ways of life and values.

B – Kuwait

C – Oil-producing countries in the Middle East

Database: Saudi Arabia and Kuwait

		Saudi Arabia	Kuwait
Life expectancy	1981	60	71
	1995	71	76
Literacy rate (%)	1981	25	60
	1995	61	77
People/doctor	1981	1819	589
	1995	749	N/A
GNP ($)		7040	17 390
Infant mortality		29	13
Access to sanitation		86%	94% (est.)
Access to safe water		93%	98% (est.)
N/A = not available			Data: 1995

Questions

1. Use the data in A to identify the wealthiest and the poorest regions of Brazil. Explain your choices.

2. Why does physical geography often make some areas of a country difficult to develop?

3. What effect has development had on standards of living in Kuwait and Saudi Arabia?

4. Why have countries with other types of raw material not been able to develop as rapidly as Kuwait and Saudi Arabia?

9.4 Reducing the development gap

The information on pages 176–179 shows that there is a large gap between the richest and poorest parts of the world. This difference is further illustrated by **A**.

Why does a development gap exist?

Recognizing that there are differences in levels of development is relatively easy, but understanding why such a 'development gap' exists is far more difficult. There are many reasons why countries have different levels of wealth and often these are unique to individual places. The following are some of these reasons:

- *Level of industrial development:* some countries have few industries and rely on a narrow range of industrial opportunities.
- *Reliance on primary products:* some countries rely on a narrow range of primary products (minerals, agricultural products) to earn money. When the price of these products falls there is nothing they can do about it.
- *Lack of technology:* this means that it is difficult to compete with other areas and much time is spent performing basic tasks.
- *Using resources to survive:* in some parts of the world every effort is spent on basic survival — gathering food and water, providing shelter, etc. — which leaves little time or energy for development.
- *Lack of power:* modern, highly developed industrial areas use massive amounts of power (electricity). If a country does not have energy supplies it has to buy them from abroad.
- *The nature of trade:* many poorer countries rely on exporting basic goods for income but have to buy more expensive products from abroad. They have little control over prices that are dictated by the richer countries.
- *International debts:* many poor countries spend a lot of valuable money simply paying interest on debts.
- *Political instability:* some countries are unstable and are involved in external or civil wars. This uses up their limited resources.
- *Natural disasters and environmental hazards:* many countries have the added burden of natural disasters (floods, earthquakes, cyclones) or environmental hazards, like water-borne diseases.

How can the development gap be reduced?

In order to reduce the development gap, LEDCs need to be able to develop their economic and social facilities. Creating more jobs, improving agricultural output and building new roads are all examples of improving economic facilities. At the same time, if living standards are to improve, money has to be spent on improving housing conditions, healthcare and education.

How can this be achieved?

There are a number of methods being used to try to increase the level of development in LEDCs.

1 Investment

- LEDCs can borrow money and put in place development projects like multi-use river schemes and road developments.
- LEDCs can encourage transnational companies to set up industries, creating job opportunities and generating wealth.

'A child born in the poorest parts of the world will be fortunate to survive the first two years of life and will spend the rest of their short life with problems of food in squalid conditions with few amenities. Opportunities for education or personal development will be limited and little will be passed on to the next generation. A child born in the wealthiest parts of the world will be born with full medical support and will expect to develop into a healthy, well-nourished child. They will be well educated and expect to get a well-paid job which will allow them to live in a comfortable home with a full range of amenities. Leisure time and holidays will be expected and in the event of illness a doctor or hospital will be available.'

A – *Accident of birth*

2 Government aid projects

LEDCs can use aid from MEDCs to help in the development process. The main types of government aid are:

- **bilateral aid**: aid between two countries which usually involves a loan or investment from an MEDC to an LEDC.
- **multilateral aid**: aid given to LEDCs by MEDCs through international organizations like the World Bank.

Government aid can provide much-needed finance and technical help. However, there has been criticism of some aid projects because:

- money has been wasted on large-scale, unsustainable projects
- MEDCs have control of the money and often link it to trade deals
- they have been slow to be put in place and can make LEDCs reliant on aid.

3 Voluntary aid (non-governmental organizations, or NGOs)

Aid given by charities such as ActionAid, Oxfam and Christian Aid is raised by voluntary contributions. This is often used in response to disasters, or for smaller-scale development projects (**B**), which are often seen as more appropriate in LEDCs.

B – Drilling for clean water in Prey Veng province Cambodia

4 Change the terms of trade

Trade between MEDCs and LEDCs often favours MEDCs because:

- MEDCs protect their markets and do not always allow goods in from LEDCs
- LEDCs export mainly primary goods which are low in price
- the price of raw materials is usually determined in the MEDCs
- there is a significant gap in price between the basic raw material and the finished product and this difference is often earned by MEDCs.

If LEDCs could earn more through trade they would have fewer debts and be able to spend more on economic and social development. In 1994 the World Trade Organization was set up to encourage free trade between all countries of the world. It was hoped that this would give LEDCs a better chance to compete in world markets. Despite this, trade continues to be dominated by the market-led economies, with Japan, the EU and the USA accounting for more than 60 per cent of world trade.

Questions

1. Suggest five reasons why some countries are wealthier than others.

2. Figure **C** shows the breakdown of money from a jar of coffee. The coffee is grown in LEDCs but processed and sold in MEDCs. What does this suggest about the location of jobs associated with coffee, and trade between LEDCs and MEDCs?

C – The costs of a jar of coffee
- 10% Retailing
- 58% Processing, advertising and distribution
- 5% Transport
- 27% Growing and picking

3. Explain what the cartoon in **D** is trying to show.

Managing Economic Development

9.5 Large-scale development projects in LEDCs

The Three Gorges Dam scheme

The Three Gorges is a narrow, steep-sided part of the Yangtze River, one of the world's longest rivers (5000km). The Yangtze Valley is home to more than 400 million people and provides China with more than 60 per cent of its rice crop. In 1992 the Chinese government agreed to the building of the Three Gorges Dam — at more than 2km long and 150m high it will be the world's largest dam by the time it is completed in 2009. The estimated cost of the scheme is between £17 and £21 billion.

Advantages of the scheme

- It will supply more than 10 per cent of China's electricity needs and reduce the need to burn fossil fuels.
- It will supply towns and cities along the Yangtze River with electricity, and encourage industrial development.
- Large ships will be able to reach Chongqing, which is in an area where development has been stunted by a lack of communications.
- It will create thousands of jobs both during construction and after completion as new business develops.
- New towns and farms will be developed, increasing local living standards.
- The lake could be used for fishing or as a store of water for irrigation.
- It will protect millions of people and massive areas of productive farmland from the risk of flooding.

Disadvantages of the scheme

- A lake 600km in length will be created, flooding more than 150 towns and 4500 villages.
- More than 1.3 million people will be forced to move, many against their will.
- It will damage plant and animal life and may bring about the extinction of already endangered species.
- The landscape of the Three Gorges, an increasingly popular tourist area, will be changed for ever.
- Human and industrial waste, which was previously washed down the river, will collect in the lake.
- The dam will trap millions of tonnes of silt. This will reduce the fertility of the soil further downstream.
- Archaeological treasures including ancient temples will be drowned.
- The volume (weight) of water may trigger earthquake activity.

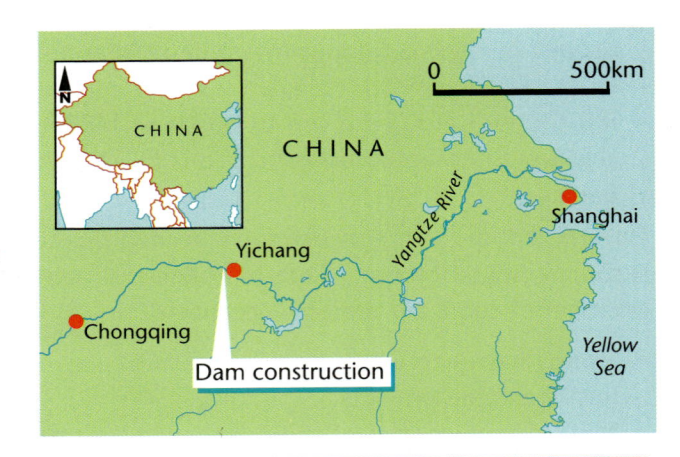

A – Location of the Three Gorges Dam

B – The Three Gorges (before flooding)

CS Tourism – Zimbabwe

Tourism can bring many benefits to LEDCs by helping the development of industry and infrastructure. It often brings much-needed money into areas and creates job opportunities for local people. At the same time, over-exploitation can put pressure on resources and environments and create conflicts with local people. (E)

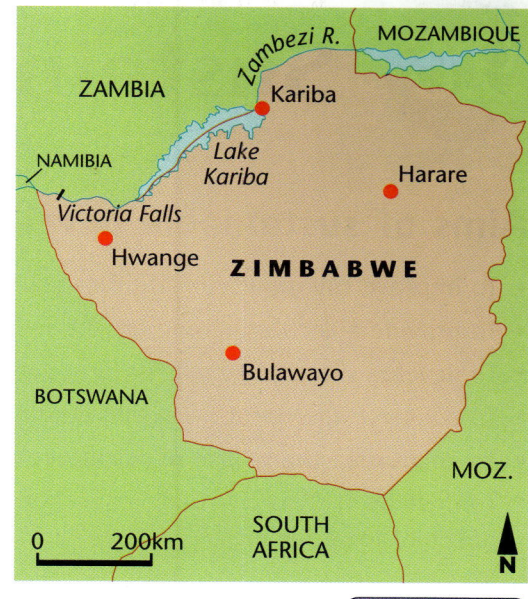

Victoria Falls, Zimbabwe

Zimbabwe attracts more than 1 million visitors a year, and tourism is the country's third largest export earner. Visitors come to Zimbabwe for the stunning scenery and wildlife parks. One of the most popular areas is Victoria Falls on the Zambezi River – a spectacular feature in an area of outstanding physical beauty (see (E) on page 241).

'Camp Fire' schemes

'Camp Fire' schemes are small-scale developments which work in partnership between local people and holiday companies. One of these schemes has been set up in the Victoria Falls area where a small number of 'eco-lodges' have been built for bird-watchers. The developers employ local people to build and run the lodges and pay rent for the land. In return, the local people look after the environment. In this way the project provides work for local people and improves local living standards while ensuring that no harm comes to the environment. This is an example of **sustainable development**.

C – Zimbabwe

D – Victoria Falls Hotel

> Many new buildings have been put up and this can affect the look of the place. The tourist facilities all have running water and electricity while many local villages only have standpipes. It does create work but wages are low and jobs can be seasonal.
> A local holiday company has given my village money because it uses part of our land. We have been able to use it for community projects like the new school, and a water supply.
> The local hotel (D) has given many of its workers education and training and we have good jobs. Tourists spend lots of money in the area and this gives work to local craftsmen and people producing souvenirs. There are few opportunities in this area, so tourism is important. Also it's really good to meet people from other parts of the world.
> A lot of tourists come here for the watersports (white-water rafting) or to see the animals. Some are not really interested in the environment – they leave rubbish behind, and expect to be driven everywhere, eroding the fragile landscape.

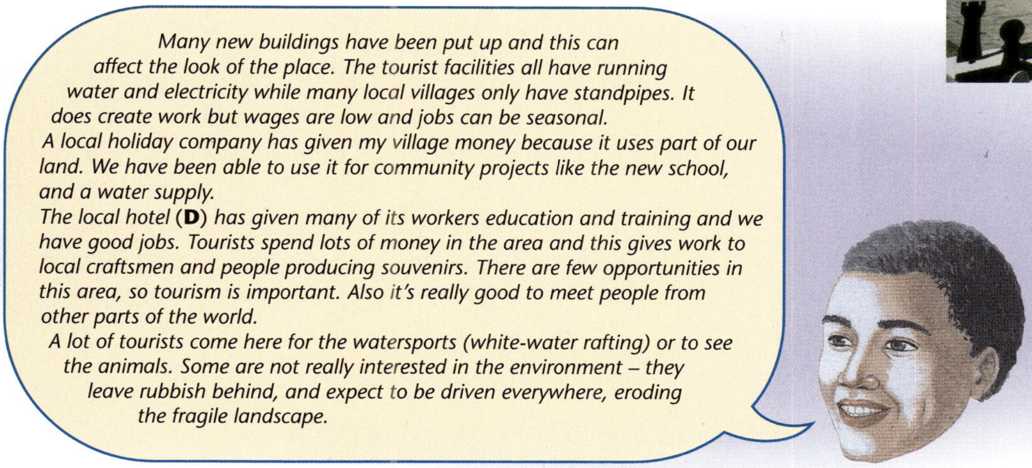

E – The impact of tourism

Questions

1. a) List five advantages and five disadvantages of the Three Gorges Dam scheme.
   b) Explain how the scheme might help the development of the area.
   c) The scheme has been described as 'economic development at the cost of people and the environment'. What is meant by this?

2. a) How can tourism help an area to develop?
   b) List the advantages and disadvantages of tourism to the Victoria Falls area.
   c) Explain why 'Camp Fire' schemes are examples of sustainable development.

9.6 Sustainable development

Aims of sustainable development

- To improve the quality of life for local people.
- To provide a secure income for the local community.
- To develop ways of increasing production without falling into debt.
- To conserve the natural environment.
- To encourage the re-use of resources wherever possible.
- To develop technology that is appropriate to the skills, wealth and needs of local people.

The Liana project, Brazil

The Liana project is run by the Rainforest Action Network (RAN). This is a non-governmental charity set up in 1985 to protect the Earth's rainforests and support the rights of their inhabitants. It aims to develop small rural community enterprises that sell liana vines and their products. These enterprises will cultivate and collect the vines in a sustainable way and produce finished and semi-finished goods locally (A).

The Liana project recognizes that the key to the preservation of the rainforest and its people lies within the local communities. Traditionally, communities clear land for short-term agricultural uses that eventually leave the land non-productive and unable to regenerate forests. Through sustainable projects like this one, local people can look after the forest.

The project has developed a wicker furniture industry in Brazil using the rattan-like lianas that grow in the rainforests. Project staff have found markets for the finished products in Brazil and the USA. They have given money, technical knowledge and equipment to the local communities who will then run their own businesses. At present the vines are harvested in the wild but RAN is working with local communities in developing methods of growing the vines. The industry is using the forest in a sustainable way and giving local people the opportunity to use the forest resources for economic development.

A – Wickerwork products

9 Contrasting levels of development

CS The Village Platform, Mali

The village of Balanfina (population 1200) in southern Mali is 48km from the nearest tarmac road. It can only be reached on foot or by a bumpy one-hour drive in a 4x4 vehicle. Consequently the villagers have to be self-sufficient (**B**).

> The village platform is an invention by a Swiss man, Roman Imboden. Each one costs £2500 and is provided by the United Nations Development Programme (UNDP). It consists of several simple machines driven by an 8 hp engine made in India. It runs on diesel and is multi-functional, as it generates electricity for lighting and cooking, pumps water, processes rice and millet, and welds metals. It takes a lot of pressure off the women, who traditionally fetch water and process crops. You cannot put a price on the opportunities electricity provides and how it can improve the situation in Mali.

> It has made our lives easier. We can prepare our food more quickly and this gives us more time to work in the fields and grow more food. We now have power for cooking and can pump clean, fresh water to our homes.

B – The Village Platform, Mali

CS Tools For Self Reliance, Africa

Every year, Tools for Self Reliance (TFSR) supports at least 700 African groups in some of the poorest countries, by providing them with tools they have requested. These requests are collected by African organizations working with TFSR who have the local knowledge, to ensure that the tools will be useful to local communities, and links that ensure the tools get to the people who really need them.

TFSR works with local organizations in Ghana, Mozambique, Sierra Leone, Tanzania, Uganda and Zimbabwe. By focusing their efforts on these countries, TFSR hopes to make best use of their resources. This might be to start up a training course so that young people can become blacksmiths, tailors, carpenters or builders.

In the UK, 70 volunteer groups collect and repair hand tools. These go to make up carpentry kits, or whatever else has been asked for, from saws and vices to hammers and sewing machines.

Since 1979 when TFSR started, well over half a million tools have been refurbished and sent overseas, assisting many thousands of people. In addition to this, recycling and re-using these well-made tools helps to prevent waste in the UK.

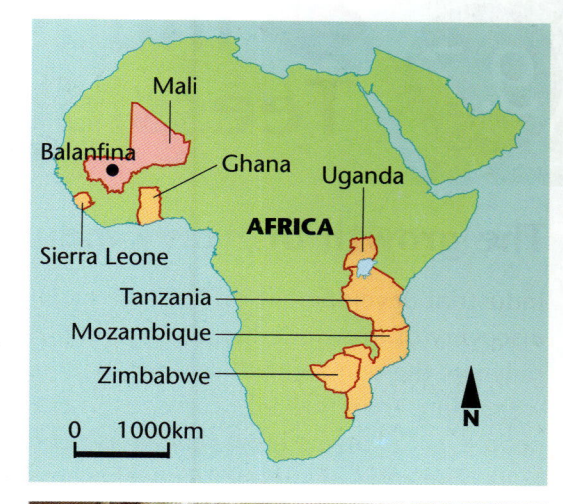

Definitions

Appropriate technology – *technology that is suited to the needs of the country and will improve living standards in a sustainable way.*

Sustainable development projects — *these aim to improve people's living standards without the risks of making anyone worse off or damaging the environment. This type of development is often called 'bottom-up' development because it starts with local communities. The projects are often small-scale and initially may only affect a small community.*

Question

Explain how each of the three projects (pages 186–187) could be defined as *sustainable* and *appropriate*.

Managing Economic Development

9.7 Industrial change – Teesside, north-east England

The growth of heavy industry 1880–1970

Industrial development on Teesside began in the 19th century with the discovery of ironstone in the Cleveland Hills. With the growth of the railways the demand for iron and steel increased and by 1900 there were more than 800 iron furnaces in the area, employing thousands of people. Local towns grew rapidly as people moved into the area for work, and rows of terraced houses were built to accommodate the growing population. By the early part of the 20th century, Teesside was one of the major urban/industrial areas in Britain, and this growth continued for the next 60 years. In the 1960s and '70s the area was seen as the 'industrial centre of the future', with efficient, modern heavy industry employing thousands of people and unemployment as low as 3 per cent (**A**).

Teesside had a number of advantages for the location of heavy industry:

- nearness of **raw materials**, including iron ore, limestone, coal and rock salt
- a wide, deepwater estuary – ideal for importing raw materials and exporting finished products
- large areas of flat, marshy land on either side of the river that could be reclaimed and used for the development of heavy industry
- nearness to the North Sea for links to the North Sea oilfields
- direct trade links to northern Europe.

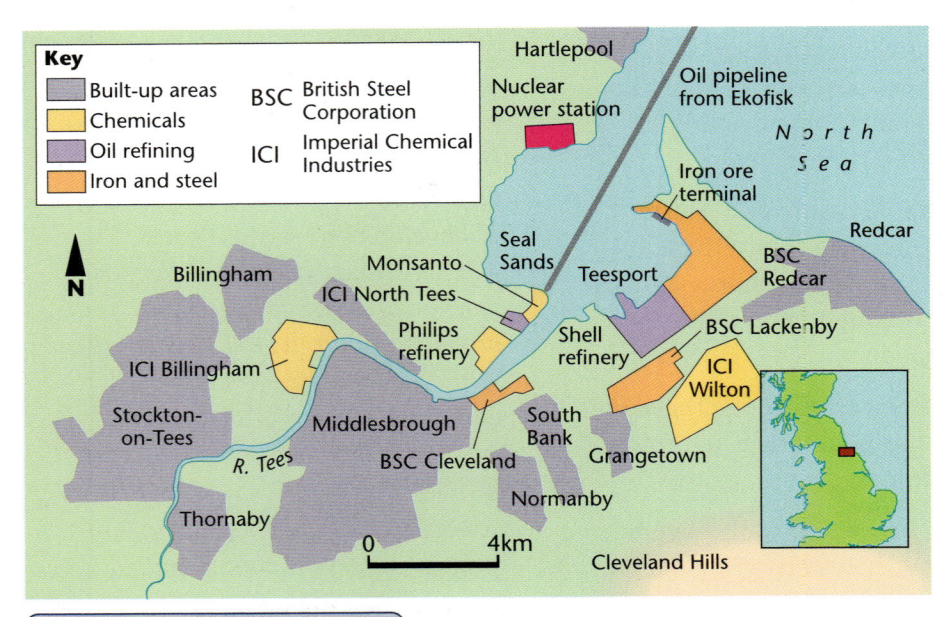

Types of industry

As well as the iron and steel industry, other heavy industries developed, including:

- *Chemicals* – initially using local raw materials to produce agricultural fertilizers and industrial chemicals.
- *Petrochemicals* – the production of oils and tars.
- *Oil refining* – the production of fuels from oil.
- *Shipbuilding* – shipyards on the banks of the River Tees used locally made steel to build ocean-going ships and vessels used in the North Sea oil industry.
- *Engineering* – using locally produced metals to manufacture machinery.

The growth of these industries provided many jobs in the area. In the early 1970s, more than 10 000 people were employed in one chemical plant alone. However, the growth of industry was not without cost to the environment. During the 1960s and '70s there was a steady increase in the levels of pollution in the River Tees, and in parts of the river no plant or animal life could survive. People were warned not to eat shellfish caught near the estuary in case they were contaminated. There was also an increase in air pollution, which was found to be affecting people who lived close to the industry. Figure **B** describes some of the environmental problems of the area.

A – Teesside in the 1960s and '70s

9 Contrasting levels of development

Breath of Blighted Life

Grangetown in Cleveland has been dubbed the unhealthiest town in Britain with the number of asthma sufferers twice the national average, rates of death from lung cancer up to three times the average and life expectancy 10 years less than the norm.

In Grangetown, Cleveland, asthma rates are twice the national average and collections for nebulizers the most common fundraising activity.

The industry-dominated area, straggling along the south of the River Tees, is also severely affected by premature deaths from lung cancer and bronchitis. In 1986, a health study showed that in South Tees women were three times, and men twice, as likely as the average Briton to succumb to these diseases. As a result, residents in Grangetown have a life expectancy of 10 years less than the norm – the same mortality rate as the average Briton in the 1930s.

Together, these grim statistics have earned Grangetown the unenviable epithet of 'the unhealthiest town in Britain'. Like all pockets of deprivation, the area suffers the social problems that have long been linked with high levels of disease. Damp housing, poverty, high unemployment, bad diet and high smoking rates among an almost exclusively working-class population have all made their contribution.

But in Grangetown, surrounded on three sides by the industrial complexes of ICI Wilton and British Steel Lackenby, an additional spectre – pollution – is emerging as a likely major factor in the disease equation. Last summer, a Cleveland Health Team community study uncovered widespread concern and resentment about environmental pollution among residents and health professionals in Grangetown, many of whom perceived the area as the most polluted in Europe. To anyone who has walked the streets of Grangetown, which sprang up in the 1880s as a steel town and has been dominated by heavy industry ever since, such a conclusion seems inescapable.

The population of 4000, one-quarter of them under 15, lives in rows of damp terraced houses which huddle matchbox-like against a backdrop of towering chimneys. The British Steel works, which employs more than 4000 to produce coke, iron and steel, runs 300 yards from Grangetown's 'frontline' Balekow Road; the 2000-acre ICI petrochemical complex, with 6500 employees, is less than half a mile away.

A rooftop monitoring device at Grangetown adult training centre registers 12 tons of grit and dust a month over a square mile. On the ground, this translates into layers of black coke dust and orange ferro-manganese deposits, coating cars and walls in a concentration that is unlikely to be matched anywhere in Britain.

B – Adapted from the Observer, 1991

The decline of heavy industry

In the early 1970s there was a big increase in the price of oil and this led to an industrial recession (decline). Industries that were dependent on oil suffered badly and consequently Teesside was one of the worst-hit areas in Britain. Unemployment rose from 2.5 per cent in 1965 to a record high of 23 per cent by the mid-1980s. In some parts of the region more than 40 per cent of the working population was unemployed. The main reasons for the decline in job opportunities were:

- the introduction of new technology in the steel-making and chemical industries, which led to the loss of more than 40 000 jobs
- decline in the demand for local engineering products leading to the closure of a number of industrial factories
- decline in the demand for shipping and a reduction in North Sea oil investment, which affected the shipbuilding industry.

By the mid-1980s the area was one of the most economically depressed regions in Europe, with high unemployment and growing urban and industrial dereliction as factories were left to decay.

C – Heavy industry on the Tees estuary in the 1970s

Questions

1 a) Describe and explain three reasons why Teesside became an important area for heavy industry.

b) How were many of these industries linked?

2 Use **B** and **C** to describe some of the environmental problems caused by the growth of heavy industry.

3 What were the effects of industrial decline in the 1980s?

9.8 Recent developments in Teesside

By the mid-1980s, Teesside had serious problems of industrial decline and rising unemployment (23 per cent at its highest point). Many of the largest industries were reducing their workforce and factory closures were increasing the amount of derelict and polluted land.

Against this background the Teesside Development Corporation (TDC) was set up in May 1987. The aim of a development corporation is to use public (government) money to improve declining regions. This is done by building new infrastructure and cleaning up derelict areas while encouraging private industry to set up in the area. The TDC covered more than 5000 hectares of land alongside the River Tees, which was described in 1987 as 'the worst area of dereliction in Europe'.

During its 10-year lifetime the TDC attracted over £1 billion worth of private investment and created over 20 000 jobs. Unemployment fell to nearly 10 per cent — still higher than the national average but significantly lower than it had been.

A – Teesside White Water Course during construction

Definitions

Development Corporation
Set up by the government to improve areas that have a high level of unemployment because of the decline of traditional industry.

Infrastructure
A network of links which can include communications (road, rail, air), telecommunications and basic utilities (water, electricity, sewerage systems).

Major projects completed by the TDC

- *Tees Barrage and White Water Course* A barrage has been built across the river linking the north bank of the river with Teesdale. The barrage controls the tidal flow and allows the river to be used for leisure purposes. Included in this development is the White Water Sports Centre which is used for major international events (**A**).

- *Teesdale* A £500 million development with a mix of housing, shops, offices and social facilities (**B**). Included in the development are residential care facilities for people with Alzheimer's Syndrome, and university halls of residence.

- *Tees Offshore Base* A derelict shipyard has been developed into a high-tech centre for offshore technology linked to the North Sea oil industry.

- *Hartlepool Marina* Parts of the original docks have been developed into a marina with 750 yachting berths. Included in the development are facilities for leisure users, and a commercial area. Hartlepool historic quay, a visitor attraction based on an 18th-century fishing village, has been developed.

9 Contrasting levels of development

- *Teesside International Nature Reserve* An area of about 1000 hectares on the north bank of the river has been turned into a nature reserve with a range of different woodland and wetland environments.

B – *Teesside office development*

Other developments included:
- Riverside Park – the new home of Middlesbrough football club.
- a new freight railway terminal at Wilton
- a number of industrial estates and shopping developments
- the University of Stockton
- the building of riverside walkways with conservation areas
- new roads linking the recent developments.

How successful has the TDC been?

- Unemployment has fallen.
- The area now has a wider range of industries.
- There is a greater range of training and job opportunities.
- The environment has been improved.
- Living standards in the area have improved.
- There are more leisure facilities.

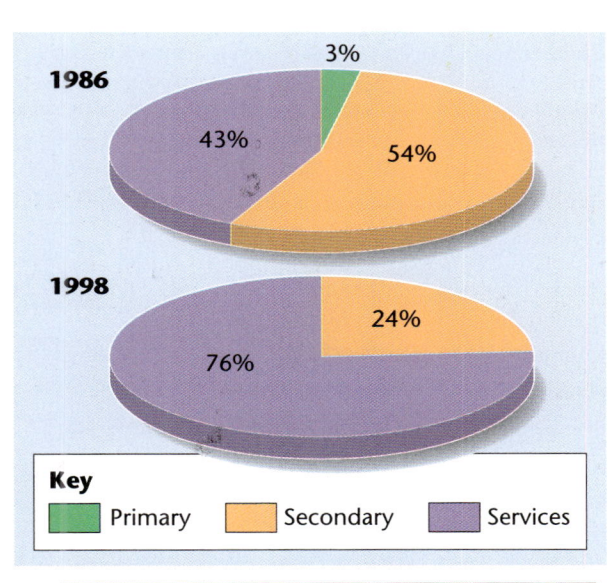

1986: 3% Primary, 54% Secondary, 43% Services

1998: 24% Secondary, 76% Services

Key: Primary | Secondary | Services

D – *Industrial structure of Teesside, 1986 and 1998*

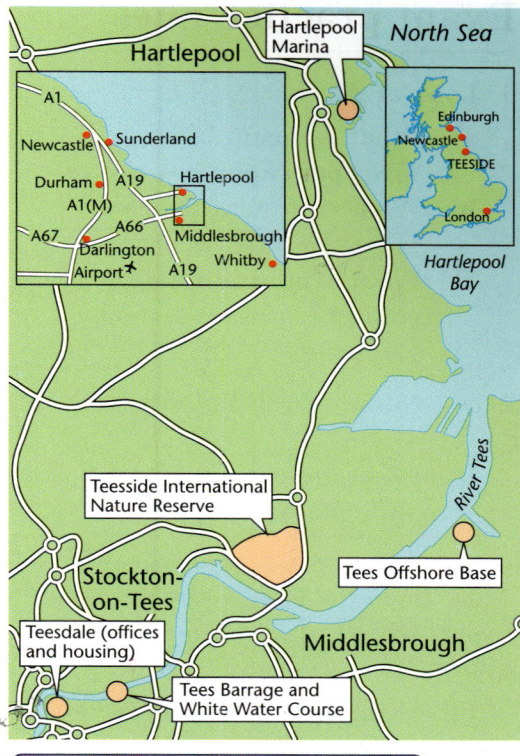

C – *Teesside in the early 21st century*

Questions

1 a) Why was the Teesside Development Corporation set up?
  b) How has it changed the economic and environmental conditions?

2 Study C and D. Describe and explain the changes in the industrial structure of Teesside.

3 In the 1990s the Tees Estuary Environmental Scheme (TEES) was put in place to clean up the River Tees. It is a joint scheme run by Northumbria Water and a number of local industries to increase the level of treatment for waste water going into the river and to reduce the level of industrial waste flowing into the river.
  a) Why was such a scheme required?
  b) How might it affect the environmental quality of the river estuary and surrounding coastal and riverside areas?

191

Exam practice questions

Mark schemes can be found on the book's website, at www.heinemann.co.uk/issuesmarkschemes

1. Look at A.
   a) What is meant by 'GNP per capita'? (2)
   b) What continent appears to be the most wealthy? (1)
   c) What other information could be used to compare countries? (4)

2. a) Name two different types of aid. (2)
   b) What are the advantages and disadvantages of aid? (4)

3. a) What is meant by 'appropriate technology'? (2)
   b) Using examples you have studied, explain why appropriate technology may be seen as a suitable method of increasing living standards in LEDCs. (6)
   c) Describe and explain the advantages and disadvantages of a large-scale development scheme you have studied. (8)

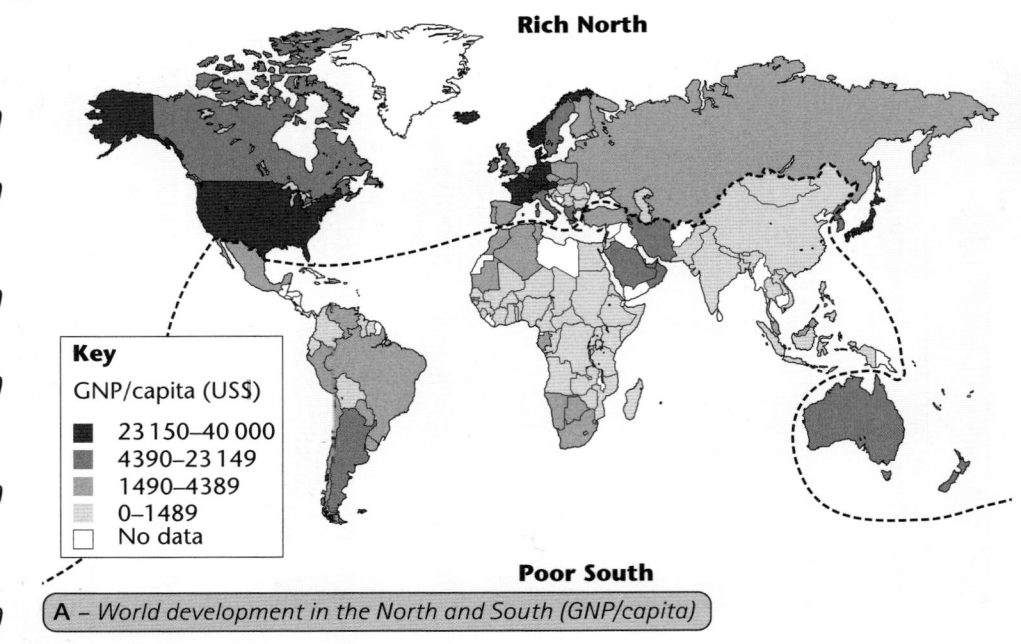

4. Explain why governments might help to encourage new industry to an area. (4)

5. Read B. The report was produced in 1996 by the charity, Save the Children Fund.
   a) How many people in the world have no access to healthcare? (1)
   b) What is the difference between the poorest countries and Britain in the amount of money spent on health? (1)
   c) How might low spending on health affect general living standards? (4)

Key
GNP/capita (US$)
- 23 150–40 000
- 4390–23 149
- 1490–4389
- 0–1489
- No data

A – World development in the North and South (GNP/capita)

HEALTH OF THE POOR WORSENING

One-sixth of the world's population has no access to healthcare. This is over 800 million people. Children's health in many countries is getting worse. The Save the Children Fund reports that healthcare systems are failing.

According to the report, diseases that can be easily treated will be killing more children by the end of the century. It says that at least £8 a year per person is needed to provide basic healthcare. However, Bangladesh, Nepal, India, Vietnam, Pakistan and sixteen African countries all spend less than this. Britain spends £723 a year per person.

Natural disasters, wars and huge debts make it impossible for many countries to spend more on health. Even simple treatments are too expensive for some countries. Immunisation programmes, which would protect children at a cost of only 40 pence per person, still cost more than many countries can afford.

B – Report on the state of health in some of the world's poorest countries

MANAGING ECONOMIC DEVELOPMENT

10 Resource depletion

How can existing resources and their alternatives be managed to ensure future supplies?

Managing Economic Development

10.1 The depletion of resources

• What is a resource?

A resource is anything that is useful to people, but this varies with time. Trees, when cut down, have long been a resource as a fuel or building material, but standing trees are now valued for their appearance — a scenic resource. Black, tarry oil, seeping to the surface in the Middle East, was only used by local people until the 20th century when cars and the chemical industry made it a most valuable resource to have and to sell. So changes in technology and changes in the way we live affect the value of a resource.

• Is anything a resource?

Water, air, soil, minerals, animals, people and anything else we use, are resources. Some are **organic**, or living (e.g. fish), while others are **inorganic** (e.g. coal). People are a resource, using their brains, or using their hands for manual labour.

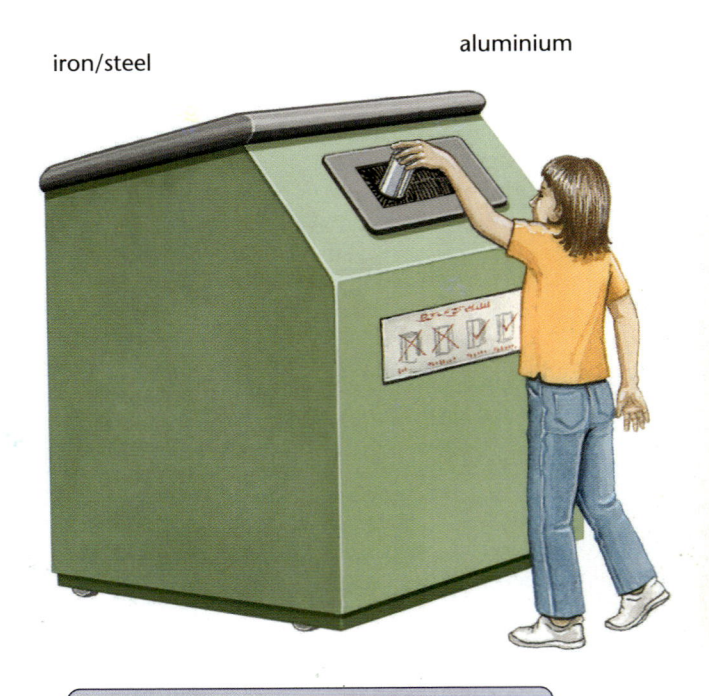

A – Non-renewable resources

B – Non-renewable but recyclable resource

• Are resources here for ever?

Resources like coal, oil and natural gas took millions of years to form, so when they are used and consumed, they are gone. These are **non-renewable** resources, 'fossil' fuels that are used to generate much of the world's electricity (**A**).

Metals can be used once and discarded, but some can be recycled and re-used, so they are recyclable — 41 per cent of aluminium in drinking cans in Europe is recycled (**B**).

Living resources like fish and trees are **renewable** unless we use too much of them. Overfishing in the North Sea has caused a reduction in the total number of fish there, so what was a renewable resource may become **non-renewable**. Some animal and plant species become extinct every year (**C**).

Air and water are **naturally renewable** but we can make them unusable through pollution. Energy from the sun, tides and wind is constantly renewable whatever people do, so these resources are also naturally renewable. They have huge potential for the future (**D**).

10 Resource depletion

• What is the difference between a resource and a reserve?

A **resource** is anything that we use. A **reserve** is a non-renewable resource (e.g. coal) which exists in a finite quantity (there is not an endless supply) in the crust of the Earth. We do not know the full extent of reserves because as technology changes, previously unknown reserves may be opened up. Oil is now extracted from oilfields under the North Sea that were unknown in the 1970s when oil drilling began.

• Are resources everywhere?

Some continents and countries have more resources than others. Some places lack basic resources, like water and soil, so life is difficult. Other countries have more resources than they can use, so they are able to sell them to other countries. Brazil, for example, has large quantities of several renewable and non-renewable resources, and can export some of these to other countries. Income from the sale of a resource like tin may be vital to sustain some poor LEDCs.

C – Water, fish, forests and soil – renewable resources, but they can be damaged by pollution

D – The sun, wind and tides are naturally renewable resources with great potential

• Who owns resources?

Resources like coal are found in fixed locations, so the landowner, a country or a company can decide how and when it is used. Air and water move, so who owns them? If they are a resource in common for the whole world, who has the right to say what happens? Should one country have the right to so pollute a resource that it becomes unusable for a neighbouring country?

Questions

1. What is the difference between a *resource* and a *reserve*?
2. Draw a large labelled diagram to show the differences between resources that are *organic, inorganic, renewable, non-renewable, naturally renewable* and *recyclable*. You could use sketches or a spider diagram. Use A–D.

195

10.2 Fossil fuels and minerals

Coal, oil and gas are **non-renewable fossil fuel resources**, created from the remains of plants and animals that lived millions of years ago. The fossil fuels that the world burns in one year took about 1 million years to create, and reserves are limited. Fossil fuels are used as energy resources in power stations, and they are the quickest and easiest way of generating the vast amounts of electricity that we now use. To generate the same amount of energy as a large modern power station you would need 300 wind turbines 60m high, or 150km^2 of solar panels, or powerful wave energy along a 100km stretch of coastline.

Estimates of future **reserves** vary widely, but at the present rate of consumption known oil reserves will last the world around 40–45 years, natural gas 50–65 years and coal 200–300 years. Reserves will last a little longer if demand declines when the price of energy goes up as supplies dwindle, or if another energy source is used.

The rich MEDCs, with one-quarter of the world's population, consume over 70 per cent of all fossil fuels. The USA uses 25 per cent of all world commercial energy, and LEDCs such as Ethiopia (Afica) or Nepal (Asia) consume the least. Countries that use other things, like fuelwood for domestic energy, consume little commercial energy. Fuelwood is vitally important to many LEDCs. It is renewable but is rapidly being depleted worldwide as more wood is burnt than regrows. It contributes approximately 6–14 per cent of total world energy.

Coal

Coal is the most used fuel for generating electricity worldwide (**A**). Some countries are more heavily dependent on it than others.

Some of the main consumers of coal also produce the most (**D**), but not all of them. Known coal reserves are found in almost 100 countries, and there is considerable trade between countries in different types of coal. Coal is a useful export for less wealthy countries like Indonesia and Colombia.

Since the Industrial Revolution, coal and steel have been used together, and 70 per cent of world steel production still relies on coal.

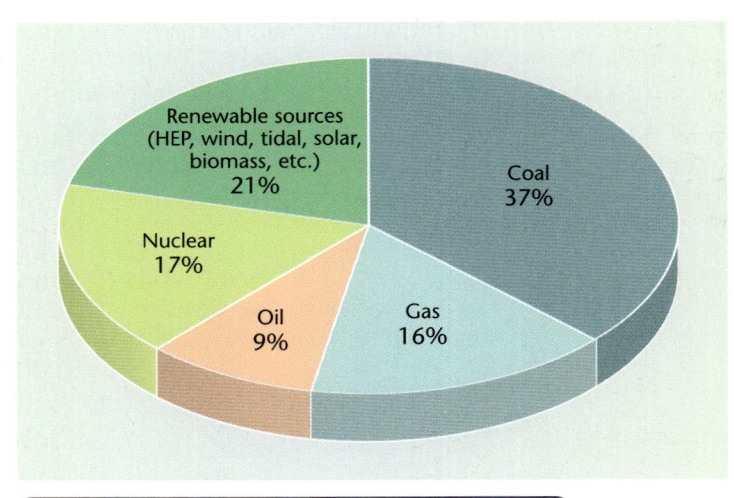

A – *Sources of world electricity generation (2000)*

- Coal 37%
- Renewable sources (HEP, wind, tidal, solar, biomass, etc.) 21%
- Nuclear 17%
- Gas 16%
- Oil 9%

Oil and natural gas

Oil is very unevenly distributed around the world but is the source of 40 per cent of the world's energy. Just 20 countries control 95 per cent of proven reserves, and over half are in the Middle East.

LEDCs produce most oil and more than half depend on oil for over 75 per cent of their commercial energy needs. Eleven exporting countries, which together manage 40 per cent of oil production and 78 per cent of reserves, have grouped together to form the Organization of Petroleum Exporting Countries (OPEC) (**B**). They co-ordinate policies and agree a price so that world oil prices do not fluctuate wildly. OPEC consider their reserves to be sufficient for 80 years at the present rate of consumption, while reserves of non-OPEC countries may last for less than 20 years.

Oil-producing countries also produce natural gas, most of it comes from Russia and the USA.

10 Resource depletion

Minerals

Iron, copper, lead, zinc, tin, potash, phosphate, etc. are all materials that exist in limited quantities in the Earth's crust, but unlike fossil fuels they are not generally destroyed in use and could be recycled indefinitely (C). However, articles made from these are often thrown away in rubbish sites so they become unusable.

World coal reserves (billion tonnes)

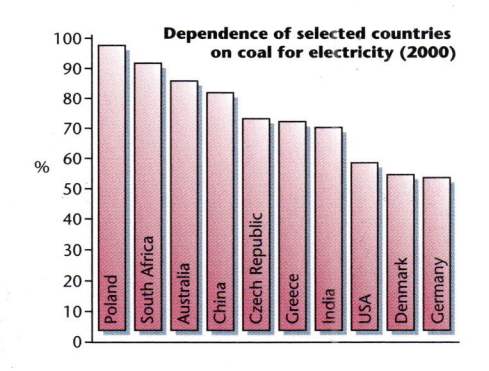

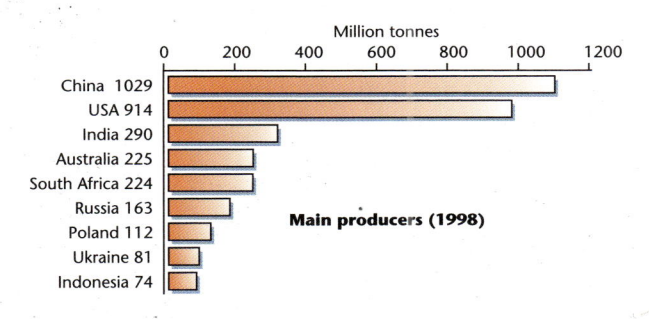

- North America 116.7
- Eastern Europe & CIS 113.3
- Western Europe 25.8
- Other Asia 74.9
- China 62.2
- South & Central America 7.8
- Africa & Middle East 61.4
- Australasia 47.3

Dependence of selected countries on coal for electricity (2000) (%)

Poland, South Africa, Australia, China, Czech Republic, Greece, India, USA, Denmark, Germany

Main producers (1998) (Million tonnes)

- China 1029
- USA 914
- India 290
- Australia 225
- South Africa 224
- Russia 163
- Poland 112
- Ukraine 81
- Indonesia 74

Main coal exporters
* Australia
* South Africa
* Indonesia
* USA
* China
* Canada
* Colombia
* Russia
* Poland

Main coal importers
* Japan
* Korea
* Taiwan
* Germany
* UK

D – Some data on coal

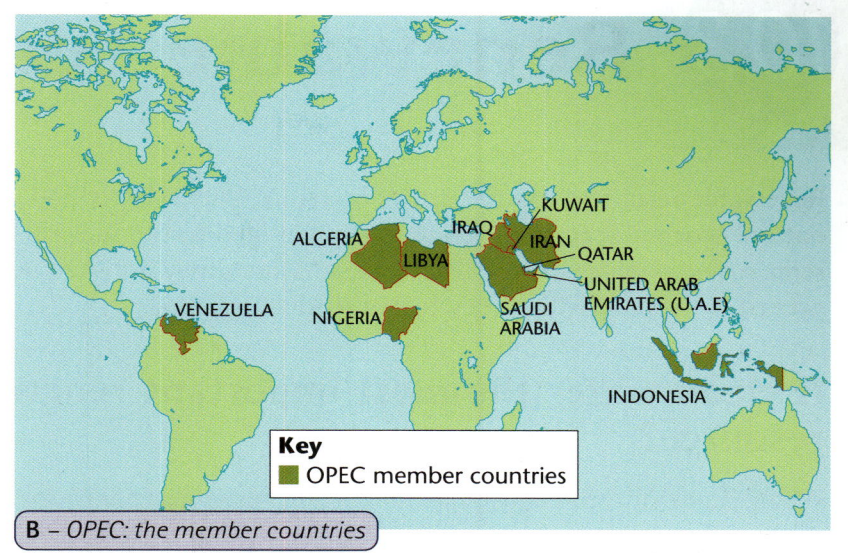

B – OPEC: the member countries

Key: OPEC member countries (Algeria, Libya, Nigeria, Venezuela, Iraq, Iran, Kuwait, Qatar, Saudi Arabia, United Arab Emirates (U.A.E), Indonesia)

C – If more minerals were recycled, less would need to be extracted from the Earth

Questions

1. Coal, oil and gas are *non-renewable resources*. What does this mean?

2. Which countries – LEDCs or MEDCs – use most fossil fuels?

3. How important in the world is coal as an energy source? (Use D)

4. Draw a table with three columns:

Who most depends on coal?	Who produces most coal?	Who exports most coal?

   Put the names of at least five countries in each column. Does any country appear in all three columns? Describe the pattern shown, using all the data in D.

5. What is OPEC? Why was it set up? How does OPEC affect global oil supplies?

6. Do you think that the world will run out of minerals? Explain your answer.

Managing Economic Development

10.3 Renewable resources

Renewable resources are those that replenish themselves through natural processes. Forests, fish stocks, water and fertile soil will all remain sustainable as long as the rate at which they are used does not exceed the rate at which they replenish themselves.

Is clean water the most important renewable resource?

Water is one of the world's most important resources. The worldwide demand for clean water continues to grow rapidly, for domestic, agricultural and industrial uses.

We each need about 5 litres of water a day to survive — but the average US citizen consumes 307 litres a day (**A**). Dishwashers, washing-machines and garden sprinklers increase the water consumption of affluent people. The challenge for many countries, particularly LEDCs, in the 21st century is how to ensure a reliable supply of clean water. Variations in precipitation may make future water supplies difficult to predict with accuracy and be the cause of conflict between countries with rapidly growing populations.

The River Nile flows through several countries to the Mediterranean Sea (**B**, on page 143). Proposals to dam the river in Ethiopia would provide water to grow food for the 86 million people in Ethiopia and Sudan, which both suffer frequent droughts, but Egypt would then be left with little water. Ninety per cent of the country's 80 million people live on the narrow strip of land on each side of the river, and depend on the Nile for irrigation.

How do we use the oceans?

The oceans cover 70 per cent of the surface of the Earth and are a vital resource but now they are at risk. Our

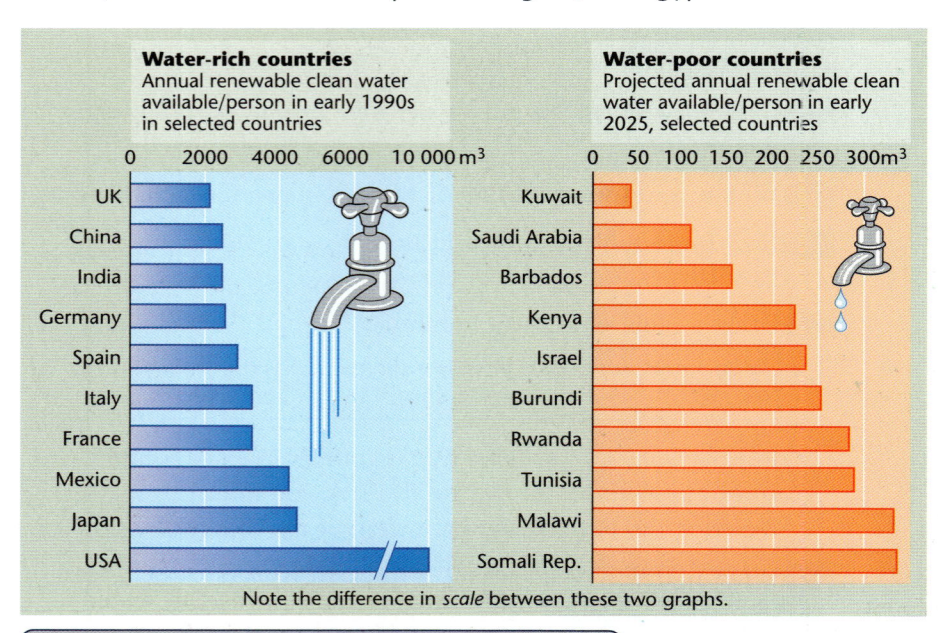

Water-rich countries
Annual renewable clean water available/person in early 1990s in selected countries

0 2000 4000 6000 10 000 m³

- UK
- China
- India
- Germany
- Spain
- Italy
- France
- Mexico
- Japan
- USA

Water-poor countries
Projected annual renewable clean water available/person in early 2025, selected countries

0 50 100 150 200 250 300 m³

- Kuwait
- Saudi Arabia
- Barbados
- Kenya
- Israel
- Burundi
- Rwanda
- Tunisia
- Malawi
- Somali Rep.

Note the difference in *scale* between these two graphs.

A – *The contrast in water availability around the world*

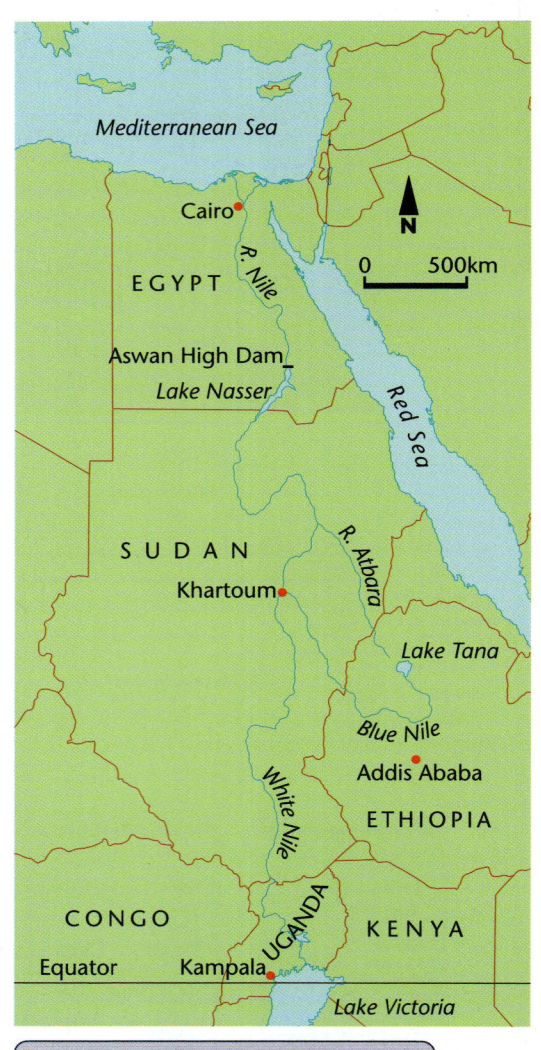

B – *Who uses the waters of the Nile?*

10 Resource depletion

ability to catch fish in huge numbers often exceeds the ability of the fish stocks to survive and all major ocean fish stocks are now in danger of depletion from overfishing (C). Fish is the biggest source of protein for many people in LEDCs but coastal fisheries throughout Asia, East Africa and West Africa are being depleted.

The seabed is an important source of sand and gravel, producing up to 10 per cent of the sand and gravel used in the UK construction industry. This is a renewable resource but over-extraction can change the surrounding coastlines. The oceans contain huge quantities of minerals, and half the world's magnesium and two-thirds of bromide are obtained from seawater. Tin, silver, iron, platinum, phosphates and diamonds are also extracted from the seabed, and of course oil from below the sea.

The sea is also used as a convenient dumping ground and sewage, chemicals, oil, toxic wastes, radioactive materials and agricultural chemicals pollute the oceans and can turn a valuable resource into a health hazard.

What about the forests?

One quarter of the Earth's surface is covered by forest, which is less than half the amount that was there 300 years ago. Forests provide timber, fuelwood and charcoal, they protect water supplies, provide a home for very diverse wildlife, create humus for soil, protect soil from erosion, absorb carbon dioxide, convert energy from the sun through photosynthesis, and contain 85 per cent of the world's biomass (the world's total organic matter). Forests are also a scenic resource and provide recreation facilities for millions of people.

Fears for jobs as fish quotas cut to bone

HUNDREDS of fishermen will lose their jobs under the new European catch quotas for 2001, but fish stocks around Britain are likely to go on plummeting.

Cod stocks are so low that the North Sea quota has been cut by 45% from 81 000 tonnes to 48 500 tonnes. But even this figure is unlikely to be reached: fishermen have been unable to find their cod quota since 1995, and cod is likely to become a luxury fish. A few years ago the average catch was 300 000 tonnes.

From the Guardian, 16 December 2000

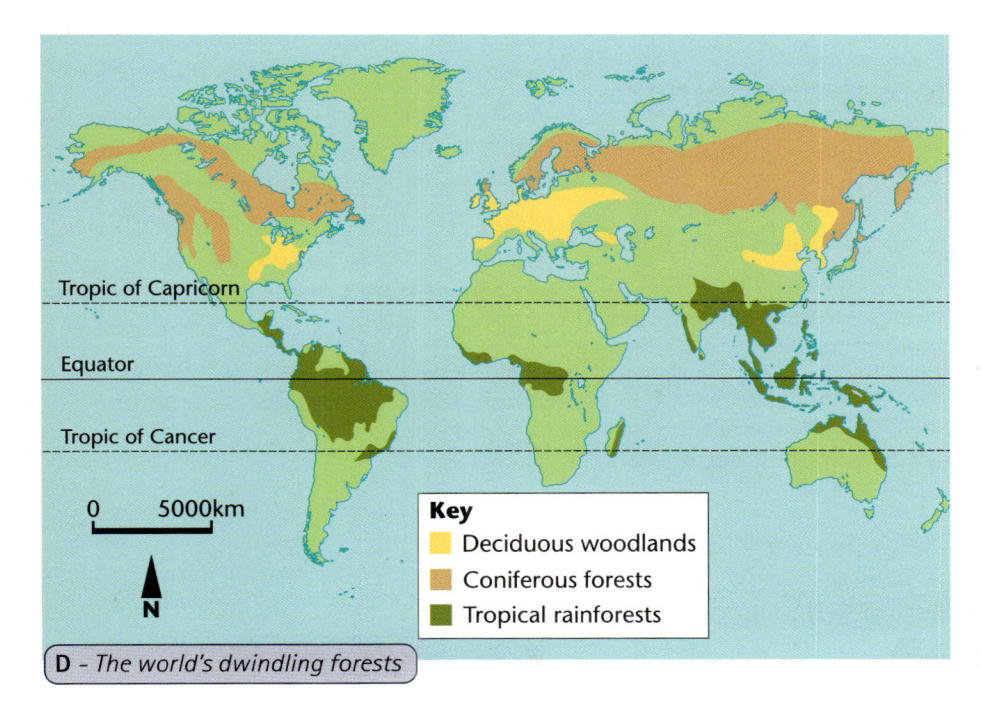

C – Fish quotas in the North Sea

D – The world's dwindling forests

Key:
- Deciduous woodlands
- Coniferous forests
- Tropical rainforests

Questions

1. What are renewable resources?
2. Why do MEDCs use so much clean water?
3. Sketch map B and annotate to show the importance of the Nile to the countries it flows through.
4. How do we use the oceans? Can the oceans' resources be exhausted?
5. Draw an outline of a tree in the middle of a page and annotate it with 10 reasons why trees are essential to the environment.
6. Describe the contrasts in water availability shown in A.

Managing Economic Development

10.4 Brazil, the Amazon Basin and the effects of deforestation

Tropical rainforests cover 7 per cent of the Earth's land surface: 58 per cent in South America, 19 per cent in Africa, and 23 per cent in South-east Asia (page 199). The fragile rainforests contain about half of all living species, 80 per cent of insects and 90 per cent of primates, with a greater variety in Brazil than in any other country.

In Brazil, 58 per cent of the land area is covered by forest, and 22 per cent by grassland (see page 180) (by contrast, in the UK 10 per cent is forest and 46 per cent grassland). The Amazon river flows for 6400km through the largest area of equatorial rainforest left in the world. The Amazon forest is disappearing at the rate of 15 500km^2 a year. In 1998, 31 per cent more land was cleared than in the previous year (18 120km^2), and in 2000 the Brazilian government put forward proposals that allowed still more land to be cleared (**A** and **B**).

Indigenous people have lived a sustainable, shifting lifestyle for generations but the Indian traditional way of life is fast disappearing. There are only about 200 000 native people left, and most are now living in reservations, pushed out by the demands of logging and mining companies (**B**).

Brazil has used its substantial resources to become a newly industrializing country with a rising standard of living, but much of the wealth is now in one area, the South East, where 60 per cent of the people live.

How is use of the Amazon forest changing?

Increasing areas of forest are being lost as the resources are being exploited.

- *Timber* The forest is cleared for hardwoods such as mahogany. Illegal loggers may take out only the tallest canopy trees, but the entire ecosystem is destroyed in the process. Friends of the Earth, an environmental 'green' pressure group, claimed in 1999 that only 14 per cent of the timber was exported — most was used by Brazilians themselves, mostly in the richest south-eastern states. Green pressure groups try to counteract some of the damaging actions of governments and transnational corporations.

- *Agriculture* Since the 1970s families have left other parts of Brazil to farm small plots of land in the forest given to them by the government. However, most of the nutrients are in the plants, not in the soil, so once the forest cover is removed the soil is rapidly exhausted and washed away by the heavy daily convectional rain, and crops grow poorly. There are also more than 50 000 livestock farms in Amazonia, many run by large landowners or transnationals producing beef for export. The land is often cleared by burning, but the carbon that was previously stored in the trees is released as carbon dioxide into the atmosphere, contributing to global warming. In March 1998, fires in Roraima state

A – *Large-scale destruction of the forest*

10 Resource depletion

north of the Amazon destroyed an area equal to one-quarter the size of the UK. The smoke over the forest from all these fires was visible from space.

- *Road building* The Trans-Amazon Highway is more than 9600km long. Increasing numbers of roads are being built through the forest but they can lead to uncontrolled development. Advance Brazil, the £27 billion plan to develop the forest roads, waterways and dams infrastructure, could mean that only 5 per cent of the rainforest is intact by 2020, according to some US and Brazilian researchers.

- *Mineral extraction* There are huge deposits of minerals such as iron ore, bauxite, copper, nickel, manganese and gold. The largest iron ore deposit in the world is being developed at Grand Carajas in Para state. The ore is taken nearly 890km by train to the port of São Luis for export, providing 8 per cent of the world's iron ore. Some of the iron ore goes to the steelworks at Maraba nearby, which is fuelled by charcoal made from the forest trees. The opencast mines mean that huge areas of vegetation are stripped away, and rivers polluted. Indian land is protected around Carajas but beyond that are thousands of mining prospectors, squatters and farmers, all using the land for their own purposes. Bauxite from the huge mine at Trombetas on the Amazon is also exported, mostly to MEDCs.

- *Hydro-electric power (HEP)* provides the quantities of power needed to develop the minerals but because of the gentle gradient of the river basin, vast lakes are needed. Rotting forest under the lake water pollutes the rivers and reduces soil fertility for farmers downstream. As the vegetation rots, more gases are given off than would be created by burning fossil fuels to generate the same amount of electricity as is produced by the HEP. An HEP station was built at Tucurui on the River Tocantins to power the Carajas development, the railway and an aluminium factory. Indian reserves and villages were flooded and 800 Indians and 15 000 other Brazilians had to be resettled.

Brazil would not have been able to reach its present level of development without its forest resources, but how should this world forest resource be managed? Will ecotourism have an impact on how people see the forest (see page 239)?

TRADITIONAL AMAZONIAN INDIAN WAY OF LIFE

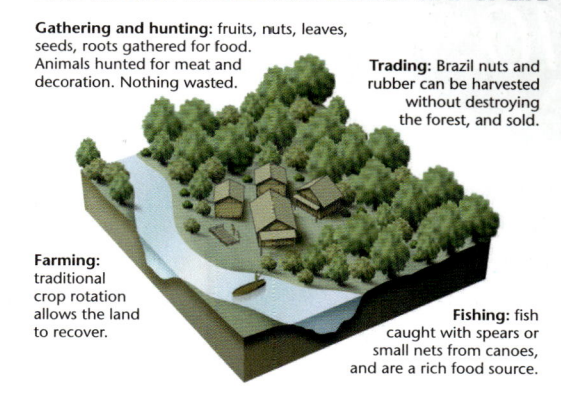

Gathering and hunting: fruits, nuts, leaves, seeds, roots gathered for food. Animals hunted for meat and decoration. Nothing wasted.

Trading: Brazil nuts and rubber can be harvested without destroying the forest, and sold.

Farming: traditional crop rotation allows the land to recover.

Fishing: fish caught with spears or small nets from canoes, and are a rich food source.

IMPACT OF DEVELOPMENT

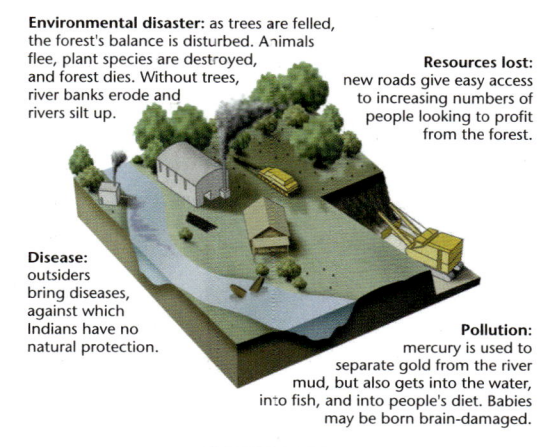

Environmental disaster: as trees are felled, the forest's balance is disturbed. Animals flee, plant species are destroyed, and forest dies. Without trees, river banks erode and rivers silt up.

Resources lost: new roads give easy access to increasing numbers of people looking to profit from the forest.

Disease: outsiders bring diseases, against which Indians have no natural protection.

Pollution: mercury is used to separate gold from the river mud, but also gets into the water, into fish, and into people's diet. Babies may be born brain-damaged.

WHAT IS LEFT

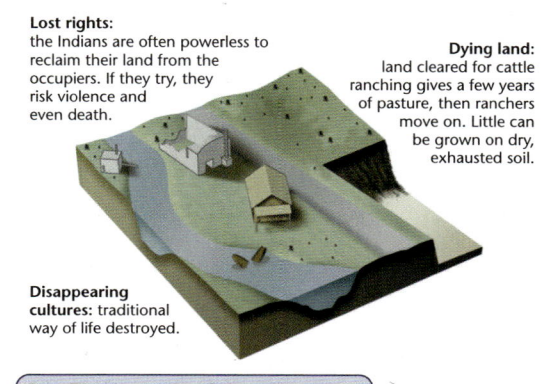

Lost rights: the Indians are often powerless to reclaim their land from the occupiers. If they try, they risk violence and even death.

Dying land: land cleared for cattle ranching gives a few years of pasture, then ranchers move on. Little can be grown on dry, exhausted soil.

Disappearing cultures: traditional way of life destroyed.

B – *The impact of development*

Questions

1. How much rainforest is left in the world? draw a pie chart to show global distibution of rainforest.

2. Draw a diagram to show why tropical rainforest is so valuable.

3. Use the text and (C) to identify what is happening to the native people of the Amazon rainforest.

4. Describe five different uses of the rainforest. Draw up a table to show in each case what is gained and what is lost, who gains and who loses from these activities.

5. Using an atlas, draw a sketch map of the Amazon Basin to show the location of the Carajas mine and the railway line to the coast. Annotate it to show effects of the mine development.

Managing Economic Development

10.5 CS The effects of coal mining in South Wales

Extracting and using minerals from the Earth's crust involves costs and benefits both for the producers and the consumers. Coal mining damages the environment and the people working and living there, and coal burning pollutes the atmosphere. On the other hand, mining the coal provides jobs, brings income into the area, and supplies an energy source that people depend on.

Coal and steel from South Wales fed the factories and railways of the UK throughout the 19th century. The first coal was dug from seams that were visible on the valley hillsides, but deep mining reached down to the rich underlying layers, and villages grew along the valley floors as people moved into the area for work. By 1920, 300 000 miners were working in the South Wales pits, but it was difficult and dangerous work. Miners developed lung problems from the dust, and accidents killed many, but these were close-knit communities (B). Then the demand for coal dropped and in the 1980s and 1990s many mines closed. Thousands of miners were made redundant and the economy of the South Wales valleys declined. There was little other work and high unemployment.

Now, opencast mining is providing much-needed work, but at what cost? The landscape is destroyed, there is noise and air pollution, new roads, lorries and mud — but there are jobs.

Opencast mining takes away the topsoil and rock (the **overburden**) to expose the coal seam, which is then dug out (C). Once a hole has been dug and the coal removed, the overburden and then the topsoil are put back and the area is landscaped. The area of active mining gradually moves across the hilltop.

At the Celtic Energy mine at Nant Helen near Abercraf, the coal is high-grade anthracite but only 4 per cent of the total dug out is coal. The hole is 10 times deeper than the mines dug in the 1920s

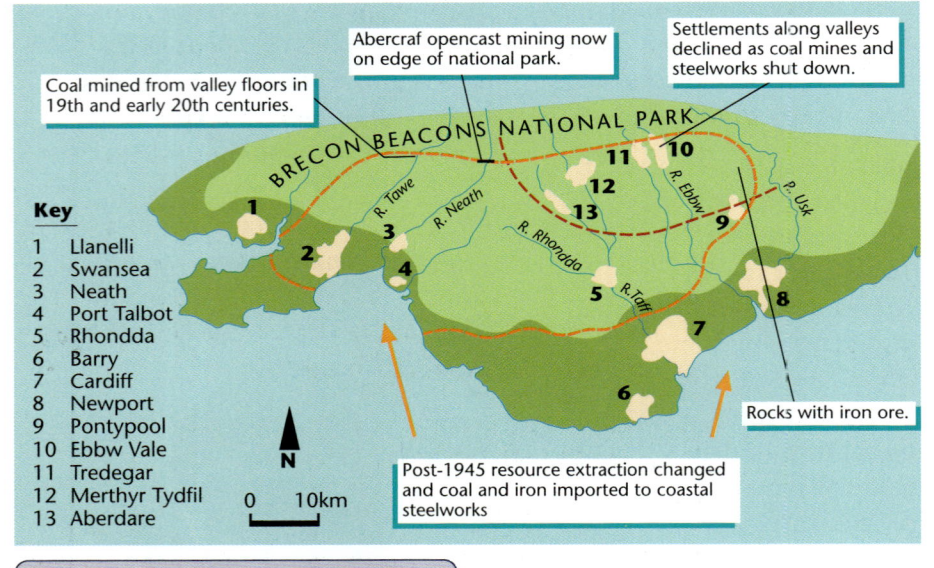

A – South Wales and the coal industry

Key
1 Llanelli
2 Swansea
3 Neath
4 Port Talbot
5 Rhondda
6 Barry
7 Cardiff
8 Newport
9 Pontypool
10 Ebbw Vale
11 Tredegar
12 Merthyr Tydfil
13 Aberdare

B – Mining in the South Wales valleys in the 1930s

C – Opencast mining in South Wales today

10 Resource depletion

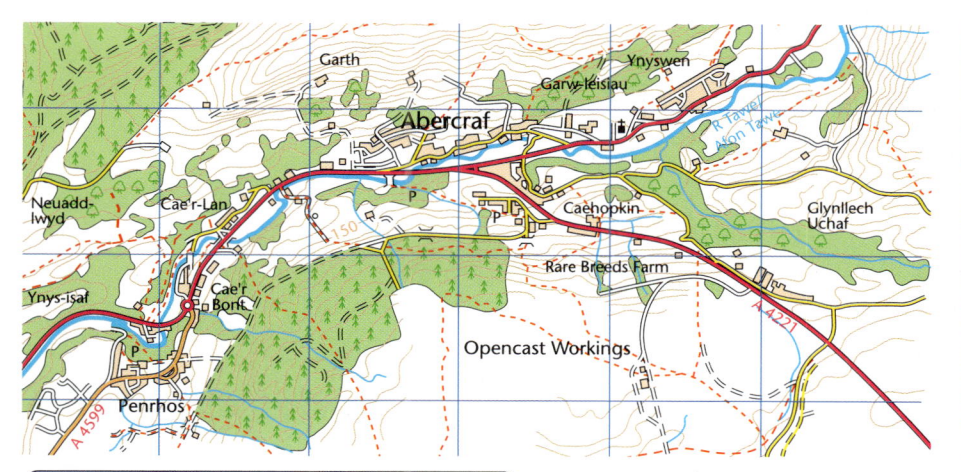

D – OS map extract 1:50 000 scale showing part of the Swansea Valley in South Wales
© Crown Copyright

E – A 'reclaimed' landscape

and '30s (165m), so it has a marked effect on the local environment. The coal is taken away by lorry, 40 per cent being used for the production of electricity and the rest for domestic fires and the steelworks on the South Wales coast. Electricity production using anthracite produces less greenhouse gases than other coals, but it is expensive and electricity companies can choose where to buy their fuel, often using the cheapest source. The cheapest coal may be from another country where damage to the environment is not a consideration. The cost of replacing a landscape has to be added to the price of the coal from Wales. Celtic Energy found that electricity is easier to sell than coal, so they use their coal in their own power station, and sell the electricity.

Changing landscapes

The landscape in South Wales is the result of generations of changing use. The people living in valley communities are there because of mining development a hundred years ago. Today, people need jobs. They have to balance what is lost with what is gained from the opencast mining, and there is disagreement. Nant Helen mine is very close to the Brecon Beacons National Park (A), but it was given permission to extend across the hilltop despite opposition from local people and the County Council, which considered the destruction of the environment and the pollution a price too high to pay.

Thirty years ago, replaced landscapes were covered with rows of conifers and often the soil was thin and easily washed away. Planning and design now go into repairing the landscape after mining, but a mature ecosystem cannot be recreated instantly. Sometimes artificial systems have to be used, e.g. plastic liners for streams. Many old deep-pit mine workings in the South Wales valleys have been successfully re-landscaped to provide recreational environments.

Friends of the Earth (FoE), an environmental non-governmental organization (NGO), is opposed to opencast mining, believing it to be one of the most environmentally destructive processes taking place in the UK today. FoE argues that the mining causes asthma in local children and damages the local economy by deterring other industries, causing a fall in house prices. It believes the disadvantages outweigh any benefits from jobs. This is quite a widely held view, and more applications for opencast mines in the UK are now turned down than approved.

Questions

1. What is opencast mining?
2. What are the advantages and disadvantages of this type of mining?
3. Explain why people in South Wales are divided in their views about opencast mining in the area?
4. a) Draw an outline grid of **D**. On your grid mark:
    - the River Tawe
    - the A roads
    - the lowest point on the map
    - the highest point on the map.
    - opencast workings
   b) Shade in the area of coniferous forest.
   c) Draw and shade in the built-up areas (approximately).
   d) Describe and explain the pattern of roads, settlements and forest areas.

Managing Economic Development

10.6 Renewable energy

Renewable energy is clean and sustainable. Wind, water and solar energy are naturally available, and biomass is renewable. The amount of energy from such sources should increase as fossil fuel reserves decrease.

- *Hydro-electric power (HEP)* – At present, HEP is the only extensively used renewable source, providing about 7 per cent of world commercial energy without pollution. HEP can be generated on a small scale where water flows down a mountainside (as in Norway) or in a large scheme like Itaipu on the Brazil/Paraguay border (A), or at a natural waterfall like Niagara Falls.

  Itaipu reservoir is 180km long and 5km wide, and was made by damming the River Paraná in 1982. Then it was the largest scheme in the world and supplied three-quarters of the power for Paraguay and one-third of Brazil's energy. Around 140 000 new trees were planted to make a sustainable environment around the lake. However, as for every major HEP scheme, there are problems:
  - silt collecting behind the dam slowly fills up the lake
  - decaying vegetation in the water releases methane and carbon dioxide
  - people are displaced by the rising water (42 000 at Itaipu)
  - ecosystems and heritage sites are lost for ever
  - the financial cost of building a big dam is huge
  - few permanent jobs are created.

- *Wind power* — Very windy places like parts of Wales, Scotland, and Cornwall offer the best sites in the UK and could provide 10 per cent of the UK's electricity. Electricity generated by the wind is cheap and clean but the turbines are large. Production from a wind farm 1km off the Northumberland coast at Blyth began in December 2000 (see page 211). The North Hoyle wind farm 6km off the north-west coast of Wales planned in April 2001 will generate enough electricity to power 50 000 homes using 30 turbines.

- *Solar power* has great potential in places where there is more sunlight than in the UK, particularly in many LEDCs where conventional energy sources are difficult to install. Solar power could only provide 1 per cent of UK electricity.

- *Geothermal energy* is very important in volcanic countries like Iceland, Japan and New Zealand. Hot rocks just below the surface heat water, and hot springs or steam are used to generate electricity. Geothermal energy is free, renewable and constant.

- *Biomass* includes vegetation and organic materials. Quick-growing willow can be used in power stations. This gives off greenhouse gases but the growing crop absorbs them. Brazil developed ethanol from locally grown sugar cane as a substitute for petrol when oil prices rose in the 1970s. Fuelwood and dung biomass are widely burnt in LEDCs, resulting in deforestation, and animal dung may be better used as a fertilizer for crops.

A – Itaipu reservoir and dam

10 Resource depletion

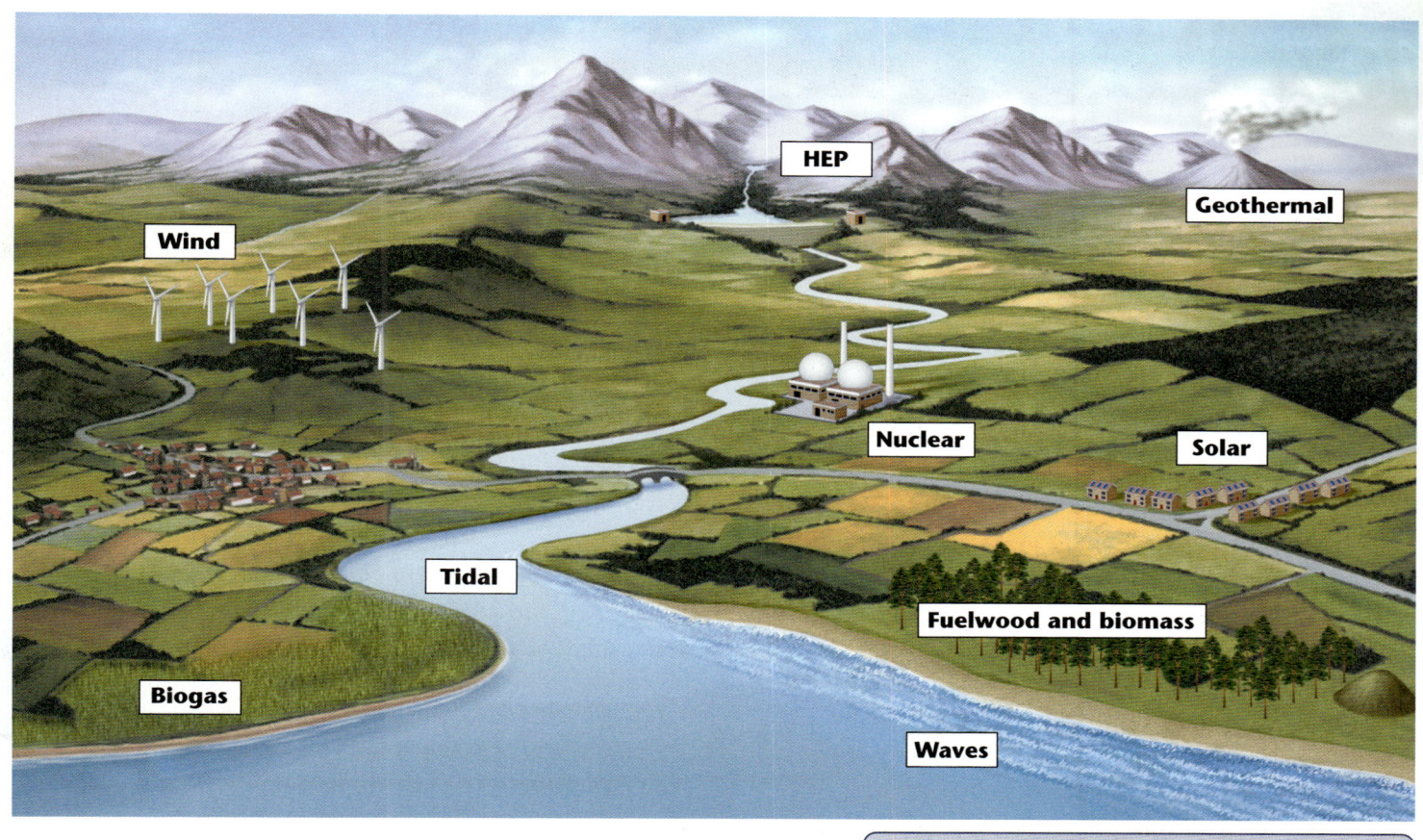

B – There is a variety of sources of renewable energy

- *Biogas* systems using animal dung and organic waste to produce methane have great potential in LEDCs where they reduce the demand for fuelwood.

- *Tidal power* has potential in the UK, and several schemes have been proposed. A successful scheme operates on the R. Rance in France

- *Wave power* has been successfully developed in Scandinavia, and there is great potential along parts of the British Coastline.

- *Nuclear power* is generated using uranium, which is used in such small quantities that it can be regarded as 'renewable'.

Questions

1. Complete a table with the headings *Renewable energy, Advantages, Disadvantages, Best location, Where used*.

   Add data from websites (search for 'Renewable energy' or 'Wind farms', for example).

2. a) Describe the pattern shown in C. Use dates and figures in your answer.
   b) Do you think that the target of 5 per cent will be achieved by 2003, or 10 per cent by 2010? Give three reasons for your answer.

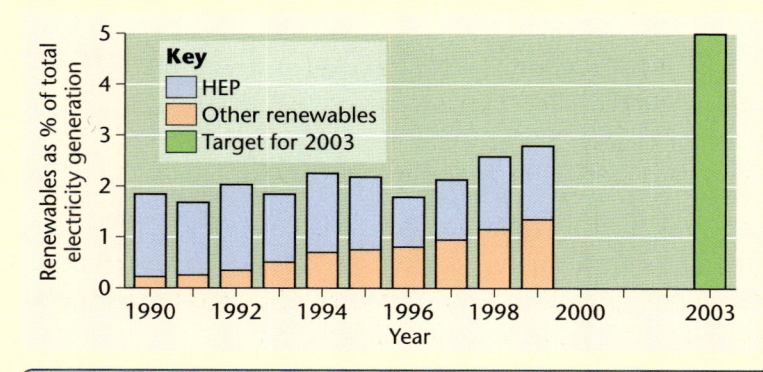

C – Growth in UK electricity generation from renewable sources, from 1990

10.7 Recycling — a way to conserve resources

Recycling means using things more than once so that resources can be saved and waste reduced. People in LEDCs are very efficient at making use of everything, as money and resources there are limited, but richer people tend to throw more away. Minerals can be used time and time again, and steel and aluminium are widely recycled. In MEDCs, paper, glass, metals, clothing, plastics and garden waste are now being successfully recycled.

Recycling:
- cuts waste disposal costs
- saves energy
- conserves resources
- creates jobs
- keeps streets clean
- raises public awareness about resources.

Should we recycle everything possible?

- *Plastics* made from oil can be recycled but they have to be collected and taken by lorry to the few places that can deal with them. So is it worth burning oil to conserve oil? If the value gained (financially and environmentally) is greater than the value of the resource lost, then it is worth recycling.

- *Glass* is 100 per cent recyclable and is collected in 20 000 bottle banks around the UK — one for every 2800 people. Up to 10 per cent of average household waste is glass, and a typical family uses 500 glass containers a year. Most bottles contain recycled glass, but green bottles can be up to 60 per cent recycled (A). The government aim is to recover and recycle 50 per cent of all packaging (glass, aluminium and paper) — currently the figure is only 25 per cent.

- *Aluminium* is very efficiently re-used and it is currently the most valuable recycled material. Recycling saves 95 per cent of the energy needed to produce new aluminium. Half of all cans worldwide are recycled (but only 36 per cent in the UK). We still throw away the equivalent of 12 million dustbins-full, or £30 million worth, of aluminium.

Who is involved in recycling?

Governments set targets for recycling, local authorities put policy into practice, and environmental NGOs (e.g. Friends of the Earth, Greenpeace, the Sierra Club, Planet Aid and One World) make us aware of the need to recycle. Various companies extracting and using raw materials and, on the wider scale, the United Nations and the European Environment Agency, are also now involved in the policies and processes of recycling. In most cities in LEDCs (e.g. Cairo in Egypt and São Paulo in Brazil), small groups of people work around the city's rubbish dumps, recycling the waste materials that are an important part of the economy.

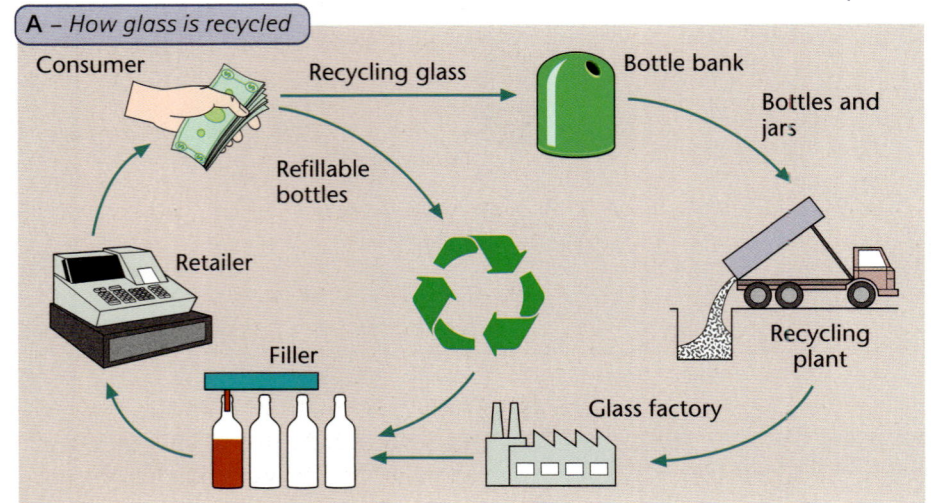

Curitiba, the environmentally friendly LEDC city

The people of Curitiba (Brazil) have their recycling well organized. They separate their waste into two parts, organic and inorganic. This is picked up by different trucks. Poor families living in squatter

A – How glass is recycled

settlements that cannot be reached by truck carry their waste to neighbourhood centres, to exchange for eggs, milk, oranges and potatoes, which are brought in from the surrounding rural areas.

The waste goes to a plant (itself made of recycled materials) where people separate the bottles, cans and plastic. Useful materials are sold to local industries. Polystyrene is shredded and used to make quilts for the poor.

The recycling programme costs no more than the old landfill, but the city is cleaner, more people have jobs, and local farmers are supported. Two-thirds of the city's waste is now recycled.

CS Waste management on the Isle of Wight

The Isle of Wight is a small island with a population of 138 000 but the number of people doubles in the summer. As in many parts of the UK, the landfill sites now have a limited life (about 12 years), so waste management is important. The UK recycling rate is about 6 per cent, but in 1998 in the Isle of Wight, 34 per cent of waste was recycled, and by 2001 that figure could be 50 per cent.

- *Waste 2 Energy waste derived fuel (WDF) plant* — all general waste that can be burned is converted into fuel pellets and used in the nearby power station. Sufficient energy is produced to power 500 homes.
- *Steel and aluminium* are recycled.
- *Paper* is separated by each household and collected fortnightly.
- There are *old clothing* banks in all recycling centres.
- *Composting* began with garden waste in 1995, and the scheme now operates the largest composter in Europe. Domestic organic waste is collected in special buckets from each household and added to garden waste (up to 60 tonnes a day). Composting saves on large volumes of landfill (7200 tonnes of organic waste were being landfilled each year), and the compost can be sold for garden use after 14 days.

Item	% of total landfill
Household packaging	3
Other household waste	13
Commercial and industrial packaging	3
Other commercial/industrial waste	50
Construction/demolition waste	18
Other waste	13

C – The contents of landfill sites in the UK

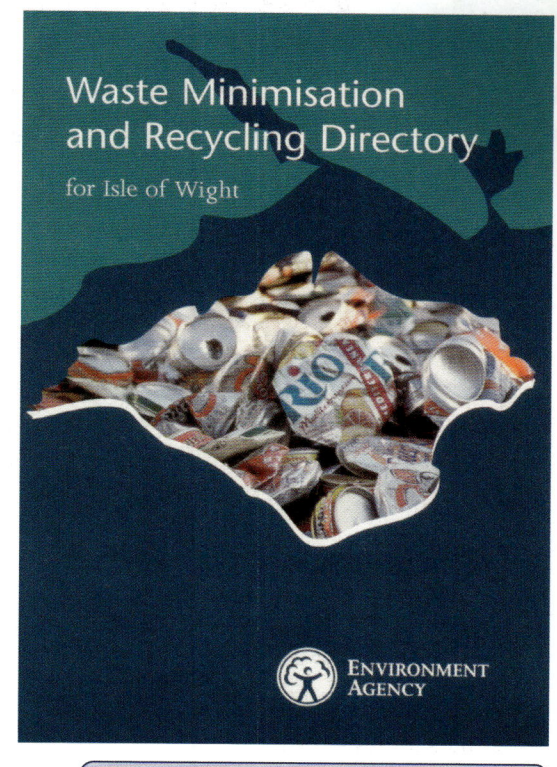

B – Recycling success on the Isle of Wight

Questions

1. Why is recycling so important in LEDCs and in MEDCs?
2. Which materials can be recycled most effectively?
3. When is recycling *not* the best thing to do?
4. Use C to draw an annotated graph illustrating the contents of our landfill sites.
5. Find out what facilities for recycling there are within access of your home. Do you use them? Explain your answer.

Managing Economic Development

10.8 A changing resource: the US temperate forests

Logging has already destroyed 90 per cent of the USA's temperate forests and 60 per cent of Canadian temperate rainforests (see **D** on page 199). Temperate forests include coniferous forests in Russia and Canada, and rainforests along the western coast of the USA where trees can live for 800 years and grow to 100m in height. The world's first national forests were established over 100 years ago in the USA.

How important is the forest in the USA?

More than 3000 species of fish and wildlife, including salmon and grizzly bears, and 10 000 plant species, need the forest habitat. The trees stabilize hillsides, protect against floods and purify the water that flows through the area. When the trees are cut down, water gushes down the slopes and causes floods and dangerous mudslides, and pollutes the water supplies. These are expensive problems to manage.

When the forest is also used for recreation, the gains for just a few people in the logging industry are outweighed by the need to cherish this valuable resource for future generations. The 1992 Rio Conference on Environment and Development set out standards for sustainable resource use. Implementing those standards will involve many groups of people, governments, NGOs, transnationals, pressure groups and individuals everywhere.

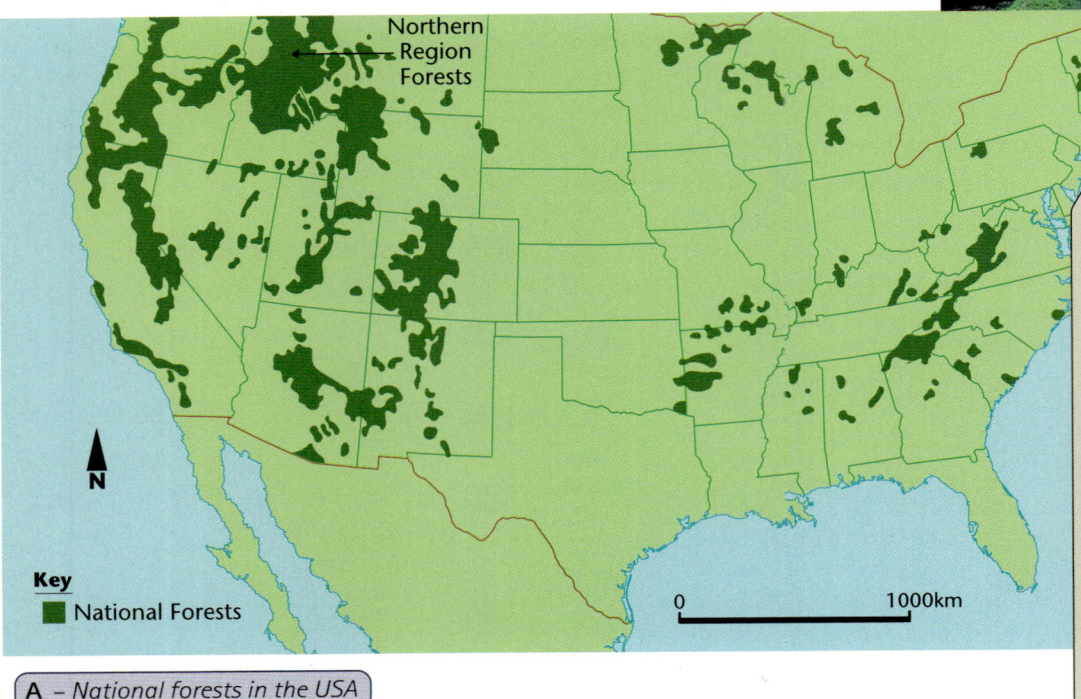

A – *National forests in the USA*

Dale Bosworth, Regional Forester:

'Our focus must be on what we leave on the land, rather than on what we take from the land.'

The Northern region includes 12 national forests in northern Idaho and Montana, and four national grasslands in north and south Dakota; 25.4 million acres.

The forests supplied:
- 18.7 million visitor days
- enough timber to build 28 000 3 bedroom homes
- forage for 203 000 cattle
- habitat for 9 endangered species.

10 Resource depletion

B – Changing values of the forests

The changing perception of a resource
The US forests were destroyed because they were valued for just one resource: timber. Now, though, the forests are also valued for their scenic appearance, recreational potential, and for their ability to protect the land and absorb greenhouse gases like carbon dioxide. Different forest uses all have social, environmental and financial benefits to various groups of people.

Managing the resource
Management of the forests is based on three principles: preservation, biodiversity, and sustained development. This means managing the land in order to preserve unique ecosystems and plant, animal and fish species. It also means preserving the landscape. Different uses are in balance to provide best use of the forests for the greatest number of people.

How can people help in the conservation of forests?
MEDCs import a lot of hardwood and softwood from tropical and temperate forests. The timber should come from sustainable sources, and the policies of major companies like DIY chains in the UK can affect the timber-supplying countries. B&Q, for example, states that timber products 'will be independently certified from well-managed sources as our customers buy our products to improve their quality of life, so it would be bizarre if this was at the expense of other people's quality of life.'

About the national forests
National forests are America's 'favorite playground':
- 835 million visitor-days are spent in national forests
- tourists bring in 38 times more income than logging
- the forests provide 31 times more jobs than logging
- 4400 campsites, 96 scenic rivers, 121 000 miles of trails.

Questions

1. Design an A5-size leaflet that could be used by an environmental group to publicize the changing values of the US temperate forest. Mention at least five disadvantages of clearing the forest, and five advantages of the forests now. Include sketches or an annotated map. Visit www.fs.fed.us or www.sierraclub.org/forests to find some web addresses.

2. Who can prevent rapid resource depletion? List five possible groups of people, and suggest what sort of effect they can have.

Managing Economic Development — Resource depletion

Exam practice questions

Mark schemes can be found on the book's website, at www.heinemann.co.uk/issuesmarkschemes

'A planning application for the superquarry at Lingarabay on Harris was lodged nine years ago but has been opposed by environmental groups, who say it would scar the landscape.'
November 2000 statement made in ongoing planning report

Use the information above and in A to answer the following questions.

1. a) What is the name of the place in the south of the Isle of Harris where the superquarry is proposed? (1)
   b) How many jobs have been proposed by the developers? (1)
   c) Suggest two new jobs that might be created for local people, other than quarrying, if the superquarry goes ahead. (2)

2. Explain two possible environmental impacts if the superquarry goes ahead (4)

3. Use the information in A and your own knowledge to suggest why some islanders:
   a) may not be in favour
   b) may be in favour
   of the proposed superquarry. (4 + 4)

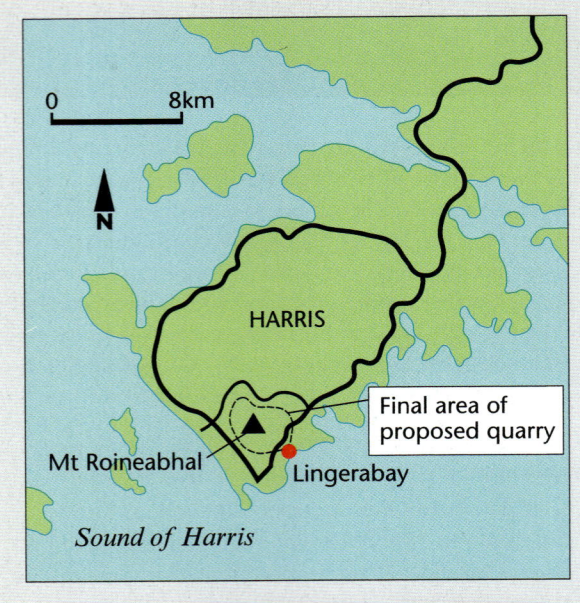

SUPERQUARRY DIVIDES ISLE DESPERATE FOR EMPLOYMENT

ISLANDERS, conservationists and developers are arguing over plans to develop a superquarry at Lingerabay on the south coast of the Isle of Harris.

Objectors say that the island would be totally changed. The quarry would involve removing most of Roineabhal, a 460 metre high mountain. Landscape scars would be visible from the Isle of Skye, 32 kilometres away, and the noise and dust would be horrific for local people.

A farmer born and brought up on Harris says, 'You're talking about an ugly white scar you could see from the moon. You're talking about a hole big enough to put 80 pyramids in! Waste rock will be dumped in the sea, which will ruin the fishing industry'.

But supporters of the quarry point out that without jobs the island's economy will die. The population has halved since 1920 to just over 2,000 as islanders have moved to the mainland to find work.

The quarry developers have promised to create 100 jobs and have offered £100,000 a year to develop social facilities for local people on the island.

The director of Friends of the Earth, Scotland says, 'It is not simply a case of jobs versus the environment.

'The impact on tourism and the fishing industry has not been thoroughly looked at. There will be huge ships coming in and out of the bay. New work is important, but so are the existing jobs.'

Sixty per cent of the islanders are in favour of the proposed superquarry, but those living closest to it are against the plan.

A – From *The Times*, 4 October 1994

11 Managing economic development

MANAGING ECONOMIC DEVELOPMENT

How can economic development be sustained without damage to communities or the natural environment?

11.1 Economic development and the global environment

'Economic development' implies a better quality of life for people, but not all people benefit and in many cases the environment has suffered. People in some industrial regions have been badly affected by air and water pollution. Soil erosion and water pollution have increased with intensive agriculture. Global environmental problems such as acid rain and ozone depletion have also resulted from economic development. Global environmental damage is happening and it is unlikely that it will be stopped, but the rate of damage can be slowed through international co-operation. Global warming and sea-level rise are now affecting all 6 billion people in the world.

Sustainable development is one way forward. The UN definition of sustainable development is: 'Development that meets the needs of the present without compromising the ability of future generations to meet their needs.' A rainforest can be sustainable if a tree is planted for every one cut down. A damaged environment that will never be the same again is unsustainable.

Economic development may damage people and the environment.

- Digging up coal damages the environment at a local scale. Burning coal creates global air pollution and acid rain, and accelerates global warming.

- Leaks from oilwells and pipelines in Siberia and Nigeria have badly contaminated land and reduced the quality of life of the people who live there. The money from the oil sales has benefited these countries and aided development, but is the widespread environmental loss worth the gain?

- Widespread deforestation has increased the levels of carbon dioxide in the atmosphere, contributing to global warming. In 1997 and into 1998, large areas of rainforest in Indonesia and other parts of South-east Asia were destroyed by fire (**A**). Traditionally, local farmers and loggers use fire to burn off the undergrowth in the rainforest at the end of the dry season. The monsoon rains put out the fires but the rains failed. The fires raged unchecked, creating considerable air pollution, and huge smoke fogs hung over Singapore, Malaysia and Indonesia. People in several countries suffered breathing and lung problems, and environmental damage was extensive. Huge quantities of carbon dioxide were released into the atmosphere.

- Water pollution, of rivers, lakes and the sea, has always followed economic development (**B**). The pollution can be restricted to part of a river, but it usually affects a wider area. The North Sea, for example, receives water

Pollution chokes South-east Asia

Fire in the East. Storms in the West. Who said greed is good?

by David Harrison
Environment Editor

THE CAUSES of the pollution disaster in South-east Asia are many, but the biggest is greed. Human greed. For years, giant logging companies have plundered the forests of Indonesia with impunity, welling their profits and moving on. Greed.

In their wake came plantation owners and farmers who wanted to clear the brush to grow lucrative palm oil and other crops. They could have bulldozed or burned the debris. They chose to burn because it was cheaper and faster. Greed.

TRAIL OF HAVOC

- Cargo ship collides with supertanker 28 crew missing — Medan
- Forest fires cover thousands of hectares — Sarawak/Borneo
- Aribus crashes killing all 222 passengers and 12 crew — Sumatra

A – From the Observer, 28 September 1997

11 Managing economic development

Europe awakes to Danube cyanide threat

EUROPE awoke to an environmental catastrophe yesterday, with whole ecosystems left dead by a huge cyanide spill from a gold mine in northern Romania, affecting rivers from Belgrade to the Black Sea.

More than 80 tons of dead fish have already been pulled from the cyanide-laced water of the Tisa river in Hungary alone. The river flows through Hungary and on into Serbia, and more damage is likely as the polluted water moves downstream. According to initial reports, it will take 10 years for the ecosystem to regenerate.

Pollution of the River Tisa in Hungary

B – *Adapted from the* Daily Telegraph, *February 2000*

from several rivers flowing through industrial areas in the UK, Germany and the Netherlands. Industrial, domestic and agricultural waste is carried into the sea — the only way to reduce the pollution is through international controls and agreement.

- Industrial accidents have had devastating effects on the environment and on people. People in countries struggling with development have generally been worst affected. Pollution is worst at the site of an accident, but the impact may be felt over a wide region. Poisonous gases escaped from a US-owned pesticide plant in Bhopal, India in 1984 (page 222), injuring 500 000 people. The explosion in the nuclear power plant at Chernobyl (Ukraine) in 1986 (**C**) badly contaminated the immediate area and also affected the whole of Western Europe. Radiation levels in the atmosphere increased right around the world.

The challenge for the future is to manage development without further global damage.

C – *Disaster at Chernobyl nuclear power station, 1986*

Questions

1. What is meant by the term 'sustainable development'?
2. How can economic development change the environment? Use A and B.
3. Describe three examples of activities that can aid development but also damage the environment. Your answer could be in the form of a table:

Unsustainable activity	Where?	What happened?	Who was affected?	What could be done?	Can development be made sustainable?

213

Managing Economic Development

11.2 Acid rain

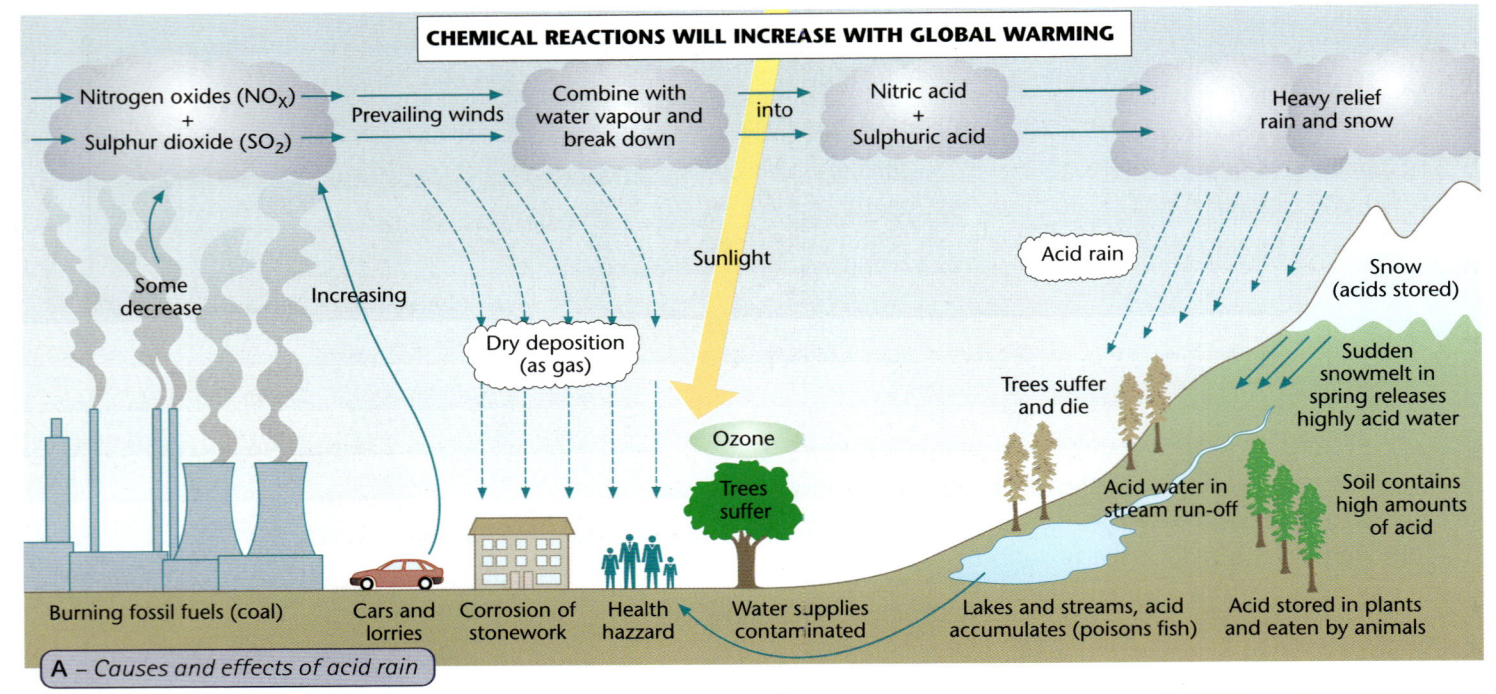

A – Causes and effects of acid rain

CHEMICAL REACTIONS WILL INCREASE WITH GLOBAL WARMING

Nitrogen oxides (NO$_X$) + Sulphur dioxide (SO$_2$) → Prevailing winds → Combine with water vapour and break down → into → Nitric acid + Sulphuric acid → Heavy relief rain and snow

Some decrease · Increasing · Sunlight · Dry deposition (as gas) · Ozone · Trees suffer · Acid rain · Snow (acids stored) · Trees suffer and die · Sudden snowmelt in spring releases highly acid water · Acid water in stream run-off · Soil contains high amounts of acid

Burning fossil fuels (coal) · Cars and lorries · Corrosion of stonework · Health hazzard · Water supplies contaminated · Lakes and streams, acid accumulates (poisons fish) · Acid stored in plants and eaten by animals

The widespread damaging effects of acid rain were seen as long ago as the 1970s. Burning fossil fuels creates emissions of sulphur dioxide and nitrogen oxides (**A**). These combine in the atmosphere with water vapour, sunlight and oxygen to make dilute sulphuric and nitric acids. These acids are washed out of the atmosphere by rain, hail or snow or fall as dry particles to the ground. Rivers, lakes, forests, buildings and the soil are all affected by acid rain.

The acid particles are carried by the wind, so their impact depends on the atmospheric circulation. Acid found in the ice in Antarctica is thought to come from the industrial regions of South America and the Asia-Pacific region, while power stations in the UK are known to damage the forests of Scandinavia.

What is the problem?

The acidity of water and soil is measured by its pH value (**B**). Rainfall is naturally acidic with a pH of 5.6, but rain falling in Norway can be as acid as lemon juice. A pH of 2.4 has been recorded at Pitlochry in Scotland.

Acid rain passing through soil leaches out nutrients and dissolves heavy metals such as lead, mercury and zinc. Crops grow poorly in the contaminated soil, and when the water reaches streams and rivers, fish die. Dry acid deposition can cause breathing and health problems in people. In southern Norway, 80 per cent of lakes and rivers have little

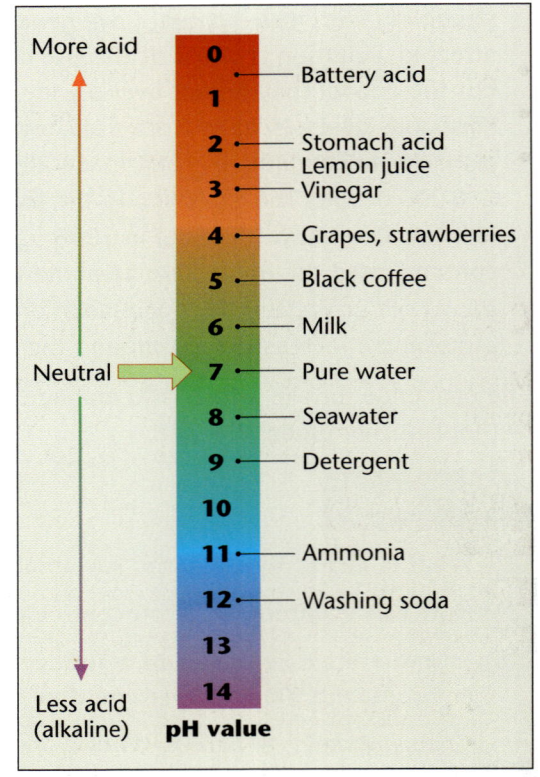

B – The pH scale

More acid
- 0 — Battery acid
- 1
- 2 — Stomach acid / Lemon juice
- 3 — Vinegar
- 4 — Grapes, strawberries
- 5 — Black coffee
- 6 — Milk

Neutral → 7 — Pure water

- 8 — Seawater
- 9 — Detergent
- 10
- 11 — Ammonia
- 12 — Washing soda
- 13
- 14

Less acid (alkaline)

pH value

or no life left in them, because nothing can live in very acid water. A quarter of the 90 000 lakes in Sweden are acidified, and 4000 have no fish. Trees are weakened by the acid, and die.

Can the consequences of acid rain be treated?

Lime neutralizes acid and it is regularly added to lakes in Scandinavia, but it is expensive. Sweden spends $15 million a year on liming. Loch Fleet in south-west Scotland was full of trout in the 1960s but by the 1980s it was dead. Lime was spread over the loch and the surrounding moorland and the loch is now recovering but the cost was high (£1.5 million). Few places can be treated at this cost. Who should pay for the clean-up: those who create the emissions, or those experiencing the damage?

C – Effects of acid rain on a forest in the Czech Republic

Can acid rain be reduced or prevented?

Acid rain can spread far from the point where the pollutants are produced, so who can prove where the acid rain comes from? Acid rain can be reduced, but cross-border agreement is needed – and a lot of money.

- International agreements were reached in the early 1980s when most European countries agreed to reduce their emissions by 30 per cent.
- In 1994, further sulphur dioxide reductions were agreed for 2003.
- Sulphur emissions at power stations can be reduced by 95 per cent by fitting flue gas desulphurization equipment, known as 'scrubbers'. These add to the cost of the electricity.
- Low-sulphur coal or gas can be used.
- Clean energy supplies would be a better solution.
- Emissions from cars have been reduced, although at a cost (the price of a car is now higher). An alternative would be to reduce the number of cars on the road.

Can all countries afford to reduce acid rain?

Many countries depend on coal for energy, but cannot afford to pay for pollution control, particularly poorer countries such as India. Should the more wealthy countries help to pay for cleaner energy?

Questions

1. Draw an annotated diagram to show how acid rain is created.
2. Make a copy of B. Add labels to your diagram to show the acidity of:
   - average clean rain
   - precipitation in Norway
   - the most acid precipitation ever recorded in Scotland.
3. What are the effects of acid rain? and how can the problems be dealt with?
4. Use D to describe the changes in areas affected by acid rain in europe.

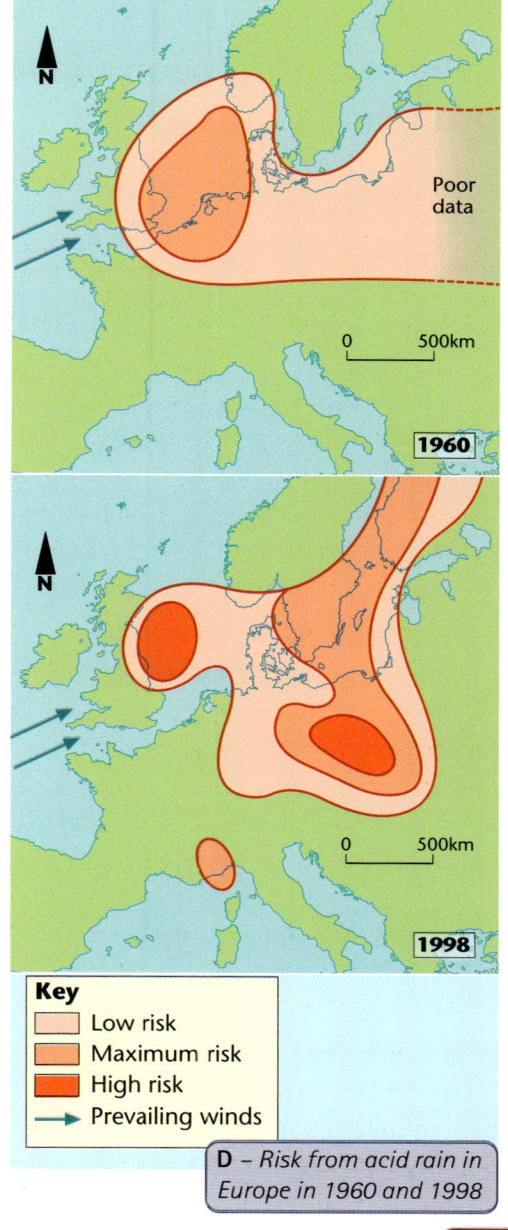

Key
- Low risk
- Maximum risk
- High risk
- → Prevailing winds

D – Risk from acid rain in Europe in 1960 and 1998

Managing economic development

11.3 The ozone layer

The ozone layer filters out the sun's ultraviolet (UV) shortwave radiation, which damages living things. Ozone is a natural gas that is found in small amounts in the atmosphere, but **chlorofluorocarbons (CFCs)**, originally used in refrigerators and aerosols, **halons,** used in fire retardants, and other polluting substances released into the atmosphere as a result of people's activities, cause ozone to break down. The layer above the Arctic and the Antarctic has thinned since the 1970s (A and B).

Why is a thin ozone layer a problem?

A thin ozone layer allows UV radiation to reach the Earth's surface (A) — a 10 per cent depletion of the layer allows in 20 per cent more UV radiation. Over-exposure to UV radiation can cause skin cancer and sunburn and a reduction in the body's ability to fight disease. The UK could expect 30 000 more cases of skin cancer by 2050 if pollutant levels remain the same. Photosynthesis and plant growth are also reduced by increased radiation, which in turn affects our food supplies.

A UV index was developed by Environment Canada (C). A reading of 10 represents a typical midsummer sunny day in the tropics, and sensitive, light skin may burn in less than 15 minutes. Summer weather forecasts now give the estimated sunburn time. Children are especially vulnerable to sunburn now that the ozone layer is thinner.

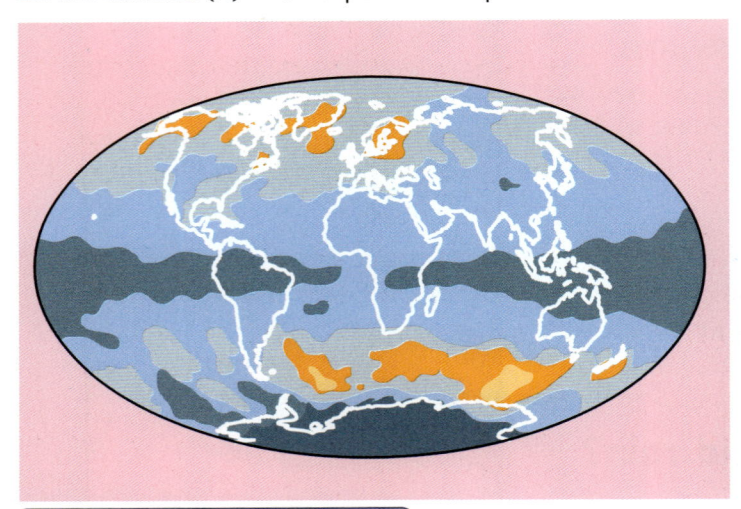

A – The thinning of the ozone layer

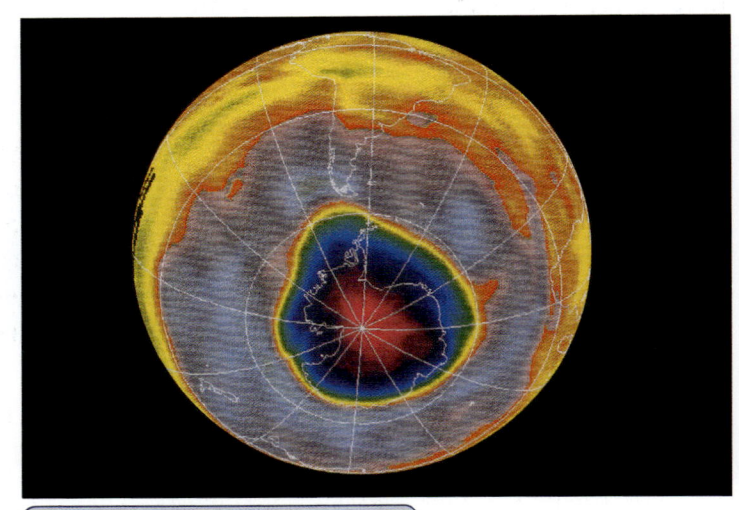

B – An ozone hole over Antarctica

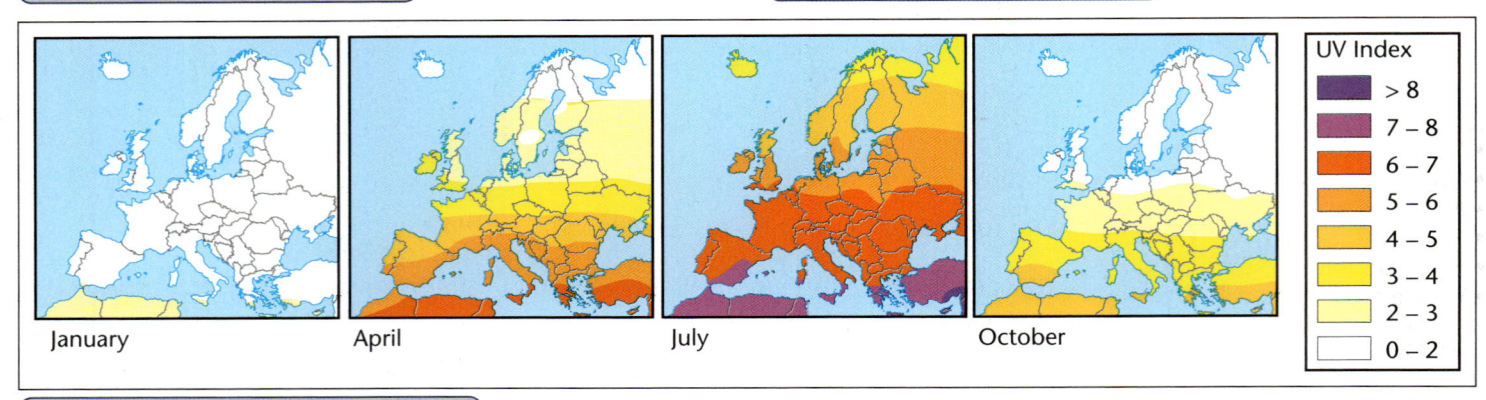

C – UV intensity in Europe during the year

January　April　July　October

UV Index
- \> 8
- 7 – 8
- 6 – 7
- 5 – 6
- 4 – 5
- 3 – 4
- 2 – 3
- 0 – 2

11 Managing economic development

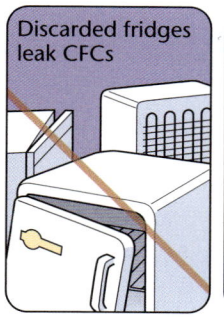

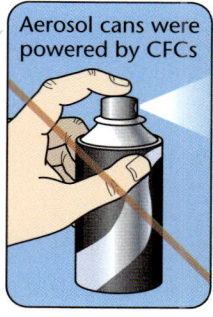

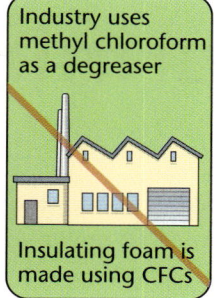

Discarded fridges leak CFCs	Aerosol cans were powered by CFCs	Air-conditioners in cars and buildings leak CFCs	Industry uses methyl chloroform as a degreaser
			Insulating foam is made using CFCs

D – *Where the pollution comes from*

How has the ozone layer been damaged?

Chlorine is released into the atmosphere by CFCs, and this causes ozone to break down. Unfortunately, economic development increased the use of ozone-damaging chemicals. Eventually CFCs were banned in most countries, but they can take seven years to reach the stratosphere and last for 50 years. The concentration of CFCs in the atmosphere is falling, but other harmful substances, such as halons, are increasing. Vehicle and aircraft exhausts also destroy ozone by reacting with UV radiation.

Can ozone depletion be prevented?

The Montreal Protocol (1987) was an international agreement, to phase out the use of ozone-damaging chemicals. By 1992 the Copenhagen Agreement committed governments to a rapid end to using the most damaging CFCs, although developing countries like China have until 2010 to find alternatives to halons. Levels are still rising, the ozone layer is still being depleted and the holes get bigger each year.

SMOG
Summer smog → Deaths → Hospital

- Sun's heat
- Carbon monoxide
- Nitric oxide
- Nitric dioxide
- Hydrocarbons
- Volatile organic compounds (VOCs)
+ Ozone

- Asthma
- Allergies
- Breathing problems

E – *Summer smog*

Will the ozone layer stabilize?

Most governments have now banned the use of CFCs, and try to control their disposal. CFCs are carefully extracted from old fridges at waste disposal sites. But people continue to use CFCs, often illegally. Some LEDCs may not be able to use the more expensive alternatives. The future of the ozone layer may well depend, in the end, on individuals rather than on governments.

Urban air pollution and ozone

Air pollution causes breathing difficulties and illness, reduces life expectancy and can even kill.

Summer air pollution affects millions of people. Ozone and vehicle pollutants react together in high temperatures and long sunshine hours to give summer smog, which seriously damages health. MEDCs set air-quality standards but they are not easy to monitor or enforce.

Most large urban areas have serious air pollution, whatever the state of their economic development (from Tokyo to Mexico City, Athens to Delhi) and some have to ban the use of cars when conditions get too bad (e.g. Athens, Greece in 1999).

Questions

1. a) What are the causes of thinning of the ozone layer? (use D)
   b) What are the effects of a thin layer?
2. a) How can ozone depletion be prevented?
   b) Do you think the measures taken will be successful? Make three different points in your answer.
3. a) What are the causes of summer smog?
   b) What can be done about it?

Managing Economic Development

11.4 Global warming

The Earth is getting warmer and the global climate is changing. There is evidence in tree-ring patterns and deposits in ice of previous dramatic shifts in temperatures associated with carbon dioxide levels in the atmosphere, but scientists increasingly agree that a proportion of the present warming is caused by human activity. The speed of warming is increasing. The climate warmed by about 0.6°C on average in the 20th century but this could increase to 2–4°C by 2050 and possibly 6°C by the end of the 21st century.

What causes the warming?

The atmosphere around the Earth naturally contains greenhouse gases such as water vapour and carbon dioxide, which act like glass in a greenhouse and trap heat around the Earth (**A**). The gases let heat through but prevent some of it being radiated back into space. Without these gases the Earth would be too cold for life. In the last 200 years, emissions of greenhouse gases from human activities have added to these natural gases. The amount of heat trapped has increased. MEDCs have emitted most additional greenhouse gases in the past, and the USA still adds 25 per cent of the global total.

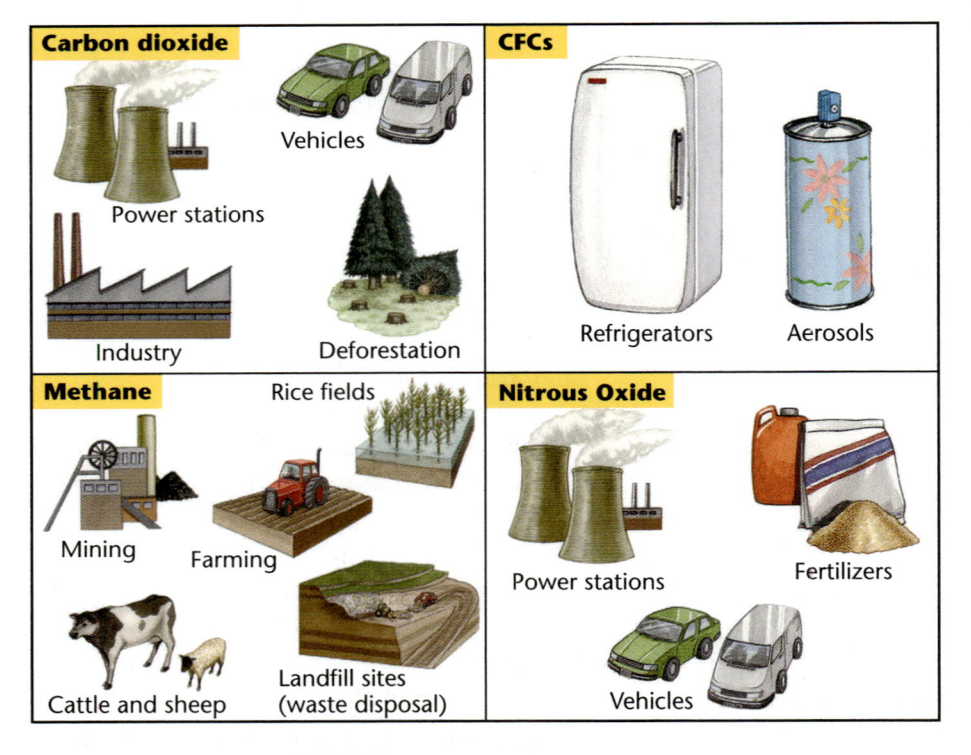

A – The greenhouse effect

B – Sources of greenhouse gases

What are the major greenhouse gases added to the atmosphere by people?

- *Carbon dioxide* comes from burning fossil fuels (approximately 50 per cent from industry, 30 per cent from power stations, 20 per cent from vehicles) and deforestation (possibly 2 billion tonnes).

- *Chlorofluorocarbons (CFCs)* are used as refrigerants and were propellants for aerosols.

- *Methane* comes from farming (about 50 per cent), waste disposal and mining. Rice growing and flatulent cows and sheep produce lots of methane – New Zealand has 50 million sheep (**D**).

- *Nitrous oxide* is emitted from power stations and vehicles, from agriculture (1 per cent) and in the use of fertilizers.

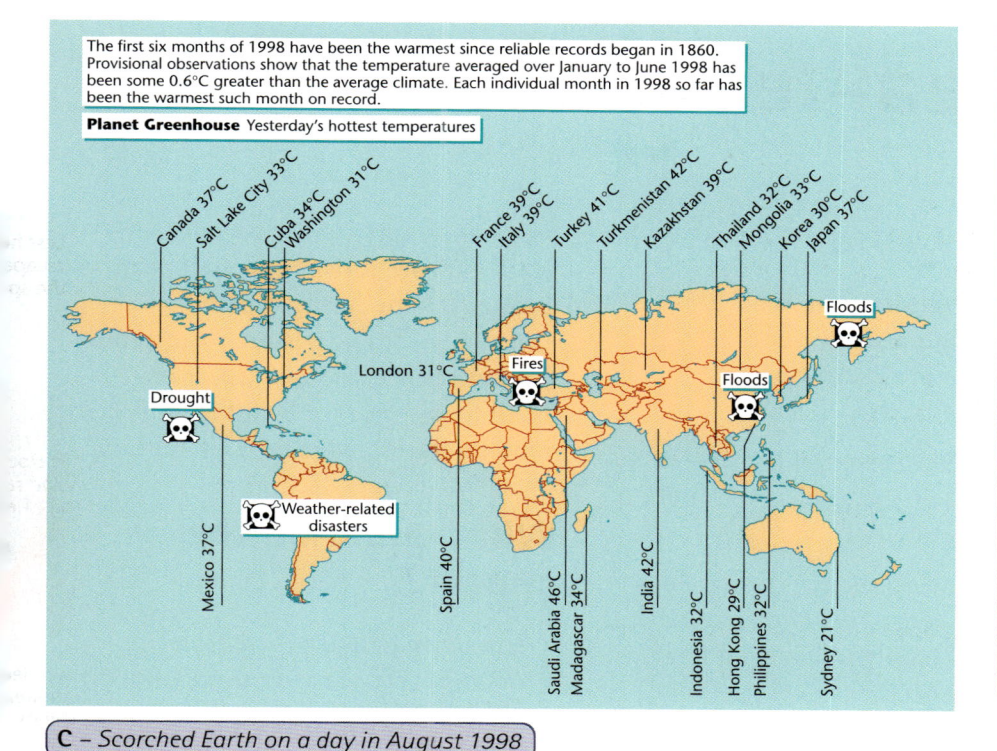

11 Managing economic development

The first six months of 1998 have been the warmest since reliable records began in 1860. Provisional observations show that the temperature averaged over January to June 1998 has been some 0.6°C greater than the average climate. Each individual month in 1998 so far has been the warmest such month on record.

Planet Greenhouse Yesterday's hottest temperatures

Canada 37°C, Salt Lake City 33°C, Cuba 34°C, Washington 31°C, France 39°C, Italy 39°C, Turkey 41°C, Turkmenistan 42°C, Kazakhstan 39°C, Thailand 32°C, Mongolia 33°C, Korea 30°C, Japan 37°C, London 31°C, Fires, Floods, Drought, Mexico 37°C, Weather-related disasters, Spain 40°C, Saudi Arabia 46°C, Madagascar 34°C, India 42°C, Indonesia 32°C, Hong Kong 29°C, Philippines 32°C, Sydney 21°C

C – Scorched Earth on a day in August 1998

Wind velocity test on flatulent sheep
By Roger Highfield, Science Editor

SCIENTISTS have set up instruments downwind of flatulent and burping sheep to investigate methane gas emissions thought to contribute to global warming.

The study is being conducted in New Zealand, where there are 50 million sheep and 3.7 million humans. Ruminant livestock are responsible for 60 per cent of New Zealand's methane emission, and belching sheep account for half of that.

The nation generates eight times the OECD average of methane emission per head of human population, said Dr Mark Ulyatt of the Grasslands Research Centre, Palmerston North.

D – From the *Electronic Telegraph*, 27 August 1997

Global warming is expensive to manage. Costs include the damage from storms, fires and rising sea-level. The cost in human lives may be high. Can it be prevented? Can the rate of change be slowed? Yes, possibly, with global agreement and co-operation.

Indications

- *Heatwaves and periods of unusually warm weather:* six of the ten warmest years ever recorded were in the 1990s and the other four were in the 1980s. In 1998 summer temperatures in India averaged 42°C.
- The *Arctic and Antarctic ice is shrinking and thinning.* Permafrost is thawing, causing the break-up of roads, railways and buildings.
- *Global sea-level* has risen about 50mm over the last 100 years.
- *Glaciers melting:* half the glaciers in Spain that existed in 1980 have since melted, and Glacier National Park in Montana, USA will probably not have any glaciers by 2070.
- *Ocean current changes* are happening more frequently — the last El Niño caused billions of dollars of damage all around the world.

Impacts

- *Droughts* in Africa and India have caused famine and a breakdown in farming. *Desertification* has increased. Over 15 000 *fires* burned in Nicaragua in 1998.
- *Heavy rain, flooding, blizzards, storms:*
  — The rainfall and river flooding in England in autumn 2000 were the worst ever recorded there.
  — In 1999, Mount Baker in Washington, USA had 28 956mm of snow in six months — a world record.
  — More rain, and more frequent high winds and storms are being recorded right around the world.
- *Spreading disease:* deadly malaria outbreaks in 1997 in Kenya and Tanzania, in previously malaria-free mountain areas, killed hundreds of people. Malaria reappeared in Europe in 1999.
- *Changing seasons:* the growing season in Europe is 11 days longer than it was 30 years ago and birds are nesting 17 days earlier than they did in the 1960s.
- *Changes in the location of plants and animals:* birds are living 20km further north, on average, than they did 20 years ago. Northern conifers are dying from heat. Farm crops are changing (for example, maize and vines are now commonly grown in the UK).
- *Coral reef bleaching* has been recorded in 32 places from the Seychelles Islands, Kenya and Madagascar to Indonesia. Microscopic algae that colour and nourish coral die as water temperatures rise by 2°C.

E – Indications and impacts of global warming

Questions

1. Draw a labelled diagram to explain the greenhouse effect.
2. a) What is causing global warming?
   b) List five different indicators of global warming (use E).
3. What are the impacts of global warming?
4. Use data in C to explain the title 'scorched earth'.

219

Managing Economic Development

11.5 Rising sea-level

Why are sea-levels rising?

Sea-levels are rising because there is more water in the sea from melting ice-sheets and the water is expanding as temperatures rise. Millions of people living close to the sea are at risk. In the USA, 75 per cent of people live on or within 80km of the coast.

The global rise in sea-level is about 2mm/year. Sea-level is affected by a number of things including the movement of the land, the salinity of the sea and the number and strength of storms.

Sea-levels have always fluctuated, falling during ice ages and rising during periods of global warming. The most recent ice age ended about 10 000 years ago and the rising sea-level inundated low-lying land, forming the North Sea and the English Channel. Sea-level rise has been relatively constant during the last 6000 years but global warming is now accelerating that rise.

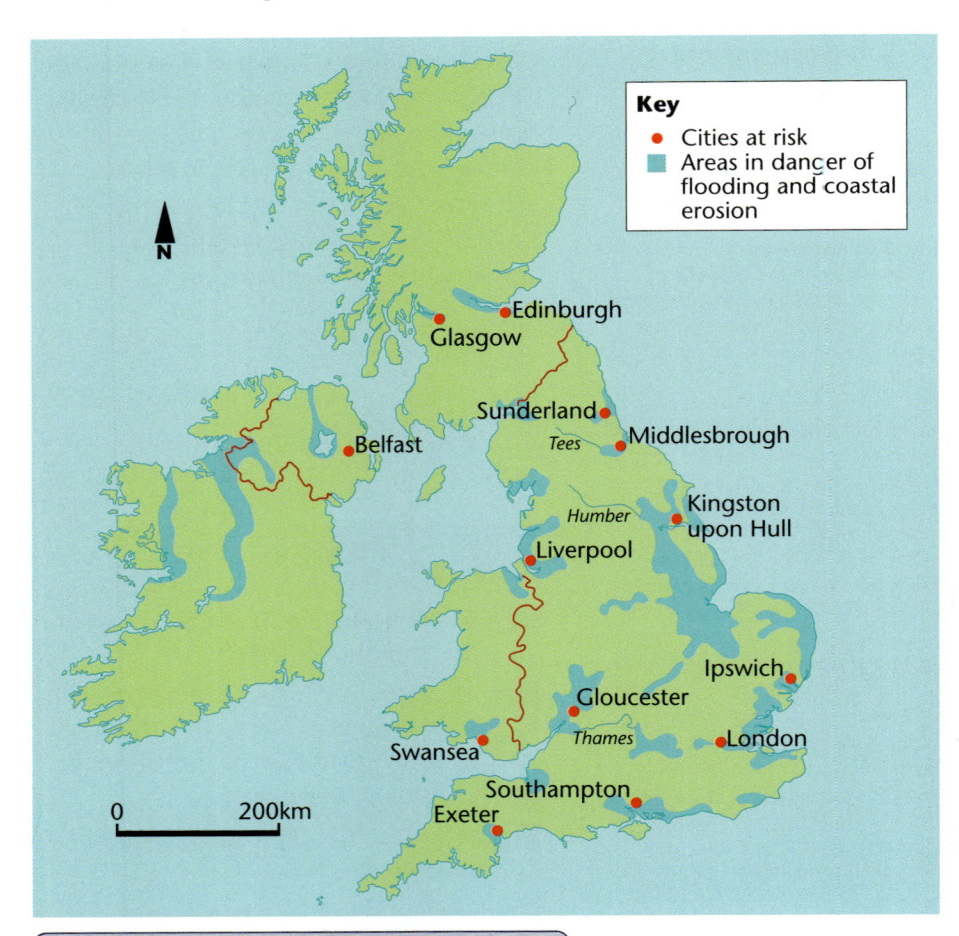

Tide-gauge records dating back 100 years indicate a rise in global mean sea-level of 50mm during that time. Average UK sea-levels are expected to rise between 2 and 9mm/year or possibly up to 67cm by 2050, which is an acceleration over the last century.

What could be the impact?

- *Low-level land is at risk from flooding* The sea may simply flood the land if there are no sea defences, and storm surges with high tides and high sea-levels may overtop defences:
  — East Anglia in particular could be at risk in the UK
  — 75 per cent of Bangladesh is only 1.5m above sea-level, so millions of people there are vulnerable to storm surges and flooding.

A – Effect of a rising sea-level on the British Isles

B – Flood defences against the sea in LEDCs are often inadequate

11 Managing economic development

When the sands of time run out

Erosion is threatening to ruin an exclusive Dorset resort favoured by the rich

By Sarah O'Grady
PROPERTY CORRESPONDENT

A BEACH at the bottom of the garden makes a perfect millionaire's playground, and celebrities determined to enjoy themselves turned a modest seaside resort into one of the world's wealthiest neighbourhoods.

But residents of Dorset's Millionaires' Row now fear playtime is over as they watch their beautiful beach disappear day by day despite all the efforts of the local council to stem the erosion.

'The beach is vanishing very quickly,' said Jeff Lambert, 63, who retired there four years ago. 'there is definitely a difference to the way it was when I first arrived.'

'A lot of locals are saying that some of the area's richest residents will get a shock whey they next come down. They all have houses backing on to the beach with their own private paths or ladders leading down. Now those paths have crumbled and the ladders are just left swinging because they are no longer long enough because so much sand has been swept away. 'The beach and the peace are the reasons why people spend millions of pounds on property here.

'But the beach is disappearing and the peace is disrupted by lorries arriving every 10 minutes with 40-tonne loads of rock which the council is laying to protect the beach from further erosion.'

C – *From the Sunday Express, 18 February 2001*

— the Maldive Islands could become uninhabitable

— a rise of 46cm would submerge 10 000 acres (4000ha) of Massachusetts (USA) at roughly $1 million per acre

— a recent study in California (USA) concluded that a 60cm rise in sea-level in Ventura county by 2040 could swamp hotels, power plants, a military base, roads, railways, recreational facilities and 4100 homes

— worldwide, a 46cm rise would put 92 million people at risk of flooding, which would be accompanied by storm surges.

- *Salt water* will spread further inland up estuaries and inlets, and the types of plants, animals and ecosystems will change. Wetlands around estuaries may become saltmarsh. In the UK, the Norfolk Broads and the Fens are particularly at risk.

    — The amount of sediment in estuaries will increase. Dredging will be necessary to maintain harbours and ports.

    — Pollution could increase. Tidal wetlands and estuaries which often receive polluted water will not be flushed out by fresh water.

    — 14 key estuaries in England and Wales are currently being monitored by the Environment Agency.

- *Coastal erosion* will increase, especially where sea defences are overcome by storm surges. In the UK, the coastal nuclear power station at Dungeness is above a shingle bank that now has to be constantly maintained. It is seriously threatened by rising sea-level. Housing along the south coast where the defences are shingle banks at places like Shoreham-by-Sea, are very vulnerable (**C**). Cliffs will erode more rapidly if sea defences are overcome, and waves can then break against the cliff, putting at risk considerable areas of the south coast.

- *Cities on low-lying estuaries*, such as London, may be flooded. Bangkok in Thailand is vulnerable and is already sinking as the water table falls. Economic development and increasing water extraction accompanied by sea-level rise will make many coastal cities more susceptible to flooding. A 90cm rise in sea-level with a storm surge would flood Wall Street in New York and put the subway system at risk.

- *Travel and tourism* is the largest industry in the world, worth $2.9 trillion globally. As much as $750 billion of the USA's GNP comes from travel and tourism, and the majority of tourists go to coastal states. The Government already spends $30 million a year in beach replenishment because of increasing coastal erosion.

Questions

1 Why are sea-levels rising?

2 Draw a table to show five impacts of sea-level rise:

Impact	Examples	Damage and costs to people and places
1		
2		
3		

221

Managing Economic Development

11.6 Development, pollution, health and accidents

Pollution and economic development have always gone together, but many people now object to pollution. Regulations have been introduced to control processes and emissions that harm people and the environment. People also need jobs and so may put up with poor working conditions, especially in LEDCs.

MEDCs try to safeguard people but safety always costs money, which LEDCs may not have.

Bhopal in India, 1984

Bhopal is sometimes described as the world's worst industrial accident and half a million people are still suffering from its effects.

Bhopal is in the state of Madhya Pradesh in central India. A US transnational company (Union Carbide) built a pesticide plant on the edge of the city. A high-density population of poor shanty housing grew around the plant — something that planning regulations would have prevented in an MEDC. On 2 December 1984, 40 tonnes of the toxic chemical methyl isocyanate leaked, then mixed with water and exploded. A cloud of toxic gases spread over 79km^2 and over 600 000 people. People were affected in different ways (**A**), both at the time and later. Even now 4000 victims a day visit the local hospitals.

Accurate figures are not available, but it seems that 8000 people died within a week, and the final death toll could be between 10 000 and 16 000. Union Carbide claimed that 2000–3000 died or were disabled. Possibly 400 000 people fled, some of whom died. Official figures (probably an underestimate) suggest that over half a million people suffered from gas poisoning.

Union Carbide claimed that the leak was the result of sabotage, the Indian government claimed that there was negligence but agreed to compensation of £470 million from Union Carbide instead of the £1.5 billion claimed.

What were the costs?

The economic damage from the accident is thought to be around $2.5 billion, but the biggest cost is in human suffering. Most survivors were very poor people, and work for them now is very difficult. The government made small payments to the victims in the 1990s. Children born since the accident with genetic defects prolong the suffering of families already struggling to look after disabled survivors.

If such an accident had occurred in an MEDC, victims would have been dealt with more quickly and would have received more compensation, faster.

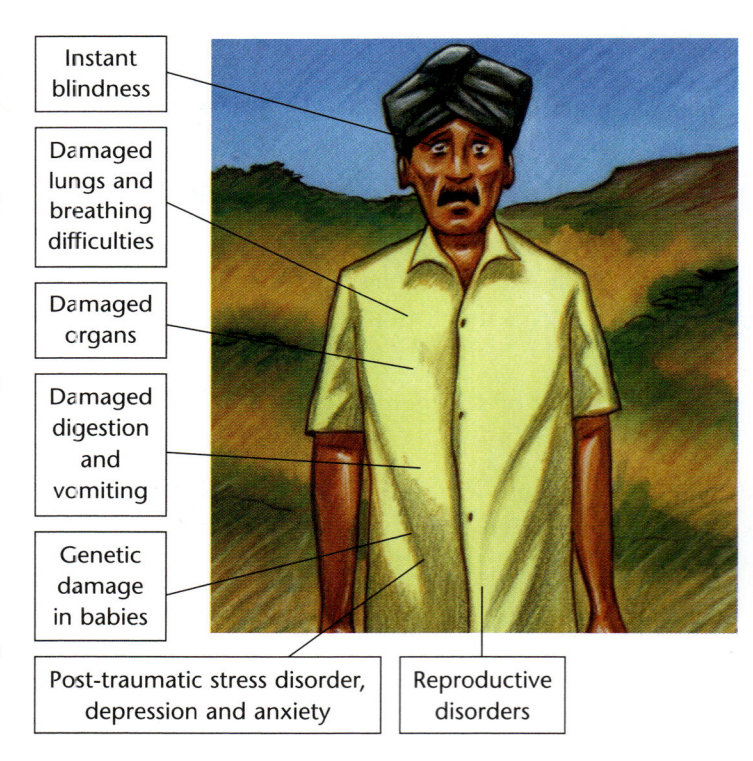

A – *Suffering caused by the Bhopal disaster*

- Instant blindness
- Damaged lungs and breathing difficulties
- Damaged organs
- Damaged digestion and vomiting
- Genetic damage in babies
- Post-traumatic stress disorder, depression and anxiety
- Reproductive disorders

CS Chernobyl, 1986

Economic development depends on power supplies and nuclear power should be one of the cleanest.

On 26 April 1986 there was a catastrophic explosion and fire at the Chernobyl nuclear power plant in Ukraine, then part of the Soviet Union (C). A nine-tonne radioactive cloud of debris blasted into the atmosphere and spread over north-west Europe as far as the UK (B).

The fire was put out and the reactor encased in concrete by 'liquidators', who could work for only 40 seconds before they received a lethal dose of radiation, and many have since died. The surrounding people, animals, and land were badly contaminated.

Perhaps 375 000 people were eventually evacuated from the area. But 10 days passed before any evacuation. Caesium-37 caused radiation throughout much of the northern hemisphere, and iodine-131 triggered thyroid cancer in local people, particularly children.

What has happened now?

- 160 000km^2 remain contaminated. Even sheep farms in the Lake District (UK) still face restrictions on selling their lamb because of continuing contamination of the vegetation.
- 1000 people stayed in Chernobyl because the power plant continued to generate much-needed electricity until it finally closed in December 2000.
- Some elderly people have moved back to farm the land because they have no other way of getting food. The crops they grow are contaminated.
- The Ukraine branch of Greenpeace estimates that more than 32 000 people have died and 1.25 million people are directly affected. Children are badly affected.
- All the evacuations, medical care, etc. have cost over $250 billion.
- The economies of local states have been devastated, economic development has almost ceased and the quality of life has deteriorated throughout the region.

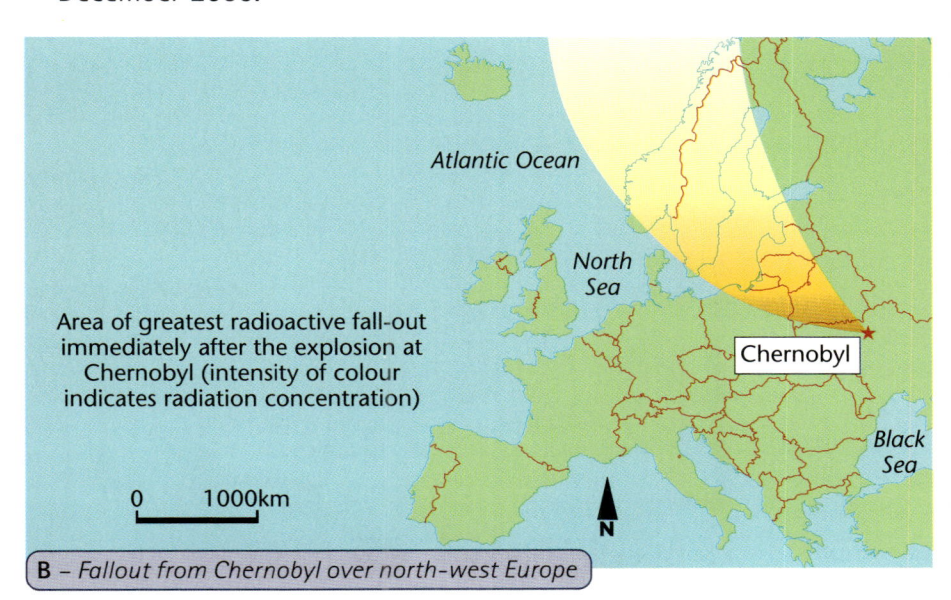

B – Fallout from Chernobyl over north-west Europe

C – Radiation testing after the destruction at Chernobyl

Questions

1. a) Why did each accident happen?
   b) What happened to the people?
2. How widespread were the effects?
3. What are the long-term costs and dangers of such accidents?
4. Why are poor people often affected the most in industrial accidents?

Managing Economic Development

11.7 Sustainable strategies for development

Cubatao, Brazil

'Some say the dirty air is the price of progress' said a doctor in Cubatao in the 1980s, 'but is it? Look who pays the price, the poor.' Cubatao in Brazil was known as the Valley of Death and the most polluted place in the world. The air was so polluted with toxins that breathing made your lungs ache, cancer rates were high and infant mortality was 10 per cent higher than in the rest of the state.

The Brazilian government in its drive for economic development in the 1950s thought the valley near the port of Santos, 60km south of São Paulo, was an ideal location for industry. Chemical and fertilizer plants followed a giant oil refinery and a huge state-owned steelworks. The town grew to 100 000 people, most of them poor and desperate for work. The concentration of industry increased to become the largest heavy chemical industry site in South America, operating with no environmental controls. Toxic air pollution became trapped in the valley by surrounding mountains.

From the late 1970s there was a series of disasters that made the government and companies involved think about the environmental impact of economic development.

Several babies were born without brains. This could not be directly linked to the pollution, but the people living there thought it was. The air pollution was like a chemical defoliant, killing the lush vegetation on the mountainside. In the rainy season, soil on the bare slopes was washed away, sending mudslides and floods into the valley and causing extensive damage. Pipeline explosions under shanty settlements caused widespread damage. People lived and died in appalling conditions.

The government recognized the need for a more sustainable approach to development, and environmental laws in the 1980s began to control the worst effects. Local and regional authorities worked with the industries, local people and international agencies. Air pollution was cut by 80 per cent in 10 years, the slopes were reforested and the water quality

A – Cubatao in Brazil

B – Cubatao as it is today

11 Managing economic development

Are Bangladeshi tanneries to blame for health problems?

Hell from leather

Arshad Mahmud in Dhaka

Mirazul Hossain Chowdhury is angry. The 40-year-old businessman throws his arms in a gesture of helplessness. 'I wish I could move elsewhere permanently,' he says. 'This is like living in a hell where you slowly, but surely, embrace death.'

Chowdhury is talking of Hazaribagh, a crowded residential district of almost 500 000 people in the Bangladeshi capital, Dhaka. His wife died of kidney problems two years ago and, like so many others in the district, he fears the health risks from the toxic chemicals being released daily from leather tanneries dotted among their homes.

With no one apparently interested in countering this pollution, many people wonder if they are doomed to die by slow poisoning.

The leather processing plants have sprouted up haphazardly over the last 30 years. Of Bangladesh's 300 tanneries, Hazaribagh has 90%, with 277 small and medium-sized plants concentrated in 25ha of land. According to a recent study, the tanneries release 7.7 million litres of liquid and 88 tonnes of solid toxic substances daily. With no proper drainage system for waste disposal and no treatment plant, the toxic waste dumped in the area is left to accumulate unchecked.

Experts say the industrial waste causes dangerous levels of ground and air pollution. Several chemicals used in the tanneries are blamed for the pollution, but it is the sulphur dioxide and chromium that are considered the most harmful to the environment and to human health.

The stench produced by the tanneries is so overpowering that visitors are overcome by nausea.

No wonder most of the Hazaribagh residents suffer from a host of ailments, including jaundice, lung infections, skin diseases, ulcers and cancer.

Environment department officials take exception to the charge that they do not care: 'It's not true that we're doing nothing. Numerous studies have been carried out aimed at finding a solution. Most recommend shifting the tanneries out of Hazaribagh to a place far from the capital city.'

But so far all attempts to move the tanneries have been torpedoed by powerful industrial interests. 'They're rich and powerful and the politicians don't want to antagonise them,' says one official.

The leather sector earns a substantial part of the country's hard currency. Last year it earned about $280m (£190m) out of the country's total export earnings of $5.7 billion.

Unable to relocate the factories, the government has promised to build a treatment plant in Hazaribagh. So far only one factory has installed a plant.

C – *From* Guardian Society, *7 February 2001*

---

improved. The last time industry was shut down here because of pollution was in 1994.

Pollution has not been eliminated but it is under control. The air is still bad and cancer rates are high, but Cubatao is no longer Death Valley, and it is regarded as sustainable. Now most factory workers have a higher standard of living and live elsewhere, although there is still a local population of 120 000, many of whom are a new wave of poor people moving in from even poorer places.

What if the government has other priorities?

Some people and even some governments are willing to trade the environmental destruction of one place for economic development in another or the country as a whole (**C**). Mining and fossil fuel extraction are especially damaging activities, and have had devastating effects on some regions that may not have even benefited from economic development.

Some countries may not have the money to control pollution, and some may choose not to, but the actions of just one country may have global implications.

Questions

1
a) Why was industry established in Cubatao?
b) What were the industries?
c) Why was air pollution trapped?
d) When, why and how did the government take action?
e) What is the area like now?

2 Study **C**.
a) Where are the tanneries in Bangladesh?
b) What are the problems created by the tanneries?
c) Who suffers the most?
d) What could be a solution to the problems?

Managing Economic Development

11.8 Appropriate technology and sustainability

From the 1960s many people thought that economic development came through large-scale projects. Brazil saw big developments as the way forward — roads through the Amazon rainforest, industrial plants at Cubatao, and transnational corporations (TNCs) like General Motors bringing work. People eventually realized that there are disadvantages as well as benefits from this approach. Small enterprises can be cheap to run, low on energy consumption and efficient at using, re-using, and recycling resources. Worldwide, people in small workshops, family businesses and farms use materials and technology that are appropriate to their lives, which is an efficient and sustainable way forward.

Traditional appropriate technology

Clothing, furniture, utensils, jewellery, food, drink... the list of things made in local workshops and homes is endless, from the back streets of Cairo (Egypt) to remote villages in Nigeria. Local and recycled materials help people get products that they need but cannot buy, either because they have no money, or because access to supplies is limited. Some of these traditional products are now sold as tourist souvenirs or commercial exports.

Newer appropriate technology

Newer technologies can help small-scale developments. For example:

- Small portable solar power generators are efficient in remote areas, for homes, clinics, etc. where other sources are not available, or where resources like fuelwood are being depleted.
- Small HEP systems provide easily managed, renewable power.
- Simple, strong mechanically operated hand pumps have brought good-quality water supplies to many parts of India and Africa.
- Wind-up radios and torches (cheap, robust, non-polluting) can improve the quality of people's lives.
- Developments in information and communications technology influence how people live and work all over the world. Small companies in rural parts of the UK can use the internet and video-conferencing, so car travel and commuting are reduced, which is better for the environment.

Appropriate farming

Appropriate technology for subsistence farmers may mean strong basic tools, easily maintained watering systems, and methods that use the number of hands available, rather than expensive diesel-driven machines.

Organic farming helps to preserve the soil and maintain a sustainable environment, in contrast to many extensive commercial farming methods that have led to soil erosion, increased run-off and flooding.

A – Goods made using traditional appropriate technology

B – New appropriate technology: solar cells heat underground water store

Sustainability, transnational corporations and pressure groups

International groups such as Friends of the Earth, Greenpeace, WWF and the United Nations focus attention on global and local problems of economic change. Non-governmental organizations (NGOs) like Oxfam, Save the Children Fund and ActionAid work with communities in LEDCs and MEDCs to raise the quality of life without environmental damage. TNCs, most of them with their head offices in the USA or Asia, dominate global markets and search for the physical and human resources that can be exploited for the lowest cost. Governments have to respond to all of these.

Various groups react to environmental and pollution problems (e.g. the oilspill in the Galapagos Islands in February 2001) and anticipate problems (e.g. the Three Gorges Dam in China). They try to get governments and businesses working together towards sustainable development. In the UK, for example, the WWF is working with the Scottish Parliament to encourage better care of freshwater environments, marine life, and important natural areas. Parts of Nigeria are badly polluted by oil extraction and local people need help from international pressure groups to tackle the oil company BP and the government that supports it. National groups like the Sierra Club in the USA, which has 700 000 members, focus attention on US actions that have local and international effects.

What can a pressure group do?

'Greenpeace blocks import of waste for incineration' was the headline in February 2001 when 50 activists stopped a ship from docking 40km south of Stockholm. On board were 3700 tonnes of waste from the Netherlands on the way to an incinerator. The waste contained high levels of heavy metals like copper, lead and mercury. Incineration is cheap in Sweden, using HEP, and additional money can be made locally by selling the heat that is generated. Imports of waste have increased dramatically in the last five years. 'Sweden is not a dumping ground for waste from other countries,' said Greenpeace Sweden, and added, 'If countries are allowed to evade their own waste problems by exporting them, there will be no incentive to reduce, re-use or recycle waste.'

C – A pressure group working through the Web

D – Greenpeace in action

Questions

1. Why are some appropriate traditional methods of production sustainable?
2. How can newer appropriate technologies help people to improve their quality of life?
3. a) What is appropriate technology for subsistence farmers?
   b) Why might intensive farming be unsustainable in some places?
4. What can pressure groups do, and whom do they influence?
5. Who benefits and who loses when waste is taken to another country for disposal?

Managing Economic Development

11.9 International agreements and responses to climate change

Global problems can only be solved through global agreement. A succession of conferences has agreed certain aims, but not exactly what each country will do or how to make every country take action.

- The first UN conference on the human environment was held in Stockholm in *1972*.
- In *1992* in Rio de Janeiro the Earth Summit on Environment and Development discussed climate changes, forest loss, biodiversity and sustainable development. The conference set out standards for resource use that led to Agenda 21.
- The Kyoto Conference in *1997* continued to consider climate change.
- In conferences in *2000* and *2001* people were still trying to get countries to ratify previous agreements.

What are some of the difficulties?

Scientists and governments agree that the climate is changing but they do not agree on the extent to which people are causing the change. Some people believe the changes are a natural process. There are arguments on both sides, but LEDCs and MEDCs tend to have different viewpoints:

- LEDCs have to use the energy sources available to them, which may mean burning fossil fuels and so creating more acid rain and contributing to global warming and ozone depletion.
- LEDCs may not have the money to clean emissions from their power stations, factories and vehicles.
- MEDCs have made most of the pollution in the past.
- The USA still produces most greenhouse gases and has consumed most resources.
- LEDCs at risk of flooding from sea-level rise see activities in the MEDCs as the greatest global threat.
- MEDCs see newly industrializing LEDCs as the greatest threat because of their uncontrolled fossil fuel burning and pollution.
- Voters influence many governments. In democratic countries, elections are held every four or five years, so governments are forced to react to people's views.

How can governments respond?

They can:

- agree targets for reducing greenhouse gas emissions

When it comes to polluting the atmosphere, the US rules the world, mainly because the car is king. There are 1.3 people per car in the US compared with 125 people per car in China.

World may be warming up even faster
Climate Scientists warn new forests could make things worse
9 November 2000

Global warming: it's with us now

Climate change
Floods in Yorkshire. Millions facing drought in China. Permafrost melting in Russia. Malaria spreading across Africa. And that's just the start.

- Climate change talks begin at the Hague
- Fears that US will block progress

14 November 2000

Energy targets would change face of Britain
James Meikle
A British landscape and coastline dominated by wind farms, with turbines on and under the sea and on much of the land, was yesterday sketched out by scientists who recommended a 60% cut in carbon dioxide emissions over the next 50 years.
The Guardian, 17 June 2000

The great climate sell-off
Big corporations are buying their way out of environmental curbs

Pace of global warming 'could double'

China wants the car economy but not the fumes

WORLD: CLIMATE SUMMIT
US plays dirty as planet chokes
Squabbles as America fights to avoid reducing emissions
The Observer, 19 November 2000

Exhaust fumes, industry and weather conditions form lethal cocktail
Dangerous ozone levels could be regular feature of hot summer days

Future fear as global temperature hits 1000-year high
23 January 2001
The movie horror-fantasy of the sea engulfing major cities on the east coast of the USA could become reality this century if nothing is done, scientists believe
14 November 2000

A – Aspects of economic development that may contribute to global problems

11 Managing economic development

- trade emissions with countries that have not used all their allocation (the USA trades with developing countries that are still developing so have not yet created lots of greenhouse gases)
- control the depletion of resources
- plant forests to absorb carbon dioxide.

What can local people do?

They try to persuade governments to support actions that would improve the quality of life for all people and make economic development sustainable, including:

- controlling pollution
- making working conditions safe and fair in every country
- stopping child labour
- cutting Third World debt
- reducing greenhouse gas emissions
- developing clean, renewable energy.

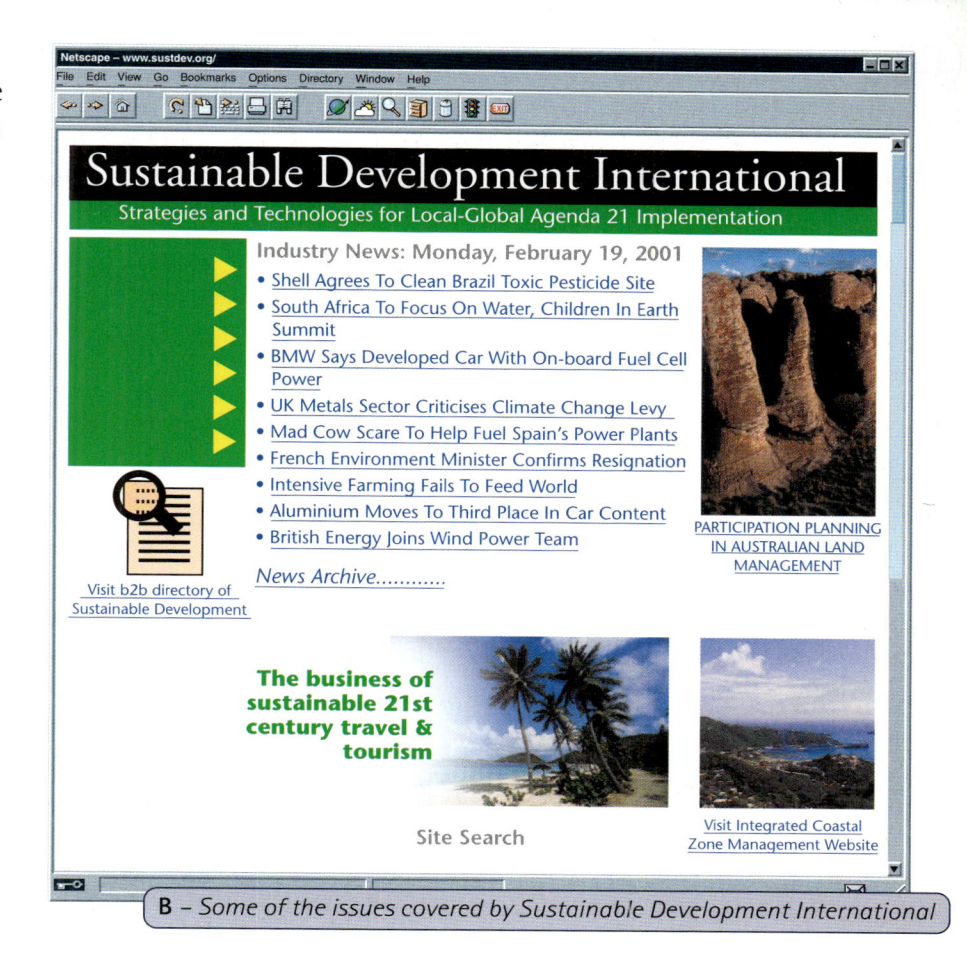

B – Some of the issues covered by Sustainable Development International

How can governments manage their own needs and global needs?

They can:

- pass laws to reduce harmful air, water and land pollution from vehicles, power stations and factories, and fine people if they continue to pollute the environment
- encourage people to use less fossil fuel by putting up the price of petrol and making it difficult to use cars
- support recycling and products that can be recycled (e.g. VW cars can be recycled)
- educate people and raise awareness about the environment.

There are still many unknown factors linked with economic development and global climate change. Rainforests absorb and store carbon dioxide from the atmosphere, but by 2050 changes in rainfall may begin to kill the forest. Will the released carbon and methane cause more change?

Conifers are being planted in Uganda to grow quickly and absorb carbon dioxide that could be counted against the US total, but they are dark and absorb the heat, so are they contributing to global warming? What happens when they die?

Questions

1. What major international conferences have taken place?
2. List five differences in the views of LEDCs and MEDCs on global agreements.
3. Design an A4 poster for a global pressure group to explain five ways in which the quality of life could be improved for all people.
4. Suggest three popular and three unpopular measures that the UK could take to reduce pollution and resource depletion.
5. Plan a letter to a US President to persuade him to reduce gas emissions.
6. Use A. Which do you think are the 5 most important global problems? Explain your answer.

Managing economic development

Exam practice questions

Mark schemes can be found on the book's website, at www.heinemann.co.uk/issuesmarkschemes

1. a) What is global warming? *(1)*
   b) Which of the problems shown in A may be caused by:
      - an increase in temperature
      - a decrease in rainfall
      - a rise in sea-level? *(6)*

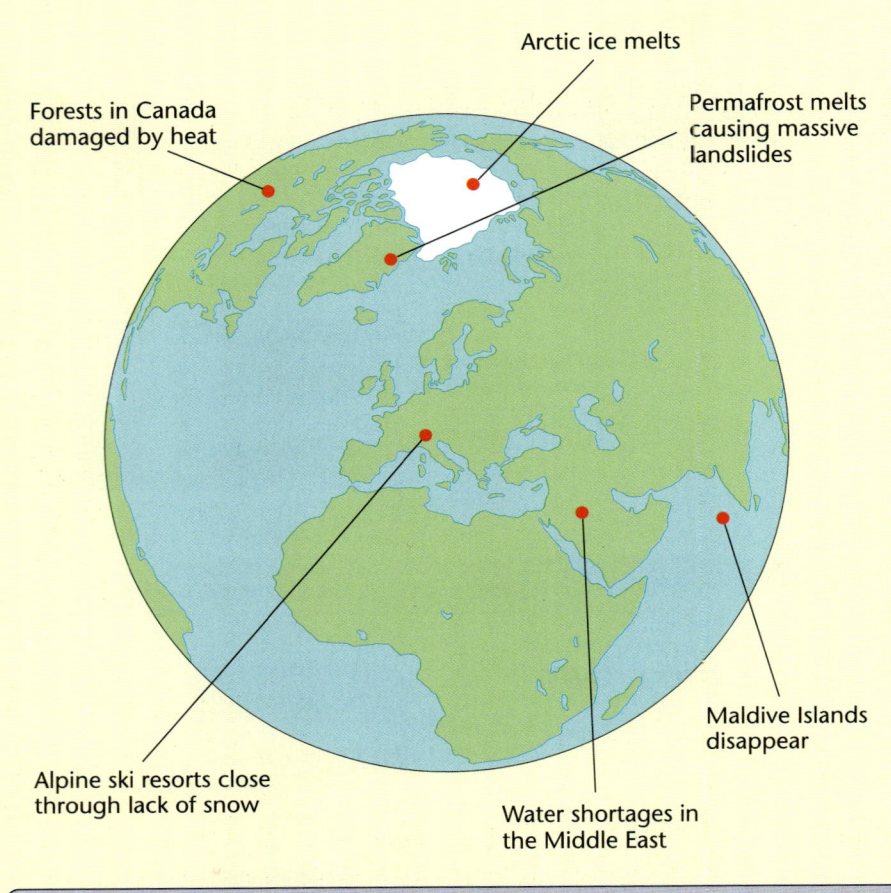

Labels on diagram A:
- Arctic ice melts
- Forests in Canada damaged by heat
- Permafrost melts causing massive landslides
- Alpine ski resorts close through lack of snow
- Water shortages in the Middle East
- Maldive Islands disappear

A – Some of the problems that may be caused by global warming in the next 50 years

2. Economic activities can cause large-scale changes in the Earth's environment, e.g. global warming, acid rain, ozone depletion, deforestation.

   Choose *one* example of a large-scale change in the environment.
   a) Describe the change and suggest reasons for it. *(6)*
   b) Suggest steps that could be taken to reduce further environmental damage. *(5)*

3. 'Sustainable development' is a term used to describe how economic development can continue without causing too much damage to the environment. Explain how recycling can help to reduce damage to the environment. *(4)*

MANAGING ECONOMIC DEVELOPMENT

12 Tourism and development

How can tourism create economic opportunities and help areas to develop?

Managing Economic Development

12.1 The growth of global tourism

Tourism is not a new industry. In the 19th century, wealthy Victorian families left the cities and travelled to the coast for their summer holidays each year. Places with good rail links developed into busy seaside resorts with good-quality hotels and other facilities such as piers and amusements. This is how traditional British resorts like Brighton, Blackpool and Scarborough developed. At the same time children from the richest families were often sent on a 'Grand Tour' of Europe for several months. However, other foreign travel was rare at this time, and journeys to distant continents like Africa and South America were viewed with a sense of adventure and discovery.

A – *On the Spanish costas*

Growth of holiday destinations, 1950–2000

- *1950* The traditional British holiday resort was still popular, with many people visiting places such as Brighton, Blackpool and Scarborough for their summer holidays. By the end of the 1950s, an increasing number of people were going abroad for their holidays using package tours organized by travel agents.
- *1960s* There was rapid growth of a small number of European coastal areas, including southern Spain (**A**), France, Italy and Greece. These destinations were able to offer cheap organized holidays with clean beaches and the guarantee of hot, dry weather.
- *1970s* Development of existing European resorts continued, and there was further development in places like Portugal, Turkey, and the North African coastal areas of Tunisia and Morocco. An increasing number of people took long-haul holidays — the USA became increasingly popular.
- *1980s* The tourism industry expanded throughout the whole Mediterranean region and there were increasing numbers of tourists going to the USA, with places like Florida becoming popular. Less economically developed parts of the world such as the Caribbean islands and Goa (India) (**B**) became increasingly popular.
- *1990s* The increasing globalization of tourism, with package holidays available throughout the more economically developed world and in many areas of the less economically developed world. People were increasingly interested in more remote areas such as northern Australia and Alaska (**C**) and areas with spectacular environments, such as southern Africa and the Amazon rainforest.

B *Varanasi, India, an LEDC tourist destination*

C – *A more unusual holiday environment: Antarctica*

12 Tourism and development

Reasons for the growth of global tourism

- Air transport destinations have developed throughout the world, with more regional airports.
- Airfares have become increasingly affordable.
- People have more money to spend on holidays.
- People have longer holidays and can travel to distant places or visit a number of places on one holiday.
- The growth of package tours to all parts of the world has made organizing holidays much easier.
- Specialist travel agents can arrange holidays to more remote places.
- There is an increased awareness of a wider range of places because of holiday programmes on television and travel reports in newspapers.
- Many parts of the world have developed holiday destinations or special attractions because they recognize that tourism is important to the local economy.

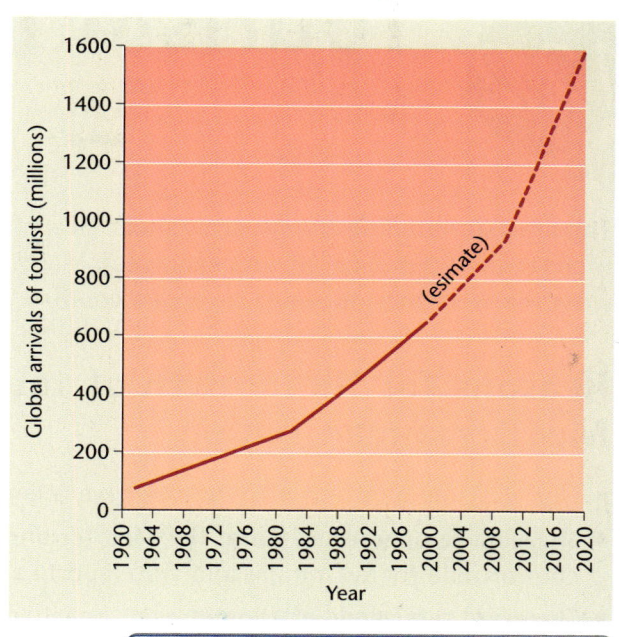

The pattern of growth

It is estimated that the number of global tourists will continue to rise over the next 20 years (**D**). The rate of growth will probably increase as people become wealthier and have more spare time. Rates of growth vary between continents. In 1995 Europe had the slowest rate of growth and Oceania the fastest (**E**).

D – The growth of mass tourism since 1960

Region	Average annual growth (%)
Oceania	10.5
Africa	9.0
Asia	8.5
Americas	7.5
Europe	5.5

E – Growth of the tourist industry, by region, 1995

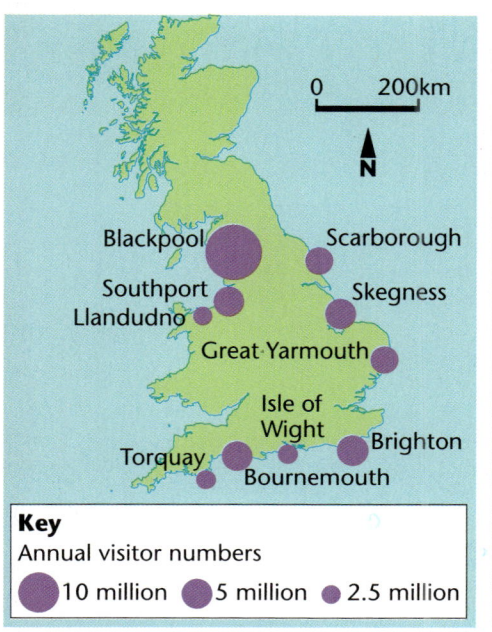

F – Annual visitor numbers to British seaside resorts

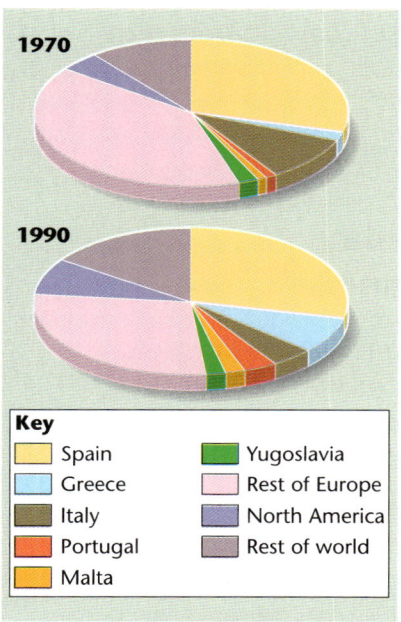

G – Foreign holiday destinations of the British, 1970 and 1990

Questions

1. The number of visitors to British seaside resorts has declined since the 1950s, but they are still popular with day visitors (**F**).
   a) Describe the distribution of resorts.
   b) Why are the resorts still popular with day visitors?
   c) What could British resorts do to increase the number of visitors, and why have numbers declined?

2. Study **G**.
   a) Describe the changes that took place between 1970 and 1990.
   b) Explain the changes.

3. Why might the number of global tourists continue to rise?

4. Why are more unusual tourist destinations becoming increasingly popular?

233

Managing Economic Development

12.2 Tourism in Europe

The area surrounding the Mediterranean Sea is a holiday location for more than 120 million visitors each year. Many of these people come from the wealthier northern European countries.

Reasons for the growth of tourism in the Mediterranean region

- Hot, dry summers and mild winters give a long holiday season (**B**).
- The high temperatures warm the Mediterranean Sea and make it comfortable for swimming and watersports activities.
- There are thousands of kilometres of beach, much of it fine golden sand. In a recent survey carried out amongst British holidaymakers, over 80 per cent said that the climate and the beaches were the two most important reasons for their visit.
- There is a long history of tourism in the area, and many people return year after year.
- Access is fast and relatively cheap, with an increasing number of regional airports. This makes short breaks of a few days or just a weekend possible.
- Most big holiday companies offer 'package holidays' throughout the area, making it easy to choose and buy a holiday.
- Holidays in southern Europe and on the north coast of Africa were relatively cheap, at least until the early 1990s.

The interview with a travel agent in **D** helps to explain the development of tourism in Europe in recent years.

The location and type of holiday destinations in the Mediterranean

This area developed mainly as an area for 'sun and beach' holidays. There are many islands in the Mediterranean Sea and a number of these, including Majorca, Malta and the Greek islands, have become important holiday destinations.

The area offers a growing number of other tourist opportunities as well as beach holidays, including:

- cruising holidays visiting a number of Mediterranean destinations
- watersports and sailing holidays (**A**)
- historical and cultural holidays, visiting sites such as the Acropolis in Greece, or the Alhambra Palace in Andalucia.
- city breaks for sightseeing or shopping
- holidays away from the coasts for the scenery or the natural environment.

A – *A Mediterranean holiday destination*

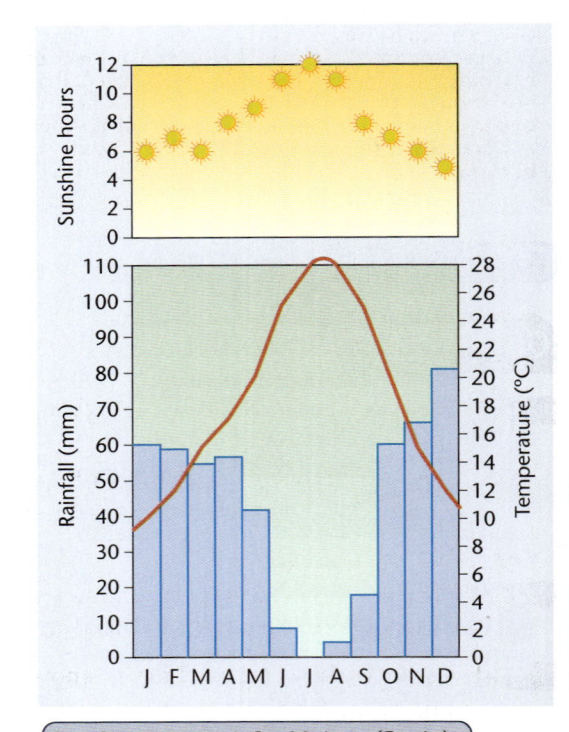

B – *Climate graph for Malaga (Spain)*

12 Tourism and development

Although the Mediterranean region has been the major focus for tourism in Europe, many other areas are also visited (C).

Tourism and the European Union

The importance of tourism within Europe was recognized in the early 1990s when the EU produced a policy document for the development of tourism. Some of the aims included:

- promoting Europe as a tourist destination to make jobs in the industry more secure
- using tourism to help poorer regions develop by giving aid to tourist developments
- making it easier to travel within the EU and throughout Europe
- making sure that holiday companies put accurate and detailed information in their brochures
- improving the quality of tourist facilities, beaches and bathing water
- protecting sites of environmental and historical value.

This document makes two points very clear:

1. Tourism and its related industries are very important to the economy of Europe.
2. There is a need to protect areas from over-development and environmental damage.

C – Holiday destinations in the EU

Interviewer: How have holidays in Europe changed in the last 30 years?

Answer: There has been an enormous change in the last 30 years. Most holidaymakers in Europe in the 1970s would have taken a beach holiday, often a week in Greece or Spain. The range of beach resorts has increased – now just about every Mediterranean country offers beach holidays. Spain and France are still very popular, but places such as Turkey and Portugal are increasingly popular. Of course flights are more frequent and they now go to many more destinations, which makes travelling a lot easier. The other thing that has changed a lot is the type of holiday. More people are renting villas or going self-catering, instead of staying in a hotel, and beach holidays now often include a range of watersports and other activities. Activity holidays have always been popular, especially winter skiing, but people today want a wider choice, including walking, sailing, golfing and touring. Many large leisure resorts have opened since 1980. Perhaps the most famous in Europe is Eurodisney, which is very popular all the year round. Then there are still many people who want to visit cities and historical sites. The Italian cities and Greece have always been popular locations. There has been a lot of growth in short-break and weekend holidays – cities like Dublin, Stockholm and Bilbao are very popular at the moment – and the opening of the Channel Tunnel has led to the increased popularity of Paris and Brussels. Tourism seems to be doing well. Thirty years ago I was told that it would be the biggest industry by the year 2000, and I think it must be close!

D – Interview with a travel agent

Questions

1. a) Describe the climate of Malaga and explain why it attracts tourists.
   b) Suggest three other reasons why there has been a growth of tourism in the Mediterranean region.

2. What have been the major changes to holiday destinations in Europe in the last 30 years?

3. a) Using E, draw a bar chart to show the top five European tourist 'earners'.
   b) Why is tourism 'very important to the economy of Europe'?

4. Why is there a need to protect areas from overdevelopment and environmental damage? Describe two ways that this might be done.

Rank	Country	Income ($ millions)
1	Italy	30 000
2	France	28 000
3	Spain	26 000
4	UK	20 000
5	Germany	16 000

E – The top five European tourist 'earners'

Managing Economic Development

12.3 Changing patterns of tourism in Spain

The Mediterranean coast in Spain has seen massive development in the past 40 years. In the 1950s there were just a few small coastal villages and fishing ports. Now the area attracts more than 60 million tourists each year, mainly from other parts of Europe. The key factors that led to this development included:

- the attractive climate with hot dry summers and mild winters
- the long coastline and warm sea temperatures
- easy access to other European countries
- the relatively cheap hotels and restaurants
- sight-seeing, and spectacular mountain scenery in southern Spain
- the highly developed night-life in some places.

A – Benidorm – a popular Spanish resort

The impacts of growth

In the 1960s the Spanish government realized that tourism could bring a much-needed boost to the economy. Tourism was encouraged along the Mediterranean coast, and in some areas fishing villages developed into busy towns with high-rise hotels and main roads (**A**). There were few planning restrictions and developers were able to build densely packed hotels and other tourist facilities without any objections. This linear development was at first focused along the south coast, the Costa del Sol (the Sun Coast), but later other areas were developed. More recently there has been infilling between tourist centres as villas and golf courses have been built. Today little of the Spanish Mediterranean coast remains undeveloped.

The tourism crisis in Spain

By the late 1980s and early 1990s it was clear that the popularity of Spain as a holiday destination was beginning to decline (**B**). There were several reasons for this:

- The area had reached saturation point, and many resorts were overcrowded.
- The standard of accommodation had fallen.
- The quality of the environment had declined. Beaches were dirty, and in some areas raw sewage discharged into the sea causing health problems.
- Other Mediterranean areas such as Turkey or Greece provided better-quality and cheaper beach holidays.

Regeneration of tourism

'A Plan for Spanish Tourism' was drawn up by the Ministry of Industry to try to reverse the downward trend. Some of the measures included in the plan are:

- a ban on the building of any new hotels unless they are 4- or 5-star quality
- stricter building regulations that stop the building of high-rise hotels and ensure more open space between buildings
- the demolition of many of the poorest high-rise hotels

Year	Total visitors
1987	50 544 874
1988	54 178 150
1989	54 057 562
1990	52 035 508
1991	53 494 964
1992	55 330 716
1993	57 263 351
1994	61 400 000
1995	58 350 000
1996	61 785 000

B – Visitors to Spain, 1985–96

12 Tourism and development

C – Tourism in Spain today

'Green Spain': Northern coast/Inland mountains; recent growth, smaller scale, more expensive settlements. Appeals to tourists who want to explore scenic landscape and enjoy traditional Spanish culture.

Pyrenees mountains: between Spain and France have spectacular countryside, walking holidays, tours and winter sports.

Tourists on short stay/ longer holidays visit major cities (Madrid, Barcelona, Seville, Granada).

Inland southern area with high mountains, hill towns, traditional villages; many have famous historical connections (e.g Granada, Ronda).

Most recent coastal development on Atlantic coast; protected area with many nature reserves. Development here is very sensitive, but still many golf course and hotel holiday developments.

Original growth areas; typical sun, sea, beach holiday, package tours. Massive growth in tourism and development 1960-90.

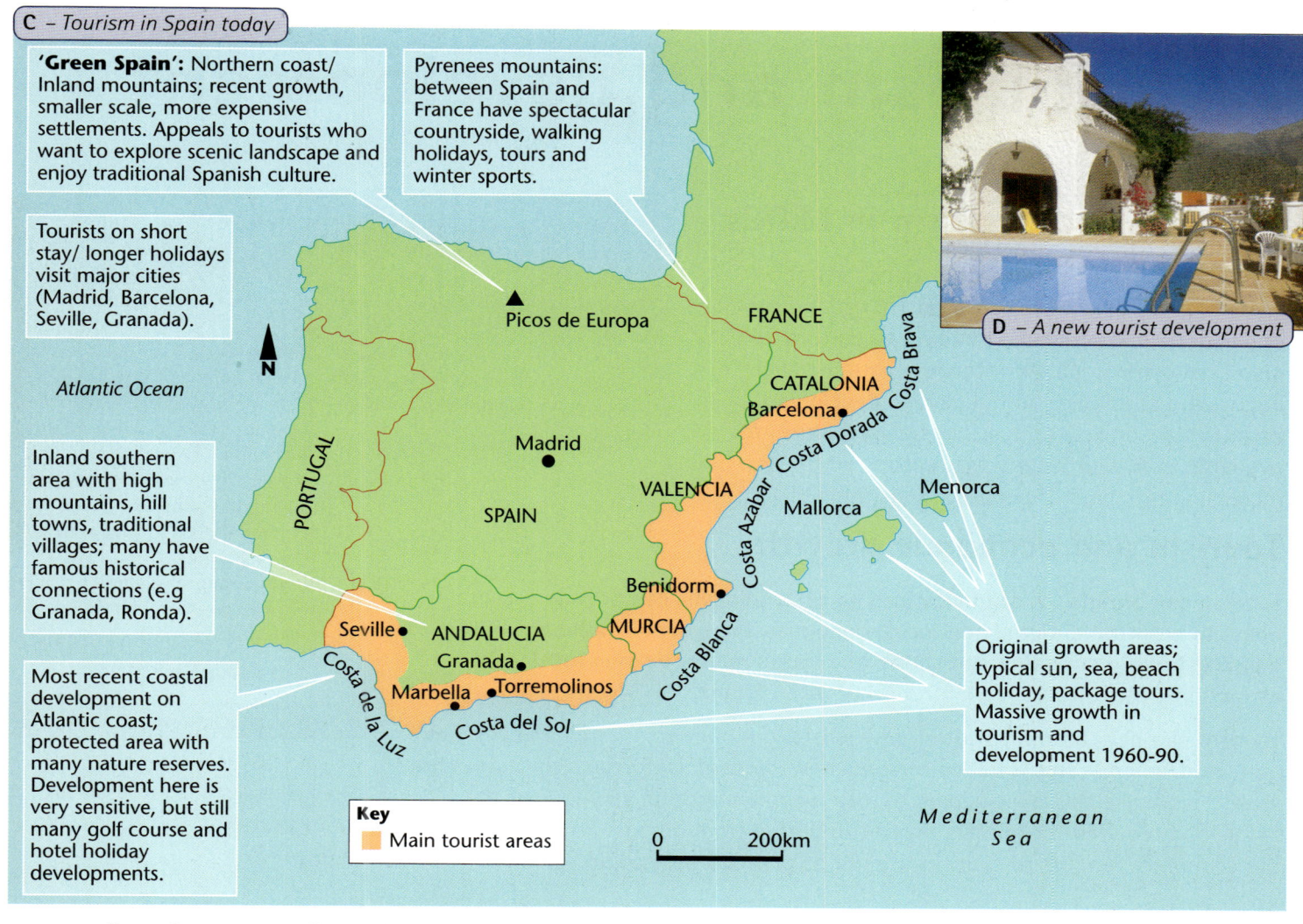

D – A new tourist development

Key: Main tourist areas
0   200km

- upgrading of water supplies and sewage disposal
- improvement in seawater quality and beach cleanliness
- encouragement of tourism development in other parts of Spain (C).

Today the tourist map of Spain looks very different, with a wider range of destinations across the whole country and newer developments showing a greater level of sensitivity to the environment (D).

Have recent changes in policy been successful?

Although it is too early to say conclusively, it does seem that recent changes have reversed the decline of tourism. The number of visitors increased during the 1990s (B), and there has been an increase in tourists from the USA, largely as a result of the improved quality of hotels. Spain appears to have a more positive environmental image and now has over 200 Blue Flag beaches (recognized as being high quality). However, there are still concerns that development in some areas is taking too much of the natural landscape and that more environmental protection is required.

Questions

1. What physical attractions does the Spanish coast have for holidaymakers?
2. Describe photograph A, and suggest why visitors might find it unattractive.
3. Why did the number of visitors to Spain decline in the early 1990s?
4. a) Why was it important for the Spanish government to try to regenerate tourism?
   b) Explain how three of the measures taken by the Spanish government might encourage more visitors.

Managing Economic Development

12.4 Tourism and development

The growth of tourism in LEDCs

There are few places today that do not attract visitors. Every continent can offer tourists a range of opportunities, from beach holidays to cultural or historical centres (**C**). An interview with a travel agent who specializes in holidays in developing countries describes the types of holidays that are available in **A**, and **B** suggests reasons why increasing numbers of people are visiting LEDCs.

Tourism and economic growth

Tourism can bring a lot of money into an LEDC and this can provide a useful boost to both the national and local economies. For example, a holidaymaker may use taxis, restaurants and shops, and spend money visiting local visitor attractions. This creates work for a lot of local people.

Tourism can help to bring a lot of new jobs and money to an area and can help an area develop — this is called *regional development*. Unfortunately it does not always work like this. Wages paid to local people might be very low, or the extra food required for tourists may be imported from abroad. So in some areas the economic benefits of tourism are not as great as they could be.

There are a large number of popular places for tourists to visit in LEDCs. Some have been popular for many years, for example safari holidays in Kenya and historical tours to Cairo (Egypt). More recently the coastal regions of Venezuela and western India have become popular. It really depends on what kind of holiday you are looking for. If you want sand, sea and sun, the Caribbean or Goa (India) may suit you. For a more historical or cultural holiday, Cairo or China might be interesting. Those who want more adventure might choose mountain trekking in the Himalayas or even a river trip in the Amazon rainforest. There are so many different places to go where package holidays are already arranged, or you can make your own arrangements and travel independently.

A – An interview with a travel agent

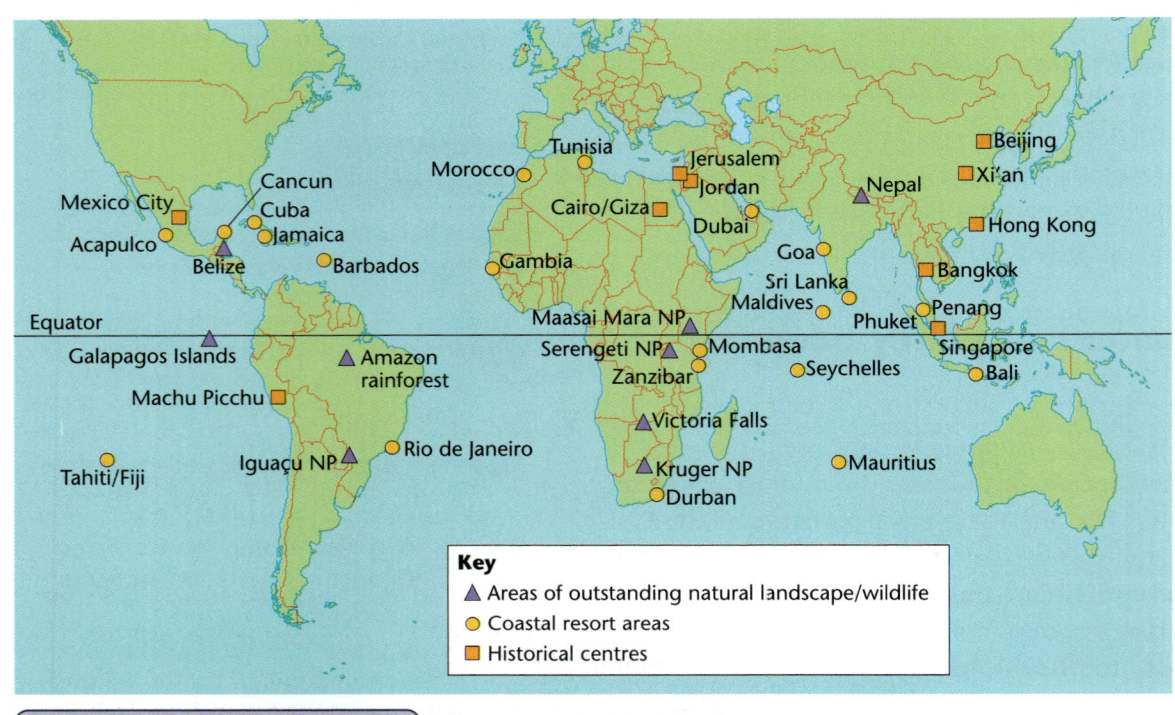

C – Tourism in developing countries

12 Tourism and development

Speech bubbles:
- It is interesting to see another culture, and the environment is so different from ours.
- We like to explore the history of places and see what they were like in the past.
- The weather is more reliable and the beaches are not polluted.
- It can be just as cheap as Spain or Greece, and far less crowded.
- Long-haul flights are so much cheaper today.
- It is interesting to go to cities and see different shops and taste different foods.
- We saw it in a holiday programme and it looked interesting.

B – Why go on holiday to an LEDC?

The environmental and cultural effects of tourism

There have been growing concerns that tourism can also have negative effects on LEDCs, especially on the environment and the way local people live.

Some concerns about the environment

- Vegetation is cut down and wild animals are killed during the building of large holiday resorts.
- Too much water is used in some areas. Each visitor can use up to 1800 litres of water a day, while a golf course may use up to 4.5 million litres a day.
- With the arrival of millions of visitors, existing services cannot always cope and untreated sewage may be pumped into the sea.
- Increased building changes the look of an area and places become 'urbanized', losing their natural beauty.

Some concerns about local people

- If electricity and water are limited, holidaymakers may have first call on the services while local people are cut off for several hours a day.
- Wages in many sectors of the tourist industry are low, and local people may be exploited.
- Working conditions are often poor.
- Land used for tourist development is not available for local people to use for housing and agriculture.
- Young people may be encouraged to move away from their families to work in tourism.

- Tourists are often very intrusive, taking photographs without permission and walking into people's homes. This may affect local people's privacy and their quality of life.

Ecotourism

Because of these concerns there has been a growth in ecotourism, or 'green tourism'. This is the development of tourism that looks after the environment and takes into account the needs of local people.

Ten commandments for tourists

BRITISH holidaymakers need to be more sensitive to foreign cultures when travelling abroad, according to a new report into the social impact of tourism.

Many tourists still go on holiday without researching the customs of the country they are visiting, do not bother to learn foreign phrases, and often haggle with shopkeepers to such an extent that locals are being ripped-off, it claims.

The report, *Don't Forget Your Ethics!*, published by Tearfund, a Christian charity, urges travellers to adopt ten steps to make themselves more culturally aware. These 'ten commandments' of ethical travel include reading about the country you are visiting before going on holiday, using local shops, minimising your environmental impact, and avoiding 'conspicuous displays of wealth' as this can 'distance you from the cultures you came to explore'.

Other advice includes asking permission before taking pictures and not 'making promises to local people that you can't keep when you return home'.

Tour operator Kuoni says that its sales staff are trained to give customers cultural information, and advise people on excursions in which they can sample local culture. Reps also tip off customers about what to wear when visiting monasteries in Thailand.

E – From *The Times Weekend*, 22 July 2000

Questions

1. Suggest three reasons why people might want to visit an LEDC.
2. Explain how tourists might bring wealth to an area.
3. Describe and explain three ways the environment might be put under pressure by the development of tourism.
4. What could governments do to make sure that the environmental effects of tourism are kept to a minimum?
5. Look at E. Why is it important for visitors to be sensitive to foreign cultures when travelling abroad?

Managing Economic Development

12.5 Tourism in Africa

Few continents offer tourists the range of opportunities that Africa can. From the Mediterranean coast in the north, the continent stretches right across the tropics to nearly 35° South. This means that its natural environments include hot deserts, tropical rainforests and savannah grasslands.

Some parts of Africa have been popular holiday destinations for many years, including Cairo and the River Nile and the wild animal reserves of southern Africa. More recently the Mediterranean coastal countries of Morocco and Tunisia, and the Gambia on the Atlantic coast, have been developing coastal holiday resorts similar to those in Mediterranean Europe.

The main appeal of Africa as a holiday destination is the physical environment and the climate (particularly for visitors from Europe in the winter). Other reasons for holiday visits include:

- the many historical attractions found throughout the continent
- the opportunities to experience different cultures
- the variety of wildlife to be found in the game reserves.

North-west Africa

North Africa is easy to reach from most European countries and the weather is usually warm. This makes it an ideal destination for beach holidays. Both Tunisia and Morocco have many miles of clean, uncrowded beaches. There has been a lot of coastal development in recent years, with the building of large modern hotels with swimming pools and a range of sporting activities. Away from the beach there are trips inland to visit the desert regions of North Africa with their spectacular sand-dunes. From the coast of Morocco it is possible to get to the Atlas Mountains or visit the city of Marrakesh with its medieval architecture and street markets.

B – A beach resort in Tunisia

West Africa

Many companies offer package tours to The Gambia, which has many miles of beaches now fringed by modern hotels. Temperatures are reasonably high throughout the year, so the area has become popular with winter visitors from Europe.

Away from the coast it is possible to visit traditional villages and rural markets.

In recent years there has been increasing tourism development based on the varied local environment, which includes coastal forests and mangrove swamps which are excellent for bird-watching.

C – Table Mountain, Cape Town

Southern Africa

Southern Africa offers some of the most spectacular scenery in the whole continent, from Table Mountain in South Africa to the Victoria Falls in Zimbabwe.

South Africa has miles of beaches and a well-developed tourism industry with high-quality hotels and resorts. Inland the area can offer visits to the famous wine-growing regions and game reserves, including the Kruger National Park.

The Victoria Falls in Zimbabwe has developed a tourism industry based entirely on the environment of the River Zambezi with its spectacular waterfalls. Tourists come to admire the scenery, look at the local wildlife or to hunt. Whitewater rafting is an increasingly popular sporting activity.

The coast of Mozambique has hundreds of miles of white sandy beaches with opportunities for diving and deep-sea fishing expeditions.

12 Tourism and development

A – Some tourist destinations in Africa

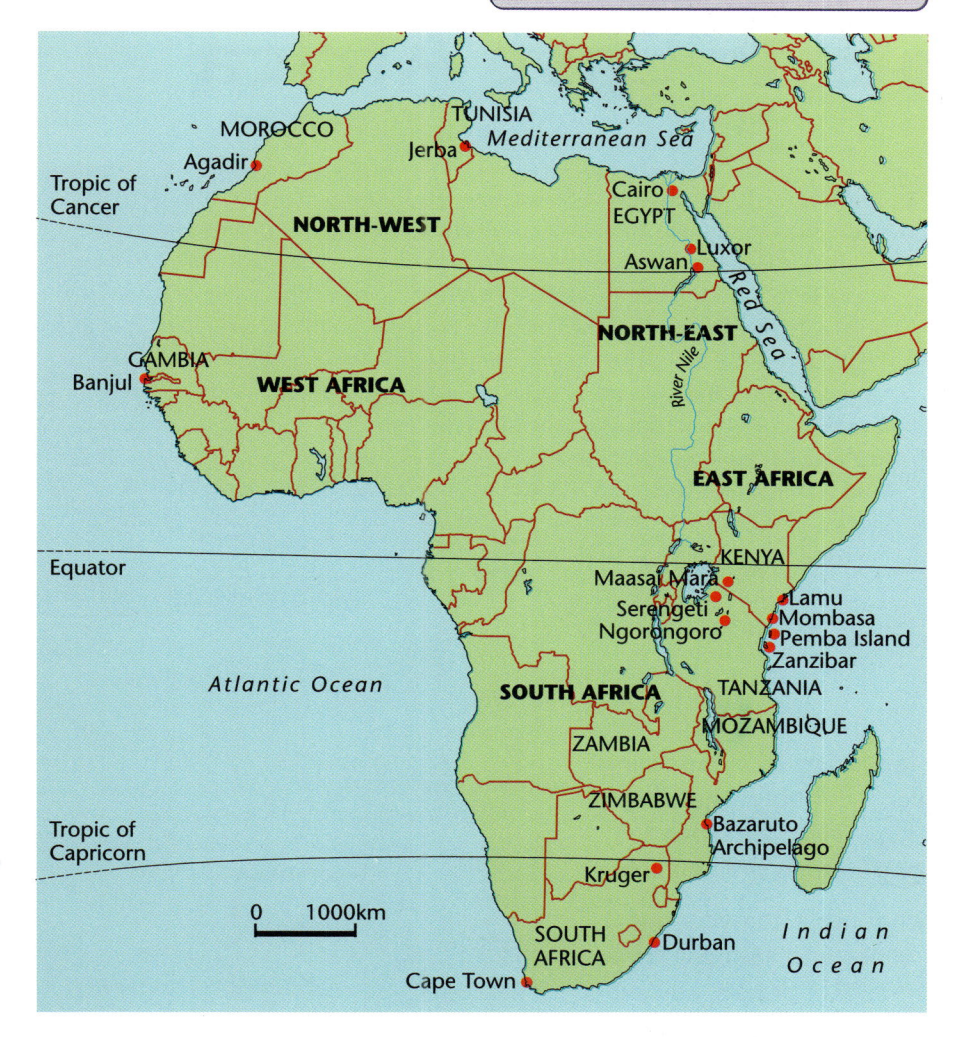

North-east Africa

Tourists have been visiting Egypt for many years to see the Ancient Egyptian sites including the Valley of the Kings where the Pharaohs are buried, and the Pyramids. Cruising the Nile is a popular way to see the country. Cairo, the largest city in Africa, is a popular holiday destination, with people from all over the world visiting the city to see the relics of the past. The Red Sea is the most recent area of tourism development and has a large number of resorts offering beach holidays with a range of watersports. The area also offers specialist diving holidays.

D – The Pyramids near Cairo

East Africa

Tourists have been visiting Kenya and Tanzania for many years, taking trips to the mountains and the savanna grasslands. These countries have nearly 100 game reserves and national parks, including the world-famous Serengeti National Park in Tanzania. Safari holidays are very popular — visitors can travel through a game reserve and stay in a game park lodge for a few days.

The Kenyan coast, with its warm dry weather, white beaches and coral seas, has developed a thriving tourism industry. The area around Mombasa has seen considerable development, with the building of many large hotels and resorts.

E – Victoria Falls on the Zimbabwe/Zambia border

Questions

1. Draw up a table like the one below and for each of the five areas in A make brief notes describing its major tourist attractions.

North-west Africa	• Miles of clean, uncrowded beaches • Lots of modern hotels • Trips inland to deserts

2. How important is the physical geography in attracting tourists to Africa?

Managing Economic Development

12.6 Tourism and the environment: East Africa

The East African countries of Kenya and Tanzania offer the visitor an enormous range of physical landscapes (A) — for example:

- mountainous areas including Mount Kenya at 5199m and Mount Kilimanjaro at 5895m above sea-level
- Lake Victoria and Lake Turkana — two of the largest lakes in Africa
- hundreds of miles of white sandy beaches and coral reefs
- vast plains of savanna grassland where wild animals roam in nature reserves.

> ... with over 50 national parks Kenya has a great deal to offer the holidaymaker who wants to observe and photograph wildlife. Many of the parks and game reserves have good access, so it's possible to visit for a day or two. If a longer break is required game lodges are found in many of the parks. A popular holiday is a week's safari in the Serengeti National Park (Tanzania) staying at a safari lodge. The excitement as you search for the 'big five' (buffalo, elephant, leopard, lion, rhino) and many other animals is truly unforgettable. A holiday combining the game parks and the beach 'surf and turf' is easily possible, since this area has hundreds of miles of clean beaches.
> And don't forget the cities of Nairobi and Dar es Salaam with their lively markets and fascinating cultural opportunities.

A – From a holiday brochure

Wildlife tourism

Kenya has protected nearly 10 per cent of its landscape by designating it as national parkland. A number of safari lodges and hotels have been built within the national parks and game reserves. These cater for the visitors who come to the area to look at and photograph the wildlife.

Visitors provide a major source of income in what are often very poor areas. Money from tourism can provide local wages and help pay for schools and health centres. However, large numbers of people visiting the area can put pressure on the wildlife and local people.

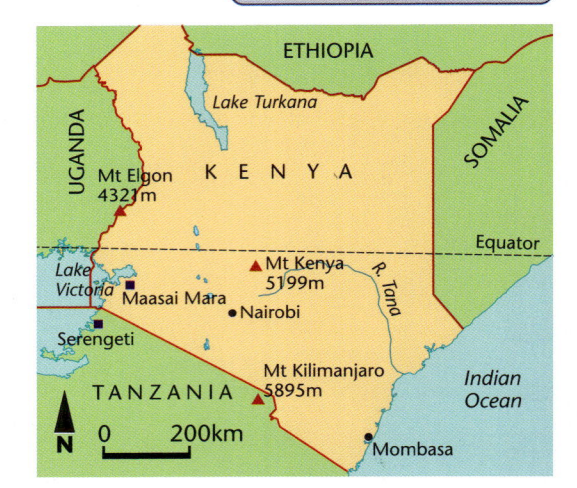

B – East Africa tourist locations

Pressures on the area

The environment
- Large numbers of minibuses can cause tracks to become eroded in the dry season or churned up in the wet season. Tracks are often widened by vehicles driving on verges, which damages the vegetation.
- Although the minibuses are supposed to keep to the stated routes they often go off the tracks to get closer to the animals and in doing so destroy fragile grasslands (C).

The wildlife
- Minibuses often try to get near the animals so that the tourists can take close-up photographs. Animals can be frightened off and forced to move to other areas.
- The increasing use of light aeroplanes and hot-air balloons disturbs the wildlife.
- Although poaching is illegal, some people ignore the laws.

C – On safari in an East African game reserve

The local people

- The setting up of a national park can mean that nomadic tribes, like the Maasai, have to be moved from their lands. They often find themselves on poor-quality land where it is difficult to make a living.
- Some nomadic peoples have been forced to live in permanent settlements and now have to make a living by selling souvenirs or performing dances for the tourists.

Coastal tourism

Thousands of tourists are attracted to the coastal areas by the hot climate and the large expanses of clean sandy beaches. The area around Mombasa is especially popular for beach holidays, with many people coming to explore the coral reefs and marine life.

The growth of tourism has given a massive boost to the local economy, providing work for nearly 20 per cent of the population. It has helped to develop the local building and transport industries and provided thousands of jobs in a range of services. However, this growth has not been without cost to the environment and to the local culture.

Impact of tourist development...

... on the beach areas

- linear development and hotels making the area urbanized
- increases in road development and traffic
- loss of farmland, natural vegetation and wildlife habitats.

... on the coral reefs

- damage of the fragile coral reef by divers, and pollution from boats
- pressure on the marine life as coral is damaged.

... on the local people

- loss of farmland has led to the movement of traditional farmers
- break-up of families as young men move to the coast to work in the tourism industry.

The way forward?

Echoheaven – Pemba Island

Pemba Island is just off the coast of northern Tanzania and is known as 'Emerald Isle'. A new resort has been built in a 7ha nature reserve where visitors can explore mangrove swamps and forests and see bush babies, eagles and parrots.

The reserve also has a 5km strip of white sandy beach and offers the opportunity for diving and sea fishing. The resort has only 20 chalets built in the forest to fit in with the natural environment and designed to cause as little damage as possible.

12-NIGHT SAFARI AND BEACH HOLIDAY

Day 1
Departure from Heathrow.

Day 2 Nairobi
Morning arrival in Nairobi for 1 night at the Holiday Inn Mayfair Court.

Day 3 Nairobi/Samburu
Set off on safari. Lunch en route. Afternoon game viewing in Samburu Nature Reserve. 2 nights at Samburu Lodge.

Day 4 Samburu
2 game drives.

Day 5 Samburu/Treetops
To the Aberdare Mountains. Lunch at the Outspan Hotel in Nyeri, before continuing to the world-famous Treetops. Watch the animals come down to the waterholes.

Day 6 Treetops/Lake Naivasha
After an early morning call, return to Outspan Hotel for a full breakfast. Then continue via Thomson's Falls to Lake Nakuru National Park. Overnight at Lake Naivasha.

Day 7 Naivasha/Masai Mara
A morning at leisure. After lunch, drive to the Masai Mara for 3 nights at Keekorok Lodge.

Days 8 and 9
The vast plains of the Mara stretch to the Tanzanian border and are home to thousands of animals including lion, rhino, leopard, elephant and buffalo. Morning and afternoon game drives are included.

Day 10 Masai Mara/Mombasa
Return to Nairobi and fly to Mombasa for a 4 night stay at the medium-class Jadini Beach Hotel.

Days 11--13 Mombasa
At leisure.

D – *Safari in Kenya*

Questions

1. How important is physical geography in attracting visitors to East Africa?
2. Draw up a table to explain the advantages and disadvantages of tourism to the people who live in and near the popular wildlife areas.
3. What impact is the growth of tourism having on wildlife and coastal environments?
4. a) What is meant by ecotourism?
   b) Why do you think holidays on Pemba Island might be expensive?

Economic Development

12.7 Tourism in fragile environments: the Amazon rainforest

Tourists from MEDCs have become increasingly adventurous and now look for holidays in places where they can experience different cultures and environments. There are several reasons for this:

- Many people have longer holidays and they can spend longer periods away from home.
- People have more money to spend on holidays.
- There has been an increase in the number of flight destinations.
- Holiday programmes and newspaper articles have made people more aware of different places.
- Organized tours are available to more remote places.

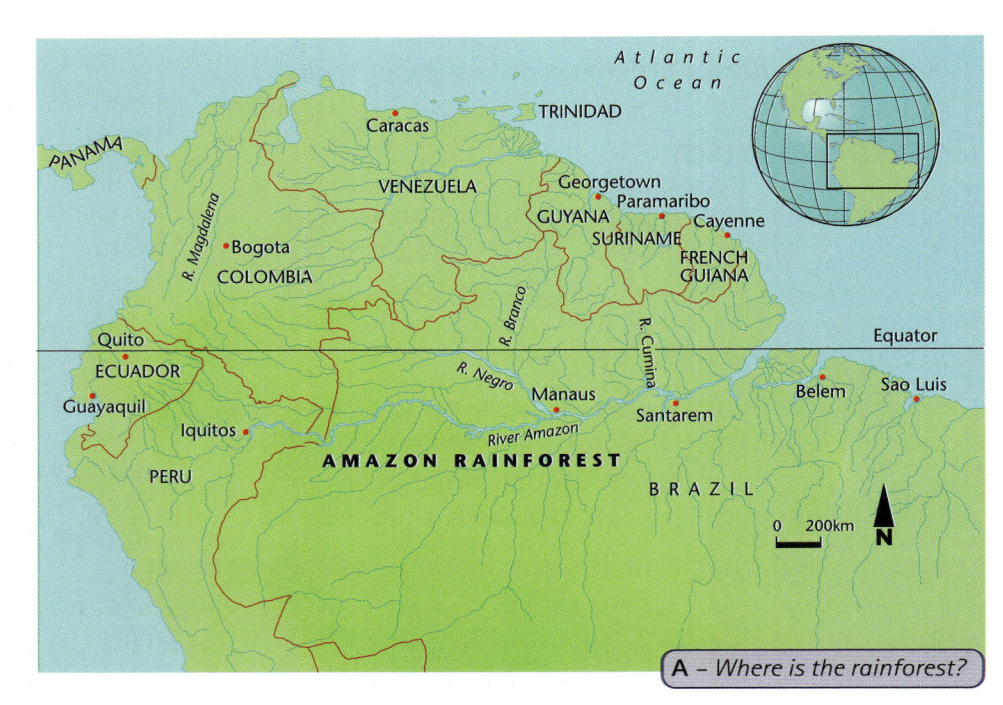

The Amazon rainforest in South America is one place that is attracting an increasing numbers of visitors (**A**).

Below are some of the questions that travel agents are often asked by people interested in visiting the area.

What is the Amazon?

The Amazon is one of the world's biggest river systems running through the world's largest rainforest. The river takes water from the countries of Colombia, Ecuador, Peru, Bolivia and Brazil and flows in an easterly direction through Brazil before reaching the Atlantic Ocean. At its widest point the river is over 60km wide. It is possible to take a boat from the Atlantic to the inland part of Iquitos, travelling right through the centre of the Brazilian rainforest (**A**).

What is the rainforest like?

The Equator runs through the rainforest, so it is always hot and humid and it can be uncomfortable. The high rainfall and constantly high temperature mean that the forest has a larger variety of plants than anywhere else on Earth (**B**). There is also a huge range of animal life, including giant insects and brilliantly coloured frogs, over 2000 species of birds as well as jaguars and monkeys.

A – *Where is the rainforest?*

B – *Inside the rainforest*

Why go there for a holiday?

There are many reasons why people might go to the Amazon for a holiday. The most obvious is to see the great variety of plant and animal life there. Other reasons might be:

- enjoy a relaxing holiday sailing down the river in the comfort of a modern ship, viewing the changing scenery and wildlife
- whitewater rafting where the river flows fast near its source
- exploring the forest on foot with an organized tour guide, staying in modern lodges in the forest and exploring remote areas by canoe
- visiting the local people (C). The Amazon is still home to many of the original Indian tribes, although their way of life has been changed by the introduction of industry, and many now live in reservations. Tourists can visit Indian villages for displays of dancing and locally made souvenirs.

When is the best time to go?

The climate is hot and wet all year, so there are no real seasons. But there are big differences in the level of water in the river. In the low-water season from September to November, the streams are narrower and with more shallows it is easier to spot marine animal life. There are also fewer biting insects at this time, which makes it more comfortable for the visitor. The high-water season from April to June is when many of the trees are in flower, and with the river wider and deeper it is possible to visit more remote areas and see a greater variety of plant and animal life.

Does tourism damage the area?

Tourism in fragile areas such as the Amazon can have advantages and disadvantages (C).

What can be done to protect the area?

Many organizations are trying to balance the impact of tourism so that the area can benefit without, significant loss of the environment and traditional culture. This is called *sustainable tourism*.

Some of the ways that the area can be protected are:

- encouraging specific types of holiday, for example bird-watching which is well organized and avoids causing extensive damage
- encouraging tourists to only buy wooden objects certified to be from sustainable forests
- promoting only the most environmentally friendly tour operators and lodges, with a good record in protecting the local area
- educating tourists to respect the local people and environment
- limiting the number of tourists visiting the area
- encouraging the development of ecotourism, where developments are small and fit in with the local environment.

C

Advantages
• Brings money into the country
• Brings income to local people
• Tourism can help to educate people about the environment
• Can help preserve the local culture where tourists pay to experience it
• Could help preserve the environment
• Can improve communications networks

Disadvantages
• Building roads, airstrips etc. changes the landscape
• Building means cutting down vegetation
• Tourists might destroy habitats
• Increased pollution, spread of new diseases to area
• Local people exploited and their lifestyles permanently altered

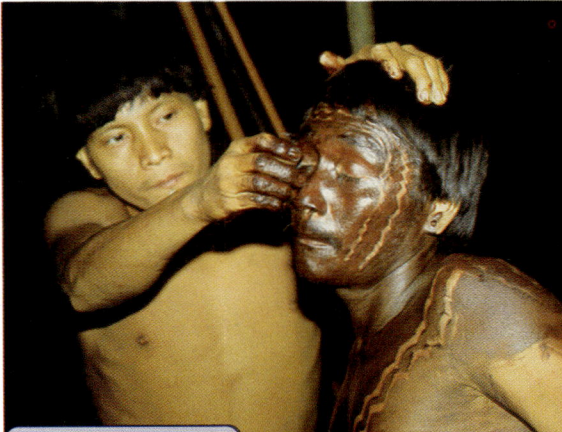

D – Amazon Indians

Questions

1) Why are more people visiting the Amazon?

2) a) Describe the attractions of the Amazon rainforest for visitors.
   b) What problems might visitors to the area face?

3) a) How might the growth of tourism harm the environment?
   b) What could be done to protect the area from overdevelopment?

economic development — Tourism and development

Decision-making exercise

A potential tourist development in Barbados

In 1995 a company put forward plans to build a development in Barbados, a Caribbean island.

General background

Barbados is a Caribbean island that has been visited by tourists from North America for many years. More recently it has become increasingly popular with European holidaymakers. There are now many direct flights between European countries and Barbados each week. As a holiday destination it has much to offer, including spectacular beaches and a subtropical climate.

Questions

Look carefully at all the resources on these two pages, then answer the following questions.

1. Why is Barbados an attractive holiday destination?
2. What are the advantages and disadvantages of the proposed development?
3. 'Tourism in areas like this is always a balance between the economy and the environment.' What does this statement mean?
4. Do you think the development should go ahead? Give reasons for your answer.
5. If it were to go ahead, what could be done to reduce its 'environmental impact'?

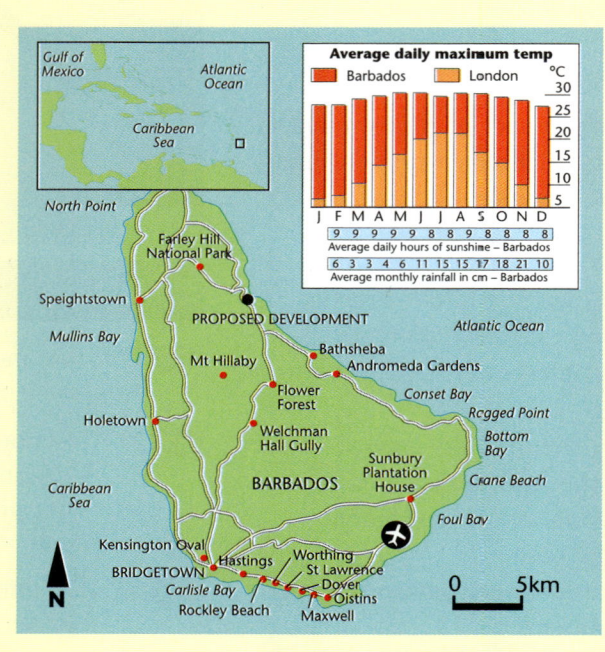

A – *Barbados: climate and location*

Your guide to Barbados

"The perfect holiday island with the finest sandy beaches and a wide variety of watersports and nightlife"

In Barbados the welcoming atmosphere is as warm as the weather. The tropical heat is blissfully fanned by trade winds, giving this island paradise possibly the best climate in all of the West Indies. Barbados really is a place of discovery – where a maze of little roads chase across the island over rolling hills of sugar cane down to luxuriant dales, surrounded by a coast of sandy beaches slotted into beautiful rocky bays.

To gain an even more spectacular view of Barbados there are a number of ways to take in its splendour – helicopter rides, submarine trips and a choice of boat excursions enable you to make the most of the island's many beauty spots. As well as providing a wonderful opportunity for you to spend leisurely hours exploring and sight-seeing, Barbados hosts an array of exciting activities such as riding, championship golf and watersports.

Living up to its reputation for elegance, Barbados houses some of the most sophisticated shops in the Caribbean. You can purchase duty-free goods in Bridgetown, and stroll around boutiques selling a wide range of smart casual wear in the resorts and capital.

Barbados – the holiday island where paradise awaits your arrival.

B – *From Thomson Holidays Caribbean and Mexico brochure*

Tourism and development

Hotel Giant Takes Caribbean Plunge

IT WAS ANNOUNCED this week that Paradise Hotels have shown an interest in building a holiday complex on the east coast, 3km south of Barclays Park.

This area is recognized as an area of outstanding natural beauty, and no large-scale developments exist here at the present time.

The company, an American multinational, would like to build a large hotel with over 300 rooms, as well as 40 villas in landscaped grounds. They plan to develop a watersports centre in the area which could also be used as a private club. A golf course may follow.

This will be a multi-million-dollar investment for the area and is bound to bring significant changes with it. A spokesperson for the company stated that 'this is a golden opportunity for the area to develop its natural resources – the sun, sea and wonderful scenery. Of course it will mean change, but it will also bring jobs and wealth. Tourism in areas like this is always a balance between the economy and the environment.'

PARADISE HOTELS

This is an exciting project for both our company and the local area.

During the building phase over 400 jobs will be created and when it is in operation the holiday complex will employ nearly 500 people. This area has few opportunities and this development will give it a tremendous boost. As well as these jobs, the development will also generate other jobs: supplying us with day-to-day goods, transportation, entertainment, etc. – the list is endless! Our intention is to develop a new road in the area so that visitors can reach us quickly. If the scheme is successful it could be expanded. Many holiday complexes have golf course and other large-scale leisure facilities. Of course, any development means change, and there is no doubt that the local environment will be changed.

However, our changes will be carefully managed; we have no wish to damage the area – it would not be in our own interest. Our other developments show that we are sensitive to the environment and wherever possible aim to build in sympathy with the local area.

SAVE OUR COAST!

The Environment Commission Fights to Preserve the East Coast

The Environment Commission is spearheading the fight to stop the tourist development on the east coast. The site outlined by the developers falls within an area designated for special environmental control, and is within the area proposed for a national park. This is one of the most scenic parts of the island, virtually unspoilt for thousands of years. The area contains a rich mixture of plant and animal life existing in a delicate balance of nature. The area is largely agricultural, where local farmers have tended the land for generations.

The area would be greatly changed by this development. Land would have to be cleared, slopes levelled for building and streams put in pipes underground. The beach would be spoilt by the building of huge breakwaters to create sheltered water conditions. The human effects of the development would be equally damaging. Many farmers would lose their land and there would not be enough water for the local people during the dry months. The local sewage works would not be able to cope, and untreated sewage could end up on the beaches or in the sea, damaging the fishing industry.

The Newsletter of the Barbados Environmental Commission

C – *East coast development*

Managing Economic Development — Tourism and development

Exam practice questions

1. a) Use A to describe the location of long-haul holiday centres offered to European holidaymakers. (3)

   b) Which factors have encouraged the development of tourism in these areas? (4)

2. a) Make a copy of the following table, and use B to complete your table.

Location	Reason for visiting	Flying time from the UK
Hollywood, USA	Film studios	11 hours
Himalayas		10 hours
River Nile		5 hours
Sydney, Australia	City tour	
Florida	Theme parks	

   (4)

   b) Why are more British people able to visit distant locations? (6)

3. Using an example you have studied, describe the advantages and disadvantages that tourism has brought to an area. (6)

4. Using examples that you have studied, explain how mass tourism can put pressure on different environments. (6)

5. a) What is meant by *ecotourism*. (2)

   b) Describe an example of ecotourism. (4)

   c) Why is it important to protect fragile environments? (6)

6. How can tourism help a country to develop? (6)

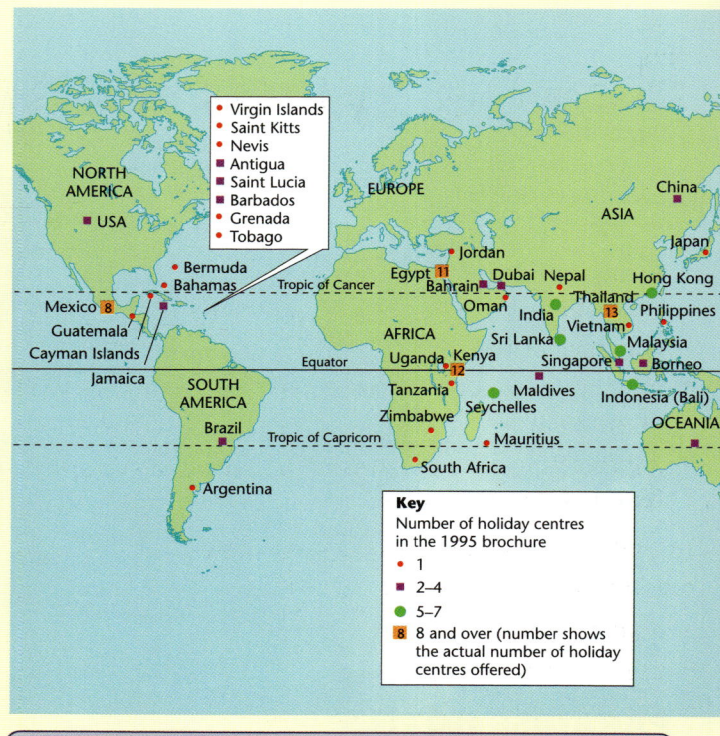

Mark schemes can be found on the book's website, at www.heinemann.co.uk/issuesmarkschemes

A – Holiday destinations featured in a 1995 holiday brochure

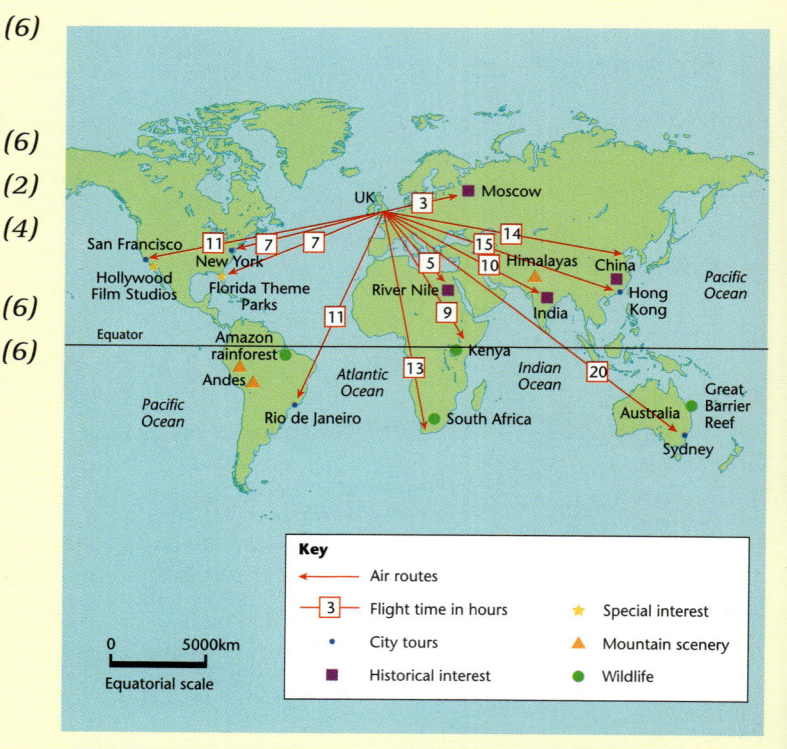

B – Some more distant locations for British holidaymakers

Revise your map-reading skills

Ordnance Survey (OS) maps can be useful for:
- locating places or features
- drawing location or base maps (particularly for coursework)
- understanding the physical and human characteristics of an area
- appreciating the relationship between places and features on the ground.

To make the best of an OS map, a number of skills are required. These include the ability to:
- read conventional signs
- use grid references
- use scale and calculate distance
- use compass directions
- interpret relief.

1 Reading conventional signs

Conventional signs are symbols and colours showing features on a map. They are not completely standardized, but every map should have a key providing all the information needed to be able to understand the symbols.

2 Using grid references

Every OS map is covered by grid lines. These enable particular points on the map to be located. The grid lines on all OS maps are spaced 1km apart, regardless of the map scale. This means that the approximate distance between places can be judged by counting the squares. The vertical grid lines are called **eastings** and are numbered along the top and bottom of the map. The horizontal grid lines are called **northings** and are numbered on each side of the map.

How to use grid references
Key points:
- Always start from the bottom left-hand corner of the square.
- Always quote eastings *before* northings. ('Along the corridor and up the stairs!')

Four-figure references describe a whole square, so in Figure A the reference for square A is 4788.

Six-figure references describe a point and are read by subdividing a square into 10 further eastings and northings, each representing 100m. The method is the same: the third and sixth numbers are the tenths. So in Figure A the reference for point B is 482867, and for point C is 495875. If the point lies on a grid line, a zero must be used – so the reference for point D is 465870.

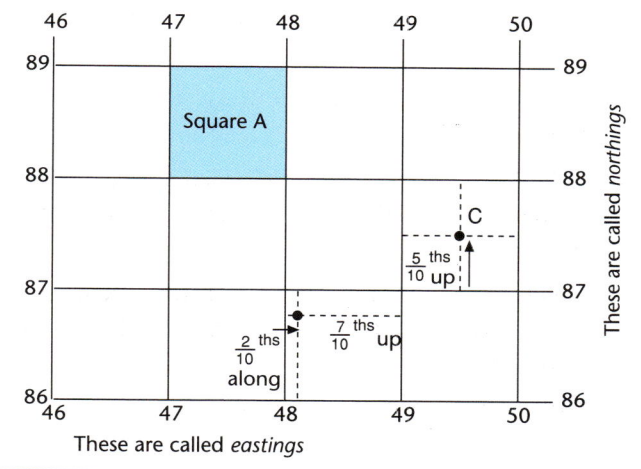

A – Using grid references

3 Using scale and calculating distance

Scale is the relationship between distance on the map and distance on the ground. By measuring the distance between two points and using the scale-line at the bottom of the map, the real distance can be calculated. If the distance along a road is required, a piece of string can be laid along the road and then measured using the scale-line. Always remember to state the unit being measured (kilometres or miles).

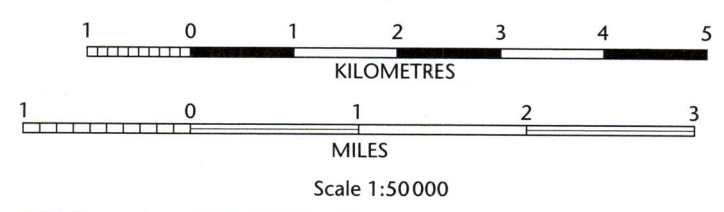

Scale 1:50 000

B – Metric and imperial scale-lines

Revise your map-reading skills

4 Using compass directions

All OS maps have north at the top. Compass bearings are described using the grid on the map. In order to find a compass bearing between two places, put the centre of the compass on the starting point and read off the direction (bearing) to where you are going.

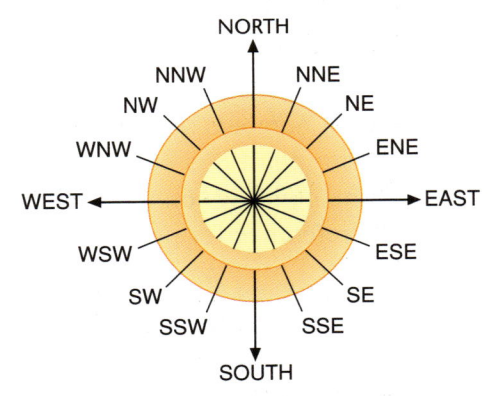

C – Points of the compass

5 Interpreting relief (shape of the land)

Height is shown on a map by:

- spot heights:
- triangulation pillars
- contour lines: lines joining points of equal height, at 10m intervals

Key points about contour lines

- Every fifth contour line is thicker.
- The numbers on contour lines face upslope.
- Contour lines close together = steep slope.
- Contour lines further apart = more gentle slope.

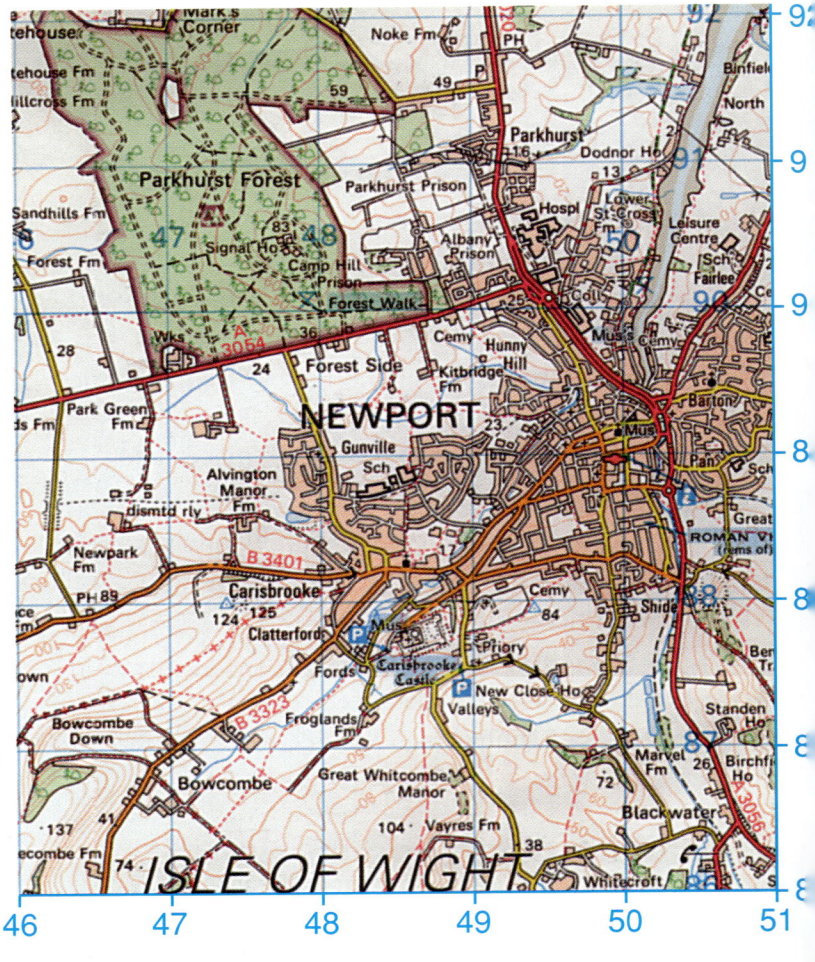

D – OS map extract 1:50 000 scale showing Newport on the Isle of Wight

© Crown Copyright

Questions

1. Name the Manor found in grid square 4886.
2. Give the four-figure reference for the square containing Carisbrook Castle.
3. Name the features at:
   a) 506895
   b) 495904.
4. Give the six-figure reference for Noke Farm (middle square at top of map).
5. What is the straight-line distance, to the nearest km, from Newport bus station (499889) to Park Green Farm (468893)?
6. Which direction are the following places from Newport bus station:
   a) Parkhurst Forest
   b) Marvel Farm (500870)?
7. Name three ways that height is shown on this map.
8. Describe the relief of the land on a walk from Newpark Farm (464884) to Bowcombe (470866).

Glossary

Accessibility	A measure of how easily a place can be reached.
Acid rain	Precipitation that contains dilute concentrations of mostly sulphuric and nitric acids.
Aftershocks	Series of movements after a major earthquake.
Ageing population	Population where the proportion of older people is increasing, becoming greater than the proportion of young people.
Aids or AIDS	Acquired immune deficiency syndrome: a condition caused by a virus transmitted in the body fluids, marked by severe loss of resistance to infection and so ultimately fatal.
Anticyclone	Area of high pressure where weather is calm.
Appropriate technology	Technology appropriate to the needs, skills and knowledge of the people.
Attrition	Rocks rubbing against each other as they move.
Bilateral aid	Aid given by one government to another government.
Biological weathering	Breaking down of rocks by the action of plants and animals.
Biomass	Living organisms — rotting waste matter from plants and animals produces methane which can then be collected and used as fuel.
Birth rate	The number of births per year per 1000 people.
Brownfield site	A derelict site in an urban area that could be redeveloped.
Cash crop	Crop grown for sale.
Catchment population	The total population with access to a particular place or service.
Census	An official count of the number of people in a country and the collection of other related information, usually taken every ten years.
Central Business District (CBD)	The commercial centre and focus of a town or city.
Chemical weathering	Where rocks are dissolved by the action of water as a dilute acid.
Climate	Average weather conditions.
Collision zone	Where two continental plates meet and form fold mountains.
Commercial farming	Production of farm products to sell.
Commuter	A person who travels some distance to work.
Conservative margin	Where two plates move alongside one another.
Conurbation	Large urban area formed by the merging of several smaller urban areas that have expanded to meet each other.
Convenience goods	Products needed by households as daily requirements.
Corrasion/abrasion	Wearing away of cliffs or valley sides by material rubbing against them.
Corrosion	Rocks dissolved by acids in water.
Counter-urbanization	The movement of people from larger urban areas to smaller urban or rural areas.
Crust	Thin outer layer of the Earth.
Cycle of poverty	A circle of poverty which happens when poor people cannot get enough food or money to improve their existing situation and so remain poor or get poorer.
Death rate	The number of deaths per year per 1000 people.
Demographic transition model	A model to show the sequence of change in birth rates, death rates and population growth over time in a country or a number of countries.
Depopulation	When the total population in an area declines through outmigration or an increasing death rate.
Depression	Area of low pressure where weather is unsettled.
Deprivation	The state of having inadequate housing, facilities, employment, etc.
Desertification	Spread of desert-like conditions in semi-arid areas.
Destructive margin	Where two plates are destroyed as they push towards one another.
Development	General improvement in standards of living.

Glossary

Development Corporation	Government body set up in the UK to help areas with high unemployment.
Drought	Long period without rainfall.
Dyke	Embankment built to prevent flooding.
Earthquake	Shaking of the Earth's crust.
Ecotourism	Tourism that does not damage the local environment or people.
Epicentre	Point on the Earth's surface directly above the epicentre.
Erosion	Wearing down and removal of material by water, ice and wind.
Fertility rate	The average number of children born to a woman in her lifetime.
Firewood (Fuelwood)	Wood that is collected on a daily basis by people in LEDCs as their energy supply for cooking.
Floodplain	Flat area of a valley floor which floods regularly.
Focus	Point in the Earth's crust where an earthquake originates.
Footloose industry	An industry not tied to the location of raw materials but dependent on a good infrastructure.
Formal sector employment	Work within a specific organization or structure, usually with a regular paid contract.
Fossil fuels	Fuels consisting of hydrocarbons that were laid down in geological times, e.g. coal, oil.
Freeze-thaw action	Breakdown of rocks by constant freezing and thawing.
Garden city	Town or city built with the attractions of many trees and open spaces.
Gentrification	Run-down houses in a poor area are bought and improved by more affluent people, so the neighbourhood becomes fashionable and property prices rise.
Geothermal power	Power obtained using water that is heated naturally underground.
Geyser	Ejection of steam and hot water from underground.
Glaciation	Action of ice on a landscape.
Global warming	The raising of average global temperatures due to the greenhouse effect.
Globalisation	Processes at a global scale.
Green belt	Area around a city, usually farmland, where development is restricted.
Green Revolution	A term applied to a number of measures developed by MEDCs and adopted by LEDCs to increase agricultural output, e.g. improved seeds.
Greenfield site	An agricultural or green site that has not been previously built on.
Greenhouse effect	Process that traps heat in the lower atmosphere.
Gross National Product (GNP)	Total value of goods and services produced in one year.
Growth rate	The rate at which a total population grows, considering birth rates, death rates and inward and outward migration.
Habitat	Environment where plants and animals live.
High-technology (high-tech) industry	Industry associated with advanced technological development, especially in electronics and computing.
Honeypot site	Small area that attracts an exceptionally large number of people.
Hot spot	Area of volcanic activity away from a plate margin.
Human Development Index (HDI)	Measure of development using income, education and life expectancy.
Hurricane	Tropical storm; also known as *cyclone* and *typhoon*.
Hydraulic action	Force of water.
Hydrological cycle (water cycle)	The cycle or system of water between air, land and sea.
Hydrology	Study of water movement.
Immigration	Entry of individuals into a country other than their own with the intention of staying.
Impermeable	Rock that does not allow water to pass through it.
Infant mortality	The number of deaths of babies under the age of one year, per 1000 babies born per year.
Informal sector	The work that is done by people on an informal basis, perhaps for exchange of goods rather than money, unregulated, e.g. recycling rubbish in Cairo.
Infrastrucure	The fixed networks of communications and services in an area, such as roads, railways, gas, electricity, water, drains, sewerage and telecommunications.
Intensive farming	Using large inputs of labour or capital.
International migration	Movement of people between countries.

Inter-urban migration	Movement of people from a town or city to another town or city.
Irrigation	Artificial watering of the land for farming.
Isobar	Line joining places of equal air pressure.
Landfill site	Area of land used for the disposal of solid waste, e.g. domestic rubbish.
Lava	Molten rock flowing on the surface of the Earth.
Levée	Natural or artificial raised bank alongside a river.
Life expectancy	Average number of years a person at birth can expect to live.
Light railway	A railway constructed for light traffic.
Locational factor	Something that influences where development takes place.
Longshore drift	Movement of material along a beach.
Low-density housing	Small number of dwellings on a large area of land.
Magma	Molten rock beneath the surface of the Earth.
Mall	A self-contained undercover shopping precinct.
Malnutrition	Lack of the right kinds of food.
Mantle	Layer of the Earth between the crust and the core.
Mega-city	City with a population over 10 million.
Mercalli scale	Scale used to measure the amount of shaking during an earthquake.
Migration	Movement of people from one place to another, often permanently.
Millionaire city	City with a population over 1 million.
Mortality	Ratio of deaths to the total population in an area.
Multilateral aid	Aid organized by development agencies.
National Park	Area of special environmental interest that is set aside and protected by law.
Natural increase	The difference between the birth rate and the death rate.
New town	Planned urban centre designed to be a self-contained town both socially and ecomonically.
Non-governmental organization (NGO)	Organization that concerns itself with issues but is neither funded nor controlled by a national government.
Opencast mining	Extraction of a mineral from the surface of the Earth.
Overpopulation	When the population is so great in relation to resources and the ability to use them, that the majority of people do not have an acceptable standard of living.
Ozone depletion	Loss of ozone from the ozone layer due to the use of chlorofluorocarbons, halons, etc.
Pensionable age	Age at which people receive a pension and generally stop work. This may be different for men and women and is not the same in each country.
Plate	Section of the Earth's crust.
Plate margin	Boundary between two plates.
Pollution	Contamination or fouling of the environment caused by human activity.
Population change	Change in a population measured in terms of the birth rate, death rate and migration figures.
Population explosion	Very rapid increase in population when the death rate declines and the birth rate remains high with a falling infant mortality rate.
Population pyramid	Graphic method of illustrating the age and sex structure of a population.
Population structure	Proportion of the total population in each age group and gender.
Porous (impermeable)	Rock that allows water to pass through it.
Precipitation	Water in any form that falls from the atmosphere.
Primary industry	Extraction of raw materials: mining, farming, forestry, fishing.
Primate city	Urban centre that dominates a country, with a population much bigger than the next largest city.
Proactive pressure group	Pressure group that exists all the time and monitors or reacts to changing situations, e.g. Greenpeace.
Pull factor	Something that motivates people to move to a place.
Push factor	Something that motivates people to leave a place.
Quaternary industry	Research and development; information technology.
Raw materials	Items used in the manufacture of goods.
Reactive pressure group	Pressure group that gets together in reaction to a situation.
Recycling	Re-use of materials that would normally be discarded.

Redevelopment	Rebuilding of part of a town or city, either by demolishing all existing buildings and putting in new ones, or modernizing some of the old buildings.
Regeneration	Social, environmental and economic improvement of a declining area in order to encourage new economic development.
Renewable resource	One that is naturally replaced after use so that it never runs out.
Reservation	Area set aside for the groups of people who live there.
Reserve	Estimated lifespan of a non-renewable resource.
Resource	Any natural feature that can be used to meet human needs.
Retail park	Out-of-town or edge-of-town area with a variety of large shops, food outlets and parking.
Richter scale	Scale used to measure magnitude of earthquakes.
Rural	Areas of countryside with low population densities, small settlements and primary industries.
Rural/urban fringe	Land at the edge of the suburbs of a town where the land use is a mixture of rural and urban activities.
Rural-urban migration	Movement of people from the countryside to towns or cities.
Sahel	The region across North Africa between approximately 10° and 20°N.
Sanitation	Water and sewerage facilities.
Science park	Purpose-built area, dedicated to knowledge-based industries, research and development.
Secondary industry	Manufacture of finished or semi-finished products.
Service activity	Activity that provides a service, e.g. banking.
Shanty town or squatter settlement	Informal and usually illegal settlement of self-built houses made from whatever is around, often lacking services.
Smog	Pollutant combination of smoke and fog.
Soil degradation	Decline in the fertility of soil.
Storm surge	Rapid rise in sea-level as a result of low pressure and strong winds.
Subduction zone	Area where a plate descends and melts.
Subsistence farming	Small-scale farming to supply the needs of an individual family.
Suburbanized village	Village like the suburbs of a city (mostly housing) where people live and work as they would in a city rather than in a rural area.
Superstore	Retail store covering a large surface area.
Sustainability	Meeting the needs of the present without compromising the ability of people in the future to meet their own needs.
Synoptic chart	Map showing weather conditions.
Tertiary industry	Providing services to people or industry.
Tornado	Violent rotating winds, up to 300km/hr.
Transnational corporation (TNC)	Large corporation usually based in an MEDC with operations in many other countries.
Undernutrition	Too little food for good health.
Underpopulation	Insufficient number of people to use the resources available.
Urban function	A land use associated with an urban area, such as retail, residential, industrial.
Urban growth	Expansion of town and cities.
Urbanization	Process in which the proportion of the population living in urban areas increases.
Volcano	Place in the Earth's crust where lava, gas and ash erupt at regular intervals.
Voluntary aid	Aid organised by non-governmental organizations.
Weather front	Boundary between air masses of different temperature.
Weather	Day-to-day conditions of temperature, precipitation, wind, cloud, etc.
Weathering	Breaking up of rocks by the actions of the weather, chemicals or plants.
Zone of advance/assimilation	Area around a CBD that is in demand for CBD functions, and so the use of the area changes.
Zone of retreat/discard	Area of decline around a CBD where buildings are abandoned or changed to a non-CBD function.
Zone of transition	Urban area subject to change.

Index

acid rain 212, 214-15, 228, 251
air pollution 15, 39, 48-9, 188-9, 212, 213, 214-19, 222-5
anticyclones 112, 113, 133, 251

Bangladesh 20, 22, 176, 220, 225
    flooding 124-5, 130
Brazil 42, 176, 180, 186, 195
    Amazon rainforest 200-1, 244-5
    Curitiba 40-1, 206-7
    rural-urban migration 25, 29, 30, 36-7, 40
Britain see UK
British Isles 108, 126-7, 220, 221
    see also UK

California (USA) 148-9, 221
    earthquakes 93, 106
CBDs (central business districts) 31, 45-9, 56-7, 62-3, 77, 84-5, 251
China 8, 11, 20-1, 22, 139, 184
cities 50, 60-1, 66-7, 109, 217
    LEDCs 13, 26-7, 31-3, 38-41, 138-9
    MEDCs 46-7
    see also CBDs; inner cities; shanty towns; transport
climate changes 125, 214, 218-19, 220, 228-30
coal 196, 197, 202-3, 212, 215
coastal processes 156-7, 221
Curitiba (Brazil) 40-1, 206-7

deforestation 200-1, 212
demographic transition model 10-11, 251
depressions 110, 111, 251
deprivation, urban 54-5, 251
desertification 136-7, 219, 251
development 8, 23, 84, 176-83, 192, 252
    environmental impact 184-5, 212-25
    impact of tourism 185, 238-9, 243
    sustainable development 185, 186-7, 212, 226-7
drought 132-3, 135, 136-7, 219, 252

earthquakes 90, 91, 93, 94-9, 106
economic development see development
ecotourism 239, 245, 252
Egypt 31, 38-9, 142-3, 241
energy 193, 194, 196, 204-5, 211
    use 22, 176, 177

environmental protection 84
erosion 155, 252

flooding 121-9, 130, 219, 220, 228
food 12-13, 22, 23, 43, 132-5, 142
forests 199, 200-1, 208-9
fossil fuels 194, 196, 197, 214, 225, 228, 252

glaciation 158-63, 174, 252
global warming 125, 214, 218-19, 220, 228-30, 252
green belts 78, 80-1, 252
greenhouse gases 218-19, 228-9

honeypot sites 167, 252
housing 68-9, 72-3, 78-9, 84, 176
hurricanes 114-19, 124, 125, 135, 252
hydrological cycle 120-1, 252

India 21, 26, 30, 34-5, 132, 146-7, 213, 222
industrial change 188-91
inner cities 47, 54-5, 58-9, 62-3, 77

Japan 11, 12, 14-15, 179

Kenya 29, 30, 44, 133, 135, 179
    population change 16-17
    tourism 241, 242-3

Lake District (Cumbria) 164-7
LEDCs (Less Economically Developed Countries) 7, 176-9, 180, 182-3, 196, 206-7, 228-9
    cities 13, 26-7, 31, 32-3
    impact of natural hazards 95, 98-9, 101, 104-5, 115, 116-19, 124-5
    pollution 215, 217, 222
    population change 6, 8, 9, 12, 20-1, 23
    and resources 22-3, 195, 204
    rural-urban migration 13, 16, 25-30, 40, 42
    tourism 185, 238-48
    water supplies 12, 22, 35, 38, 138-41, 226

MEDCs (More Economically Developed Countries) 7, 136, 176-7, 179, 183, 196, 222
    greenhouse gas emissions 218, 228-9
    impact of natural hazards 95, 96-7, 101, 102-3, 115

population change 6, 8, 9, 12, 18–19
    see also cities
microclimates 109
Middle East 181
migration 7, 8, 69, 253
    rural-urban 13, 16, 25–30, 40, 42
mining 197, 201, 202–3, 225, 253

national parks 153, 164–71, 242–3, 253
natural hazards, perceptions 92–3
new towns 39, 68, 78, 81–3, 86–7, 253

OS (Ordnance Survey) maps 249–50
ozone layer 216–17, 228, 253

plate margins 90–1, 253
pollution 13, 32, 35, 132, 167, 212, 253
    air 15, 39, 48–9, 188–9, 212, 213, 214–19, 222–5
    water 146–7, 188, 212, 212–13, 221, 225
    see also acid rain; greenhouse gases
population change 5–19, 22–3, 27, 68–9, 253
poverty 8, 13, 32, 132, 134, 176, 179
pressure groups 76–7, 227, 253

quality of life 35, 58, 62–3, 178–9

rainforests 200–1, 229, 244–5
recycling 41, 194, 206–7, 229, 254
redevelopment 45, 46–7, 54, 60, 62, 84–5, 254
regeneration 54, 58–9, 60, 254
renewable energy 193, 194, 201, 204–5, 211
resources 12–13, 22–3, 194–201, 209, 210, 254
retailing 48, 49, 56–7, 70, 74–5, 77
rivers 120–3, 128–9, 146–7
rural change 26, 28–9, 33, 42–3
rural-urban migration 13, 16, 25–30, 40, 42, 254
rural/urban fringe 56, 65–7, 68, 70–7, 78–9, 254

sea-level rise 212, 220–1
services 30, 73, 74, 254
    see also retailing
sewage disposal 138–9, 140, 236, 237, 239
    in LEDCs 32, 35, 38, 146, 147
shanty towns 30–1, 34, 35, 36–7, 38–9, 40, 254
squatter settlements 30–1, 34, 35, 36–7, 38–9, 40, 254
sustainability 40–1, 84, 144–5, 206–7, 226, 245, 254
sustainable development 185, 186–7, 208, 212, 226–7

Teesside (north-east England) 188–91
Three Gorges Dam (China) 184
tourism 103, 185, 209, 221, 231–3, 238–9, 243
    Britain 164–7, 172–3, 232, 233
    Europe 232, 233, 234–7
    impact on environment 236–7, 239, 242–7
    LEDCs 185, 238–48
    national parks 153, 164–7, 168, 170–1
    natural landscapes 152–3, 161, 174, 209
traffic 13, 32, 39, 48–53, 60, 61, 75
    Lake District 166, 167
transport 41, 50–3, 61, 64, 67
tropical rainforests 200–1, 229, 244–5
tropical storms 114–19, 124, 125

UK (United Kingdom) 10–11, 18–19, 153, 232, 233
    see also British Isles
urban areas see cities
urban deprivation 54–5, 251
urban redevelopment 46–7, 54, 60, 62, 254
urban regeneration 54, 58–9, 60, 254
urbanization 26, 121, 127, 254
USA (United States of America) 11, 21, 22, 148–9, 170–1, 208–9
    greenhouse gas emissions 218, 228, 229

villages 68, 73, 78–9
volcanoes 90, 91, 100–5, 106, 254

waste 33, 35, 39, 207, 227
water management 142–3, 146–9
water pollution 146–7, 188, 212, 212–13, 221, 225
water supplies 32, 142–3, 145, 198, 239
    LEDCs 12, 22, 35, 38, 138–41, 226
weather maps 110, 113, 130
weathering 154–5, 254